# Cold War Camera

# Cold War Camera

THY PHU ANDREA NOBLE ERINA DUGANNE EDITORS

Duke University Press *Durham and London* 2023

Printed in the United States of America on acid-free paper ∞
Designed by Courtney Leigh Richardson
Typeset in Elephant, Fuura, and Minion Pro by Copperline Book Services

Library of Congress Cataloging-in-Publication Data
Names: Phu, Thy, [date} editor. | Duganne, Erina, editor. |
Noble, Andrea, editor.
Title: Cold war camera / edited by Thy Phu, Erina Duganne,
and Andrea Noble.
Description: Durham : Duke University Press, 2022. |
Includes bibliographical references and index.
Identifiers: LCCN 2022007314 (print)
LCCN 2022007315 (ebook) |
ISBN 9781478015956 (hardcover)
ISBN 9781478018599 (paperback)
ISBN 9781478023197 (ebook)
Subjects: LCSH: Cold War—Photography. | War photography. |
World politics—1965–1975. | Cold War in mass media. | BISAC:
PHOTOGRAPHY / Criticism | PHOTOGRAPHY / History
Classification: LCC D843 .C653 2022 (print) | LCC D843 (ebook)
DDC 909.82/50222—dc23/eng/20220707
LC record available at https://lccn.loc.gov/2022007314
LC ebook record available at https://lccn.loc.gov/2022007315

Cover art: (Detail) Discarded Soviet air force training film,
from the series Lost Emulsion (2019). Light box. © Tong Lam.
Courtesy of the artist.

*For Andrea*

# Contents

## Structures of Seeing

# Illustrations

# Acknowledgments

Of the many collaborations we have been part of, work on *Cold War Camera* was by far as stimulating as it was challenging. What started in Mexico City, where Andrea Noble was then based, as an informal discussion about global Cold War photography prompted us to realize how little we knew about how and why images were made, where they went, and what cultural work they did both during and in the aftermath of this prolonged conflict. Even then, we realized that the only way we could even begin to take up these questions was through collaboration, an undertaking that saw us meeting in Canada, the United States, and the United Kingdom, where our home institutions are located, and to Guatemala and back to Mexico City, where our research and academic networks took us. We are grateful to the University of Toronto, Western University, Durham University, Texas State University, the Social Sciences and Humanities Research Council of Canada, and the Arts and Humanities Research Council (UK) for their support of this project.

Although building and maintaining this collaboration across daunting distances and many time zones was a larger challenge than we had anticipated, we were fortunate to have generations of feminist models to sustain and inspire us. We also had loads of help, and we would like to thank our research assistants, Zeinab Mcheimech, Kelsey Kilgore, and Mike Sloane. Muriel Hasbun and Luis Albertos also provided invaluable translation support. We are also fortunate to have worked with many talented researchers, some of whom shared their expertise in lively discussions at events held in Guatemala and Mexico City, and with the critics whose work made the 2015 co-edited special issue of *Visual Studies* on "Cold War Visual Alliances" such a valuable contribution to our understanding of photography in mediating this prolonged conflict. These researchers and critics include Marcos Armstrong, Tani Barlow, Sarah Bassnett, Jordana Blejmar, Kevin Coleman, John Curley, Deepali Dewan, Heather Diack, Molly Geidel, Eva Pluhařová-Grigienė, Kevin Hamilton, Martha Langford, Stephen S. Lee, Johanna Lozoya, Nicolas Mirzoeff, Gabby Moser, Ned O'Gorman, Pippa Oldfield, Jason Pribilsky, Daniel Hernández-Salazar, Eric Sandeen, Ileana Selejan, Joseph Slaughter, Linda Steer, Dot Tuer, Kelly Wood, and Andrés Mario Zervigón. Our conference and workshop could not have been organized without the support of many institutions including, in Guatemala, the Bone Laboratory of the FAFG (Fundación de Antropología Forense de Guatemala), the Museum of Martyrs, the National Police Historical Archive, the Catholic Church Human Rights Bureau, La Fototeca (Centro de Investigaciones Regionales de Mesoamérica); and, in Mexico City, Centro de la Imagen. We were also able to share early drafts of our work in developing the concept of the *Cold War Camera* with European colleagues at the Cold Atlantic conference, hosted at the Museo Nacional Centro de Arte Reina Sofía, in Madrid, Spain, an event co-organized by Paula Barreiro López and Fabiola Martínez. While collaboration does not necessarily entail agreement, we are constantly reminded of how productive even the most heated of discussions can be.

We are humbled by and grateful for the support of the brilliant contributors to this volume, who undertook numerous revisions with grace, humor, and patience as we shaped and reshaped the project. The final, polished form is the result of their hard work. It is also the result of insightful and incisive feedback from our anonymous reviewers, whose careful and thoughtfully prepared reports are most appreciated. We also thank Nadine Attewell, Greg Barnhisel, Elspeth Brown, Yi Gu, and Darren Newbury for their generosity in reading and commenting on early drafts; our editor, Ken Wissoker, for believing in the book; and the entire editorial team at Duke University Press, most especially Joshua Gutterman Tranen, for guiding us to publication.

We dedicate this book in loving memory of Andrea Noble, world traveler, renowned critic, and dearest friend. Andrea was the one to whom we looked for inspiration, who unreservedly cheered our successes, and whose strength we leaned on. She sometimes liked to say, with a glint in her eye and a lightness in her voice, that she would pick us up if we fell. We knew she meant every word. And at an event in Mexico City, she did exactly that. When one of us fainted, whether from exhaustion or stress or the venue's high elevation, she was the one who did the lifting, literally and figuratively. This moment and so many others showed us just how much she had our backs, how deeply her friendship was rooted, and how widely it extended. Her untimely death in 2017 left so many of us who followed her work and benefitted from her intellectual generosity devastated and heartbroken. At the time of her sudden passing, Andrea was working on three projects, her own monograph on the cultural history of tears in Mexico, an ambitious series of collaborative exhibitions that traced Cold War visual legacies in Latin America, and this book. While the first two projects remain unfinished, we are honored to be able to complete *Cold War Camera* and hope this book fulfills her vision. We are grateful to have known her and will always cherish her memory.

THY PHU ANDREA NOBLE ERINA DUGANNE

# Cold War Camera

## AN INTRODUCTION

In 1970, Bui Cong Tuong, communist chief of Propaganda, Culture, Education, and Training, surrendered to US officials in South Vietnam. Included among the sensitive documents he delivered to his handlers was a set of photographs. One of them depicts soldiers evicting a peasant from his hut, and a second shows other soldiers watching over a funeral. While not all the images depict war in an obvious way—a third shows a Catholic pastor marching with villagers in a religious procession—still, as Tuong explained, communists produced and disseminated photographs as weapons against American advisers and their South Vietnamese allies. The people in the photographs, he said, were members of a theater troupe who acted out scenes for the camera, which were meant to depict the injustice of the enemy's pacification programs, the cruelty of surveillance, and religious freedom under communism. In his debriefing, Tuong repudiated his role in "telling lies to the people" and provided instructions on how to decode what was visible—and discern what was disguised—in the photographs (figure I.1). In short, his debriefing reveals the pivotal role that photography played in the global Cold War, the broader context in which the Vietnam conflict unfolded.[1] His instructions show that images, whether spectacular or mundane, whether "objective" or staged, were used to win hearts and minds.

*Cold War Camera* explores photography as integral to the cultural practices of this prolonged conflict. The chapters collected here contribute to an emerging body of work on Cold War cultural politics, which, as Eric Zolov

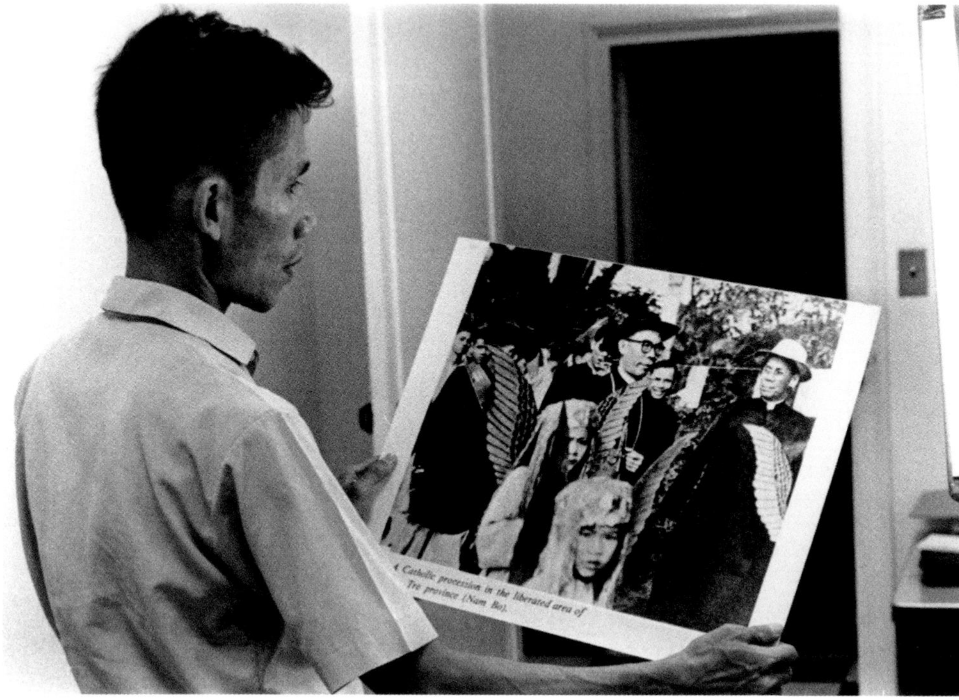


states in relation to the Global Sixties, aims "to expand the narrower notion of the 'political' to include the terrain of culture and everyday life, carefully seeking to map out and make sense of the complex ideological threads that bind culture and politics together in this period."[2] The cultural turn in Cold War scholarship has revealed the impact of opera, jazz, art, and literature in promoting ideological positions.[3] However, photography's function in the global Cold War has yet to be fully investigated. With the exception of the extensive critiques and reassessments of *The Family of Man* exhibition as a Cold War phenomenon (which we discuss briefly below), and, more recently, Martha Langford and John Langford's reflections on the visual bridging of war and tourism, commentary is limited.[4] This oversight is due, perhaps, to photography's diffuse operation over multiple sites, which poses a challenge for a single scholar or single study to trace, or which leads to a tendency to view photography as simply illustrating rather than playing an active role in this conflict. As the opening discussion of Bui Cong Tuong suggests, to grasp photography's meanings one must not only take account of the image object, but also consider the full range of photography as cultural practice, including the conditions of production, the actors who participate in this process, the

**Figure I.1.** Bui Cong Tuong contemplates a photograph that he had orchestrated when he served as communist Chief of Propaganda, Culture, Education and Training in Ben Tre Province, South Vietnam. Photographer unknown. Robert F. Turner Collection, 74040-10 A.V, 1970, Envelope S., Hoover Institution, Stanford University.

ways that images are remediated, the dispersed sites of circulation, and the cultural work that images undertake.

To address this challenge, we adopt a multifaceted approach, examining photography as a practice and a diffuse medium that is integral to prosecuting war across far-flung regions. In so doing, we take up the call made by John Lewis Gaddis and Odd Arne Westad, among others, to attend to subjects and sites marginalized in the debates in Cold War studies, which tend to focus exclusively on the bipolar struggle between the superpowers, the United States and the USSR, or on the European "long peace." Specifically, the Cold War is often understood as beginning in 1947, unraveling in 1989 (with the fall of the Berlin Wall), and ending in 1991 (with the dissolution of the Soviet Union). This periodization has reinforced a bipolar framework, by bracketing, at one pole, the ascendance of the two superpowers after World War II, and at the other pole, the triumph of the United States. While the influence of this framework is undeniable, it is limited because it forecloses analysis of the global scope of the Cold War. Significantly, the superpower struggle unfolded on multiple fronts across Africa, Asia, Latin America, and beyond. As Greg Grandin, Gilbert Joseph, and Daniela Spenser have observed, there was nothing cold about it, particularly in locations across the global South, where it played out in vicious civil wars and terror on "an almost inconceivable scale,"[5] in a process that reconfigured geopolitical boundaries. Moreover, the discovery of archives in Guatemala, Cambodia, and beyond, contest accounts that emphasize the linear, progressive trajectories of the global Cold War, which highlight 1947 and 1991 as watershed moments.[6] Indeed, Joseph suggests a longer genealogy that stretches before World War II, when Latin America served as training ground where the United States "studied how to execute imperial violence through proxies,"[7] which, after 1945, morphed into the violent containment of communist threats.

So, while we neither dispute the importance of the US-USSR rivalry nor disregard the East-West axis, this book reorients criticism to include the function of photography along the frequently disregarded North-South axis. Whereas an emphasis on the East-West axis underscores just how cold this prolonged conflict was, our critical expansion, in highlighting the North-South axis where violent proxy wars took place, lays bare its hotness. Just as importantly, attending to the visual networks that link these axes helps to reveal the impact of decolonization, or "decoloniality," as Walter Mignolo puts it in the case of Latin America, in these geopolitical reconfigurations.[8] Or, it helps to reveal a "decolonizing Pacific," as Simeon Man conceptualizes it, wherein anticolonial movements in the United States, Asia, and the Pacific converged with US imperial ambitions.[9] Decolonization, as these critics contend, did not just occur coincidentally with, and as a backdrop to, the global Cold War; rather, they must be understood and reckoned with as crucial to and inseparable from this prolonged conflict. Accordingly, *Cold War Camera* highlights the significance of photography from parts of the global South—including West and South Africa, Vietnam, China, Central America, and Chile—in exploring possible decolonized futures, in establishing affinities and solidarities, and in supporting efforts toward transitional justice in reckoning with the violence of proxy conflict. In particular, we build on the work of critics who have reexamined how metaphors of the Iron and Bamboo Curtains construct a false sense of fixity that belies vibrant cultural exchanges within and between ideological blocs.[10] As Michael David-Fox observes, the Iron Curtain functioned more as a "semipermeable membrane" than an opaque boundary.[11] As our contributors show, visual exchanges provided ways of envisioning political life beyond the bipolar imaginary; indeed they support a vision more attuned to the aspirations of, say, the Non-Aligned Movement, which under the leadership of India's first prime minister, Jawaharlal Nehru, Indonesia's Sukarno, Egypt's Gamal Abdel Nasser, and Ghana's Kwame Nkrumah, sought to envision a new world order.[12]

We contend that photography is crucial to these expanded investigations for it enables us to reexamine what can be seen and known. In this regard, the phenomenon of covert operations is instructive, particularly when it comes to the prosecution of the global Cold War along the North-South axis, where it heated up in Latin America's "dirty war" or *guerra sucia*.[13] The purpose of covert operations in a dirty war is to obscure collusion between state and nonstate actors in counterinsurgency operations. Covert operations are noteworthy in part because they give rise to "percepticide," Diana Taylor's phrase for the compulsory collective blindness produced by state terrorism, whereby spectators know and plainly see atrocity and yet are forced to avert their gaze.[14] How might photographic practices of the global Cold War selectively and strategically render subjects visible as well as invisible? What has been obscured and what remains unrecognized?

Through the development of a comparative analytic, we address these questions. This book examines how the camera, as a set of cultural practices, has been productive and generative, variously employed by states, media, and individuals to promulgate visions of socialist utopias, to advance capitalist desires, to give form to nonaligned political affinities and communities, and to portray quotidian experiences that unfold alongside, while also in contrast to imperial discourses that persist despite decolonization. At the same time, we consider the ways that the camera has exerted a repressive and destructive force, as the logic of percepticide potently demonstrates. We argue that photography was not only crucial to the conduct of the global Cold War and its aftermath but also central to our understanding of it.

## LOOKING AWAY: PHOTOGRAPHY CRITIQUE AND THE COLD WAR

Although some of the most influential ways of seeing and understanding photography were shaped in response to the global Cold War, strangely enough, they have not been fully grasped as such. Consider, for example, Roland Barthes's revered *Camera Lucida*. In this book, Barthes introduces the much-cited concepts of *studium*, the cultural, linguistic, or political elements of interpretation, which he contrasts with *punctum*, an image's capacity to wound, which is crucial for his affectively charged and personal approach to criticism.[15] However, as Erina Duganne argues in her chapter for this volume, Barthes developed his theory of the inextricably linked *punctum* and *studium* in the course of his brief musings on a specific image: a 1978 photograph, made by Dutch photojournalist Koen Wessing, of the conflict in Nicaragua, a major proxy battleground of the Cold War (figure I.2). The significance of

**Figure I.2.** Koen Wessing, *Nicaragua*, 1978. Collection Stedelijk Museum Amsterdam.

Barthes's attention to and ultimate disregard for the full significance of Wessing's photograph can best be understood in terms of *Camera Lucida*'s peculiarly selective focus.

Sensitive readers of Barthes have expounded on the importance of the numerous photographs included—and not included—in *Camera Lucida*, most famously the cherished Winter Garden photograph of his mother as a young girl.[16] In an essay published in *Photography and the Optical Unconscious*, Laura Wexler provides a way of explaining this oversight, positing that the Winter Garden photograph is important precisely because its absence from, yet discursive prominence in, *Camera Lucida* disowns the troubling legacy of Barthes's grandfather, Louis-Gustave Binger, who was a powerful colonial administrator in Côte d'Ivoire.[17] That is, this act of visual negation obscures Barthes's own family ties to France's legacy of colonialism, a history he invoked more explicitly (though without touching on his connections to this history) in an earlier book, *Mythologies*. Published in 1957, *Mythologies* introduced a semiotic method of ideology critique that invoked France's crumbling empire during the turmoil of decolonization in Africa and Indochina.[18] In contrast, however, to *Mythologies*' analytic method, *Camera Lucida*'s personal approach more clearly withdraws from context and history. While we do not suggest *Camera Lucida* links decolonization directly with the global Cold War, its deflections are suggestive.

Notably, obfuscation can be discerned at two key moments. As observed above, obfuscation takes a negative form; specifically, by refusing to withhold the Winter Garden photograph, the book obscures Barthes's personal linkage to the family's role in French colonialism. At the same time, obfuscation operates in what might be described as a positive or productive way, through the showing of Wessing's image from the Nicaragua conflict. That is, the inclusion of Wessing's image to exemplify the mutual influence of studium and punctum, context and feeling, in a manner that glosses over the precise context that produced the image, suggests Barthes's—and readers'—recognition yet simultaneous repression of photography as a global Cold War practice. The inclusion of Wessing's photograph reveals the ways that *Camera Lucida*

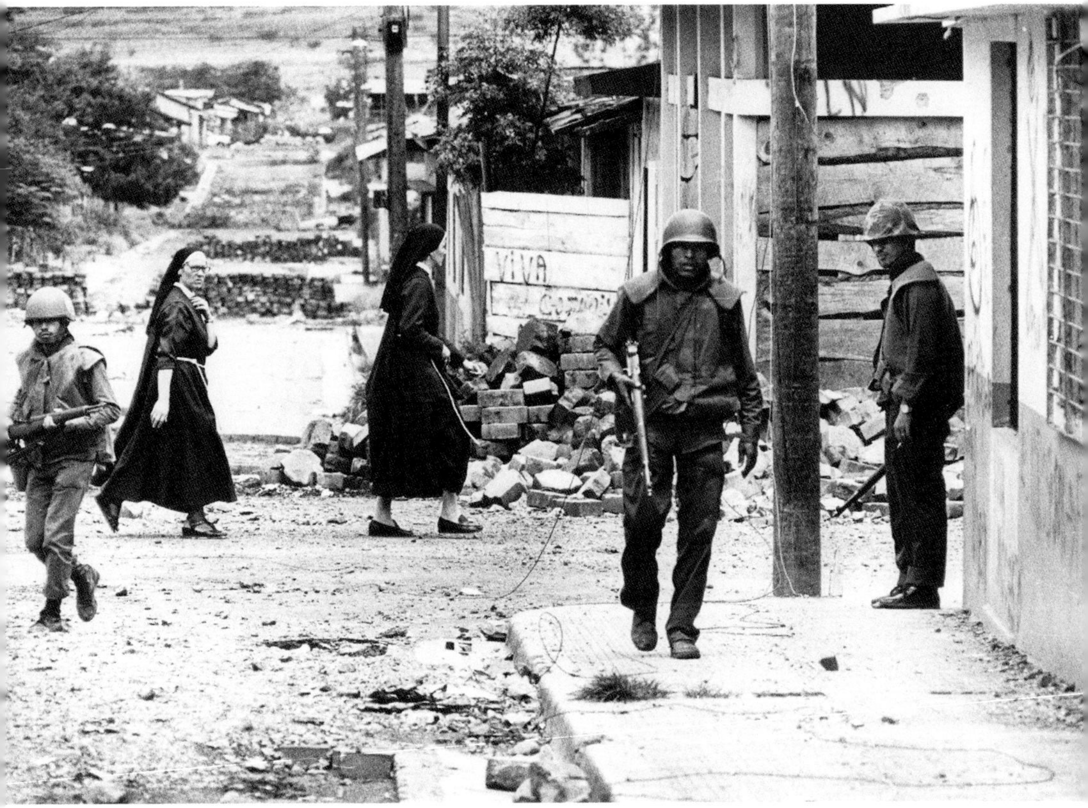


invokes the global Cold War only to disavow its importance for grasping how photography functions visually as a political force within it.

Susan Sontag is even more clearly conflicted in her perspective on photography, which was shaped in response to two excursions to Hanoi, North Vietnam, in 1968 and 1972, as part of a contingent of antiwar activists participating in "radical tourism" during the global Cold War.[19] Her landmark 1977 book, *On Photography*, is striking for wholly excluding images. In a world that Sontag described as increasingly "image-choked," the excessive circulation of images, she worried, diminished their political usefulness.[20] In *Trip to Hanoi*, her 1969 memoir about her experiences, Sontag confessed that photographs of this Cold War conflict formed preconceptions that distorted her view of Vietnam. As Franny Nudelman has pointed out, Sontag's lessons from these trips convinced her that an image-choked world would captivate, not liberate, viewers from the thrall of ideology.[21] In 1973, after Sontag's return to the United States from her second trip to Hanoi, the set of essays expressing her ambivalence about photography's political efficacy appeared in the *New York Review of Books*; they would eventually be published in *On Photography*.

Sontag was not alone in harboring suspicion about the image world. As one of the principal architects of a Euro-American tradition of critique, Sontag shared with her contemporaries, Roland Barthes, Guy DeBord, Victor Burgin, Allan Sekula, and John Tagg, among others, a Leftist, even Marxist intellectual orientation, marked for its misgivings about images.[22] Despite their diverse concerns, these critics questioned images as dangerous spectacles, seductive commodities, beguiling agents of ideology, and forceful state apparatuses. Their shared critical approach evinces, in other words, a "hermeneutics of suspicion," to invoke Paul Ricoeur's term to describe the practice of reading texts against the grain to uncover their concealed meanings. This hermeneutics of suspicion is by no means a Cold War phenomenon but rather part of a broader philosophical tradition that includes the works of Karl Marx, Friedrich Nietzsche, and Sigmund Freud.[23] However, distrust formed a distinctive mode of response from the 1950s to the 1980s, the period that saw the emergence of the paradigms in critique that we have been describing.

Our point in sketching this historiography, which is well known, is to underscore its Cold War connection, which is less often recognized. The foundations of contemporary photography criticism not only were laid at the height of the global Cold War but also form and are largely informed by a commitment to Marxist methodologies, which are rooted in a hermeneutics of suspicion and a corresponding concern with excavating hidden ideologies. Given how generative this Cold War hermeneutics has been in exposing photography's implication with institutional power structures, the continuing influence of this critical approach is hardly surprising. Indeed, Cold War photography criticism has helpfully drawn attention to propaganda as a visual form and has provided a useful method of unmasking disguised messages. However, as Xiaobing Tang observes in his study of Chinese visual culture, critics assume that the production and dissemination of images is predicated on a capitalist political economy whose masked motivations need to be revealed.[24] In contrast, they disregard socialist infrastructures and their attendant motivations, objectives, and modes of expression, which, unlike their capitalist counterparts, might declare rather than obscure ideologies. Take, for example, the New Museum's 1984 exhibition, *The Nicaragua Media Project*. Organized by a group of New York–based photographers and critics, the exhibition interrogated how photography fostered public support of US interventionist policies in Nicaragua. Yet, when it came to the region's own newspapers, including the news daily *Barricada*, these images were largely assumed to stand on their own.[25] Though this assumption of codelessness likely arose from organizers' naive set of relations of rescue politics, nevertheless, its effect was to miss the ways that these images from Nicaragua functioned outside an oppositional us/them framework. Scholarship adhering to a hermeneutics of suspicion provides limited guidance when it comes to images that blatantly proclaim rather than conceal their status as propaganda, foreclosing the opportunity to address other functions, particularly photography's potential to forge international solidarity in visual terms. As Sabine Kriebel observes in the context of Weimar Republic agitprop photography, critics have yet to grapple fully with the multifarious functions and effects of propaganda. Simply labeling images as propaganda, Kriebel asserts, forecloses rather than prompts scholarly inquiry.[26] *Cold War Camera* expands on foundational critical approaches by attending to propaganda's visual tropes and by taking seriously their cultural function. Just as importantly, close examination of the varied practices of photography provides alternative ways of understanding the broader parameters of the Cold War, and desires that extend beyond suspicion and paranoia.

During the global Cold War, propaganda operated most obviously through visual manipulation, which served as a technique that not only captured momentous occasions but also disappeared events—and people—from history. Beginning in the early twentieth-century and continuing until his death in 1953, Josef Stalin demanded that retouchers erase from official records the figures of former allies, whom he had purged from the Communist Party as state enemies. The Soviet empire asserted its power through ruthless management of the visual field so that when leaders set their sights on nonaligned African nations, they sought to enforce their authority by controlling visual production.[27] In Ethiopia, for example, to prevent their power from being threatened by rival Marxist-Leninist groups, the Derg prohibited the production of photography outside government sanctioned studios.[28] Eric Gottesman's photographic series, *The Preservation of Terror*, a selection of which appears in this volume, includes images that families collected and saved during this turbulent period, which the artist then rephotographed. Together, these images constitute a counterarchive that attests to quotidian ways of resisting the repressive late-1970s period known as Qey Shabir, or the Ethiopian Red Terror.[29] Likewise, in Poland during the Cold War, the state regulated visual production to support and promote a vision of its ostensible successes.[30] Yet,

**Figure I.3.** Tong Lam, *#B1*, from *Lost Emulsion* series, 2019. Courtesy of the artist.

as the chapter by Gil Pasternak and Marta Ziętkiewicz in this volume shows, domestic images of Polish Jews during this period contested the Soviet empire's metanarrative of national cohesion, which disavowed the existence of ethnic difference.[31] Meanwhile, in China, figures who threatened Mao's star status in the photographic frame could be eliminated as readily as Stalin's enemies.[32]

The practice of manipulation was particularly commonplace during China's Cultural Revolution, as Laura Wexler's, Karintha Lowe's, and Guigui Yao's chapters in this volume also detail. The Cultural Revolution demanded such steadfast loyalty to the state that seemingly inoffensive domestic images became dangerous as they threatened to expose ideologically suspect affiliations and unacceptably bourgeois tastes. Careful examination of family photographs that survived the purge provides, according to Wexler, Lowe, and Yao, a means of reckoning with the impact of this suppression. And yet, communists also produced photographs under trying conditions of war, with limited resources, to give form to socialist ideals and to recruit supporters, locally and globally, to their cause.[33] These are just some of the ways that communists delineated the contours of what could and could not be seen, drawing on photography both to conjure and destroy. Tracing the practices of photography during the global Cold War accordingly requires that we account for the missing and the disappeared, to look beyond what is visible, beyond, that is, the image. Here we follow the insightful work of scholars such as Elizabeth Edwards and, especially, James Hevia, who call on critics to expand paradigms of photography beyond the image, to take account of what Hevia describes as the "photography complex," which is shaped by a confluence of forces and histories.[34] This book emphasizes the Cold War *camera* to acknowledge an intricate material and ideological apparatus, that is, the photography complex, wherein the workings of power are manifest in what can be perceived, in the repression of sites and subjects from the visual field, and in the production and preservation of images that circumvent these operations.[35] An image, from a series titled *Lost Emulsion* by historian and pho-

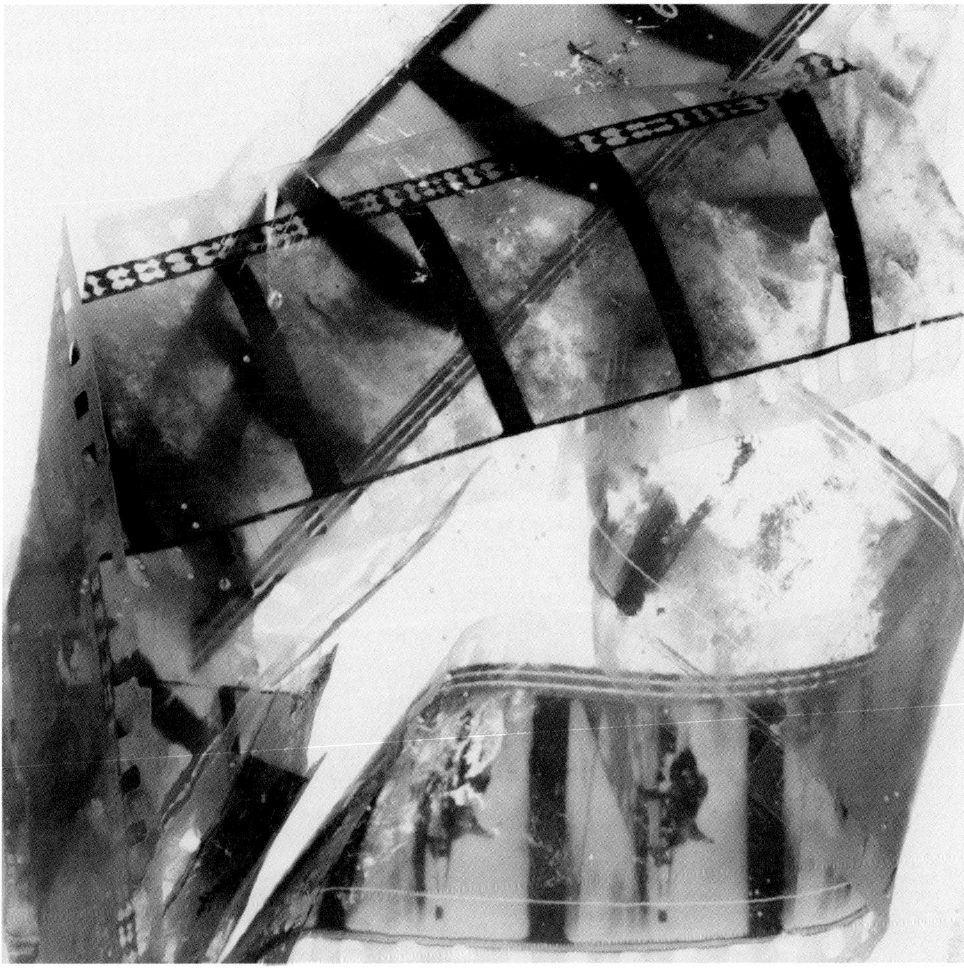

tographer Tong Lam that also serves as the cover of this book, exemplifies this entanglement (figure I.3). Describing the series, which depicts a former Soviet long-range bomber base in eastern Kazakhstan more than two decades after it had been decommissioned, Lam notes that, even though missing information on damaged film might be irrecoverable, "analog residuals are reminders of the continuing perils of self-annihilation and mutual destruction as new geopolitical rivalries have been exacerbated by weaponized digital infrastructures."[36] The images of these "analog residuals" expose the political unconscious of the global Cold War's visual regimes.

Even as photography was used to repress during the global Cold War, it also offered ways of constructing transnational visual alliances. Visual alliances take manifold forms, including exhibitions, which, as Susan Reid shows in her work on the culture of the communist bloc, provided venues for painters and photographers to showcase their work and share ideas on the relationship between politics and aesthetics.[37] Visual alliances also materialized through circuits for the exchange of photographic equipment and technical knowledge. As Thy Phu points out elsewhere, the development of "socialist ways of seeing" in North Vietnam depended on East German training and on Soviet cameras and rolls of film sent through Hong Kong and China, the same routes that images were sent out for exhibitions.[38] Crucially, then, we invoke visual alliances to denote affinities, collaborations, and solidarities that circuits of production, remediation, and circulation—crisscrossing East to West as well as North to South and vice versa—were meant to conjure and the futurities and political formations these solidarities sought to bring into fruition.

As an example of the photographic activation of alternative political formations we need only look to the 1955 exhibition, *The Family of Man*. This well-known show has inspired voluminous commentary, initially in the form of objections against the universal humanism deployed through the domestic trope of "family," which according to critics, denoted a sentimental form of belonging that masked the exhibition's corporate sponsorship and ideological collaboration. Critics further charged that, by invoking the idea of family, this exhibition mobilized domesticity as a means of advancing US hegemony.[39] However, recent reassessments have drawn attention to how this universal humanism conjured alternative possibilities, that is, other ways to imagine forms of belonging and to conceptualize futurities beyond conventional metanarratives of linearity and progress.[40] As numerous critics have observed, *The Family of Man* was not only on exhibit at the Museum of Modern Art in New York City but also circulated internationally by the United States Information Agency (USIA), in the form of five replicas, which toured as many as forty-eight countries, stretching from Europe to Latin America, from India to Africa, and from the Middle East to Japan.[41] Significantly, visitors at many of these international venues responded in ways that did not align with the USIA's imperialist intentions and ideological expectations.[42] For instance, when the exhibition toured West Berlin, during a time when East Germans were able to cross the border more freely than after the construction of the Berlin Wall, observers from the German Democratic Republic were surprised, remarking that the vision of unity promoted by *The Family of Man* aligned with socialist ideals, or, in other words, with a political formation completely outside the USIA's scope.[43] We draw inspiration from this important recent work but are also keenly aware of how the robust attention given to this exhibition has obfuscated the ways that other organizations, including the UN and the World Health Organization, have likewise harnessed the medium in the service of a "critical photographic futurism."[44]

In addition to forging unlikely visual alliances, *The Family of Man* also challenged modern conceptions of historical time. Critics such as Monique Berlier have interpreted the exhibition in ways that emphasize linear progress, namely, as constituting a post–World War II politics of reconciliation through the foregrounding of themes such as reconstruction, liberation from economic and military domination, and the end of colonial rule.[45] However, *The Family of Man*'s innovative design and creative juxtapositions provided a rejoinder to this metanarrative of linearity.[46] That is, the exhibition, by providing a limited amount of text, and especially by juxtaposing a multiplicity of quotidian photographs of birth, love, labor, hunger, and death, dislodged the supposed fixity of individual photographs and opened them up to the reconsideration of modern historical time. Juxtaposition, in other words, made possible the visualization of forms of countertemporality that helped unhinge teleological notions of linearity, homogeneity, and progress.

In addition to unsettling chronological time, *Cold War Camera* also attends to time as "conspicuous" or "out-of-joint" with history's progressive unfolding of past-present-future. In his exploration of temporality and political action, David Scott ruminates on how, in the wake of the tragic collapse of the Grenada Revolution (1979–83) and the emancipatory future that it anticipated, "time had found itself *betrayed* by history."[47] More precisely, he observes that, because revolutions are often conceived as chronological in time, their failure, whether in the case of Grenada or in the case of potential political configurations like the Bandung project, disrupts this chronology, resulting in a sense of disjointedness. We believe that the camera is especially suited to Scott's "demand for a new sensitivity of time" and, following his lead, reckon with the "aftermaths" and "afterness" of the global Cold War and its foreclosed revolutionary potentials by considering how photography might help destabilize chronological or historical time.[48]

As an index or a trace, photography is fundamentally a temporal medium; it represents something in the past that is seen in the present. But this "now time," as Walter Benjamin famously argues, is not the past "cast[ing]

**Figure I.4.** Florencio López Osuna beaten and detained during the Tlatelolco massacre, 2 October 1968. Photograph by Manuel Gutiérrez Paredes. iisue/ahunam, Colección Manuel Gutiérrez Paredes, mgp-3079.

its light on what is present or what is present cast[ing] its light on what is past." Rather, Benjamin continues, it is "that in which the Then and the Now come together, in a flash of lightning, into a constellation."[49] The meaning of a photograph, in other words, is never finished but exceeds the moment of its taking, or even exists despite the fact that an image might never be produced or be preserved. Moreover, this moment is subject to contingency and therefore has the potential to enact further encounters, as is the case when photography supports calls for transitional justice or serves as forensic evidence of atrocity.

For a glimpse of how temporalities become conflated and why they need to be pried apart, consider an example from Mexico. Although this nation-state is not usually associated with the bipolar politics of the global Cold War, nevertheless, the circulation and remediation of select icons there offer lessons on how discrete histories of violence are repeated and fused together.[50] One such photograph depicts the brutalized, seminaked body of student leader Florencio López Osuna, beaten and detained (figure I.4). Concealed from view for over three decades by the state, the photograph is an icon of the Tlatelolco Massacre (October 2, 1968), an event at which socialist student leaders were brutally crushed by the state. This massacre, which has come to be seen in Mexico as a watershed moment in the global Cold War, has gone on to symbolize other violent events, as is evident in the photograph's prominent display in the 2015 exhibition, *The Lessons of 68: Why Should October 2 Not Be Forgotten?*, at Mexico City's Museo de la Memoria y Tolerancia (Museum of Memory and Tolerance).[51] In the exhibition, visitors had first to pass a series of photographs of the 1968 Tlatelolco victims before ending up at a set of empty chairs adorned only with posters that included identification photos of the forty-three student teachers murdered in 2014 as part of Mexico's drug wars. Through this juxtaposition of Tlatelolco 1968 and what is now known

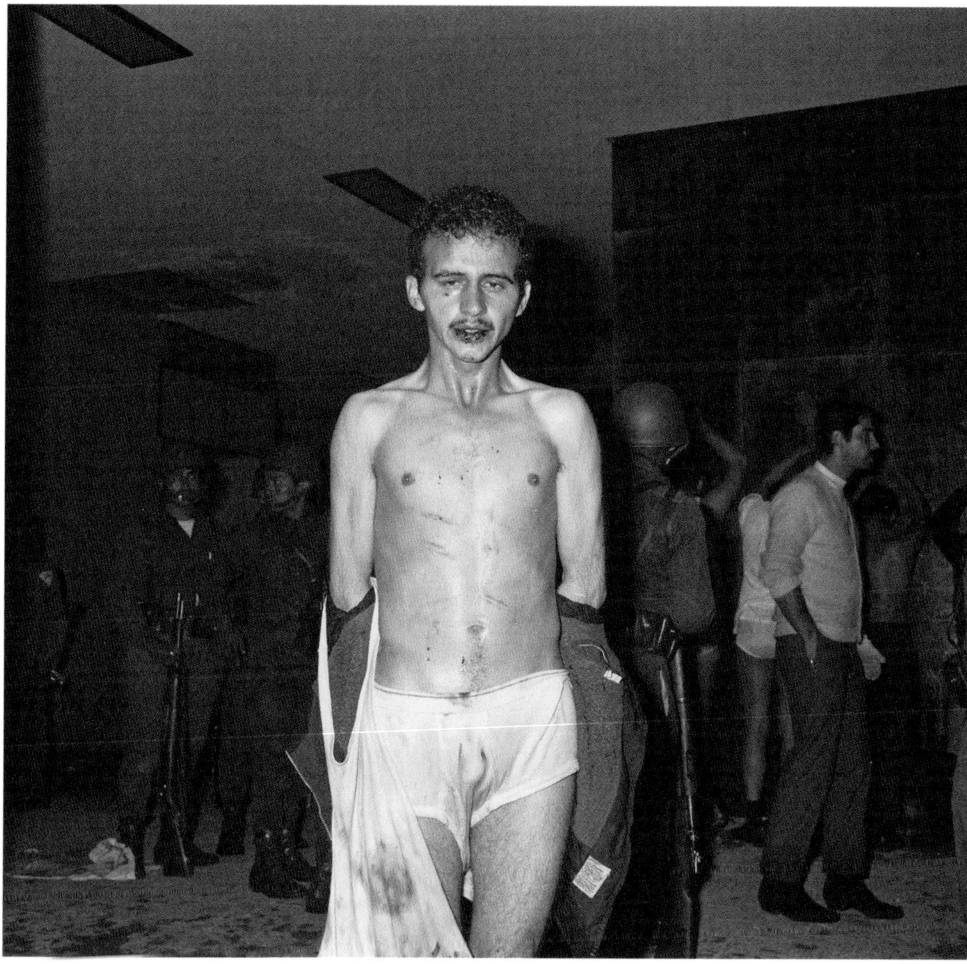

as Ayotzinapa's 43, the exhibition visually connected two moments and two massacres. Significantly, the insertion of the Ayotzinapa case into this larger linear narrative provides a convenient way for the police to avoid being held accountable. Indeed, police handed over the students to the cartel, and the Governor of Guerrero (the state where the students were taken, tortured, and disappeared). In other words, this juxtaposition helps to perpetuate the practice of "seeing red," whereby the image of the largely socialist-leaning members of the student movement in 1968 provides a cultural shorthand to grapple with the deaths of the forty-three disappeared student teachers, who were misrecognized by their kidnappers as members of Rojos (or Reds), a rival gang. On the one hand, recent remediations of the Tlatelelco photograph help highlight the ways that covert operations during the global Cold War have directly contributed to the clandestine global narcotics industry, escalating the drug wars in Mexico.[52] On the other hand, these remediations conceal the Mexican state's own complicity in drug-related violence. In short, the icon of Tlatelelco operates as a screen memory for Ayotzinopa, wherein a highly visible image serves as a means of repression, enabling the state to perpetrate violence.

Reflecting critically on visual juxtapositions enables us not only to disrupt the linearity of Cold War chronological time but also to perceive more clearly the concerns and aspirations that brought together disparate sites outside the bipolar geopolitics of the Cold War. In art history, for instance, the Bandung Conference, held in Indonesia in 1955, and seen by many as the beginnings of the Non-Aligned Movement, is notably absent from the discipline's reconsideration of the Cold War's impact on the visual arts. Instead, as Saloni Mathur points out, "its account of cold-war culture continues to privilege the art-historical divide between a dominant prewar France and American hegemony after the war."[53] Yet, some recent projects are beginning to elucidate the potential of other visual exchanges.[54] For example, Bojana Piškur has examined cultural exchanges between the newly emerging postcolonial states in Latin America, Asia, and Africa, which sought independence outside the major power blocs.[55] Moreover, as the collaborative project *Red Africa* further suggests, cross-cultural exchanges between Africa and the Soviet Union helped build a politics of "affective community," a network of affinity and friendship.[56] *Cold War Camera* contributes to the critical conversations sparked by this exciting recent work.

## STRUCTURES OF SEEING: THE COLD WAR CAMERA

Another key component of our book is photography's enlistment in structuring ways of seeing war. Here we invoke and respond to the theoretical insights of John Berger's concept of "ways of seeing," which highlights the unsettled relationship between what we see and what we know, as well as Raymond Williams's notion of "structures of feeling," which denotes that not all thought processes can be described in terms of conscious and fully formulated ideas and attitudes, nor do they wholly align with dominant ideologies or worldviews.[57] Tuong's visual pedagogy, as shown in the photographs with which we began, provides another instructive approach to structures of seeing. After all, his debriefing demonstrated an object lesson in how to see, a moment that brings together theory and practice. *Cold War Camera*, then, establishes the conditions through which war is made visible—a process that, conversely, entails ensuring that components of this act of waging war remain invisible.

We invoke the term Cold War *camera*, then, in order to emphasize how the history of photography is enmeshed in war, whether in heavy-handed or more subtle ways. Shortly after the inception of photography in 1839, the first cameras were taken onto the battlefield to document the Mexican-American War (1846–48). Experiments in battlefield photography continued on the ground in subsequent conflicts, including the Crimean War (1853–56) and American Civil War (1861–65).[58] However, the limitations of early cameras, posed by slow shutter speed and cumbersome equipment, made it all but impossible to capture combat instantaneously and with immediacy. The visual idiom of war changed dramatically with the invention of the "vestpocket" Kodak, which soldiers took into the field, and the development of the Leica camera, which was lighter and more compact than earlier equipment, thereby making it discreet or, at times, even unseen. As a genre, war photography is generally characterized by these up-close and gritty depictions of combat by photojournalists with Leicas or similarly small, handheld cameras. Its images, then, implicitly present themselves as an authentic record of a moment of conflict, unaffected by any photographer's bias. Even today, objectivity and immediacy are valued when it comes to spot news reporting of war.

The concept of the Cold War camera enriches our understanding of war photography beyond a generic category that, with some notable exceptions, is still largely defined by expectations of authenticity and associated with visual tropes that tend to linger on the devastation of battle, the glorification of soldiers, and the suffering of civilians. However, the task of reckoning with the global Cold War, which, as noted above, was experienced as hot proxy conflicts in the global South *and* as "the long peace," requires us to grapple with war's visual conventions in a more expansive way. The hotness of the global Cold War, our contributors show, is visible not just through violent spectacle. In addition to combat, war photography includes the repressive reach of state censorship; the subtle and ham-fisted rhetoric of propaganda; the lull between battle; the erasure of images; the desire to make and preserve images in the face of violence; the seemingly mundane pleasures of leisurely consumption; the depiction of everyday life; the resilience of survival; and the struggle for justice.

When it comes to the global Cold War, the practice of photography developed in a manner that extended a long-standing concern with verticality, the view from above, which Nicholas Mirzoeff elsewhere associates with the "overseer."[59] This preoccupation with verticality, as Caren Kaplan and other critics note, dates back to nineteenth-century surveillance expeditions. Undertaken in tandem with, and as part of, colonial expansion, these expeditions evinced a desire to render territory intelligible and thereby impose dominion over it. Verticality supported and advanced military objectives, starting with the colonial wars of the nineteenth-century and continuing throughout the twentieth-century. Initially, experiments with photographic elevation began with the mounting of cameras on hot air balloons for aerial surveys. Subsequently, the enlistment of the camera for the purposes of war became unmistakable when photographic equipment was brought on board the very planes that carried munitions and dropped bombs.[60] Hackneyed or not, the camera-as-gun analogy is hard to dismiss.[61] In the case of World War I aerial reconnaissance missions, the limited load of planes meant that cameramen doubled as gunners.[62] By the start of the global Cold War, engineers had not only solved such technological limitations, they also went on to test drones in the Vietnam conflict to amplify the scope of the visual field. Widely considered a milestone in visual history because of the rise of television news reporting, the Vietnam conflict also marked the first helicopter war, with the heavily armed UH-1 "Huey" transporting photojournalists to battlefields, often on the way to military missions.[63]

Perhaps the most potent example of verticality is also the most recognizable Cold War icon: the mushroom cloud of nuclear annihilation. Taken from above, the mushroom cloud helped construct what amounts to a nuclear optic, or what Joseph Masco describes as a discourse that lingers on the sublimity of the abstract view from unfathomable heights by obscuring ground-level devastation.[64] The view from above also served the ends of state surveillance, when US aerial photographs taken from U-2 spy-planes played a key role during the 1962 Cuban Missile Crisis by providing evidence of USSR ballistic missile deployment near the coast of Florida, bringing the superpowers to the brink of nuclear confrontation. As these examples illustrate, the producers of the most well-known Cold War images often adopted an aerial perspective wherein, as Paula Amad has argued, invocation of a biblical "God's-eye view" helped them assert territorial mastery.[65] And yet, viewers had to be shown what and how to see. The claim of territorial mastery was not convincing when images mounted in its support were fuzzy. The sheer volume of surveillance photographs, not to mention their abstract content, required teams of specialists, so-called imagery analysts, to decipher their meanings.[66] Notably,

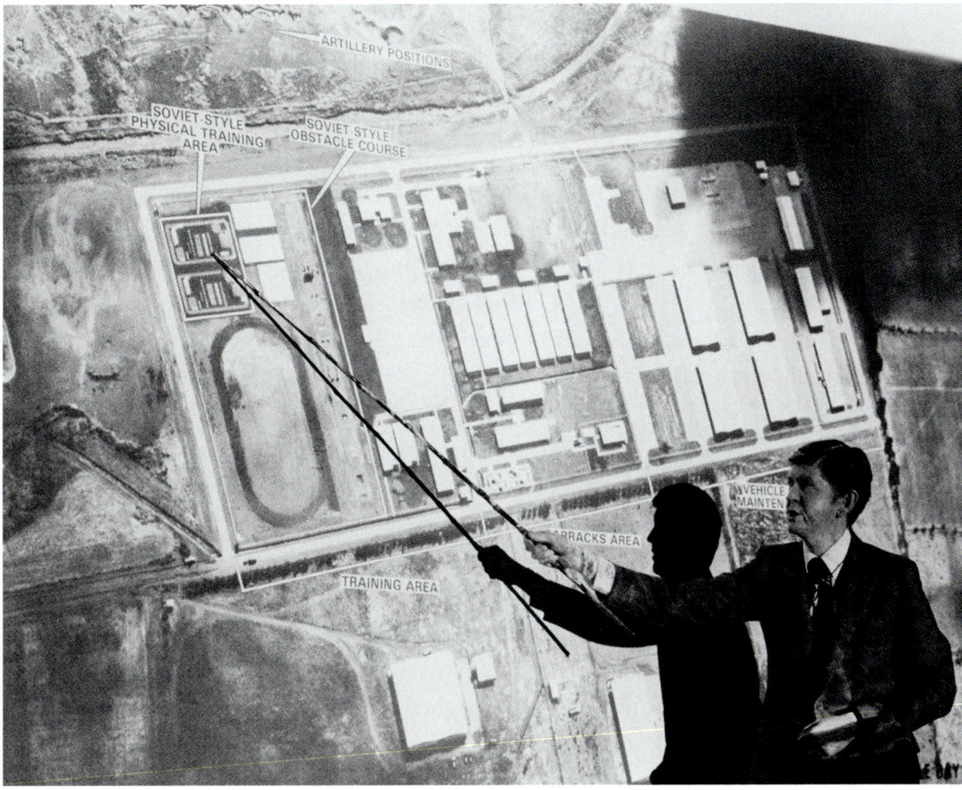


**Figure I.5.** **John Hughes, deputy director of the Defense Intelligence Agency, uses a slide of a reconnaissance photo to support Reagan administration claims that Nicaragua has engaged in a major military buildup. This slide, shown during a State Department News Conference Tuesday, March 9, 1982, in Washington, DC, purports to show a Soviet-style training area and obstacle course in Managua, Nicaragua. AP Photo by Ira Schwarz.**

John T. Hughes, perhaps the most famous of these experts, was called upon to interpret aerial reconnaissance photos during the Cuban Missile Crisis and, again in the 1980s, as part of the monitoring by the United States of alleged Soviet military support to Nicaragua (figure I.5).[67]

At the same time, it was not only verticality, nor for that matter spectacular icons, that structured ways of seeing the global Cold War.[68] Just as important is what might be described as a horizontal perspective, the ground-level view at a more human scale. To provide a fuller understanding of the concern with global Cold War photography's "dimensionality," Rebecca Adelman's term for the preoccupation, on the part of state and nonstate viewers, with the scope and scale of visual warfare, we also highlight the importance of horizontal perspectives.[69] We began this introduction with Tuong's photographs, which are unremarkable in form and mundane in content, to highlight how the quotidian might shape what could and could not be seen, an influence often overshadowed by spectacles and icons of war. When it comes to the relationship between verticality and horizontality, as Sarah Parsons shows in her contribution to this book, aerial surveillance did not sufficiently delineate the High Arctic's territorial boundaries. Photographs of Inuit people taken on the ground and on a human scale provided the Canadian state with a paternalistic means of appropriating indigeneity and thus authenticating their sovereignty against competing claims. By drawing attention to the significance of horizontal structures of seeing, this book complements studies that have illuminated the importance of verticality, while also taking heed of Caren Kaplan's reminder that verticality and horizontality are by no means binary modes of operation but instead work in tandem to reveal and obscure.

Our contributors also consider the significance of horizontal perspectives as they unfold in domestic images, taking seriously the quotidian as a means of resilience. Domestic images, they show, activate the potential for a "positive" contrast to the negating abstractions of state surveillance and provide a visual form for imagining other ways of living. Through reexamination of the contexts for the production and preservation of family photographs, our contributors also reckon with the impact of domesticity as a discourse that links the seemingly discrete sphere of the home to a broader, often more overtly violent theater of operations.[70] The famous 1959 "kitchen debate" between US vice president Richard Nixon and Soviet premier Nikita Khrushchev, set against the kitchen of a Long Island modular house at Sokolniki Park in Moscow so as to showcase the triumphs of capitalism over the so-called backwardness of Soviet communism, foregrounds how domesticity functioned as principal organizing feature of the global Cold War.[71] That is, though domestic images may be made for personal reasons, they are by no means fixed at any one site but rather, as our contributors show, move between personal and public spheres, even as the latter has historically set the terms for what can be photographed and shown. As Gillian Rose has argued, following Marianne Hirsch and others on the circuits that indelibly bind the personal and the public, domestic images operate in ways that expand beyond what she describes as a "familial practice," especially as they intersect with mass media.[72] And yet, without denying the ways that domestic images were operationalized for the assertion of soft power, we assess how they might also offer a means of envisioning alternative modes of belonging and relationality, particularly when situated within a broader global Cold War context that politicized the concept of family.[73] *Cold War Camera* examines family photographs, then, as exemplars of horizontality that not only served the ends of US hegemony but also expressed aspirations for survival and remembrance. At the same time, we acknowledge the limits of our subject positions as critics based in the global North, whose training—and ways of seeing—are shaped by the very structures we call into question here. Our attempts to engage in transnational research, we recognize, are also limited by language; this book's composition and publication in English delineates a particular way of seeing and risks confirming the hegemony of what is known as global English. We hope that by drawing attention to structures of seeing, including our own, this book will inspire critics to further widen frameworks for seeing the global Cold War.

## CHAPTER OUTLINES

This book explores photography as a cultural practice that can both facilitate and impede global interconnectedness in the long Cold War. Attending to photography in an expansive way requires a multidisciplinary approach, which is why this book includes visual artists in addition to photography scholars, historians, and literary critics from fields that range from American to Latin American studies, from transpacific and literary critique to art history. The first section, "Visual Alliances," explains how photography brokered Cold War solidarities between diverse and dispersed groups and considers the contexts in which it enabled nonaligned communities to form. The section begins with Darren Newbury's chapter, which explores continuities and discontinuities of the global Cold War through the tangled visual histories of apartheid South Africa and the United States. Focusing on the unlikely alliance that Ernest Cole, a black South African photographer, made with the USIA, Newbury examines contradictions that pulsed through international racial solidarity and conduits through which photography, here understood in terms of a politicized social biography, traveled.

In their collaborative chapter, Thy Phu, Evyn Lê Espiritu Gandhi, and Donya Ziaee show that the icon of the revolutionary Vietnamese woman provided a means for solidarity across multiple liberation movements. By tracing the photographic circulation of this contested figure within Vietnam, Palestine, and Iran, the authors argue that the icon called into being, if only temporarily, a vexed form of solidarity, taking visual form through juxtaposition or "parallelism," which nevertheless needed to grapple with the internal and external political rifts associated with the intertwined causes of decolonization, women's emancipation, and national liberation. Erina Duganne meditates further on how "visual solidarities" are constructed, focusing on the activist work of New York City–based artist collective Group Material and their 1982 exhibition *¡LUCHAR! An Exhibition for the People of Central America*. Rather than promoting commonalities and acts of identification, Duganne proposes that visual solidarities also create misrecognitions and contingencies, which demand a reconsideration of the temporalities of the global Cold War. Ángeles Donoso Macaya also takes up US–Latin American solidarity networks in her chapter on the book *Chile from Within* (1990), edited by Chilean photographers in collaboration with Magnum photographer Susan Meiselas. Produced in the wake of Augusto Pinochet's military regime, this book, as Macaya argues, is the product of a "situated visuality," or a partial and incomplete perspective, which disrupts the bipolar framework of the Cold War by providing a means of historical reckoning with US intervention in the region. In her chapter, Jennifer Bajorek takes us backward in time. Though cautioning against the "lure of redemptive narratives" that would negate the recolonizing realities of so-called decolonization, Bajorek considers how newly discovered archives might provide a means of tracing an alternative world order based on the principles of African solidarity and unity, and a resource for reckoning with notions of futurity that have been foreclosed.

We connect the two sections with an interlude that features two photo-essays. Tong Lam's photo-essay meditates on Cold War aftermaths by juxtaposing a set of paired images of Cold War ruins from often overlooked locales to establish unexpected parallels between them. In so doing, Lam's work pries apart superpower binaries. Eric Gottesman's photo-essay examines how domestic images might form a counterarchive in the context of Ethiopia's communist government, known as the Derg, which prohibited public photography during the Ethiopian Red Terror. His deployment of domestic images contests discourses about the nuclear family and constructs visual kinships.

The second section, "Structures of Seeing," traces some less familiar and, in certain cases, familial ways that photography was used to structure what could be seen and known during the global Cold War and, conversely, what remained hidden and unknown. The section opens with a chapter by Ariella Aïsha Azoulay, which examines the theoretical implications of the emergence of a new world order, at the end of World War II, under the auspices of the

United Nations. Although Azoulay's approach diverges from the contextually grounded and archivally based methodologies employed elsewhere in this volume, the chapter provides a provocative framework for understanding which histories become documented and which icons become recognizable—and which scenes of violence and repression remain unseen. At a moment when the world was violently divided into two blocs, Azoulay reflects on how photographs became didactic tools to preserve a system of differential sovereignty, which flattened complex subject positions between victims, perpetrators, and spectators and rendered certain catastrophes unrecognizable as a violation of rights. Meanwhile, Sarah Parsons's chapter situates the forced relocation of Inuit families within a global Cold War context of competing claims to Arctic territory and its abundant natural resources; she argues that the Canadian state produced photographic evidence of the presence of Indigenous peoples through the deployment of a horizontal perspective. Laura Wexler, Karintha Lowe, and Guigui Yao also explore horizontality as manifest in the politicization of family in China, evident through the production and preservation of family photographs during the global Cold War.

Oksana Sarkisova and Olga Shevchenko further examine horizontality through a series of visual tropes as they emerge in family photography archives, which facilitate the traversal and unification of far-flung Soviet sites. We conclude the volume with a chapter by Gil Pasternak and Marta Ziętkiewicz, which provides a counterintuitive analysis of the potential of photographs not just to look back on Cold War histories but also to re-narrate these histories and their legacies. Whereas the work of Sarkisova and Shevchenko attests to the lasting power of travel photography to appropriate space and mark it as generically Soviet, even while asserting nominal differences, Pasternak and Ziętkiewicz consider how the family album in Poland was used to expose ethnic differences—the presence of Jewish subjects—as a means of contesting Soviet discourses that disavowed these differences.

While no single volume can be comprehensive or exhaustive in covering global Cold War photography, this book suggests new directions in Cold War cultural criticism and reveals how photography as a practice provides a means of tracing the circuits through which visual alliances were brokered and a means of delineating the complexities of structures of seeing. In shifting the focus to take account of cold *and* hot entanglements along a North-South axis, *Cold War Camera* offers new insights on the visual rhetoric of seeing and not seeing, resistance and struggle, solidarity and collaboration. The critical reorientation we develop here also approaches photography as a practice about the future, regardless of whether these aspirations were ever realized, and helps disrupt the linearity and homogeneity of metanarratives about the global Cold War by drawing attention to the political formations and imaginaries that serve as alternatives to the superpower paradigms. Though the book emphasizes the hotness of proxy battlegrounds in the global South, in adopting this approach we do not mean to suggest that temporal disruptions are limited to this region. Rather, these disruptions, as Erina Duganne's chapter shows, reverberate more widely along the North-South axis. In these ways, *Cold War Camera* contributes to an emerging groundswell of scholarship that questions the boundaries of this conflict and suggests ways of understanding how photography delineated, navigated, and stretched the spatiotemporal parameters of the global Cold War.

*Notes*

1 The war in Vietnam was a conflict that involved more players than just the United States in alliance with the South Vietnamese government against communists from North Vietnam. Through Lyndon B. Johnson's "More Flags" campaign, Filipino and South Korean mercenaries joined the fighting and assisted in the logistics of warfare. Moreover, the war spilled over to Laos and Cambodia, when covert bombing campaigns were authorized in those countries in an effort to destroy the Ho Chi Minh Trail, which wound through the mountainous jungle border. See Blackburn, *Mercenaries and Lyndon Johnson's "More Flags."*

2 Zolov, "Introduction: Latin America in the Global Sixties," 353. Serge Guilbaut's seminal work on the political utility of Abstract Expressionism during the Cold War pioneered the cultural turn in Cold War studies. See Guilbaut, *How New York Stole the Idea of Modern Art*. For even earlier interventions, see Cockcroft, "Abstract Expressionism"; and Ashton, *New York School*.

3 The scholarship on Cold War cultural studies is too voluminous to survey fully. Some representative influential studies include May, *Recasting America*; Von Eschen, *Satchmo Blows Up the World*; Shaw, *Hollywood's Cold*; Falk, *Upstaging the Cold War*; C. F. Fox, *Making Art Panamerican*; Saunders, *The Cultural Cold War*; Barnhisel, *Cold War Modernists*; Bradley and Werner, *We Gotta Get Out of This Place*; Fosler-Lussier, *Music in America's Cold War Diplomacy*; Kodat, *Don't Act, Just Dance*; Iber, *Neither Peace nor Freedom*; and Wulf, *U.S. International Exhibitions*.

4 See Langford and Langford, *A Cold War Tourist*. See also Bassnett, Noble, and Phu, "Cold War Visual Alliances"; and Hamilton and O'Gorman, *Lookout America!*

5 Grandin, "Living in Revolutionary Time," 2. See also McMahon, *The Cold War in the Third World*. In addition, there is a groundswell of soon-to-be published books taking up similar questions around expanding both the chronological and geographic boundaries of the Cold War. Peter Kalliney's *Bandung Generation: Decolo-*

*nization and the Aesthetic Cold War* is among these forthcoming monographs and edited collections.

6 For example, Stephen G. Rabe seems to insist on this rigid periodization when he opens his concise interpretive history, *The Killing Zone*, with the bold statement: "The Cold War is over" (xxv).

7 Grandin, *Empire's Workshop*, 4.

8 For a general overview of the analytic and practice of decoloniality, including its relationship to modernity/coloniality, see Mignolo and Walsh, *On Decoloniality*.

9 See Man, *Soldiering through Empire*.

10 See Yale, *Cultural Exchange and the Cold War*. Sarah E. James has also detailed how the internationally touring exhibition *The Family of Man* impacted a divided Germany during the global Cold War in her book *Common Ground*.

11 See David-Fox, "The Iron Curtain as Semipermeable Membrane," 14–39.

12 The Non-Aligned Movement included twenty-nine newly liberated countries of Asia and Africa, the self-declared "underdogs of the human race," as Richard Wright called them. Wright wrote one the first substantial and, in many ways, still the most seminal account of the Bandung conference and its role in the foundation of the Non-Aligned Movement in 1961. See Wright, *The Color Curtain*. More recent publications include Lee, *Making a World after Empire*, as well as special issues of the journals *Australian Journal of International Affairs* 70, no. 4 (2016); and *Inter-Asia Cultural Studies* 17, no. 1 (2016). For a visual exploration of the residue of as well as contradictions within the Non-Aligned Movement, see Naeem Mohaiemen, *Two Meetings and a Funeral* (2017), a three-channel digital video installation, which premiered at documenta 14.

13 Though the term *dirty war* derives from the French phrase *la sale guerre*, where it was used by French leftist intellectuals to describe the First Indochina War, it subsequently came to be associated with state repression, first as part of the Algerian conflict of 1954 to 1962, and then, most notably, in Argentina from 1976 to 1983, during which some ten thousand persons were disappeared by the military junta. For a discussion of the etymology and shifting meanings of dirty war, see Smith and Rogers, "War in Gray," 377–98.

14 See D. Taylor, *Disappearing Acts*.

15 See Barthes, *Camera Lucida*.

16 Many scholars guess at what the actual Winter Garden photo looks like and question whether it even exists; they posit that, if it does exist, it may not be as Barthes describes. See, for example, Olin, "Touching Photographs." See also the essays included in Batchen, *Photography Degree Zero*.

17 See Wexler, "The Purloined Image," 264–79. See also *Vita Nova* (dir. Vincent Meessen, 2009), a film that returns to Barthes's engagement with French colonialism.

18 See Barthes, *Mythologies*.

19 See Wu, *Radicals on the Road*.

20 See Sontag, *On Photography*.

21 See Nudelman, "Against Photography."

22 See, for example, Sekula, "The Traffic in Photographs"; Burgin, *Thinking Photography*; Tagg, *The Burden of Representation*; Sekula, "The Body and the Archive"; and Jay, *Downcast Eyes*.

23 See Ricoeur, *Freud and Philosophy*. In "Suspicious Minds," Felski suggests that suspicious reading has an even longer provenance, dating back to medieval witch-hunts. Morris Reich also argues for the importance of a hermeneutics of suspicion to racist deployments of photography in the 1920s and 1930s. See Reich, *Race and Photography*.

24 See Tang, *Visual Culture in Contemporary China*.

25 For a more detailed discussion of this exhibition, see Duganne, "*The Nicaragua Media Project*."

26 See Kriebel, "Photomontage in the Year 1932." Likewise, Fred Turner has argued that reading *The Family of Man* as "an act of instrumental Cold War propaganda" is to miss the transformative potential of the exhibition. See Turner, "*The Family of Man*."

27 See, for example, King, *The Commissar Vanishes*; and Dickerman, "Socialist Realism in the Shadow of Photography."

28. Drew Thompson sheds light on the ways that visual repression operated in Mozambique in his "AIM, FOCUS, SHOOT."

29 The full series is published in Eric Gottesman, "The Preservation of Terror," *Callaloo* 33, no. 1 (2010): 155–64.

30 The extent of these guidelines and censored materials is found in a set of documents smuggled out of the country in 1977, by defector Tomasz Strzyżewski, and subsequently published as *The Polish Black Book of Censorship*. See Laszczuk, "The Visual Politics of Success and Solidarity."

31 Jung Joon Lee advances a similar argument for the case of Korea, contending that the absence of war icons and the dearth of images of civilian casualties in Korean photography reinforced this conflict as the "forgotten war." See Lee, "No End to the Image War."

32 See Yu and Chu, "Photographic Manipulation in China."

33 Phu, "Vietnamese Photography." See also Phu, *Warring Visions: Photography and Vietnam*.

34 Critics who call for an examination of photography beyond the visual include, among others: Hevia, "The Photography Complex"; Edwards and Hart, *Photographs, Objects, Histories*; Azoulay, *The Civil Imagination*; and Campt, *Listening to Images*.

35 In *Photography and the Optical Unconscious*, Shawn Michelle Smith and Sharon Sliwinski show invisibility as a core part of the camera's operation; photography, they contend, encompasses the unseen as well as the seen. See also S. M. Smith, *At the Edge of Sight*.

36 Tong Lam, email correspondence with Thy Phu, September 2, 2019.

37 See Reid, "(Socialist) Realism Unbound." For a good overview of the material and visual world of the Socialist Bloc from the late 1940s to the late 1960s, see Crowley, *Style and Socialism.*

38 See Phu, "Vietnamese Photography," xxx.

39 See, for example, Roland Barthes, "The Great Family of Man"; Sekula, "The Traffic in Photographs"; Hirsch, *Family Frames*; and Solomon-Godeau, "'The Family of Man.'"

40 The most notable of these reassessments can be found in Sandeen, *Picturing an Exhibition*; Back and Schmidt-Linsenhoff, *The Family of Man*; and Hurm et. al, *The Family of Man Revisited.*

41 For a discussion of the exhibition's world tour in relation to Cold War politics, see Sandeen, *Picturing an Exhibition.*

42 See Garb, "Rethinking Sekula." For other ways that photography has been employed in the struggle for human rights, especially in Latin America during the Cold War, see Noble, "Travelling Theories of Family." Mary Dudziak has likewise shown how the Cold War profoundly influenced the Civil Rights movement in the United States, which was previously seen only as a domestic concern. See Dudziak, *Cold War Civil Rights.*

43 Of the approximately 44,000 people who visited *The Family of Man* in West Berlin, one quarter to a third of those visitors came from East Germany. See James, *Common Ground*; and Kuehn, *Caught.*

44 Vokes and Newbury, "Photography and African Futures." See also Rodogno and David, "All the World Loves a Picture."

45 See Berlier, "*The Family of Man.*"

46 Fred Turner has convincingly argued that this design, which activated a participatory potential built extensively on the ideas of Bauhaus refugee designer Herbert Bayer. See Turner, "*The Family of Man.*" Turner's persuasive account of the significance of this design has influenced numerous critics, who have drawn on his argument to underpin their reclaiming of a more positive view of the exhibition's potential. See, especially, Zamir, "Structures of Rhyme."

47 D. Scott, *Omens of Adversity*, 2.

48 D. Scott, *Omens of Adversity*, 10.

49 Benjamin, "N [Theoretics of Knowledge; Theory of Progress]," in G. Smith, *Benjamin: Philosophy, Aesthetics, History*, 50–51. See also Cadava, *Theses on the Photography of History*; and Assubuji and Hayes, "The Political Sublime."

50 See Blacker, "Cold War in the Countryside." See also Pensado, *Rebel Mexico.*

51 In 2001, the image, which has since become an icon of the Mexican student movement, reappeared as one of a series of thirty-five photographs, published over two consecutive issues of *Proceso* (#1311 and #1312), at a pivotal moment in Mexico's democratic transition. For more on this set of photographs, see Noble, "Recognizing Historical Injustice."

52 For more on the global drug war, see Scott, *American War Machine*; and Bergen-Cico, *War and Drugs*.

53 Mathur, "Charles and Ray Eames in India," 40. This oversight extends to scholarship on *The Family of Man*, which opened in India only months after the Bandung Conference. Because the United States viewed Bandung as a threat (as did the USSR), USIA believed the exhibition could woo India from this new alliance of "third" or "non-aligned" nations. However, according to critic and novelist Mulk Raj Anand, Indian audiences were indifferent to the political framing of this exhibition, suggesting that the ideological vision of USIA did not always come across as the agency intended. See Anand, "Photography as an Art Form," 2–3, which is cited in Gupta, "Belatedness and Simultaneity."

54 The growing body of work on Afro-Asian encounters in the interdisciplinary field of Asian American studies can be traced back to a desire to engage with this moment/movement. See, for example, Onishi, *Transpacific Antiracism*. Scholars are also reconsidering the broader impact of Bandung and NAM. See Acharya and Tan, *Bandung Revisited*; and Lee, *Making a World after Empire*.

55 See Piškur, "Solidarity in Arts and Culture."

56 *Red Africa* was a series of seminars and events, including the exhibition *Things Fall Apart*, held at London's Calvert 22 in 2016. For more on this project, see Nash, *Red Africa*. For an historical analysis of the cultural connections and disconnections between Africa and the Soviet Union, see Katsakioris, "The Soviet-South Encounter"; and Vucetic and Betts, *Tito in Africa*.

57 See J. Berger, *Ways of Seeing*; and Williams, "Structures of Feelings."

58 The historiography of war photography is immense, but some seminal overviews include Brothers, *War and Photography*; Tucker, *War/Photography*; Rosenheim, *Photography and the American Civil War*; and Kennedy and Patrick, *The Violence of the Image*. See also Oldfield, *Photography and War*. On the politics of aesthetics when it comes to war photography, see Reinhardt et al., *Beautiful Suffering*.

59 See Mirzoeff, *The Right to Look*.

60 For an excellent cultural history of aerial imagery, beginning in the eighteenth century, see Kaplan, *Aerial Aftermaths*.

61 The analogy was established most influentially by Sontag in *On Photography*. The conflict in Vietnam also produced an iconic photograph that exemplified the camera-as-gun analogy: Eddie Adams's award-winning 1968 photograph of a Saigon execution. Adams managed to capture the decisive moment when two shots—that of the camera and gun—coincided.

62 The most famous of these was Edward Steichen, who commanded the aerial photographic operations of the American Expeditionary Force in France during the first World War. For more on Steichen and the problematic authorship of reconnaissance photography, see Sekula, "The Instrumental Image"; and Hardesty, *Camera Aloft*.

63 Paul Virilio perhaps put this most memorably when he posited the existence of a military entertainment complex, which enmeshes war's conduct with the suspect pleasures of spectatorship. See Virilio, *War and Cinema*.

64 See Masco, *The Theater of Operations*. For more on photography and the atomic age, see also O'Brian, *Camera Atomica*; and MacLear, *Beclouded Visions*.

65 See Amad, "From God's-Eye to Camera-Eye."

66 For more on the role played by imagery analysis during the Cold War, see Lindgren, *Trust but Verify*.

67 For a general overview of John T. Hughes, see Elder, "Faces of Defense Intelligence: John T. Hughes."

68 Aerial surveillance photography even helped usher in an appreciation for abstraction, a defining feature of modernist sensibility. In *A Conspiracy of Images*, John J. Curley situates contemporary art within the Cold War context.

69 See Adelman, *Beyond the Checkpoint*.

70 In her influential book on the "tender violence" of US imperialism, Laura Wexler argues that domestic ideologies provide a means of projecting a "peace that keeps the peace." See Wexler, *Tender Violence*.

71 For more on how the kitchen was deployed as a recurring motif in the ideological and propaganda battles of the Cold War, see Baldwin, *The Racial Imaginary*.

72 See Rose, *Doing Family Photography*.

73 Evidence of the practice of familial politicization is found in the popular characterization of communist leader Ho Chi Minh as the benevolent Uncle and leader of the national family of Vietnam in its struggle against imperial invaders as well as in the US invocation of what Elaine Tyler May calls "domestic containment." See May, *Homeward Bound*.

# Visual Alliances

Visual Alliances

Visual Alliances

1

DARREN NEWBURY

# Ernest Cole's *House of Bondage*, the United States Information Agency, and the Cultural Politics of Race in the Cold War

On April 25, 1966, just two weeks before he left South Africa to go into exile, a young black photographer named Ernest Cole went to the offices of the United States Information Service (USIS) in downtown Johannesburg to retrieve a collection of photographic negatives. He had secreted them there for safekeeping during his last few months in the country, a period in which he was acutely conscious his movements were being monitored by the security services.[1] He was not mistaken. A South African Security Police report recorded that he entered the building alone, when nobody was around, and retrieved the negatives from a steel cabinet to which he possessed a key. But, assuming this report is accurate, either he removed only a portion of his negatives on this occasion or, at some point over the next couple of weeks, he decided to return some or all of them to the USIS office rather than risk taking them with him on his departure to Europe via Nairobi. About a month later, on May 30, and now safely in London, Cole composed a letter to his friend and fellow photographer Struan Robertson instructing him to make contact with someone named Rockweiler at the USIS office in Johannesburg, and to explain the situation to him and make arrangements for the (remaining) negatives to be transported to London, as he needed them for publication.[2] A South African Department of Justice memo from 1968, requesting that the then published photographic book be banned, makes explicit the US connection and assistance, although the name of Cole's contact has been redacted: "[Cole] specialised in photographs dealing with conditions in locations, hospitalisations, police raids and the poor conditions in which the Bantu lived. He took thousands of photographs of this nature and smuggled them out of the country—mainly with the help of [BLANK] of the American Embassy."

Aside from the color it adds to the story of Ernest Cole's departure from South Africa, what is the significance of this rather obscure note retrieved from deep in the archival records? In this chapter, I argue that the episode can be best understood as a subplot within a larger narrative about Cold War visual culture, one that reveals the entanglement of two visual histories usually treated separately: the photographic documentation of racial injustice in apartheid South Africa and the representation of race in a United States convulsed by urban riots, civil rights struggle, and militant black power. In the 1950s and 1960s, the conjunction of Cold War, racial conflict in the United States and decolonization in Africa provided a context within which representations of race became subject to international contestation as part of a broader cultural politics. The political and racial circumstances of South Africa—a combination of staunch anticommunism and the perpetuation of white minority rule, underpinned by an ideology of white supremacy and enforced by the violent suppression of resistance—presented a challenge to successive US administrations. In short, the situation in South Africa shone an unwelcome spotlight on domestic racial problems. Furthermore, the policy of apartheid contradicted the postwar regime of human rights embodied in the Universal Declaration of Human Rights (UDHR), adopted by the United Nations (UN) in 1948. In a global political system where the nation state was seen as the guarantor of human rights, a state that flatly refused to guarantee such rights for a majority of its citizens, as a matter of principle and not simply in practice, represented a major contradiction.[3] Despite the fact that the US delegation worked extremely hard to avoid external scrutiny of the situation in the southern states through the lens of human rights, the issue of apartheid was one means by which the issue of racial injustice could be returned to the UN agenda and, to the chagrin of the United States, become the subject of international debate.[4] Diplomatic relations with apartheid South Africa, therefore, had the capacity to expose contradictions and reveal some unexpected connections between US foreign and domestic policies on racial equality. Moreover, the images of racial injustice in South Africa that began to circulate in the postwar period might be seen to contest what Ariella Azoulay refers to as the "the human rights curriculum" at the moment of its formation in debates at the UN.[5] The active support of the US National Association for the Advancement of Colored People (NAACP) for the campaign, led by Michael Scott, to stop South Africa annexing the League of Nations mandate of South West Africa (SWA) might be taken as a critical example. The SWA campaign was accompanied by Scott's film *Civilisation on Trial in South Africa*, viewings of which were arranged by the NAACP, including to delegates of the UN in 1949.[6] The film consisted of documentary footage and still photographs from SWA and South Africa.[7] It was intended both to indict the South African government for its treatment of the black majority and to establish the agency and right to speak on their own behalf of the SWA people, to which in some small measure it contributed. The political alignment between African Americans in pursuit of racial justice in the United States and colonial subjects in Africa suggests that it was not inevitable that such images would be read in terms of distance; rather, viewing the film could be a productive moment of racial solidarity. For African American viewers at least, the identities of spectator and victim were not entirely settled.[8] As Carol Anderson argues, the mobilization against the annexation at the UN "raised the very real possibility of penetrating national sovereignty in the face of systematic human rights violations,"[9] and was part of a broader perception on the part of African Americans that their struggle for justice at home was "inextricably linked" with those of colonized peoples across the world.[10]

It was in the interstices of these conflicts that a young African photographer was able to find support conducive to the survival of his project and its subsequent international dissemination. That this support came from the propaganda arm of the US government might initially seem surprising, but it also reveals the complex and multilayered US response to a world in which the racial order was shifting. Although Africa has often been viewed as marginal within dominant Cold War histories, the conjunction of international and domestic approaches to the issue of race has increasingly begun to draw the attention of historians of US foreign policy.[11] In an early study of US policy in Africa in the postwar period, Thomas Noer noted that "the pursuit of equality in the American South and in Southern Africa created a rare case of reciprocity between domestic and foreign policy,"[12] and that black activism acted as a spur to the Kennedy administration's approach to Africa. In her later study of civil rights and the Cold War, Mary Dudziak drew similar conclusions as she traced US efforts to articulate a narrative of civil rights that served Cold War foreign policy objectives. Yet, although there is some reference to film within these and other studies, photography plays only a minor illustrative role, with the emphasis more often placed on discourses of policy and journalism.[13]

My intention here, therefore, is to pursue the questions that surround this coming together of Cold War cultural politics and contested representations of race through the story of Ernest Cole's photographic project and his move into exile, a necessary condition of the work's publication. In doing so, I hope not only to provide an account of the impact of the Cold War context on the work of one photographer but also to contribute to a deeper understanding of the production and circulation of photographs addressed to issues of race as a significant dimension of Cold War visual culture. To achieve these objectives, the inquiry develops in two directions. The first focuses on the encounter between Ernest Cole and the South African branch of the United States Information Agency (USIA). The second locates the body of work Cole published as a photographic book in 1967 within a broader history of the circulation of images of race during the Cold War period, considering both its reception in the United States and the perception on the part of the South African authorities, who viewed it as part of a larger US propaganda effort.

## ERNEST COLE AND THE USIA IN SOUTH AFRICA

In his late teenage years and early twenties, Cole worked briefly as a layout assistant at *Drum* magazine before becoming a freelance photographer and undertaking assignments for newspapers and magazines in and around Johannesburg and Pretoria. He was largely self-taught and, although not politically active, had a strong sense of the injustice of the regime under which he lived. As his work developed, he conceived of a book-length photographic study of life under apartheid. This was a project that came to dominate his work from the early 1960s until he left South Africa at twenty-six years of age. These were the negatives he stored at the USIS offices in Johannesburg, which would be published as *House of Bondage* in 1967, a little over a year after he arrived in the United States. Although *House of Bondage* was the first and only major publication of Cole's photographs during his lifetime, the book quickly came to be seen as one of the key photographic commentaries on life for black South Africans under apartheid. It received wide coverage on its publication and, despite being banned, provided a significant point of reference for a generation of photographers in South Africa who came of age in the 1970s and 1980s and committed their photography to the service of a struggle for liberation and democracy. It is now regarded not only as a damning critique of apartheid but also as a canonical photobook.[14]

In the early 1960s, Cole was simply a young black man from a township outside Pretoria who was beginning to establish himself as a freelance photojournalist in Johannesburg. It was as such that he first came into the ambit of US public diplomacy on the continent, in the form of the USIA, or the USIS as it was known in South Africa.[15] Established in 1953, the USIA was the main agent of US informational, cultural, and educational programs through its overseas offices for the second half of the twentieth century. Its central purpose was to convince overseas publics that US foreign policy was "in harmony with and [would] advance their legitimate aspirations for freedom, progress and peace," through the use of modern media and communication techniques.[16] While the USIA has been the subject of major studies, most notably Nicholas Cull's *The Cold War and the USIA*, which I draw upon here, the South African dimension has yet to receive substantial attention. Cole's development as a young photojournalist coincided with an increasing interest on the part of the United States in Africa, its people, and its leaders and potential leaders. As Leonard Marks (USIA director, 1965–68) put it, in Africa, "our primary audiences must be leaders, present and potential."[17] The decolonization that swept across much of Africa during the 1960s meant that for the first time black African leaders and citizens were important audiences with respect to US foreign policy objectives. It was in 1960 that Africa first became an "area operation" in its own right for the USIA;[18] and a report of 1961 urged expansion of USIA cultural, educational and exchange activities in Africa, where political change had made their current operations seem inadequate. Furthermore, the USIA understood the importance of race in the perception of the United States and took a lead in appointing African Americans to its staff. It argued, with limited success, that NASA should make greater effort to train black astronauts, and it employed black lecturers to tour

Africa talking about the space program. This competition for African opinion even extended to bringing journalists to Europe to witness for themselves the erection of the Berlin Wall.[19]

At a local level, "USIS cultural officers around the world made it their business to get to know artists in their client cities." More specifically, a report on the USIS in South Africa referred to "'friendly and sometimes intimate relations' with key South Africans including the Progressive Party MP Helen Suzman and the editorial staff of the *Rand Daily Mail*, the *Johannesburg Star*, and the black-oriented daily *The World*."[20] The USIS in Johannesburg also "co-sponsored courses to train black South Africans for careers in journalism and provided a space in which otherwise censored publications could be read"; indeed, "three-quarters of [USIS] library patrons were non-white."[21] Most importantly, for a study of photography, Cull argues that "the whole history of the agency . . . serves as a valuable reminder that the images which were so much a part of the Cold War were not disseminated by accident,"[22] an observation that prompts a series of questions regarding Cole's travels and the circulation of his photographs.

It was at the USIS offices in Johannesburg and Pretoria that Cole came into contact with the agents of US public diplomacy. Details about the precise nature of his interactions with USIS staff are unclear, but it is striking that Cole was prepared to place at least a portion of his life's work into their hands for safekeeping.[23] At a time when risks to the survival of his photographic project and its successful publication abroad were all around him, it may be that the USIS was one of the few places in Johannesburg where Cole felt his negatives would be out of reach of the South African authorities. Nevertheless, the fact that he had independent access to the offices, and a cabinet in which to store his negatives, suggests a rather closer relationship than one might have expected.

As a freelancer, Cole worked for the *Rand Daily Mail* and had at one time been on the staff at *The World*; and he knew many of the journalists in and around Johannesburg and Pretoria. Most likely, his contact with staff at the USIS came through these connections. Young photographers as well as journalists were part of the USIA's routine sphere of operation. In the year or so before he went into exile, Cole also developed a working relationship with Joseph Lelyveld, a correspondent for the *New York Times*, who would have been familiar to senior staff at USIS and was himself expelled from South Africa around the time Cole departed, following his publication of articles critical of apartheid. Cole provided photographs to illustrate several of Lelyveld's pieces in the *New York Times* and its companion magazine, including a photo-essay on apartheid that accompanied a profile of Helen Suzman, published in March 1966.

At the same time, Cole's commitment to self-education, following his rejection of the apartheid system of Bantu education, would have led him to make use of resources such as those offered by the USIS libraries. As one US visitor to South Africa in 1965 recalled, "on weekday afternoons, the library was filled with black teenagers doing school work and it was hard to find a seat."[24] Although no longer a teenager at this point, Cole may well have been occupying one of those seats. It is interesting to speculate, therefore, on how the material he would have encountered via USIS shaped his perception of America and its receptiveness as an audience for the photographic study he was in the process of creating. As Cull notes, "Observers relying only on USIA sources for their picture of the African American Civil Rights movement would have the impression that the hero of the civil rights era was the federal government which came to the aid of the distressed black citizens."[25] Cole was not entirely dependent on the USIS for his view of America, however; for example, through his friend Geoff Mphakati, he had access to texts by writers such as Frantz Fanon and James Baldwin, which were unlikely to have been available in the USIS library. He was also an avid fan of modern American jazz musicians such as Miles Davis and John Coltrane. Furthermore, Struan Robertson recalls that by 1965, Mphakati had a copy of Martin Luther King's "I Have a Dream" speech on vinyl, which he played for both him and Cole at his studio.[26] King's speech would not in itself have been incompatible with the narrative of civil rights that USIA wished to present, and thus USIS could conceivably have been the source for the vinyl edition.[27] Indeed, on more than one occasion, USIA and the South African government came into conflict around the circulation of representations of race and civil rights. In 1964, the South African government sought to censor the USIA film *Years of Lightning, Day of Drums*, which had been made as a tribute to John F. Kennedy following his assassination, and which included scenes of black and white working together in Africa and the United States.[28] When USIA refused to edit the film, it was banned. Similarly, in 1965, the US was openly accused by the South African press of distributing "'frankly propagandistic' material" on civil rights.[29]

One of the defining projects of Cold War photography was shown in South Africa uncensored, however. Sponsored by the USIA, Edward Steichen's *Family of Man* exhibition arrived in South Africa in 1958; and in Johannesburg, at

**Figure 1.1.** "Teacher toward end of her day in school." From *House of Bondage*. Photograph by Ernest Cole. © Ernest Cole Family Trust. Reproduced with permission.

least, it was open to all racial groups. Whether this latter fact should be interpreted as an invitation to integration on the part of the USIA is a moot point; but, as Tamar Garb shows, a number of commentators, including the black South African writer Lewis Nkosi, took the license offered by this "radical space of reception" to reimagine human relationships beyond the entrenched racism of apartheid.[30] Although Cole was only eighteen years old at the time, and at the very beginning of his photographic career, it would prove to be an influential exhibition.[31] A number of the photographers working for *Drum* magazine acknowledged its importance in shaping their understanding of the medium's potential, but Cole seems to have studied it more closely than most. His familiarity with the accompanying catalog publication no doubt influenced his thinking about the presentation of his own photographs. There were in fact direct connections between the two projects: Jerry Mason, a driving force behind the *Family of Man* catalog, was editor-in-chief for the series in which *House of Bondage* appeared under the Ridge Press imprint. Yet, as I have discussed elsewhere, *House of Bondage* can be seen as a countertext to Steichen's exhibition. Cole's project rejects the universalizing humanist vision projected by Steichen's selection and sequencing of photographs, and might be better understood as a visual parallel to Roland Barthes's response to the exhibition, which he criticized for mistaking historical injustice for human diversity, most notably in the context of colonialism.[32] As is evident in the treatment of the theme of education, *House of Bondage* is a photographic essay on racial and social injustice, not universal human experience. Cole's photographs of the weary teacher and bare classrooms, accompanied by an analysis of education policy under apartheid, draw the viewer's attention to the politically and historically specific circumstances of black school children in South Africa. In contrast, Nat Farbman's photograph in the *Family of Man*, of an African elder in a premodern setting, holding the attention of a circle of

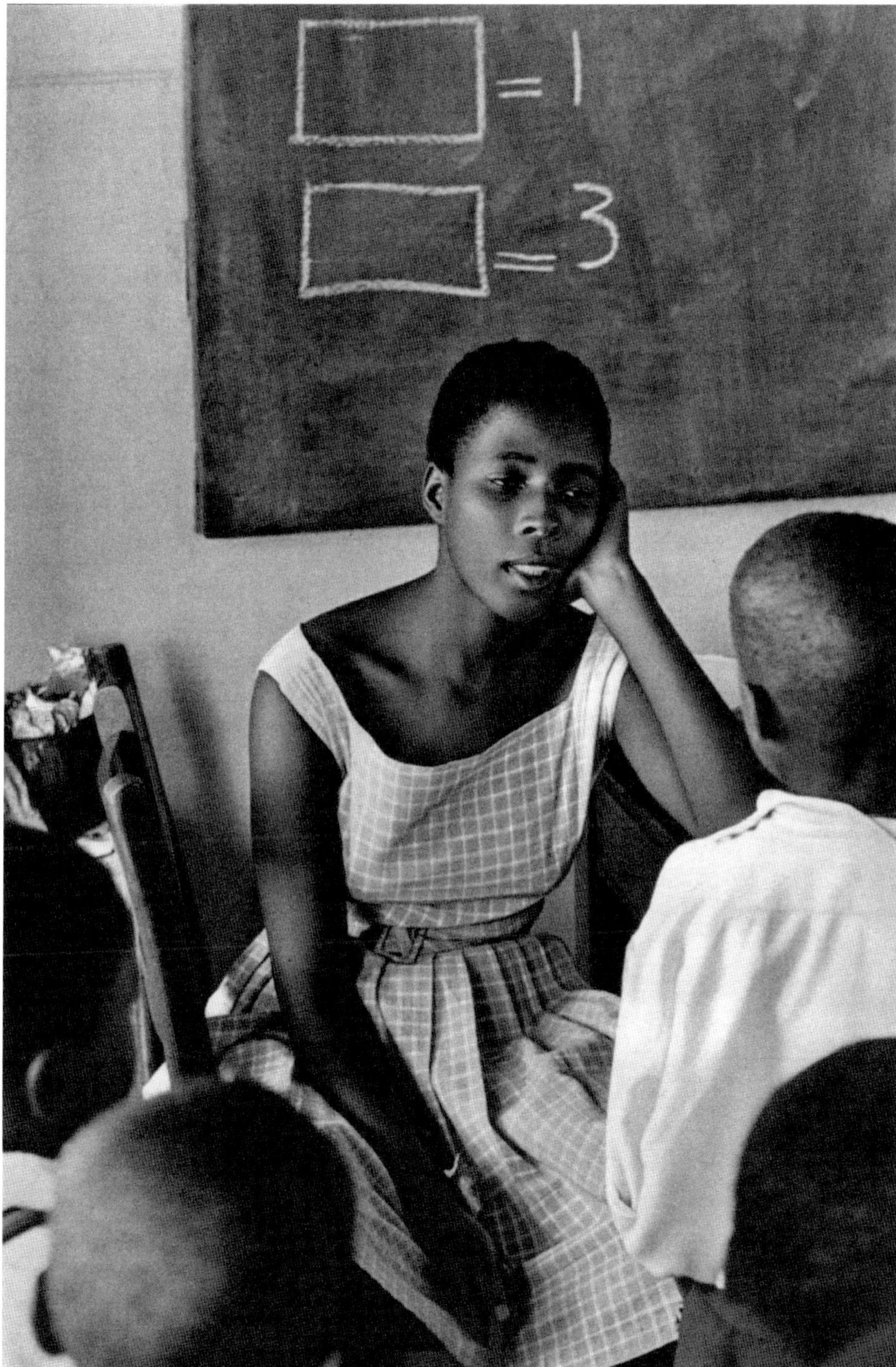
=1
=3

children, projects the idea of Africa as a timeless place, outside of history and representative of a universal ideal. Cole's book is notable too for its relentless indictment of the routine forms of oppression that apartheid imposed on the daily lives of black South Africans; education, healthcare, transportation, and policing each get separate thematic treatment. The message of the work owes as much to its overall structure and sequencing as it does to compelling individual photographs. Ultimately, Cole leaves the reader in no doubt that his is a record of specific injustice, not a visual essay on a concept as abstract as the human condition.[33] The extent to which Cole self-consciously addressed his own project to what he saw in the *Family of Man* is a matter for debate; but nonetheless, photographs and other cultural texts from the United States, many of which arrived in South Africa via channels of public diplomacy, were important points of reference.

Practically and intellectually, then, Cole benefited from a US public diplomacy that sought to bypass the National Party government and build connections directly with black South Africans, whom they believed could be influential in a future democratic dispensation. That is not to say that US policy toward South Africa could be considered progressive; there were very clear limits to its support for opponents of the apartheid regime. This was particularly so during the early part of the Cold War, when the United States largely opposed the use of sanctions. In contrast, the liberation movements in southern Africa, including the African National Congress (ANC), received tangible support from the Soviet Union and Cuba. Many in the United States were critical of apartheid, and on the ground in South Africa, US government officers were quite prepared to challenge its racial tenets through cultural means.[34] Ultimately, however, US–South Africa relations were viewed through the lens of the Cold War and larger strategic interests; what Noer refers to as Cold War realism—the view that anticommunism was the overriding threat to the United States—tended to win out.[35] The National Party government was viewed by many of those in power in the United States as a somewhat distasteful but nevertheless tolerable bulwark against communism in the region. As a consequence, US policy was limited to cultural and diplomatic opposition to the institutional racism of apartheid. This was the framework within which it was possible for Cole to establish a common interest with US public diplomacy in South Africa.

The opening up of a collection of original prints held at the Hasselblad Foundation in Sweden—the only extensive collection of Cole's prints to have survived—accompanied by exhibitions in South Africa and North America and a substantial catalog publication,[36] has prompted a renewed interest in Cole and his work.[37] These presentations, however, have emphasized the personal endeavor of Cole's journey to document the banal brutality of apartheid and his distinctive achievement as a photographer. While the story deserves telling in this way, it is very much a twenty-first-century reading, one in which the struggle against apartheid has ended, the context of the Cold War has faded away, and the status of the photographer as an artist is able to come to fore. In contrast, the task here is to offer a more historically situated reading. As the context of the Cold War influenced the production of Cole's book, ensuring its safe passage, so too did it shape its reception. It also rather tragically constrained Cole's ability to reimagine himself as a photographer in exile. *House of Bondage* was just one set of photographs on the subject of race, albeit a particularly significant set among many that circulated across the globe during the Cold War period. It was within this broader cultural context that the book's American audience would have to negotiate their reading when it emerged in the late 1960s.

Although, inevitably, the East-West ideological divide dominated propaganda efforts during the Cold War, the challenge that racial discrimination and the struggle for civil rights presented to the US image of democracy and freedom abroad meant that race was a significant site of contestation from the outset. Soviet and Chinese propagandists saw racial discrimination as a weakness in the US appeal to world opinion that they could exploit; and, in turn, the USIA put considerable effort into countering international perceptions of racial injustice. Mary Dudziak goes further, arguing that civil rights legislation was a product of the Cold War, and the priority given to civil rights under successive US administrations needs to be understood in the light of the foreign policy implications of what might otherwise have been regarded as a domestic issue. The US government realized, for example, "that their ability to promote democracy among peoples of color around the world was seriously hampered by continuing racial injustice at home."[38] In response to Communist exploitation of racial strife in the United States, the USIA sought not to deny the problem, but rather to shape the perception of American history as "a story of redemption."[39]

A brief survey of the work of the USIA demonstrates an ongoing awareness of the need to challenge negative portrayals of race in the United States and to develop a narrative around civil rights that could be presented as progressive and compatible with the US image of democracy. Even before the formation of USIA, the United States government had produced a pamphlet for international distribution entitled *The Negro in American Life*, which exposed racial discrimination as a shameful part of the national story. In contrast to totalitarianism, however, democracy was argued to provide a path to reconciliation and a means of transcending the past. But it was the ruling of the Supreme Court that segregated education was unconstitutional—*Brown v. Board of Education*—that finally gave credibility to this narrative, and which USIS offices overseas lost no time in disseminating. Although white responses in South Africa were rather diffident, reaction elsewhere in Africa was more welcoming of the decision.[40] A few years later, the battle over the implementation of this ruling, at a high school in Little Rock, Arkansas, in 1957, provided dramatic images with which to represent the conflict, including US paratroopers escorting nine African American students into the school. Predictably, white South Africans saw confirmation in the stand-off at Little Rock that "the forces against integration were gaining in the United States," whereas black South Africans were reported to have been "somewhat shocked." Yet, at the risk of sounding rather too convinced by their own propaganda, the American consulate also reported that black South Africans realized the events at Little Rock did not represent the policy of the US government.[41] In 1963, images of police using fire hoses and dogs against civil rights marchers in Birmingham, Alabama, became international news and featured extensively in Soviet news output and propaganda. A Soviet poster from that year by the graphic artist Viktor Koretsky, for example, depicts a group of African Americans confronted by police, quite possibly copied from a photograph of the scenes in Birmingham, inscribed on the face of the Statue of Liberty. The poster bears the title, "Shameful Brand of American 'Democracy.'"[42] The events in Alabama were also cited in an open letter to President Kennedy from Ugandan Prime Minister Milton Obote at the first meeting of the Organisation of African Unity.[43] And for many African diplomats visiting Washington, the fact of racial discrimination became one of which they had firsthand experience.[44] The March on Washington that followed in the summer of 1963, however, enabled the USIA to reclaim civil rights as a story of steady progress. Although controversial in Washington, the USIA film by James Blue, *The March* (1963), in the re-released version of which Carl Rowan, then USIA director, claims the event as "a profound example of the procedures unfettered men use to broaden the horizons of freedom and deepen the meaning of personal liberty,"[45] was seen positively by officers in the field—as was the subsequent, and less controversial, *Nine from Little Rock* (1964), which narrated the lives of the nine students from Little Rock in the years after 1957. Although the passing of the Civil Rights Act of 1964 underpinned the positive narrative that the USIA presented abroad, race continued to surface as an issue throughout the remainder of the 1960s, not least due to the urban unrest in US cities such as Los Angeles, Chicago, and Detroit and to the shift from the legislative focus of the civil rights movement to the more militant assertion of black pride and self-determination that characterized the black power era.[46] And if the war in Vietnam came to overtake civil rights in the international perception of the United States, it is evident that radical black activists also understood this conflict in terms of international racial solidarity.[47]

Key to the narrative on race that the United States government wished to present abroad was the idea of racial prejudice as predominantly a problem of the South. There were many challenges to this perception, not least the riots that erupted in cities across the United States in the mid to late 1960s, the period during which Cole arrived in the country; but it nevertheless retained a certain currency. It is interesting, therefore, to see this theme surface in one of the first press interviews Cole gave in the United States, shortly after the publication of *House of Bondage*. The article in the *New York Times* from December 1967 echoes precisely this contestation over the definition and location of US racism. "I had been told that being colored didn't matter at all in the United States—outside of the South that is," Cole was reported as saying, "But everywhere I saw racial attitudes that were very much like those I know from South Africa."[48] Cole did not discuss where he gained this impression of US racism as a problem only of the South—who had "told" him it was thus—but in part, at least, it can be read as a testament to the influence of the USIA narrative he had been exposed to in South Africa. In this, Cole's experience echoed that of the many diplomats and politicians from newly independent African states who, despite expectations to the contrary, suffered racism upon their arrival in Washington and New York.[49] The day after publication, Cole composed a letter to the *New York Times* (it is unclear whether the letter was printed or, indeed, even sent) setting straight several misinterpretations of his views. He was not surprised, as the article had implied, at the racism he experienced in the South, as he had been living in New York for ten months, where he had frequently been subjected to racism. He also emphasized that the grievances of blacks mentioned in the article were not his ideas but quotes from African Americans.[50] This suggests that the framing of the article owed as much to the journalist and the pervasiveness of the North-South racial narrative as it did to Cole's own words. The way in which Cole's identity as a black South African in exile was positioned in relation to US racial conflict in this article is worth further consideration in comparison with other black South Africans arriving in the United States during this period.[51] And of course Cole would have had to negotiate his own position in relation to the racial situation that confronted him in Harlem, where he was living, and as he traveled across the United States. It may be significant that the portrait of Cole illustrating the *New York Times* article showed him wearing a Black Panther style beret. Adopted by the Black Panther Party (BPP) shortly after it was founded in 1966, the beret "signified paramilitary action and serious militancy."[52] The article's publication coincided with the BPP's campaign to free Huey Newton, who was arrested after the fatal shooting of a police officer. The campaign was accompanied by a widely disseminated poster of Newton in a beret and leather jacket, holding a spear in one hand and a rifle in the other, a symbolic fusion of the African warrior and the urban American street fighter. It seems inconceivable that Cole would not have seen this image and that his choice of headgear was not a self-conscious identification with black radicalism.[53] Similarly, his explicit rejection of the term *Negro* in favor of *black* is an indication of his political sympathies. While the civil rights narrative promoted by the USIA would have dominated his perception of the racial situation in the United Sates when he was in South Africa, now living in New York, he would have seen this for the propaganda it was and aligned himself with the more militant perspectives associated with black power.

Turning to the book itself, how might it have been read in the context of the Cold War? Among those keenest to get their hands on it following its publication were, unsurprisingly, the South African authorities. They must have acquired copies relatively soon after publication, as the book was banned in South Africa the following year, making it an offense to possess or distribute copies. There were references to the book (and copies of reviews from US magazines, including *Ebony*) in Cole's police files in South Africa; and a copy was provided for the Minister of Justice to consult at the time of the book's banning. In fact, the Security Police had been aware that Cole was leaving South Africa, intent on publishing the book in the United States. *House of Bondage* was interpreted as part of an international propaganda battle being waged over the representation of the apartheid system and racial justice in the eyes of US and South African publics. The following extracts from the Security Police records demonstrate this clearly:

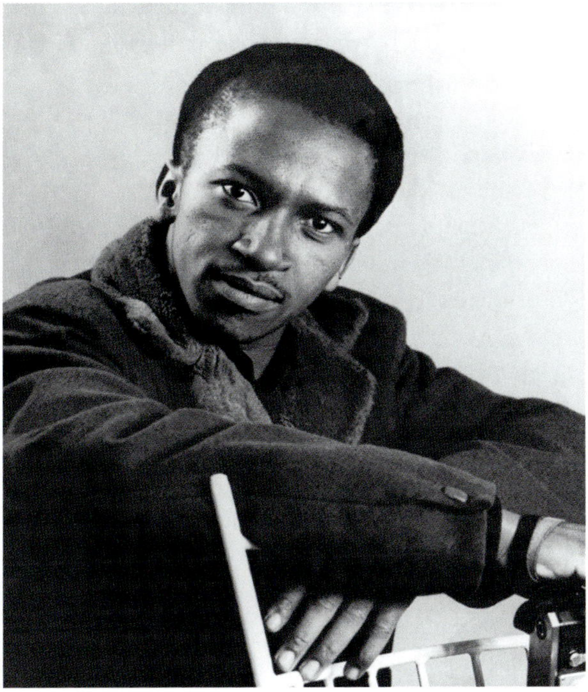

**Figure I.2.** **Portrait of Ernest Cole. Photographer and date unknown. This portrait was used as a publicity photograph for Jürgen Schadeberg's film about Cole; it appears to have been made at the same time as the image reproduced on the dust jacket of *House of Bondage* and used to illustrate a short article on Cole in the *New York Times* (1967). Courtesy Claudia and Jürgen Schadeberg, www.jurgenschadeberg.com.**

> This is not so much about the person Cole but about the influence the book will have, and it should not be forgotten that the people helping him in America are our arch-enemies. They are using Cole to spread liberalist or pink Communist views about us under the pretext that he is one of the oppressed people who have fled.
>
> I am convinced that if we do not stop this in time, these writings will be smuggled into the country and distributed to Bantu schools here, as is constantly being done with other integration propaganda from America. Coming from an escapee from the RSA [Republic of South Africa], this will have a greater impact if it is distributed.
>
> From newspaper reports reaching us from abroad about Cole and his book it is clear that even the self-confessed Communists are not having as much success with agitations against us as Cole has achieved now.[54]

The South African authorities may well have developed an exaggerated sense of the book's influence, or they may have exaggerated it in order to persuade the minister of the necessity of its banning; but it is clear nevertheless that they saw Cole's book as grist to the mill of what they referred to rather strikingly as "the fertile liberalist propaganda machine in America."

There is little direct evidence of how *House of Bondage* was read by those the South Africans authorities referred to as "American liberalists," but a number of reviews that were interested in and to some degree sympathetic to Cole's project provide insights into its reception. One theme that emerged in the US reception of Cole's book was the extent to which it showed something unique to the oppression of the apartheid system or, conversely, whether similar images could not just as easily have been made in the southern United States. For example, a review in the *Atlanta Journal and Constitution* (October 29, 1967), the only review issuing from a southern outlet that I have identified, implied a commonality between Cole's photography and the racial situation in the United States. Although the parallel is unsurprising, it is worth observing how *House of Bondage* presented a challenge largely missing from representations of Africa elsewhere in US mainstream culture, notably in the illustrated magazine *Life*. The racial anxiety induced by the prospect of decolonization, and the multiple conflicts that came with it, was assuaged for its white readers by the maintenance of a more reassuring visual discourse depicting whites in positions of authority and blacks as exotic primitives or subservient workers, who lacked the capacity to exercise agency responsibly. Where agency was accorded to newly independent Africans, it was as nascent capitalists and consumers.[55] Even in its coverage of the civil rights struggle, *Life* represented blacks primarily as victims.[56] While *House of Bondage* is not a study of black political agency, it counters the dominant positioning of Africans as essentially premodern through its concentration on modern urban settings. And in its thematic structure, addressed to issues such as housing, health care, and education, it articulates a social and economic rights agenda, which would have been legible to at least some in the United States. Equally, one should not discount the fact that the photographs were those of a black African photographer. Cole was identified as the author of the work and as speaking for a black constituency. In the United States in the late 1960s, both these things served to bring the message of the book closer to home.

Stanley Kauffmann's review in the liberal magazine *New Republic* (October 1967), entitled "Hue and Cry," first set the racial conflict represented in Cole's book in a global context, as *the* conflict of the era—"Perhaps *this* is the way the world ends: neither with a bang nor a whimper but wrecked on the color bar"[57]—before explicitly addressing the book's content from the perspective of the liberal reader: "The liberal reader's first reaction is that such a book is superfluous: he knows that apartheid is horrible. There is, admittedly, no need to break the news of venomous oppression in South Africa. But Cole's photographs . . . make it harshly vivid, in a way we have no right to call unbearable."[58] Kauffmann then used the alibi of an "American Negro friend" to compare the racial situation in South Africa with that of the US. It is worth quoting at length:

> She said that matters are basically no different in this country, they are just less overt. I think there is some truth in this, to the extent that Afrikaners are acting out the unacknowledged dreams and fantasies of many white Americans. But the difference between overtness and covertness makes for another difference. The American crisis is the result of a contrast between professions of equality and actual practice. There are no South African professions of equality—not even in the relatively liberal Verwoerd's plans for Bantu separation. If the present South African situation continues, there will not be a crisis like ours, there will simply be an explosion.[59]

He concluded the review with a call for the US to reflect on the threat that racial injustice posed to its own stability: "Cole's book holds out no hope whatsoever for South Africa; still that hopelessness may help to scare some others sufficiently."[60] Writing just a few months after race riots had exploded on the streets of Detroit and Newark (July 1967), his point may have resonated with readers. Though, as the equivocation in the review indicates, there remained the possibility that *House of Bondage* could be read in a more reassuring way by US audiences; that what was significant about Cole's image of South Africa was not its similarity to the racial situation in the United States, but its difference. Lysle Meyer made a similar observation in his analysis of US perception of South Africa in the mid-1970s: "If Americans were guilt-ridden—and many were—about their own race problem, they could always point to South Africa as an example of what was considered a more detestable system."[61] In the liberal reader, the reception of Cole and his work in late 1960s America manifested a tension within this question of similarity or difference between South Africa and the United States, which was echoed in foreign policy debates. It was a comparison that USIA officers never failed to challenge.

Although there are relatively limited sources from which to gauge the African American reception of *House of Bondage*, *Ebony* ran a feature on Cole in February 1968, under the title "My Country, My Hell!" A selection of fourteen photographs, all but one of which appear in *House of Bondage*, was accompanied by a text that recounts Cole's personal story from young photographer

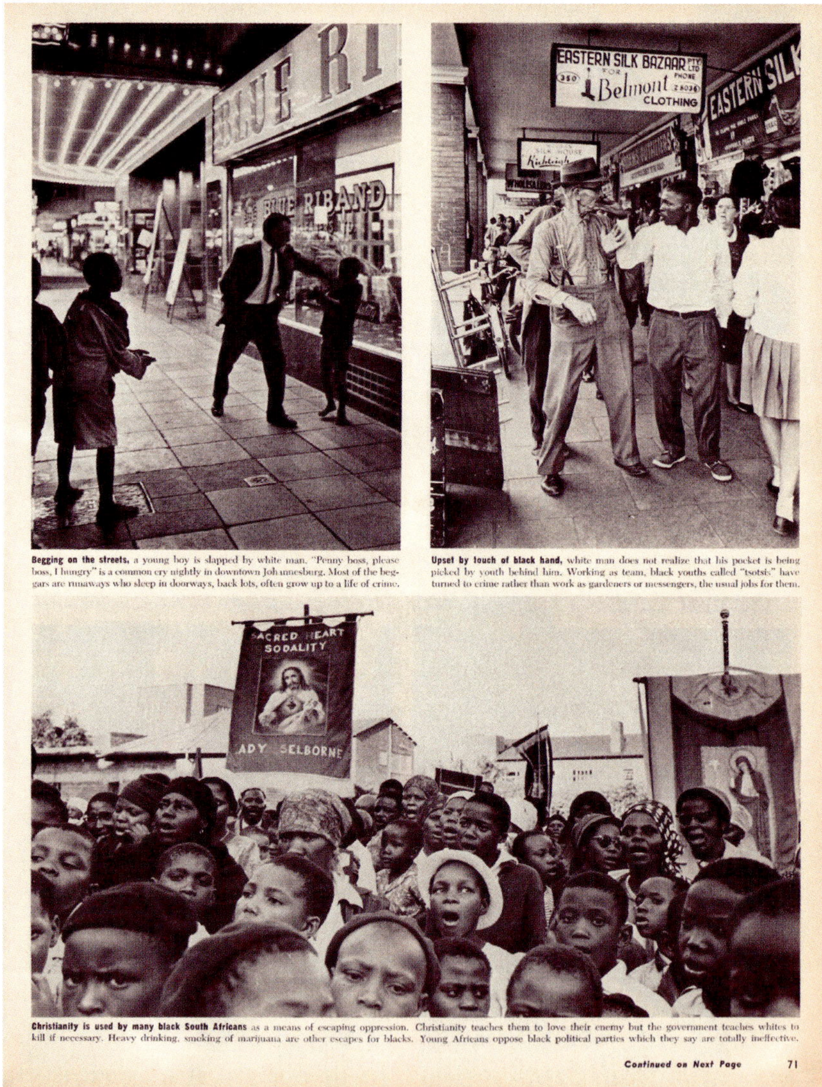
**Begging on the streets,** a young boy is slapped by white man. "Penny boss, please boss, I hungry" is a common cry nightly in downtown Johannesburg. Most of the beggars are runaways who sleep in doorways, back lots, often grow up to a life of crime.

**Upset by touch of black hand,** white man does not realize that his pocket is being picked by youth behind him. Working as team, black youths called "tsotsis" have turned to crime rather than work as gardeners or messengers, the usual jobs for them.

**Christianity is used by many black South Africans** as a means of escaping oppression. Christianity teaches them to love their enemy but the government teaches whites to kill if necessary. Heavy drinking, smoking of marijuana are other escapes for blacks. Young Africans oppose black political parties which they say are totally ineffective.

*Continued on Next Page* 71

**Figure 1.3.** "My Country, My Hell!," *Ebony*, February 1968. The photograph on the lower half of the page is the only image with this article not reproduced in *House of Bondage*. The caption reads: "Christianity is used by many black South Africans as a means of escaping oppression." Photographs © Ernest Cole Family Trust. Reproduced with permission.

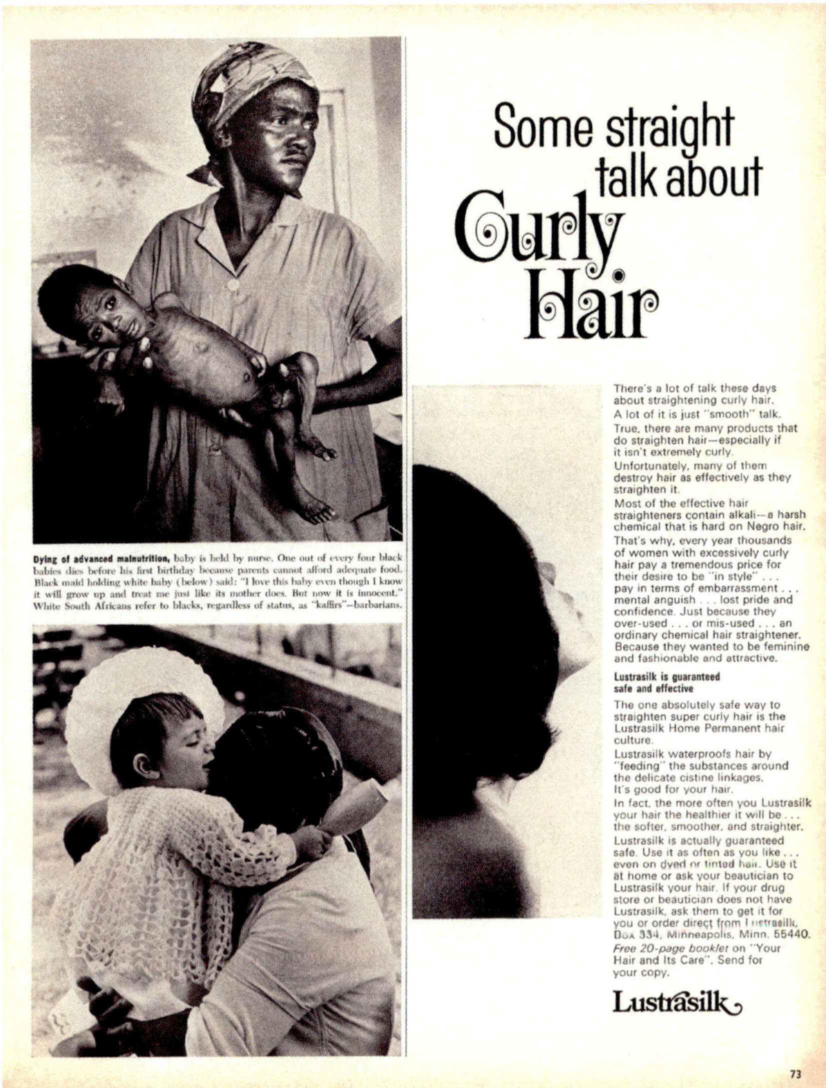

Dying of advanced malnutrition, baby is held by nurse. One out of every four black babies dies before his first birthday because parents cannot afford adequate food. Black maid holding white baby (below) said: "I love this baby even though I know it will grow up and treat me just like its mother does. But now it is innocent." White South Africans refer to blacks, regardless of status, as "kaffirs"–barbarians.

Some straight talk about Curly Hair

There's a lot of talk these days about straightening curly hair.

A lot of it is just "smooth" talk.

True, there are many products that do straighten hair—especially if it isn't extremely curly.

Unfortunately, many of them destroy hair as effectively as they straighten it.

Most of the effective hair straighteners contain alkali—a harsh chemical that is hard on Negro hair.

That's why, every year thousands of women with excessively curly hair pay a tremendous price for their desire to be "in style" . . . pay in terms of embarrassment . . . mental anguish . . . lost pride and confidence. Just because they over-used . . . or mis-used . . . an ordinary chemical hair straightener. Because they wanted to be feminine and fashionable and attractive.

**Lustrasilk is guaranteed safe and effective**

The one absolutely safe way to straighten super curly hair is the Lustrasilk Home Permanent hair culture.

Lustrasilk waterproofs hair by "feeding" the substances around the delicate cistine linkages. It's good for your hair.

In fact, the more often you Lustrasilk your hair the healthier it will be . . . the softer, smoother, and straighter.

Lustrasilk is actually guaranteed safe. Use it as often as you like . . . even on dyed or tinted hair. Use it at home or ask your beautician to Lustrasilk your hair. If your drug store or beautician does not have Lustrasilk, ask them to get it for you or order direct from Lustrasilk, Box 334, Minneapolis, Minn. 55440.

*Free 20-page booklet* on "Your Hair and Its Care". Send for your copy.

Lustrasilk

73

**Figure 1.4.** "My Country, My Hell!," *Ebony*, February 1968. These photographs both appear in *House of Bondage*, though not in juxtaposition, where they are captioned respectively, "Infant suffers from advanced malnutrition," and "Servants are not forbidden to love." Photographs © Ernest Cole Family Trust. Reproduced with permission.

**Figure 1.5.** "Rented car is status symbol at middle-class marriage. Expensive wedding can leave couple broke for a year." From *House of Bondage*. Photograph by Ernest Cole. © Ernest Cole Family Trust. Reproduced with permission.

to exile. The additional photograph depicts a Christian gathering, possibly in Lady Selborne, echoing the view presented in *House of Bondage* that religion offers a form of escape from oppression. The caption also makes the following comment on politics: "Young Africans oppose black political parties which they say are totally ineffective."[62] This photograph and caption, like the section on religion in the book, seems to convey something of Cole's personal frustration with the incapacity of political and religious institutions to effect real change in the lives of black South Africans. The rest of the selection provides a visual summary of the themes developed in the book: punitive pass laws, migrant labor, poverty, education, and health care—a visual repertoire that connects racial and social injustice—concluding with a powerful juxtaposition of a photograph of a black mother holding her malnourished child to the camera while she turns her own head away with a photograph showing a moment of intimacy between a healthy white child and its black nanny. The photographs themselves do not explicitly link the racial injustice suffered by black South Africans with that experienced by African Americans, though they are certainly legible in those terms. In his closing remarks, Cole invites just such a reflexive reading, which serves to collapse the distance between the United States and South Africa and disrupt any consoling effect: "They [the photographs] should give readers some feeling of what it is like to be a black man in South Africa. And they may also explain why in, of all countries, I should feel somewhat at home in the United States."[63]

Although the letters pages in subsequent issues were dominated by other debates, for example on the use of the term *Negro*, the styling of hair, and whether or not Lincoln might be regarded as a white supremacist, the article did receive a small number of responses, published in the April issue. William C. Jones and Celestine L. Billings of Chicago, wrote that, "the similarity

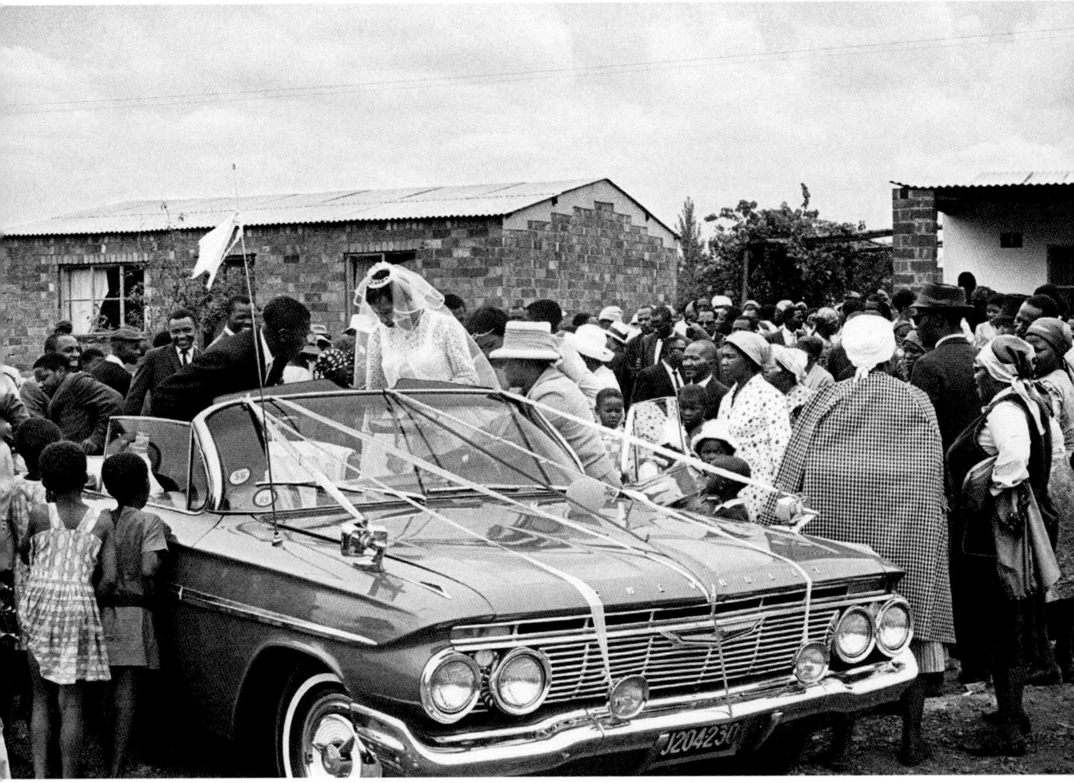


is quite evident in America's racist attitude toward her Black minority. Who is the carbon copy of whom?" George S. Carpenter of Queens, New York, on the other hand spoke from a more humanist position: "I was not angered because I am black and they (South Africans) are black, but because I am a human being, and most assuredly, they too are human beings." Herbert Hayward of Elizabeth, New Jersey, simply noted that the article "made me weep," an indication of the intense affective responses the photographs could evoke. It is worth observing too, that these African American responses refer to anger and sadness, forms of emotional identification with a capacity for solidarity, in contrast to the anxiety and guilt of white readers. To what extent African American readers interpreted the book in terms of solidarity in an international struggle against racial injustice is not a judgment that can be made with confidence. Some of the more aspirational middle-class readers of *Ebony* may not have seen it that way, but it is reasonable to conclude that others did.

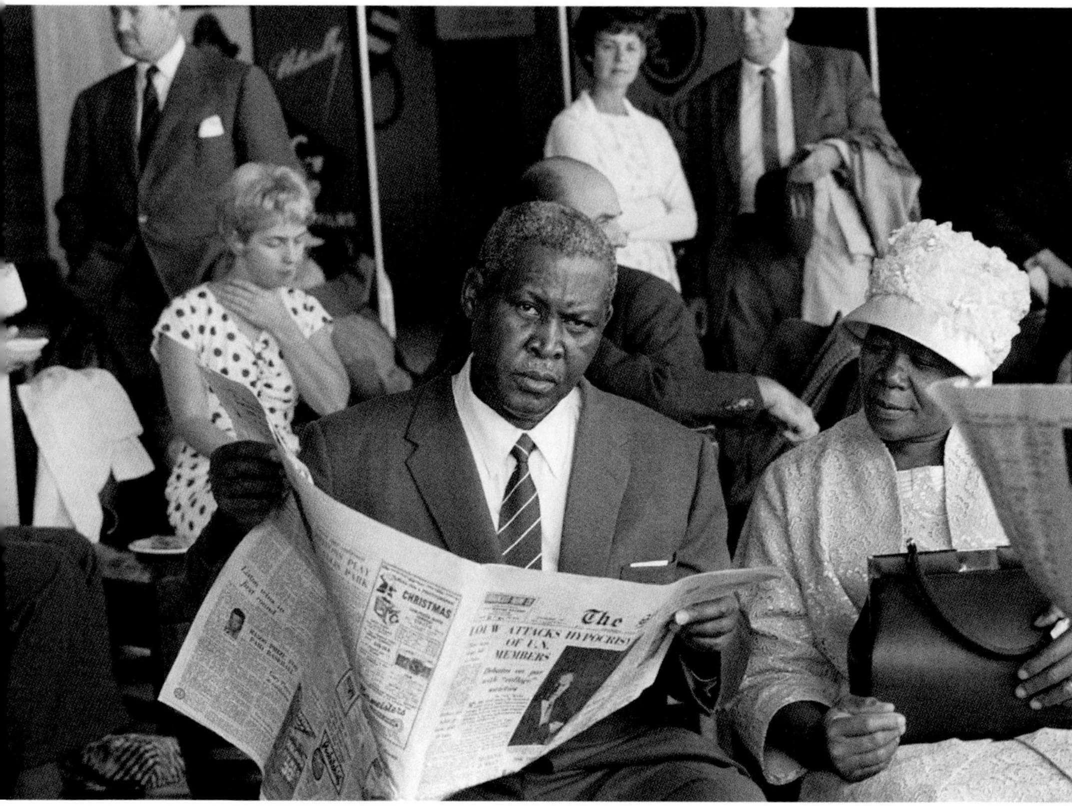


## CONCLUSION: COLE, RACE RELATIONS, AND ANTI-APARTHEID

When he left South Africa for exile, Cole was a talented young photographer determined to escape the oppression of apartheid and bring the body of work he had created to the attention of a wider world. The publication of *House of Bondage* did so emphatically, burning brightly for a moment in the late 1960s. In conclusion, however, I want to direct attention beyond the moment of Cole's departure and arrival. There are two aspects worthy of further reflection: the fate of Cole and his photographic ambitions in the United States; and the subsequent circulation of images taken from *House of Bondage* in the campaigning literature and publicity of anti-apartheid activism, as well as Cole's seeming ambivalence to such uses of his work.

If a USIA-crafted narrative of civil rights progress dominated Cole's perception of the United States from the global South, in exile he discovered

Figure 1.6. "Albert Luthuli, President of the ANC, en route to Oslo with wife to receive Nobel Peace Prize for 1960. Then—as now—he was officially in banishment." From *House of Bondage*. Photograph by Ernest Cole. © Ernest Cole Family Trust. Reproduced with permission.

something much less comforting. It was one thing to imaginatively identify with the African American experience through the images and music that arrived in South Africa; it was quite another to encounter and negotiate a place for oneself in the reality. In this respect, it is instructive to revisit one of the shortest sections in *House of Bondage*—African Middle Class. I have commented previously on this section as one of the darkest in Cole's book.[64] Several of the images, such as that of an "expensive" white wedding with the status symbol car decked in ribbons, or that of the "Miss Non-White Africa" contest, are clearly offered as condemnations of black African aspirations to Western values; and the text explicitly refers to Africans "los[ing] sight of the fact of their unalterable blackness and the realities to which this condemns them." The latter comment, clearly resonant of Fanon, indicates an engagement with the psychological consequences of racism that was equally important to black power and its critique of more moderate civil rights organizations. Whether it was assembled in the United States or South Africa, this section can be read as a commentary on where Cole had arrived and a rejection of the dominant US version of racial progress that was on offer. Moreover, the text makes clear that these are values Cole associated with the United States. He ridicules a man who, in order to establish the smallest of social distinctions in a society structured to oppress him, takes every opportunity to boast of his brief trip abroad on a sports mission and, as a result, became known as "Mr 'When-I-Was-in-America' Duma."[65] And the final image of the section, showing Albert Luthuli, president of the ANC, en route to Oslo to pick up the Nobel Peace Prize, might be interpreted as a reflection on Cole's own departure into exile. Disabused of the view of America he had formed with the assistance of the USIA, Cole realized the lim-

Figure I.7. Southern USA, c. 1969–70. Photograph by Ernest Cole. © Ernest Cole Family Trust. Reproduced with permission.

its of racial justice in the United States and the consequences for his own aspirations:

> On my departure from home I thought I would focus my talents on other aspects of life, which I assumed would be beautiful and a joy to do. However, what I have seen of this country [US] over the past two years has proved me wrong. Recording truth at whatever cost is one thing, but finding oneself having to live a lifetime of being the chronicler of misery, injustice and callousness is another. Unfortunately, such matter is about the only work magazines here want to offer me, all because of the fact that the subject matter of my first book happened to be centred on a "race issue," the colour of my skin and the fact that I endured the living hell that is South Africa. But the total man does not live by one experience. He is moulded and shaped by the diversity of other experiences into some form of the whole man.[66]

US Cold War public diplomacy assisted Cole, both in its provision of resources and networks that he could access as a young black photojournalist in the hostile environment of apartheid South Africa and, more directly, in facilitating the safekeeping of his negatives during his final months in the country and enabling their safe passage to join him in exile. At the same time, in exile in the United States, the narrative of race and civil rights the Cold War helped to construct was a trap within which, tragically, Cole became caught, unable to find a new direction for his work.[67] By the late 1960s and early 1970s, the aspirations expressed above had been replaced by a commitment to work on a project, funded by the Ford Foundation, which looked remarkably like a continuation of the USIA Cold War project to orchestrate the representation of race in the United States.[68] Cole was funded to undertake two studies: "A Study of the Negro Family in the Rural South" and "A Study of Negro Life in the City."[69] The justification was that the project would enable Cole to become "a more useful commentator on racial matters" and "do something important in the field of US race relations." This commission makes perfect

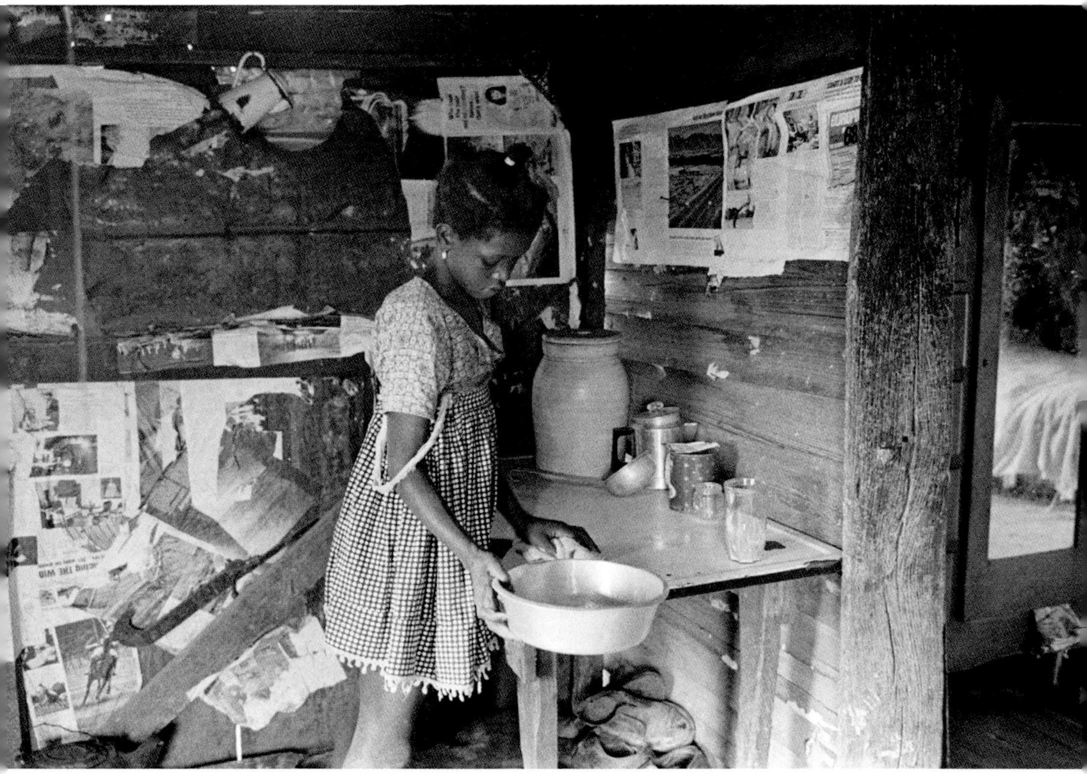

sense when one realizes that the support offered to Cole first by the USIA and then by the Ford Foundation were simply two points on an ideological continuum linking foreign and domestic approaches to race. The ideology that first embraced him in South Africa was there to accommodate him, too, in the United States, though it came at a huge personal cost. Cole would never achieve the wholeness he wished for, and from the mid-1970s on he suffered with mental health problems and long periods of homelessness.[70]

In contrast to Cole's biographical narrative, one can consider the corresponding fate of his photographs. At the time of its publication, *House of Bondage* represented the most comprehensive and penetrating photographic account of life in South Africa for its oppressed majority. It was inevitable, therefore, that beyond the publication of the book, the photographs would be picked up and disseminated in the service of the international anti-apartheid movement as its reach extended through the 1970s and 1980s. I am not aware of research that traces the full extent of the use of Cole's work, but it is clear that individual images from the book were being copied and reproduced in a

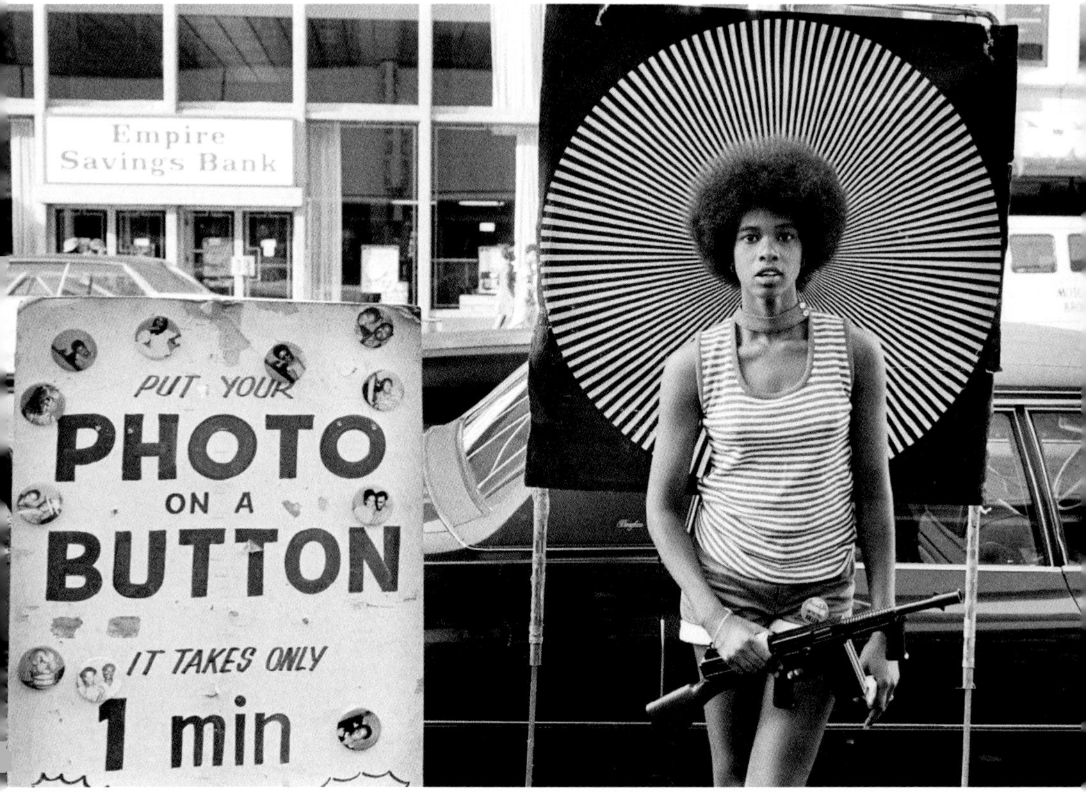


variety of political contexts, including the official journal of the ANC in exile, *Sechaba*,[71] publications produced by the International Defence and Aid Fund (IDAF), and projects in conjunction with the UN Special Committee on Apartheid.[72] Images copied from *House of Bondage* were also deployed in grassroots boycott campaigns, such as that instigated in 1970 by two African American Polaroid employees—the Polaroid Workers Revolutionary Movement—protesting against the company's complicity with apartheid through its supply of technology for the production of passbook photographs.[73]

The framing of Cole's South African images within a narrative of liberation and as a basis for international racial solidarity ought to provide a counterpoint to the attempt, symbolized by the Ford Foundation commission, to incorporate Cole the photographer within an American liberal capitalist model of racial progress. Yet, the evidence suggests Cole was profoundly ambivalent about these uses of his work. At the heart of his ambivalence, I suggest, was the deep disillusionment he experienced in the political reception

Figure 1.8. New York, c. 1971. Photograph by Ernest Cole. © Ernest Cole Family Trust. Reproduced with permission.

of his photographs during his early years of exile. In an interview by Swedish photographer Rune Hassner, first broadcast in 1969, Cole explicitly discussed the ambition for his photography to contribute to the work of the Afro-Asian bloc at the UN in its opposition to apartheid. Yet, Hassner later recalled, Cole felt disregarded by many of those to whom he tried to show his work, including ambassadors of other African countries.[74] Several people who met Cole in his later years recollected the way he felt exploited by the ANC, which used his work without acknowledgment or support.[75] And when he met Omar Badsha for the first time, in hospital shortly before he died, Cole launched a verbal attack on Badsha's political approach to photography.[76] Intensifying his disillusionment, I believe, Cole was hurt by the indifference to the integrity of his work in its use as campaigning material. More than most in the generation of photojournalists from which he emerged, or in the political generation of photographers that followed, Cole had a developed sense of the autonomy of his vision as a photographer. Fellow exile Lefifi Tladi recalls Cole saying of the ANC, "They call themselves a liberation movement and yet they're not conscious of the importance of the arts in the context of the struggle."[77] To subsume photography to the political struggle for liberation, no less than to subsume it to the betterment of US race relations, was, for Cole, an act of negation.

Yet, notwithstanding the genuine anger and disillusionment that he felt in his later years, a longer perspective must acknowledge that although Cole's life was no story of redemption, *House of Bondage* represented a key moment in the development of an "evidentiary poetics"[78] of anti-apartheid struggle and provided a source of creative affirmation for future generations of black photographers.[79] Furthermore, legible as it was within the different political discourses of US race relations and international racial solidarity, Cole's book might also be taken as paradigmatic of a Cold War critical imagination. As Octavio Paz argues, writing from a different set of Cold War coordinates: "In our age the imagination operates critically. Criticism is the imagination's apprenticeship in its second turn, the imagination cured of fantasies and determined to face the world's realities."[80] One could not better describe Cole's photography. And if, ironically, it was the cultural space opened in the service of US foreign policy that provided the conditions for Cole's work to survive and travel, it was nevertheless an act of courage and imagination to grasp the opportunity.

*Notes*

1 South Africa, Department of Justice, File No. 2/1/2265. I am grateful to the Freedom of Information Programme at the South African History Archive and, in particular, to Gabriella Razzano for facilitating my access to these documents. In most cases the original is in Afrikaans. Redactions are indicated by [BLANK]. See also Newbury, "Ernest Cole and the South African Security Police."

2 Robert A. Rockweiler was director of the USIS office in Johannesburg in the mid-1960s. In recent correspondence, he suggested that Cole's storage of negatives at the office would have been somewhat irregular and not something he would have condoned; and while he acknowledged it was entirely possible he had met Cole, he would then have passed him on to his press officer (now deceased) who had much more frequent contact with the "several young photographers who worked with *The Star*, the *Rand Daily Mail*, the *Post* and *Drum*." Robert Rockweiler, personal communication (December 1 and December 12, 2013). I am grateful to Nick Cull without whose prompting and assistance I would not have located Rockweiler. It seems probable that, rather than Rockweiler being a direct contact, Cole asked Struan Robertson to appeal to him in his position of authority at the USIS office in order to secure the safe transit of Cole's negatives. The implication remains, however, that Cole developed a relationship with the USIS that went beyond their normal support for young black photographers and journalists and that he viewed them as a source of support for his project.

3 South Africa was regularly the object of censure in UN resolutions, though despite calls for its expulsion, vetoes by the United States, along with the UK and France, ensured it remained a member. It was excluded from participating in the work of the General Assembly from 1974, however.

4 For a detailed account of the role played by African American civil rights organizations in the negotiations going on at the UN during the period in which the UNDR was taking shape, see Anderson, "From Hope to Disillusion"; and Anderson, *Eyes Off the Prize*.

5 See Ariella Azoulay, "Ending World War II: Visual Literacy Class in Human Rights," in McClennen and Moore, *The Routledge Companion to Literature and Human Rights*, 159–72. Azoulay is referring here to the submission of human rights to national sovereignty and domestic jurisdiction, and its visual corollary,

wherein the identification of human rights violations is tightly circumscribed, excluding, for example, the use of nuclear weapons at Hiroshima and Nagasaki and the forced migrations that followed the end of the war.

6 Anderson, "International Conscience," 319.

7 The photographs were taken by Leon Levson. Newbury, *Defiant Images*, 43–68.

8 Azoulay is no doubt right that the dominant pedagogy of human rights would ultimately win out over such readings, as set out in this volume. As Anderson notes, the virulent anticommunism of the 1950s precipitated a retreat from the embrace of a broader human rights and social justice agenda in the African American struggle. Anderson, *Eyes Off the Prize*, 273. But dominant readings are never entirely uncontested, and the potential for international racial solidarity, I suggest, continued to unsettle the reception of images of apartheid South Africa in the years that followed.

9 Anderson, "International Conscience," 325.

10 Walter White, cited in Anderson, "From Hope to Disillusion," 532.

11 See, for example, Dudziak, *Cold War Civil Rights*; McMahon, *The Cold War in the Third World*; and Jason Parker, *Hearts, Minds, Voices*.

12 Noer, *Cold War and Black Liberation*, 126.

13 The 2011 edition of Dudziak's book is illustrated by a number of iconic images, but neither the images nor their production or circulation are given any sustained consideration. Similarly, Jason Parker's 2016 book includes a sequence of twenty-three photographs illustrative of US public diplomacy, which are presented without further discussion. Sönke Kunkel, in *Empire of Pictures*, specifically considers the visual dimension of US foreign policy, including African case studies, though he accords television a more central place than photography. Literature, painting, and theater receive greater consideration in the wider study of Cold War visual culture, but reference to Africa is largely absent, as it is from most discussions of the highest profile photographic exhibition of the Cold War period, the *Family of Man* exhibition. See Garb, "Rethinking Sekula."

14 Cole, *House of Bondage*. *House of Bondage* features in Parr and Badger, *The Photobook*, although the accompanying interpretation contains inaccuracies.

15 To maintain a degree of continuity, the overseas offices of the USIA retained the older designation of United States Information Service (USIS), the name by which the agency was known to foreign citizens. This usage is followed here: hence, USIS refers to the South African office, and USIA to the US government agency as a whole.

16 J. Wang, "Telling the American Story to the World," 25.

17 Cull, *The Cold War and the United States Information Agency*, 278.

18 Cull, *The Cold War and the United States Information Agency*, 159.

19 Cull, *The Cold War and the United States Information Agency*, 201.

20 Cull, *The Cold War and the United States Information Agency*, 279.

21 Cull, *The Cold War and the United States Information Agency*, 279.

22 Cull, "'The Man Who Invented the Truth,'" 24.

23 The archival references to the USIS are contained in Cole's letter of May 1966 and the Security Police records, in addition to a remark that Joseph Lelyveld made about Cole conceiving of his dream to publish a book of photographs on South Africa in the USIS library in Johannesburg or Pretoria. Joseph Lelyveld, interviewed by Darren Newbury, Hampstead, London, October 18, 2006.

24 Shakespeare House, photograph by Arnold Reinhold, July 1965. Available online at https://commons.wikimedia.org/wiki/Category:Historical_images_of_Johannesburg#/media/File:USIS-Johannesburg.agr.jpg. Accessed July 17, 2015.

25 Cull, *The Cold War and the United States Information Agency*, 211.

26 Struan Robertson, personal communication (April 13, 2007). Mphakati would himself travel to the United States on a leadership program in the mid-1970s.

27 King featured extensively in USIA materials, including, to cite just one example, in "Distinguished Young Americans," a 1962 pamphlet for global distribution.

28 McKay, "South African Propaganda," 42; and Noer, *Cold War and Black Liberation*, 171.

29 McKay, "South African Propaganda," 42.

30 Garb, "Rethinking Sekula from the Global South," 47–49.

31 Cole was familiar with Steichen's exhibition and had access to a copy of the published version at Struan Robertson's studio where he often spent time. Struan Robertson, personal communication (April 24, 2007).

32 Barthes, *Mythologies*, 107–10. For more recent readings of the exhibition, and an attempt to reclaim it from Barthes's damning critique, see Hurm et al., *The Family of Man Revisited*.

33 For a more extended reading of Cole's book along these lines, see Newbury, *Defiant Images*, ch. 4.

34 See D. Whitman, *Outsmarting Apartheid*. There is, however, something uncomfortably self-congratulatory about several of the US perspectives offered in this volume, and indeed its title.

35 Noer, *Cold War and Black Liberation*, 29.

36 See Knape, *Ernest Cole*.

37 *Ernest Cole: Photographer* opened at Johannesburg Art Gallery on September 19, 2010, and has been shown across South Africa and in the United States. A smaller collection of Cole's photographs was also exhibited in *Ons hou van Suid-Afrika (We love South Africa): One Country in Three Exhibitions*, May 28–August 22, 2010, at the Museum Volkenkunde, Leiden. Cole had strong connections with Sweden during the late 1960s and early 1970s, and he spent long periods there.

38 Dudziak, *Cold War Civil Rights*, 12.

39 Dudziak, *Cold War Civil Rights*, 49.

40 Dudziak, *Cold War Civil Rights*, 108.

41 Dudziak, *Cold War Civil Rights*, 126, 144.

42 This poster is in the collection of the Victoria and Albert Museum, London (E.1739-2004).

43 Dudziak, *Cold War Civil Rights*, 169–72.

44 See Romano, "No Diplomatic Immunity."

45 Cull, *The Cold War and the United States Information Agency*, 234–35.

46 See Ogbar, *Black Power*, 2.

47 Ogbar, *Black Power*, 85. Anderson argues, however, that emphatic as it was, the BPP's internationalism was largely rhetorical, in comparison to the historiographically neglected role of black liberals working within structures of government and the UN. See Anderson, "The Histories of African Americans' Anticolonialism," 184.

48 See A. Whitman, "A South African Talks about U.S."

49 Cull, *The Cold War and the United States Information Agency*, 211; Romano, "No Diplomatic Immunity."

50 Letter from Ernest Cole to the editor of the *New York Times*, December 12, 1967 (private collection).

51 Nat Nakasa, who arrived in the US on an exit visa a few years before Cole, would be one such example. See Brown, "A Native of Nowhere."

52 Ogbar, *Black Power*, 118.

53 One can be less certain how Cole would have responded to the use of the spear and shield to signify Africa, since, under apartheid, identification with an ethnic identity risked complicity with the ideology of "separate development." Elsewhere, Cole has expressed caution over the use of his few photographs of "traditional" African cultural practices. See Knape, *Ernest Cole*, 235.

54 Department of Justice, File No. 2/1/2265.

55 Sarah Bassnett, "Photography and Insecurity: *Life* Magazine and the Emergence of Neoliberalism," conference paper delivered at *Cold War Camera*, Mexico City, February, 13–14, 2015.

56 See M. Berger, *Seeing through Race*.

57 Kauffmann, "Hue and Cry," 22. Original emphasis.

58 Kauffmann, "Hue and Cry," 22.

59 Kauffmann, "Hue and Cry," 22.

60 Kauffmann, "Hue and Cry," 22.

61 Meyer, "The American Image of South Africa," 25. For an earlier version of this same ideological narrative, the result of a USIA commission for South African author Alan Paton to visit the southern US, see Alan Paton, "The Negro in America Today," *Collier's*, October 15, 1954.

62 Cole, "My Country, My Hell!," 71.

63 Cole, "My Country, My Hell!," 69.

64 Newbury, *Defiant Images*, 203–4.

65 Cole, *House of Bondage*, 170.

66 Struan Robertson, "Ernest Cole in the House of Bondage" (unpublished manuscript, n.d.), 24.

67 Cole was not the first young black South African to find himself trapped in this way. Nat Nakasa, a young journalist who like Cole had worked for *Drum* magazine, left South Africa on an exit visa to take up a fellowship at Harvard in 1964. He soon found himself "inundated" with requests to speak on the racial situation in South Africa, which he regarded as a "display for the benefit of white liberals looking to assuage their own guilt. Had they noticed, he wondered, that there was a massive civil rights struggle underway in their own country?" Brown, "A Native of Nowhere," 55. Shaken by a visit to the southern United States in the spring of 1965, Nakasa fell into a depression; and in July of that year he jumped to his death from the seventh floor of a New York apartment.

68 Although it is beyond the scope of this paper, Karen Ferguson's excellent study of Ford Foundation support for black cultural activities in the United States provides a deeper context for understanding Cole's Ford commission, albeit Cole's project appears to be more of a one-off than part of a sustained program. See Ferguson, *Top Down*. Interestingly, in view of Cole's seeming gravitation toward a more radical separatist position, Ferguson argues that, somewhat counterintuitively, the Ford Foundation found common ground with advocates of black separatism. Ferguson, *Top Down*, 9, 50. This perceived affinity, as well as potentially useful insights for their extensive programs in racial enclaves in US cities, which were backed by massive investment, explains why Cole was seen as a useful commentator on race relations in the United States.

69 The use of the term *Negro* here may be a clue as to the extent in which this project was shaped by the Ford Foundation.

70 While Cole did make photographs during the period of the Ford Foundation commission, none of these were published at the time and the majority were considered lost. Remarkably, however, in 2017, after the first draft of this chapter was written, Cole's US negatives came to light, having apparently been stored in a Swedish bank since the early 1970s. This collection includes not only many negatives from Cole's work in South Africa but also those from the studies he conducted for the Ford Foundation, as well as later work in New York. I am grateful to James Sanders for information on the negatives' emergence and the extent of the material contained in this collection. See Sanders and Campbell, "Ernest Cole's Photographs Reveal America's Apartheid."

71 Robertson, "Ernest Cole in the House of Bondage," 39.

72 Knape, *Ernest Cole*, 243.

73 Several of Cole's photographs also appear (uncredited) alongside images of the civil rights struggle in the National Great Blacks in Wax Museum in Baltimore.

74 *Bilder för miljoner* [Images for millions], no. 5: *Lewis Hine och Ernest Cole bild som vapen* (*Lewis Hine and Ernest Cole: Photography as a social weapon*), shown in

Sweden, June 8, 1969. Rune Hassner, "Ernest Cole: Photojournalist," interview by Hans Beukes (Göteborg, Sweden, August 1993).

75 See Robertson, "Ernest Cole in the House of Bondage," 34, 39. It is not always easy to discern Cole's voice in these recollections, and some concerns may have been amplified by political differences. Geoff Mphakati, for example, is reported by Robertson as saying that Cole was "completely ripped off" by the ANC.

76 "I hear you're full of shit. You're into politics. You know man, fuck all that shit. Get rid of politics. Don't involve yourself in politics. Take your pictures. Fuck all that shit!" Robertson, "Ernest Cole in the House of Bondage," 43.

77 Robertson, "Ernest Cole in the House of Bondage," 39.

78 Garb, "Rethinking Sekula from the Global South," 52.

79 Native American photographer Hulleah Tsinhnahjinnie cites *House of Bondage* as moving her to become involved in photography when she first saw it in the late 1960s. See Newbury, *Defiant Images*, 208–9.

80 Paz, *The Labyrinth of Solitude and Other Writings*, 325.

THY PHU & EVYN LÊ ESPIRITU GANDHI

DONYA ZIAEE

# 2

# Icon of Solidarity

## THE REVOLUTIONARY VIETNAMESE WOMAN IN VIETNAM, PALESTINE, AND IRAN

In the main stairwell of the Women's Museum in Hanoi, Vietnam's northern capital city, an elegant silhouette of a militiawoman stretches across four panes of glass (figure 2.1). This silhouette was adapted and reversed from a famous photograph taken in the 1960s by Young Pioneers photographer Mai Nam to bolster support for the Vietnamese communist revolution (figure 2.2).[1] To look outside the museum, at the shaded courtyard and the boulevard beyond, one must first gaze through this idealized figure of the revolutionary Vietnamese woman. With a rifle slung across her back, she pauses

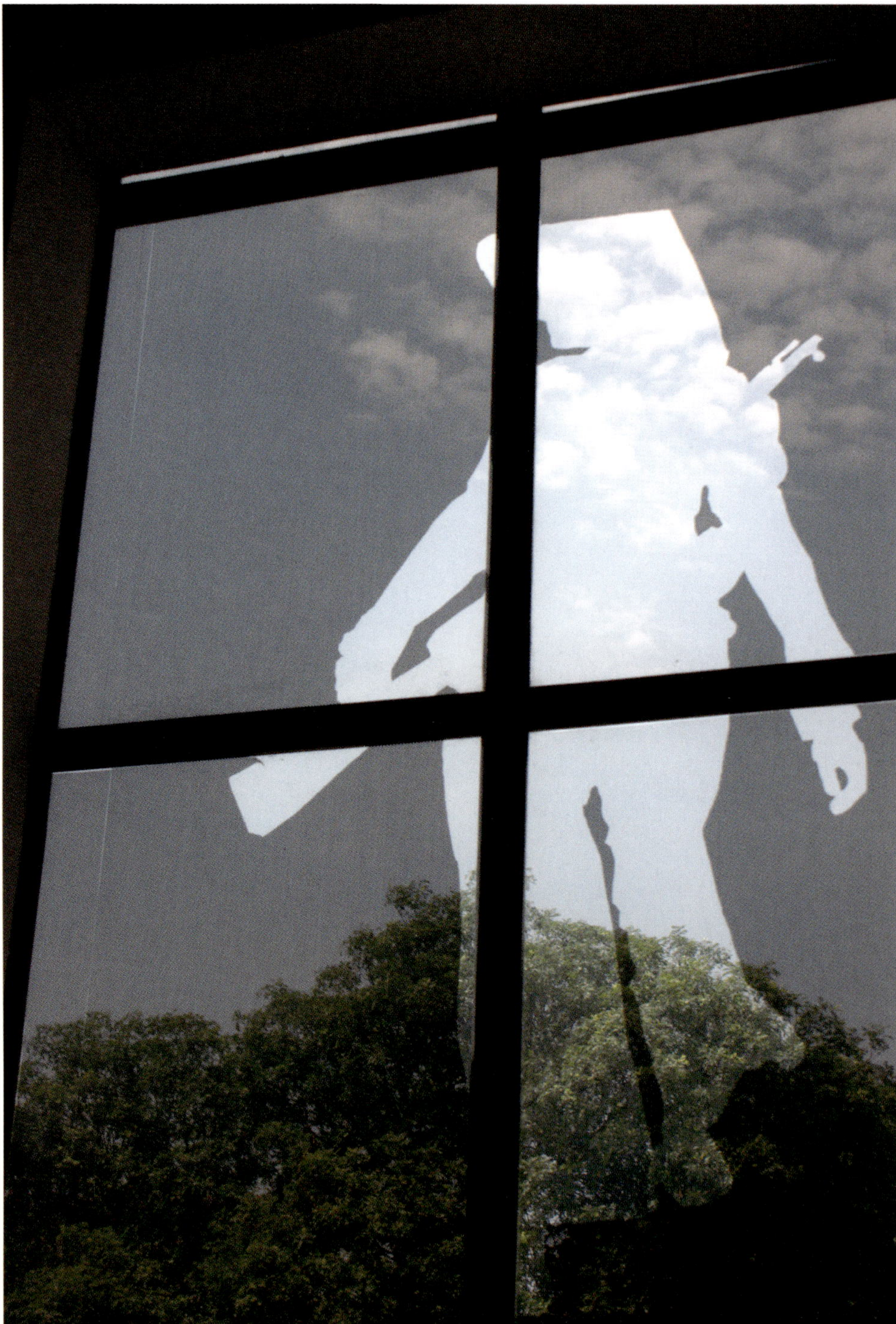

**Figure 2.1.** (*opposite*) Hanoi Women's Museum. Author photo.

**Figure 2.2.** (*below*) Militiawoman. Photograph by Mai Nam.

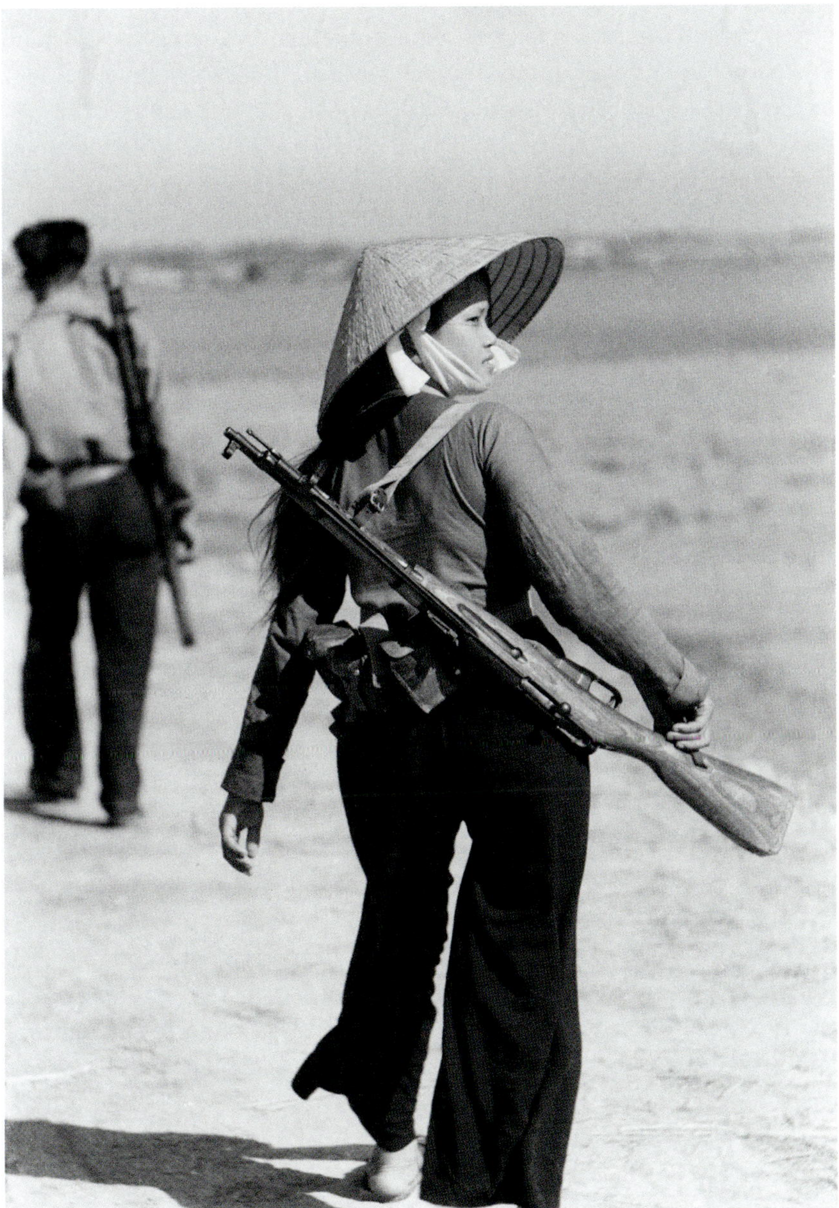

**Figure 2.3.** Peasants harvesting crops. Photograph by Le Minh Truong.

in her forward march, as though awaiting, or rather beckoning, those behind her to join. In this display, the Women's Museum in Hanoi, founded in 1987 by the Vietnam Women's Union (VWU), suggests that one must see through the silhouette inspired by the photograph taken by Mai Nam in order to grasp the role that women played in Vietnam's anticolonial resistance and national liberation. However, the museum's rhetoric of transparency belies the contested history of this figure of the revolutionary Vietnamese woman and its shifting meanings within and beyond Vietnam during the 1950s–70s global Cold War period—a period that, as Odd Arne Westad reminds us, was integrally connected to Third World decolonization.[2]

During Vietnam's war against the United States (1955–75), which simultaneously unfolded as a civil war between competing political visions of an independent Vietnamese state, the figure of the revolutionary Vietnamese woman was highly contested. Deployed by both the communist and anticommunist factions in North and South Vietnam, respectively, this figure was used to support seemingly antagonistic political ideologies. In the North, the Young Pioneers, the Vietnam Women's Union, and the Vietnamese People's Army mobilized photographers to document war efforts and shape an overall vision of socialism. The socialist state-run Vietnam News Agency (VNA) served as perhaps the most prolific producer of photographs of Vietnamese women, emphasizing themes of collective struggle, strength, and resilience. These photographs were meant to glorify women's contributions to the war, in accordance with the VWU's "three responsibilities" movement, which entailed recruiting soldiers, laboring at home and in factories, and fighting on battlefields (figures 2.3 and 2.4).[3]

Women who served in this third capacity comprised the contingent of "long-haired warriors," whom Hồ Chí Minh praised for their tenacity and patriotic fervor.[4] These photographs were printed and circulated among communist fighters to reinforce socialist ideals of unified effort and shared objectives and among peasants to recruit volunteers. Just as importantly, they were broadcast internationally to solicit sympathy and feminist solidarity from a wide array of actors, from antiwar pacifists to revolutionary freedom fighters.

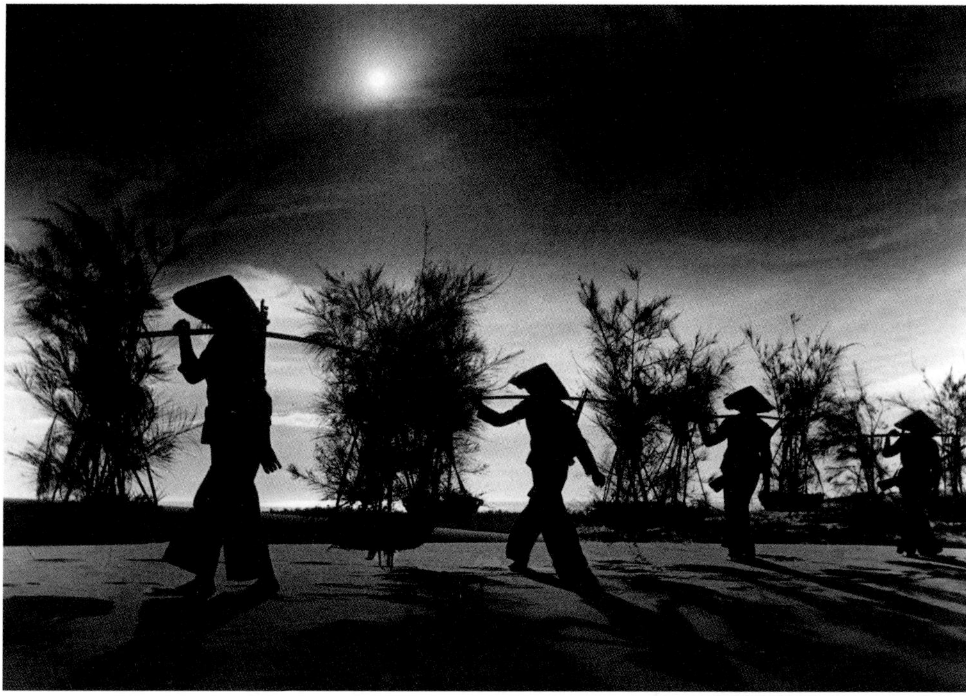

Meanwhile in the South, Madame Nhu, who as sister-in-law to Prime Minister Ngô Đình Diệm served as de facto First Lady of the Saigon-based Government of Vietnam (GVN), also lay claim to this figure of the revolutionary Vietnamese woman. She founded and led the Women's Solidarity Movement (WSM) of Vietnam, which like the North, drew on a visual idiom of collectivity and unity. Despite these convergences, Madame Nhu's rhetoric of solidarity, as detailed below, departed from the version disseminated by her political rivals in the North, leading to internal contestations over who the revolutionary Vietnamese woman was and which ideals she stood for. Ultimately, however, the northern signification of the revolutionary Vietnamese woman as a symbol of socialism won out, and it was the VWU's version that became iconic, circulating prominently outside Vietnam during this period.

Given how contested this visual rhetoric was and how influential it proved to be, we propose an analysis of the photographic representation of the revolutionary Vietnamese woman as more than just image, in line with this volume's expanded approach to photography as a cultural practice of geopolitical encounter that need not result in or even involve an image object. Instead, we explore the revolutionary Vietnamese woman as an *icon*, significant be-

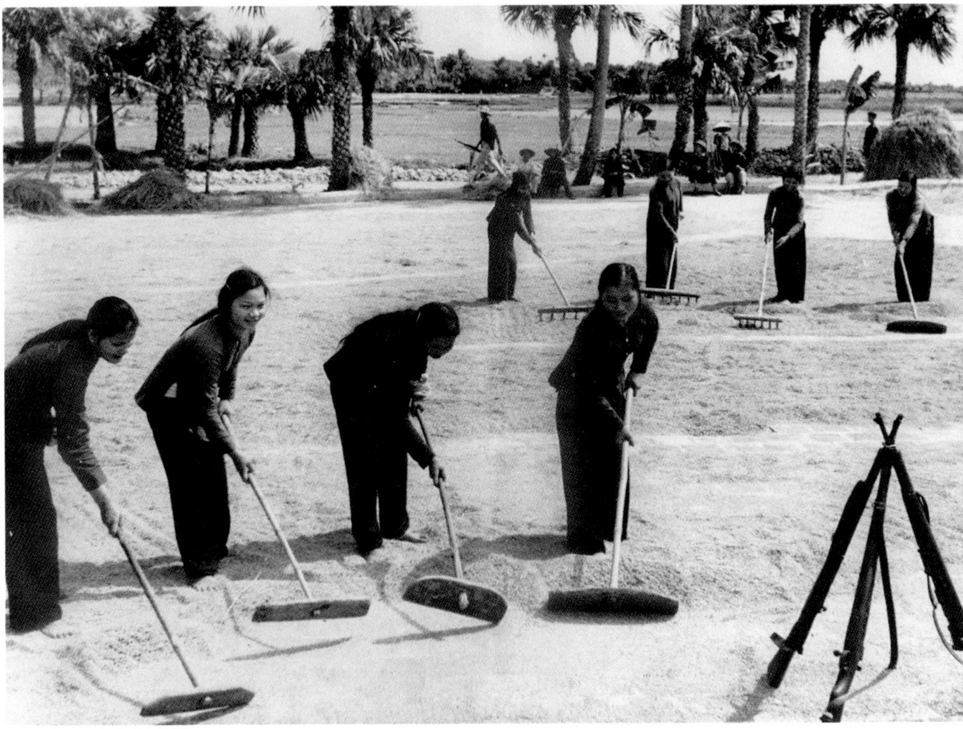

cause of the social and cultural consequences that it can bring about. We contend that the icon operates in a manner analogous to the "figure," a concept that political philosopher Thomas Nail develops to expand on notions of personhood.[5] According to Nail, the figure is neither a "fixed identity" nor a "specific person" but can instead be understood as a "mobile social position" and "social vector." When individuals position themselves in relation to a figure, their sense of selfhood is shaped by it. The icon of the revolutionary Vietnamese woman is meant to conjure a collective, a sense of solidarity made legible to individuals who position themselves in relation to the ideals associated with this icon.

Other scholars have associated the iconization of the revolutionary Vietnamese woman with objectification, depoliticization, and a lack of female agency. For example, Elizabeth Armstrong and Vijay Prashad have lamented the difficulty of pinning down the exact role of Vietnamese women during and after the war, observing: "Women in Vietnam, at their most objectified, were rendered as symbols: of revolutionary resistance, of the Third World, and perhaps most commonly, of a separatist force within the larger strug-

**Figure 2.4.** Women clearing a road. Photograph by Le Minh Truong.

gle against US occupation."[6] Mary Ann Tétreault adds that the icon's flexibility and ambiguity complicates the task of historical interpretation.[7] In contrast, we argue that attending to processes of iconization—that is, the multiple productions of the revolutionary Vietnamese woman *as icon* during the war—enables a grappling with the complex processes of signification, resignification, and interpretation that unfolded via competing visions of a decolonized Vietnam and different figurations of Third World solidarity. Furthermore, women played an important role in shaping the different manifestations of this icon, both in Vietnam and abroad.

This chapter focuses on the icon of the revolutionary Vietnamese woman in order to elucidate the ways that the complex relationships between feminism and national liberation were negotiated in Vietnam and other parts of the Third World during the 1960s–70s. Notably, the icon of the revolutionary Vietnamese woman took varied permutations, particularly as it circulated beyond Vietnam and was reinterpreted and remediated in service of manifold causes. This icon appeared as girls with guns; as militarized mothers representing a martial maternalism; as glamorously arrayed but more often than not humbly garbed peasant warriors; and, especially in the case of Nguyễn Thị Bình, as diplomatic representatives. Despite the popularity of the icon of the revolutionary woman in various struggles, the existence of localized versions suggests that no unified meaning existed, but rather that manifold meanings emerged in response to political exigencies. Moreover, the icon of the revolutionary Vietnamese woman was taken up by contemporaneous movements to advance feminist and national liberation causes in other contexts beyond Vietnam.[8] For this reason, the process of localization frequently entailed the remediation of the Vietnamese iteration of the icon. Overall, the icon of the revolutionary Vietnamese woman exemplifies what historian Bruce Cumings describes as "parallax vision," in which ways of knowing shift depending on one's viewing position.[9]

Accordingly, this chapter adopts a relational approach to understanding the contexts in which the revolutionary Vietnamese woman proliferated as an icon by focusing on the production, circulation, and remediation of this icon at three sites: within Vietnam, where internal contests for moral authority on the question of female liberation and revolution underscored the icon's fluidity, unsettling any assumption of a single "essence" of womanhood; in Palestine, where freedom fighters sought to borrow the spotlight that was focused on the then highly visible war in Vietnam to illuminate their own, relatively overshadowed, struggle; and in Iran, where feminist activists strove to advance women's emancipation against the patriarchal influence of religious authoritarianism and Leftist freedom fighters.

We choose these three sites neither because we wish to imply a seamless continuity between them nor because we claim to be comprehensive in our approach. Instead we limit our scope to these dispersed locations to emphasize how widely the icon of the revolutionary Vietnamese woman circulated and how broadly its meanings were reinterpreted. We also bring these sites into dialogue to expand the geographic and temporal framework for discussion of the visual coverage of the war in Vietnam, beyond a US-dominated culture industry, and beyond the typical coordinates of the Cold War. We contend that these three sites are linked through a visual economy of photographic icon production—that is, these three sites are linked through an uneven process of circulation and remediation of this prominent and highly visible icon—which helped to negotiate ideological connections and divergences. We ask: During the Cold War period of Third World decolonization, what was the relationship between national liberation and women's emancipation? In what ways did the icon of the revolutionary Vietnamese woman resist its instrumentalization by a larger nationalist project, and in what ways was it subsumed? Who produced these icons, and for whom? How did the signification of the icon change depending on local context? Through our relational overview of the contexts for the production and reception of these photographs in Vietnam, Palestine, and Iran, we demonstrate the malleability and portability of the icon of the revolutionary Vietnamese woman and argue that these characteristics make this icon amenable to, if not always successful in, brokering solidarity—that is, a sense of shared experiences and political objectives between different Third World liberation movements and their struggles for women's emancipation during the global Cold War.

## GENDERED VISIONS OF MODERNITY IN A DIVIDED VIETNAM

Despite being deployed abroad as a means of expressing parallels and solidarities, the figure of the revolutionary Vietnamese woman laid bare ideological differences within Vietnam, not least the tensions between socialism and women's emancipation. In Vietnam, which from 1954 to 1975 was partitioned into North and South Vietnam, this very figure became the means by which opposing administrations vied for the mantle of national liberator and champion of women's rights. As noted above, the VWU in the North was especially concerned with shaping this figure to suit its purposes and did so by elaborating on women's collective contributions to revolution. And yet, given the significance of collective struggle as a socialist virtue, the composition of some of these photographs might appear odd at first glance, for they feature a single revolutionary Vietnamese woman removed from the company of her comrades. As we saw above, the Hanoi Women's Museum opted to represent this figure as a singular presence (see figure 2.1), adapting Mai Nam's iconic photograph by cropping out the second person who appeared in his original print (see figure 2.2).

Despite the isolating effect of this excision, its seeming contradiction can be resolved when we consider that the photograph implies the presence of others. After all, visitors are encouraged to look at and, in this process, presumably, to see and sympathize with her accomplishments. The visual idiom of singularity did not necessarily emphasize the individuality of the revolutionary Vietnamese woman. Rather, this visual idiom gestures toward collectivity through an implicitly expansive notion of singularity. Specifically, the decision to frame this figure in a singular way is consistent with the VWU's broader strategy of exalting select revolutionary women as exemplary fighters in propaganda pamphlets, also called "emulation" tracts, designed to recruit more women to the cause of anticolonial struggle. Not surprisingly, the women whom the VWU addressed through the circulation of this image included not only peasants in Vietnam but also antiwar activists from among the North American women's movement, with whom the VWU sought sympathy on the grounds of a shared maternal sensibility.[10]

Perhaps the most visible model of exemplary collectivism, which is to say a singular revolutionary whose contributions laid a path for others to follow, can be seen in the representation of Nguyễn Thị Bình, particularly in her carefully calculated performance of femininity in her capacity as advocate on be-

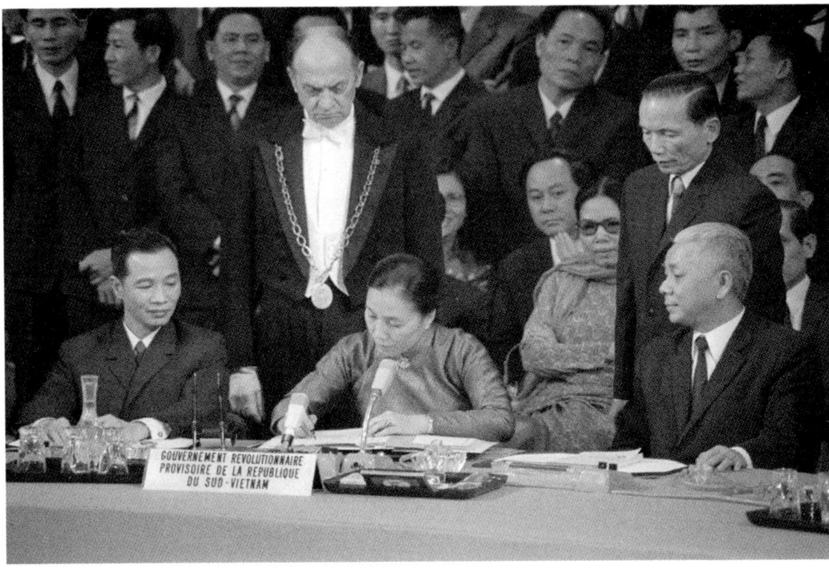


half of the Communist-sympathetic Provisional Revolutionary Government–National Liberation Front (PRG-NLF) at the Paris Peace Accords. Although she was nervous about appearing before the press, Nguyễn Thị Bình understood the profound importance of appearances. "After all," she reminisced, "a gentle, petite woman from a land where war raged had stood before them, speaking with reason and feeling. Indeed, our first steps had created sympathy among the press."[11]

Madame Bình presented herself to be seen, playfully reversing clichés about the so-called Orient (as was evident when she described herself as "gentle" and "petite"). Significantly, Madame Bình also appeared in public at the Paris Peace Accords wearing áo dài, the traditional Vietnamese dress, as a gendered display of nationalism (figure 2.5). In Vietnam, revolutionaries expressed their discipline in plainer style, with the peasants' signature black pajamas and checkered scarves. Madame Bình was well aware that her self-consciously feminine demeanor enabled the PRG-DRV delegates to appear as progressive compared to the exclusively male representatives of the Republic of Vietnam, with their overt masculinity. Her counterparts at the negotiating table failed to realize that, by sitting cozily with the all-male delegation of American diplomats, they projected an old-boys' club cronyism.

Although the connection between socialist liberation and female emancipation first emerged in the Soviet and Chinese revolutions,[12] Hồ Chí Minh expressed his commitment to women in several speeches. For example, at a

**Figure 2.5. Nguyễn Thị Bình wearing áo dài at the Paris Peace Talks, 1971. Courtesy Getty Images.**

1959 Cadres meeting, convened to debate the merits of a draft Law on Marriage and the Family, Hồ Chí Minh declared that, "[w]omen make up half of society. If they are not liberated, half of society is not freed. If women are not emancipated only half of socialism is built."[13] Indeed, the subsequent passage of the Law on Marriage and the Family in 1960 attested to the Vietnamese Communist Party's protection of women's rights by abolishing concubinage, forced marriage, and child marriage. In a speech for the Vietnam Women's Union on the organization's twentieth anniversary, Hồ Chí Minh expressed how "deeply grateful [our people are] to the mothers in both South and North Vietnam for having given birth to and bringing up the heroic generations of our country." He pointed proudly to a tradition of women and revolution in Vietnam extending two thousand years back to the rebellion led by the legendary Trung sisters against the injustice of Chinese colonialism.[14] Madame Bình's presence at the talks was thus disarming because it seemed to bring to fruition this socialist promise of women's emancipation.

Leaders in the North were not the only ones to claim women as allies and to broadcast their vision of the revolutionary Vietnamese woman, which they cast in the mold of the revered Trung sisters, the national heroines that Hồ Chí Minh celebrated. In the South, Madame Nhu projected a competing version of this figure within Vietnam, asserting that the Vietnamese women of the Saigon-based Republic of Vietnam could defend the nation against communism and foreign corruption. Specifically, Madame Nhu expressed her commitment to this vision of militarized motherhood by advancing the cause of the WSM, a South Vietnamese paramilitary organization that she founded in 1960 for the express purposes of *contesting* socialism (figure 2.6).

Madame Nhu was a powerful and polarizing leader, who performed a version of revolutionary femininity markedly dissimilar from that of Madame Bình. In contrast to Madame Bình's modesty, Madame Nhu favored an elegantly immodest style of áo dài, which Saigon-based intellectuals worried bore the taint of foreign influence (figure 2.7). Traditionalists revered the áo dài as a hallmark of a distinct Vietnamese national identity.[15] This dress, however, has evolved over the course of the nineteenth and twentieth centuries to incor-

**Figure 2.6.** Mrs. Ngo Dinh Nhu, Vietnam's First Lady, visiting female soldiers. Photograph by Larry Burrows/The LIFE Picture Collection.

porate foreign fashions, leading some historians to ponder just how national the áo dài actually is, and how it actually might be an invented tradition, even though its admirers often disavowed the extent of external influences.[16] In the 1960s, the increased presence of American advisers and soldiers brought urgency to the issue of foreign influence as the injection of billions of US dollars in aid encouraged corruption, created a market for prostitution, and stimulated a black market of illicit goods, drugs, and services. One can see signs of this influence in Saigonese fashions; women adopted elements of risqué Western dress, of which the miniskirt was perhaps the most scandalous.

Accordingly, áo dài hemlines inched higher, while the stiff mandarin collars that hid the neckline disappeared altogether. Madame Nhu favored and popularized the new designs, leading traditionalists to gossip about what it meant. Their disapproval was hardly a trivial matter, for, as the de facto First Lady, Madame Nhu symbolized South Vietnam through her comportment and dress. When magazines remarked on her open-necked áo dài, they also embarked on gendered speculation of just how open she, and by extension the Diệm regime, was to American influence. When Madame Nhu insisted that the open neck hearkened to folk traditions, she sought to quell this speculation, deflecting attention by disavowing Western sensibilities and insisting on the local origins of her signature áo dài. By the time Madame Bình entered the world stage as a prominent revolutionary and political leader at the Paris Peace Talks in 1969, the significance of the áo dài had already been firmly established. It was a sartorial sign that stitched woman to nation. Like Madame Nhu, Madame Bình deliberately crafted this sign for her purposes; however, in her more modest rendition, Madame Bình embodied a vision of gendered nationhood—and a notion of revolution—in which plainness, the virtue she upheld, contrasted with Madame Nhu's grandeur. Depending on who was looking, then, the áo dài modeled a modest and dignified North Vietnam or a more open, salacious South Vietnam.

Madame Nhu sought visibility in other ways, taking advantage of the attention afforded by the Western press to project her vision of Vietnamese

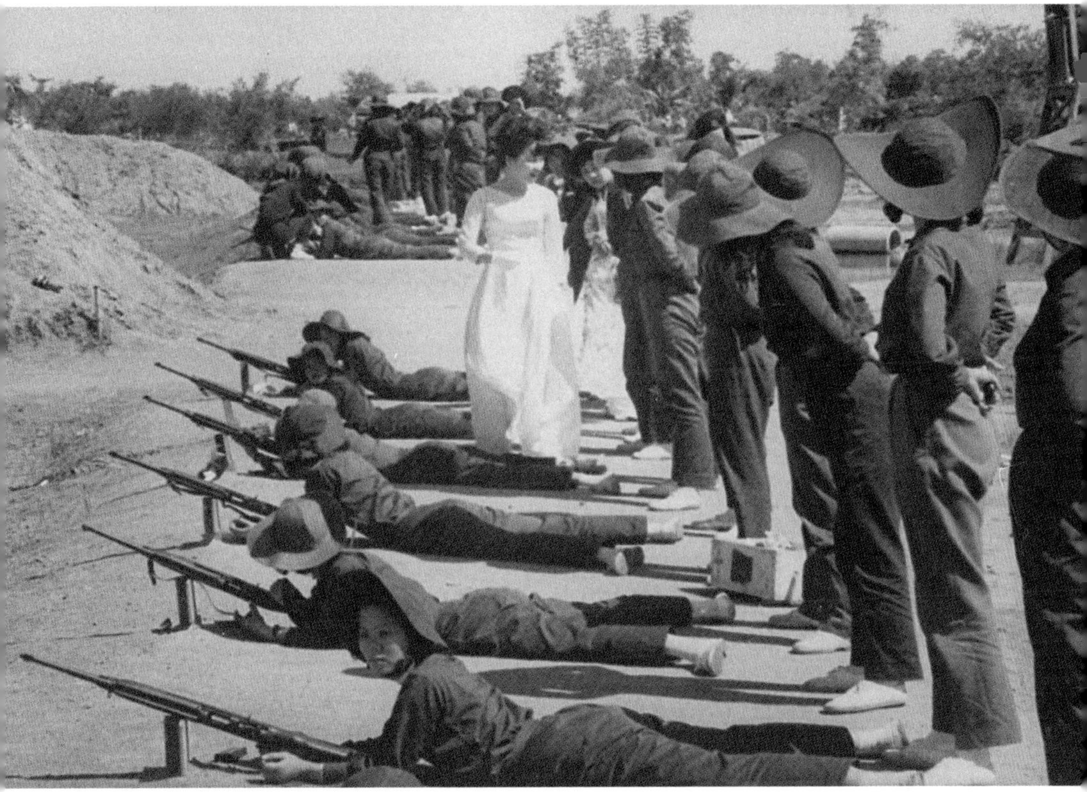

modernity for local and international spectators. In 1962, *Life* magazine featured a child at play with First Lady Madame Nhu. In this photograph, Madame Nhu and the child point toy pistols at each other. Beyond her characteristic beauty, the photograph stands out because of its theme of militarized motherhood—the very theme that would also be forcefully taken up by the VWU and the NLF-PRG, her ideological opponents. While this photograph is playful, Madame Nhu took her self-presentation of militarized motherhood seriously, even presenting her daughter Lệ Thủy a pistol as a gift on her eighteenth birthday. Madame Nhu also expressed her commitment to this vision of militarized motherhood by advancing the cause the WSM of Vietnam.

In contrast to the singularity that comprised part of the visual rhetoric of collectivism associated with Vietnamese socialism, Madame Nhu sought to represent the WSM, above all, as a tightly unified mass and part of her vision of republicanism. Accordingly, press photographs of the WSM captured the women in military formation, in training, and at drills (see figure 2.6). The image of disciplined military formation marks her understanding of solidar-

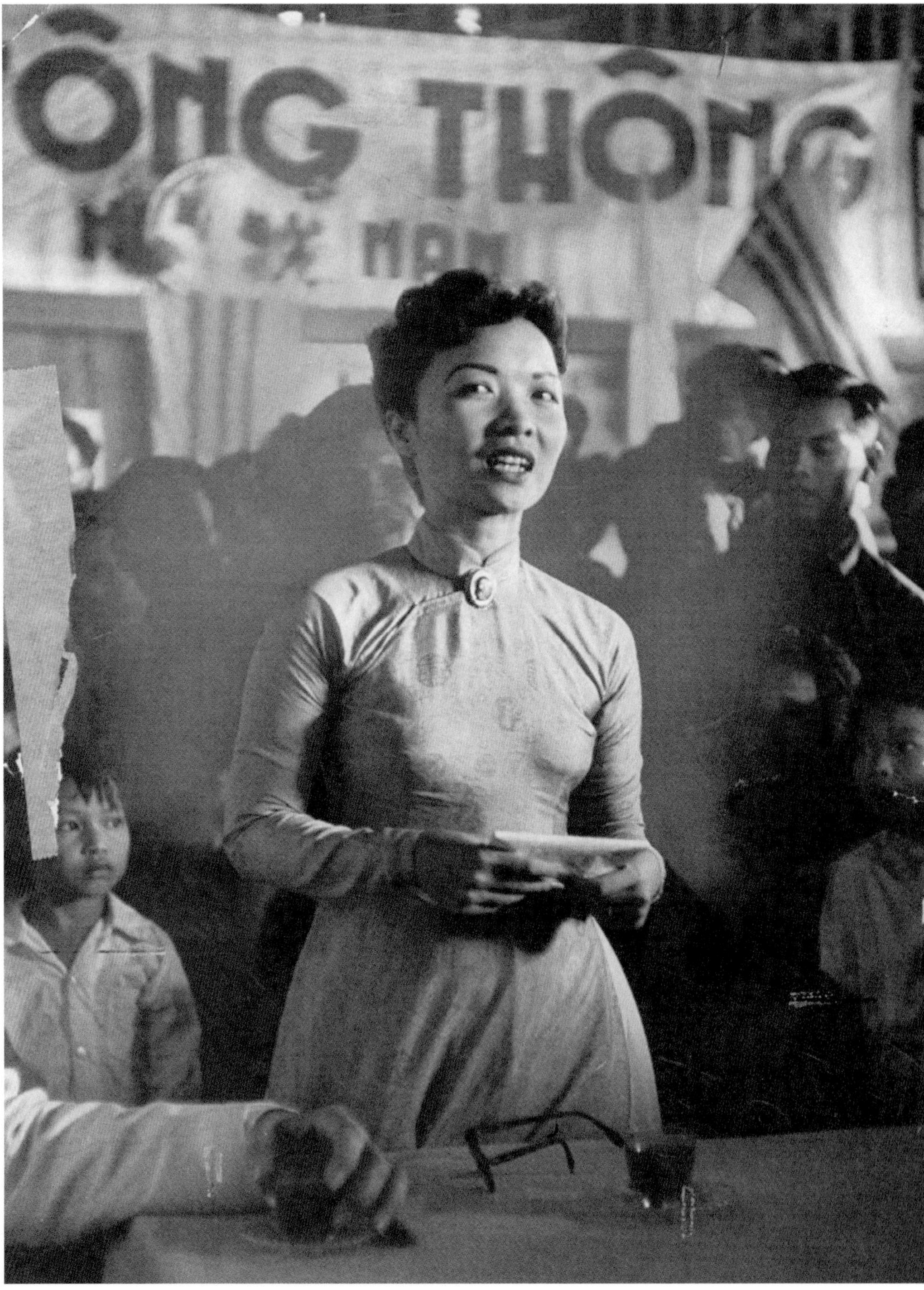
THÔNG

**Figure 2.7.** **Madame Nhu wearing áo dài. Courtesy Getty Images.**

ity; through the appearance of women in line in defense of the republic, Madame Nhu projected a sense of firm resolution. The overall picture of the WSM that Madame Nhu sought to orchestrate was a proto-feminist formation in which she strove to wrest the moral authority of women's emancipation from her opponents on behalf of the Saigon-based Government of Vietnam. However, for all that these movements were designed to communicate the unity of its members, their highly coordinated and synchronized quality belied the organization's internal divisions.

Like her counterparts among the VWU, who cast their net wide to recruit allies around the world (notably from among the liberal North American women's antiwar movement, as Phu argues elsewhere), Madame Nhu appealed abroad for support.[17] Though she particularly sought sympathy from overseas Vietnamese, she also welcomed foreign women as "associate members." This is why the organization's name was changed from the Vietnamese Women's Solidarity Movement to the Women's Solidarity Movement of Vietnam. Nonetheless, a major problem arose from Madame Nhu's very approach to "solidarity." For Madame Nhu, there were clear limits to solidarity; significantly, she stopped short of ceding national objectives to larger international organizations. Specifically, the WSM "would count on the broad reciprocity" of allies in other nations, who would, she declared, exchange "a community of ideals and objectives, though each organization is able to keep its complete independence and implement the common rules of approach in its own national field of activities."[18] In another article, she explained how her approach differed from that of others that put their energies into a "single international committee," which she dismissed because it "usually serves only to keep international contacts but is in general ignored in the national life of the member countries."[19] She rejected approaches to solidarity that subsumed national groups under the umbrella of international organizations, lest the national groups lose the specificity of their struggles for independence. Solidarity could strengthen the movement, she admitted, but only if the organization's objectives remained central. A form of solidarity that lost sight of nationalist concerns might as well not be solidarity, according to Madame Nhu. Photographs of the WSM, in emphasizing the martial choreography and uniformity of women in formation, expressed a vision of solidarity between Vietnamese women in spite of American imperialism, even as the administration Madame Nhu represented was propped up by American advisers.

In November 1963, a CIA-backed coup, led by General Dương Văn Minh, resulted in Madame Nhu's exile to Europe after the assassinations of her husband and brother-in-law. Madame Nhu boasted that her Women's Solidarity Movement, in its heyday, included more than a million members and that its Training Center had to turn away volunteers for lack of space.[20] By 1964, South Vietnam shook as one administration after another toppled in the wake of successive coups. By then, whatever semblance of cohesion the WSM had established through the force of Madame Nhu's personality had irrevocably dissolved. Thus, when other movements abroad invoked the icon of the revolutionary Vietnamese woman, they did so by taking up the VWU—that is, the communist—version of this figure, and not the spectacles staged by Madame Nhu and her paramilitary women's organization. Today, hardly anyone remembers the existence of South Vietnam's Women's Solidarity Movement.

The competing versions of the icon of the revolutionary Vietnamese woman within a divided Vietnam lay bare the contested terms in which women and revolution came into visibility. Ironically, this figure signified, depending on which group in Vietnam invoked it, socialism and its opposing ideology, republicanism. In Vietnam, the category of woman is "disorderly," according to anthropologist Ann Marie Leshkowich, who contends that the invocation of "woman" serves as a lightning rod for debates on nationhood, modernity, and solidarity.[21] Given the context in which the production of this icon exposed competing visions of modernity in Vietnam, it is hardly surprising that its contested meanings acquired further complexity through its transnational circulation, remediation, and reinterpretation at other sites of Third World liberation. In Palestine and Iran, for example, Leftist revolutionaries invoked the North Vietnamese iteration of the icon of the revolutionary Vietnamese woman—which triumphed with the collapse of the Diệm regime and demise of the GVN—to articulate varied political ideologies, competing understandings of the role of women's liberation in the larger national liberation struggle, and wide-ranging aspirations for transnational solidarity during the global Cold War.

## VIETNAM TO PALESTINE: ONE STRUGGLE, MANY FRONTS

The Vietnamese war for independence captured international attention and inspired contemporaneous struggles for national liberation around the world. In Palestine, for example, the war was praised as a "struggle of a small Third World people against the greatest power of the North," the United States.[22] Notably, this representation ignored the war's dimension of civil conflict, valorizing the northern Vietnamese project of national liberation at the expense of the southern Vietnamese vision of anticommunist republicanism. Accordingly, calls for solidarity between Palestine and "Vietnam," as detailed in this section, refer exclusively to the northern Vietnamese version of the icon promoted by the Vietnam Women's Union and its comrades.

During the 1960s–70s, Vietnam and Palestine were linked in the US's Cold War imaginary via the rhetoric of socialist containment. In the 1950s, the United States intervened in Vietnam in order to deter the spread of communism, combat Soviet Union influence, and defend its capitalist interests in Asia. In the mid-1960s, the Soviet Union began to supply Egypt and Syria with weapons for use in territorial skirmishes with the recently established State of Israel. Deploying what Jodi Kim has termed a Cold War "Manichean reading practice for making sense of the world," the United States subsequently perceived the Soviet Union as opening up a "second front" in the Middle East and moved to support Israel against a coalition of Arab states led by Egypt's President Gamal Abdel Nasser.[23] After the Six Day War of 1967, in which Israel violated the Geneva Conventions and illegally expanded its territorial occupation of Palestinian land, President Johnson agreed to sell Phantom jets, which were used in Vietnam, to Israel.[24] This sale marked the start of a sharp increase in US military, economic, and political aid to Israel at the expense of Palestinian self-determination. Vietnam and Palestine were thus connected via US Cold War policies.

However, connections between northern Vietnamese leaders and Palestinian liberation fighters also exceeded US foreign policy objectives, suggesting independent circuits of solidarity. Flouting a Cold War logic of containment, Palestinian and Vietnamese militants sought to highlight points of connection, drawing rhetorical and visual parallels between Vietnamese and Palestinian goals of anti-imperialist national liberation.[25] Importantly, the icon of the revolutionary Vietnamese woman was instrumental in solidifying the visual rhetoric of this solidarity.

**Figure 2.8. "Palestine-Vietnam." Photographer unknown. Published by Fatah (the Palestinian National Liberation Movement) as part of the Fatah 5 Series, 1970. Courtesy of the Palestine Poster Project Archives (Portfolio 1201-1300).**

In 1970, the Palestinian political party Fateh, representing the Palestinian National Liberation Movement, circulated a poster drawing parallels between the Palestinian and Vietnamese struggles for national independence by using the icon of the revolutionary Vietnamese woman (figure 2.8).[26] Established in 1959 and led by Yasser Arafat until his death in 2004, Fateh remains one of the leading political factions of the coalitional Palestinian Liberation Organization (PLO). Following the Six Day War of 1967, Fateh promoted armed struggle in the name of a diverse, democratic state of Palestine, which would embrace Muslims, Jews, and Christians alike as equal citizens.[27] This poster was part of a "Fateh 5" series celebrating five years of Fateh's prominence in the Palestinian liberation struggle.[28]

The poster draws its rhetorical power from analogy. Seeking to capitalize on Vietnam's international politics of visibility, the comparatively overlooked Palestinian liberation movement cited the visual iconography of the northern Vietnamese struggle against the United States in order to garner international support for its own cause. Black text in English frames two side-by-side black-and-white photographs of different women resisting male figures of authority. In capital letters, the overhanging text designates the left photograph as "PALESTINE" and the right one as "VIETNAM." The equal height of the two rectangular photographs suggests a parallelism, though not necessarily an equivalence: the Palestinian photograph is slightly wider, implying its rhetorical prominence and making the overall poster asymmetrical. Likewise, the Vietnamese and Palestinian national liberation struggles were not equivalent; in charting solidarities, it is important to attend to the respective struggles' social and historical differences, such as the divergent legacies of French versus British colonialism, and direct US military intervention versus US support of the Zionist Israeli state.[29]

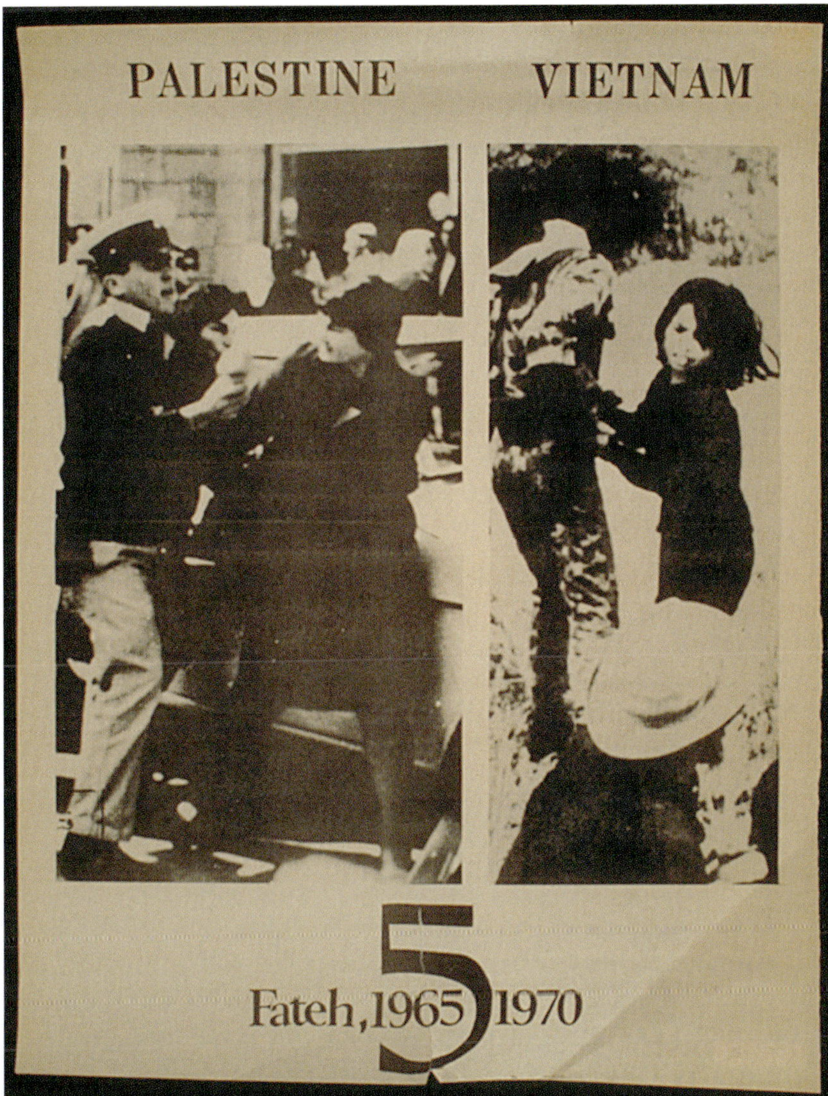
PALESTINE
VIETNAM
5
Fateh, 1965 1970

**Figure 2.9.** **"My Address: Palestine." Photograph by Hani Jawharieh. Published by the Palestinian National Liberation Movement) as part of the Fatah 5 Series, 1970. Courtesy Palestine Poster Project Archives (Portfolio 1201-1300).**

This poster's deployment of rhetorical parallelism made visible the political connections forged between Vietnam and Palestine.[30] By 1968, North Vietnam and the PLO had established diplomatic ties. In March 1970, the same year as this poster's publication, Yasser Arafat and a delegation of Palestinian liberation fighters visited President Hồ Chí Minh and General Võ Nguyên Giáp in Hanoi. During their meeting, General Giáp emphasized the two national liberation struggles' common fight against Western imperialism: "The Vietnamese and Palestinian people have much in common, just like two people suffering the same illness."[31] The Palestinian liberation fighters imagined turning the Middle East into a "Second Vietnam" and one of the surrounding Arab capitals, such as Amman or Beirut, into an "Arab Hanoi," which would serve as a revolutionary base modeled after the Vietnamese strategy.[32] Three years later, the PLO would be invited to take up the "banner of the global struggle" from communist Vietnamese freedom fighters at the 1973 Tenth World Festival of Youth and Students in East Berlin.[33]

What is surprising, then, is not Fateh's invocation of the Vietnamese liberation struggle but rather the choice to feature the revolutionary Vietnamese *woman* to symbolize that struggle.[34] This poster's paired photographs draw attention to the gendering of anticolonial resistance iconography. During the 1967–71 period of Palestinian armed struggle, the iconic image of Palestinian resistance was a young *male* freedom fighter, armed with a rifle and draped with a black-and-white checkered *keffiyeh* headdress (figure 2.9).[35] By featuring photographs of women rather than men, thus bypassing the iconic image of male Palestinian resistance for the sake of parallelism, the 1970 Fateh poster emphasizes the revolutionary Vietnamese *woman*'s potency as a transnational icon for charting Cold War solidarities. The photograph on the right features an iconic revolutionary Vietnamese woman, dressed in signature black pajamas, turning away from and resisting a soldier, whose dark face

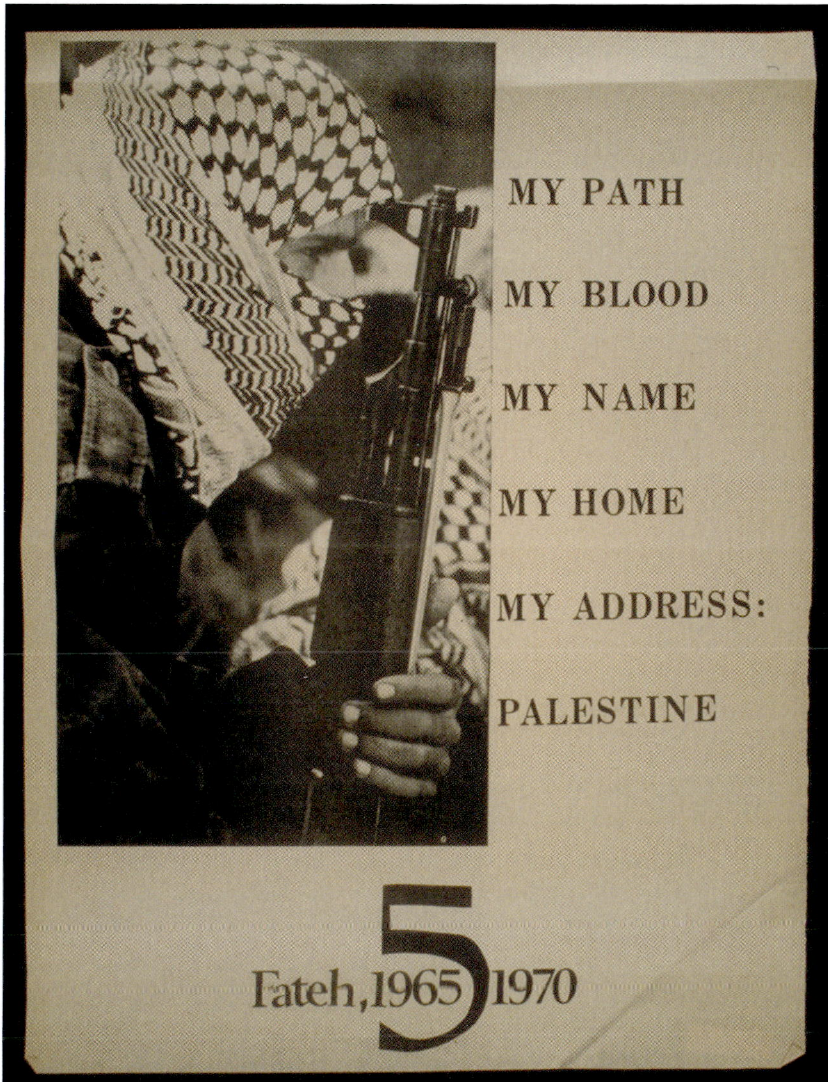
MY PATH
MY BLOOD
MY NAME
MY HOME
MY ADDRESS:
PALESTINE
5
Fateh, 1965 1970

is hidden. The soldier's obfuscated identity implicates multiple aggressors in the North Vietnamese struggle: France, the United States, and the US-backed South Vietnamese government. This gendered figure of resistance not only garners sympathy from an international audience, but also underscores the intensity of the northern Vietnamese struggle: the Vietnamese were so determined to protect their homeland and children from Western aggressors that even women were moved to join the fight.

Given the potency of this icon of the revolutionary Vietnamese woman, Fateh substituted its own default image of Palestinian resistance—an armed man wearing a black-and-white keffiyeh—for a photograph of a Palestinian woman. And yet this *particular* substitution has a limited impact, because the photograph on the left suggests victimhood as much as resistance. Not only is the Palestinian figure female; she is also unarmed and unveiled. Her hair is short, her skin is pale, and her head sports a black hat instead of a keffiyeh. The male aggressor in the left-hand photograph is Western but not easily identifiable: Is he a British soldier? An Israeli Zionist? An American supporter of Zionism?[36] The man's ambiguous identity strategically implicates multiple Western powers in the Palestinians' displacement, but it also presents the Palestinian woman as a victim of imperial aggression. Here, the woman becomes an allegorical stand-in for the homeland; the violation of this site—foreign hands on the woman's body—necessitates a gendered-male defense so as to preserve Palestinian honor. In this reading, the Palestinian woman is reduced to an allegory in need of defense, rather than an active defender of the homeland. Such a representation, however, renders invisible the important role that Palestinian women have played throughout the different stages of the Palestinian National Liberation Movement.

Palestinian women's participation in the national liberation struggle can be traced back to 1884, when women marched alongside men against increasing Jewish settlement in Palestine. In 1917, women took part in mass demonstrations in Jerusalem, Haifa, and Jaffa protesting the Balfour Declaration, which institutionalized British support for the establishment of a Jewish homeland. Four years later, the Arab Palestinian Women's Union (al-Ittihad al-Nissa'i al-'Arabi al-Filastini) was founded in Jerusalem. In 1929, the Women's Union organized the first Women's Conference (also known as the first Arab Women's Congress), which attracted over two hundred attendees. Conference participants staged the first Palestinian women's march to the office of the British High Commissioner, where they demanded the annulment of the Balfour Declaration, the cessation of Jewish immigration to Palestine, and the end of the torture of Arab political prisoners. Throughout the

1920s–30s, middle-class Palestinian women set up charitable societies to help their fellow countrymen. During the 1936–39 rebellion, also known as the Great Revolt or Arab Revolt, Palestinian women collected funds to distribute to families in need; delivered weapons, food, and water to fighting men; and instigated the boycott of foreign and Zionist products.

Following the violent establishment of the State of Israel in 1948 and the subsequent displacement of over 700,000 Palestinians from their homes, a catastrophe known as al-Nakba, women had to temporarily retreat from direct struggle. In 1964, charismatic Egyptian leader Jamal Abdel Nasser established the PLO in Cairo under the auspices of the Arab League of States, which led to the foundation of the Palestinian Women's Association. The following year, the PLO invited women's societies from the West Bank and Gaza Strip to establish the General Union of Palestinian Women (GUPW), whose stated goals were "to mobilize the efforts of Palestinian women and to organize a progressive political women's organization within the framework of the Palestinian Liberation Organization in order to represent Palestinian women everywhere and to defend women's material and moral interests, as well as to improve their social, cultural, vocational and living standards in general, and above all to achieve equality in all areas of social and economic life."[37] The GUPW was made up of representatives from the PLO's different political factions, such as Fateh and the Popular Front for the Liberation of Palestine (PFLP).[38]

The June War of 1967 marked the commencement of the armed struggle stage of the Palestinian National Liberation Movement.[39] Based in Jordan, the PLO coordinated attacks against the Zionist occupation until 1970–71, when Jordanian forces attacked Palestinian refugee camps and King Hussein prohibited the PLO from organizing inside Jordan. During this period, female fighters never gained a critical mass. However, a handful of female freedom fighters, many of whom served long sentences in Israeli prison, gained fame and were upheld as heroic models of Palestinian resistance. Of these, the "best known" female armed militant is Leila Khaled.[40]

Khaled joined the PFLP when it was founded in 1967. In contrast to the more ideologically flexible Fateh faction, the PFLP, which grew out of the Arab Nationalist Movement, advocated a Marxist-Leninist emphasis on class struggle.[41] While female leadership roles in Fateh were restricted to the wives and daughters of Fateh leaders, PFLP was more inviting of women fighters and leaders.[42] Khaled captured international attention with her high-profile hijackings of TWA 840 on August 29, 1969, and El Al Boeing 707 on September 6, 1970, conducted to bring international attention to the Palestinian

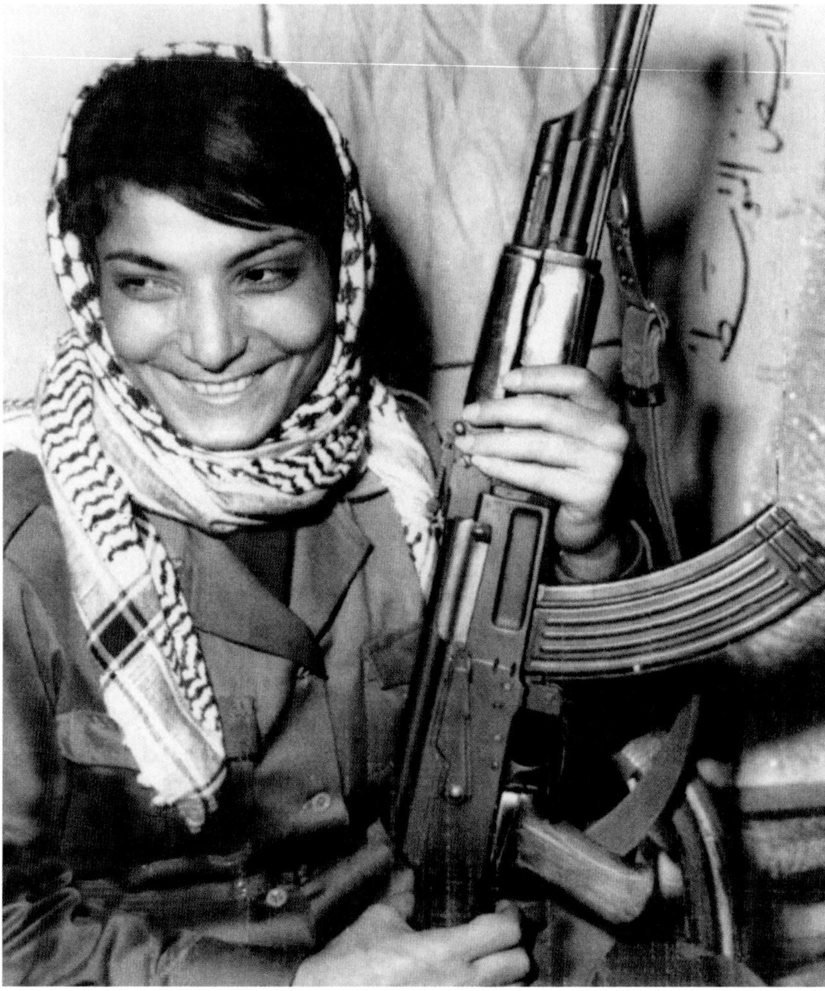

cause. This bold act, combined with an iconic photograph of Khaled—"the gun held in fragile hands, the shiny hair wrapped in a keffiah, the delicate Audrey Hepburn face refusing to meet your eye"—solidified her, in the words of the *Guardian*'s Katharine Viner, as "the symbol of Palestinian resistance and female power" (figure 2.10).[43] Although her time as a commando was brief, cut short by her rise to fame and subsequent lack of anonymity (necessary for hijacking missions), Khaled became an emblem of female Palestinian resistance, whose image has subsequently been reproduced in murals, posters, and zines, and whose story has served to inspire contemporary Palestinian women continuing to fight for social and national liberation.[44]

**Figure 2.10.**
***Hijacker Holding Machine Gun*, Bettmann, October 17, 1969. Courtesy Getty Images.**

In contrast to the ambiguous photograph of the Palestinian woman displayed on the left in Fateh's "Palestine-Vietnam" poster (figure 2.8), this photograph of Khaled would perhaps present a more appropriate complement to the figure of the revolutionary Vietnamese woman captured on the right. Indeed, in her autobiography *My People Shall Live*, published in 1973 when she was just twenty-eight years old, Khaled intimates how the Vietnamese revolutionaries were "a great source of inspiration" for her decision to join the Palestinian armed struggle: "Here was a small nation in black pyjamas fighting the mightiest empire in world history and defeating it. As Johnson intensified his bombing attacks, and as his generals promised him victory if only more tons of bombs were dropped in Vietnam, I became angrier and angrier with myself for not being able to do anything to protest or undermine American savagery."[45] Determining that the "Palestinians must learn the secrets of the Vietnamese," she connects Vietnam and Palestine via a larger Third World struggle against US imperialism: "I went to Frankfurt in the full knowledge that we, the Palestinians, the children of despair and now of revolution, were carrying the torch of freedom and human liberation on behalf of humanity: if we failed, America would have succeeded in reversing the tide of the world revolution, with the notable exception of Vietnam."[46] Khaled identifies with the Vietnam struggle so intimately that when she hears of Hồ Chí Minh's death in 1969, she feels struck by "lightning," like "a part of me had died."[47]

After her infamous hijackings, Khaled served as the PFLP's representative on the GUPW, which was constantly negotiating the place of women's social liberation in the ongoing struggle for national liberation. A GUPW poster, designed by Palestinian artist Adnan Al Sharif, sought to emphasize the importance of women's liberation to the Palestinian national liberation struggle (figure 2.11). Text in Arabic and English dominates the top of the poster. The English text, in yellow capital letters, reads: "THE WOMEN STRUGGLE A CORNER STONE ON THE ROAD TO LIBERATION." Below, a white outline of a female figure cloaked in a headscarf carrying a baby, a rifle slung across her back, is set against a pattern of dark red, black, and yellow. A circular emblem on the left side of the poster in the woman's line of sight features

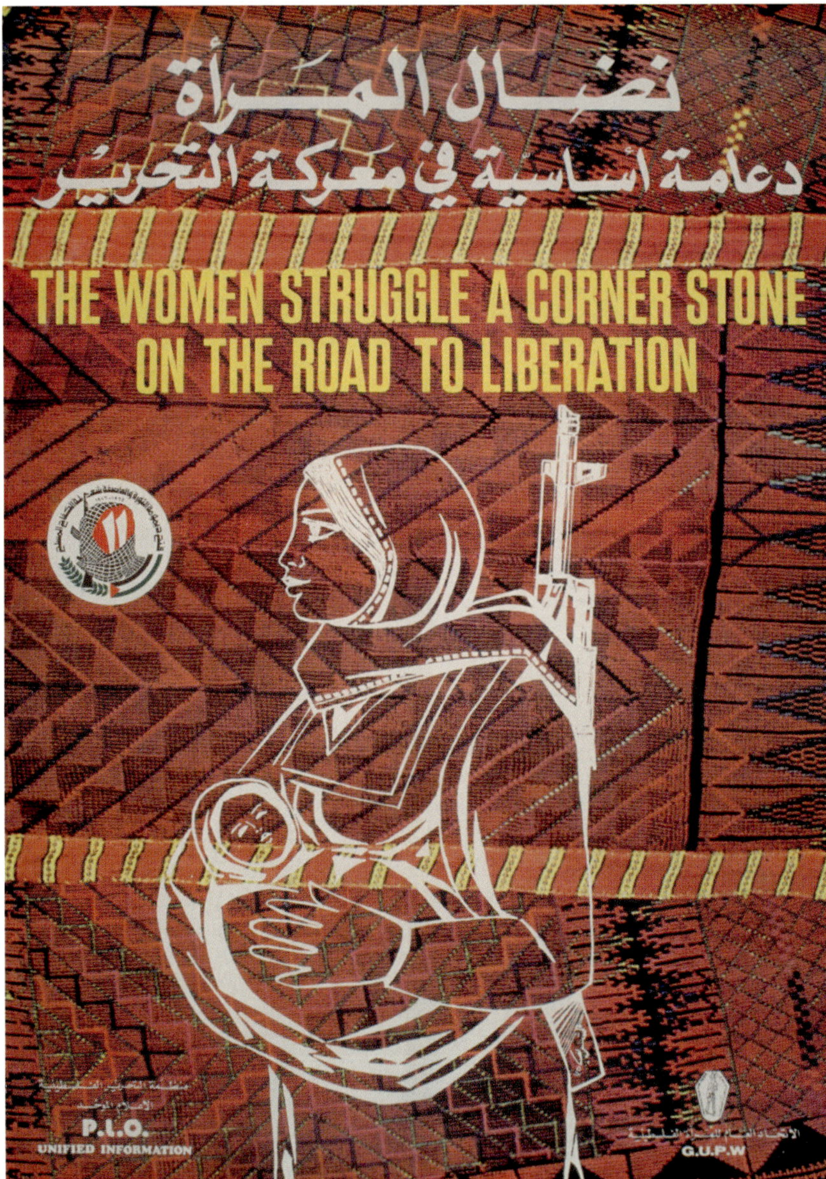
نضال المرأة
دعامة أساسية في معركة التحرير
THE WOMEN STRUGGLE A CORNER STONE
ON THE ROAD TO LIBERATION
منظمة التحرير الفلسطينية
الإعلام الموحد
P.L.O.
UNIFIED INFORMATION
الاتحاد العام للمرأة الفلسطينية
G.U.P.W

**Figure 2.11.** "The Woman's Struggle." Poster by Adnan Al Sharif. Published by FATAH (the Palestinian National Liberation Movement), General Union of Palestinian Women (GUPW), and Palestine Liberation Organization (PLO), 1976. Courtesy of the Palestine Poster Project Archives (Portfolio 1001-1100).

the black-and-white keffiyeh. Like the icon of the revolutionary Vietnamese woman promoted by the VWU, this poster features revolutionary Palestinian women as simultaneously mothers, fighters, and farmers, ready to defend their homeland and their children against foreign aggression.

This visual parallel between the images produced by the GUPW and VWU is echoed in verbal declarations of solidarity between the two organizations. At the GUPW's second conference hosted in Beirut in August 1974, Madame Ying Nol Tsnu,[48] the head representative from the National Committee of the Women's Union for the Liberation of South Vietnam, drew explicit connections between Vietnamese and Palestinian revolutionary women: "In spite of our lack of sufficient information on the struggle of the Palestinian woman, we see that her struggle to a great extent resembles the struggle of the Vietnamese woman. . . . The struggle of Vietnam is the struggle of Palestine and the struggle of Palestine is the struggle of Vietnam."[49] This declaration of a joint struggle, and the centrality of the figure of the revolutionary woman in establishing solidarity, echoes the parallelism represented in the 1970 Fateh poster (see figure 2.8).

In contrast to the Fateh poster, however, the GUPW poster insists that not only is the revolutionary woman indispensable to the liberation movement, but so too is women's liberation fundamental to national liberation.[50] Like the VWU, which was an official arm of the Communist Party, the GUPW was part of the PLO. Both sought to emphasize that women's social liberation and civil rights were entangled with the political struggle for national liberation. At the second conference of the GUPW, Fateh leader Abu Ayyad expressed support for women's social liberation and addressed "the double challenge to the Palestinian woman—from forces without who wish to liquidate the revolution and from forces within who underestimate the woman-as-revolutionary."[51] In his speech, Abu Ayyad declared: "This battle does not involve women alone, but it involves us all. It involves all the progressives who want this revolution and the women, an important element in it, to continue and progress."[52] Likewise, Yasser Arafat's brother, Dr. Fathi Arafat, insisted: "In the revolution we need women comrades who are intelligent and educated; we cannot reach victory flying on one wing."[53] Both men argued that a successful Palestinian revolution necessitated the liberation of Palestinian women.

Such rhetoric, however, was rarely translated into political action.[54] During the 1960s–70s, the Palestinian women's movement for social liberation was often put on hold in order to address the seemingly more pressing struggle for national liberation. In 1978, a group of university-educated, politically aware, and socially progressive women founded the Women's Work Committee (WWC) to develop a strategy of simultaneous national liberation and social emancipation.[55] By the early 1980s, this group had split into different women's committees aligned along the four main PLO factions, with Leila Khaled leading the PFLP's faction, the Union of Palestinian Women's Committees (UPWC).

Today, Palestinians have yet to achieve national liberation, and as such, Palestinian women continue to fight on "two fronts," negotiating the place of women's liberation in the larger struggle for national liberation.[56] The next section, which focuses on the Iranian Leftist movement, explores how women revolutionaries confront gender inequalities once the question of national liberation has already been addressed.

## IRANIAN IMAGINARIES OF THE REVOLUTIONARY VIETNAMESE WOMAN

During the 1960s–70s in Iran, the Leftist opposition to the Shah drew on the icon of the northern revolutionary Vietnamese woman as part of its own visual idiom of revolutionary struggle. Visual representations of these women almost exclusively highlighted their role as fearless fighters in armed combat—informed by the Iranian Left's own imaginaries of revolutionary womanhood. A brief survey of pamphlets produced by two Leftist groups demonstrates this remediation and its limitations. Relying on the revolutionary Vietnamese woman as an archetype for a desexualized female fighter whose emancipation was found in anti-imperialist struggle alone, these groups' reinterpretation of this icon ended up reinforcing their limited view of women's militancy and liberation. This reading would, in turn, occlude the possibility for a genuine articulation of cross-border solidarity.

The Iranian Left's construction of militant womanhood cannot be understood in isolation from the geopolitical framework of the global Cold War. Given its geo-strategic location and oil reserves, Iran was an important source of military, political and economic competition between the two great powers. Beginning with the Azerbaijan crisis of 1946, which concluded with Iran officially in the pro-American camp, the country was the site of several events central to the Cold War, most notably the CIA-led coup against Prime Minister Mosaddegh in 1953. As mass dissatisfaction grew in Iran in the 1960s and 1970s, the Shah introduced a series of preemptive reforms, in an attempt to prevent the Soviets from exploiting any domestic unrest. These reforms would instead lay the bedrock for mass opposition. Meanwhile, support for the Shah's brutal royal absolutism further contributed to discontent and a growing cultural and social backlash against the West.[57] Cold War ideologies, geopolitical maneuvering, and cultural politics definitively impacted the gendered discourses and outcomes of Iran's revolutionary transformation. Women served as predictable sites for the articulation of politics by various oppositional forces, and the figure of the revolutionary Vietnamese woman was invoked in highly politicized ways.

Among some segments of the Iranian Left, the revolutionary Vietnamese woman served as a potent icon in constructing imaginaries of militant womanhood. Several organizations described, analyzed, and provided visual representations of Vietnamese women—drawn largely from communist North Vietnamese sources—in material they produced for internal and broader circulation. Select examples from the archives of the Iranian Left's revolutionary literature demonstrate this remediation. In 1967, the Revolutionary Organization of the Tudeh Party of Iran (ROTPI) produced a pamphlet containing three lengthy essays on women in Vietnam, including firsthand reports from a ROTPI delegation to Vietnam in 1965, as well as nine photographic representations of female Vietnamese fighters. The ROTPI was a Maoist offshoot of the Tudeh Party—the most organized and influential communist party in Iran. It formed in 1964 when members of the youth section broke off from the leadership in ways that call to mind the Sino-Soviet split.[58] The second document under consideration was prepared by the Organization of Iranian People's Fedaii Guerrillas (OIPFG), a Marxist guerrilla group that, by the 1970s, had emerged as Iran's most prominent armed organization.[59] The pamphlet was designed in 1985 by a women's committee in the province of Sistan-Baluchestan on the occasion of International Women's Day and fea-

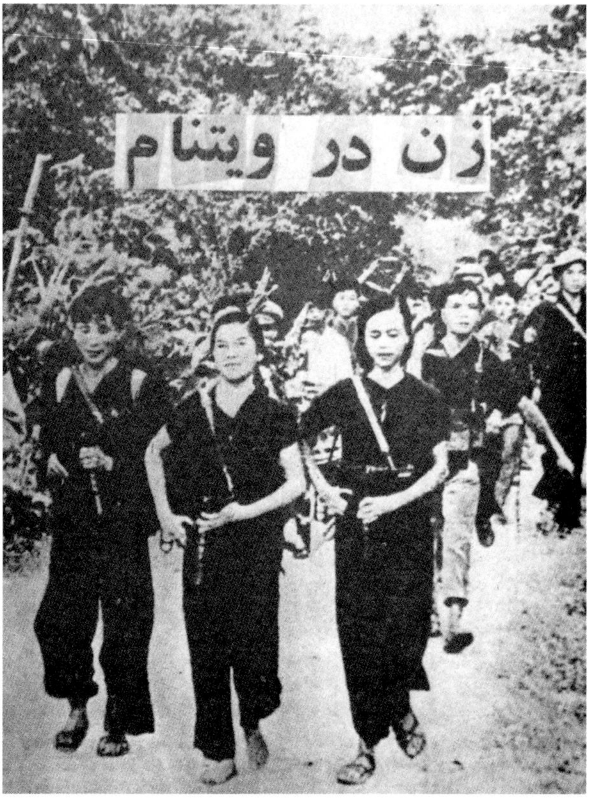


tures an essay on the role of women's struggles in Germany, Bolivia, El Salvador, and Vietnam. Despite the political differences between the two organizations, the pamphlets from the ROTPI and OIPFG share many similarities in their understanding of Vietnamese and Iranian women's struggles. These understandings, in turn, reflect much of the dominant imaginary of militant womanhood among the Left in Iran.

The visual representation of Vietnamese women that emerges in these documents is best illustrated by the cover page of the ROTPI pamphlet (figure 2.12). It features a photo of armed women fighting shoulder-to-shoulder with their male counterparts on the frontlines of combat, with the words "Women in Vietnam" in large print at the top. The image is a visual summation of a prevailing theme in the writings of both ROTPI and OIPFG: emphatic praise of Vietnamese women for taking up arms, standing alongside their brothers, and leading their people to victory. This sentiment is paralleled in an iconic poster by the OIPFG, which features an armed and resolute Iranian woman standing triumphantly next to male fighters, with the popular refrain of the

**Figure 2.12.** (*opposite*) "Women in Vietnam," cover page of a pamphlet of essays on Vietnam, published in 1967 by the Revolutionary Organization of the Tudeh Party of Iran. Courtesy Archiv für Forschung und Dokumentation Iran (AFDI).

**Figure 2.13.** (*below*) Poster from the Organization of Iranian People's Fedaii Guerrillas marking International Women's Day, n.d. The larger text at the top reads: "No revolutionary victory is possible without the active participation of women." Ken Lawrence collection, 1940–2010, hcla 6312, Special Collections Library, University Libraries, Pennsylvania State University.

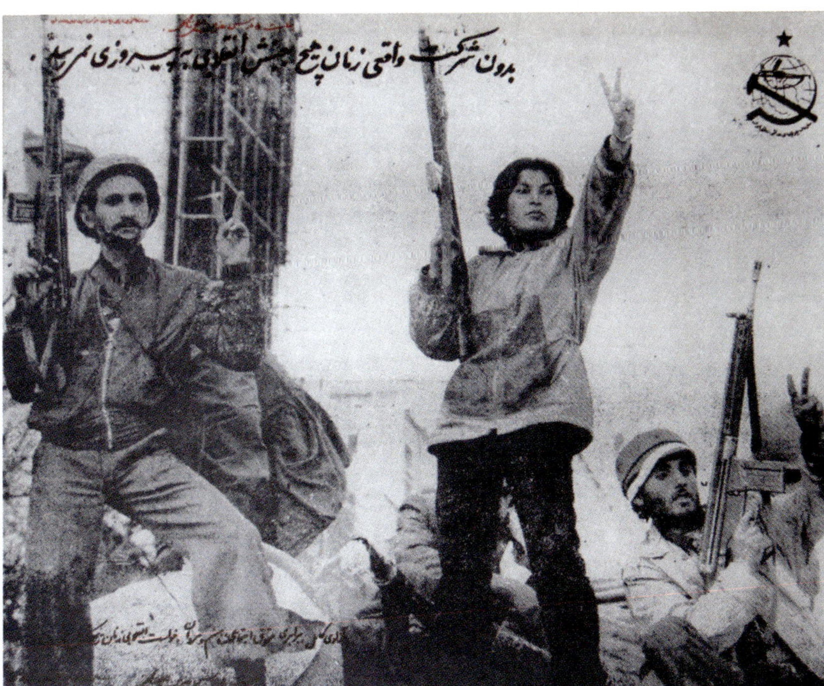

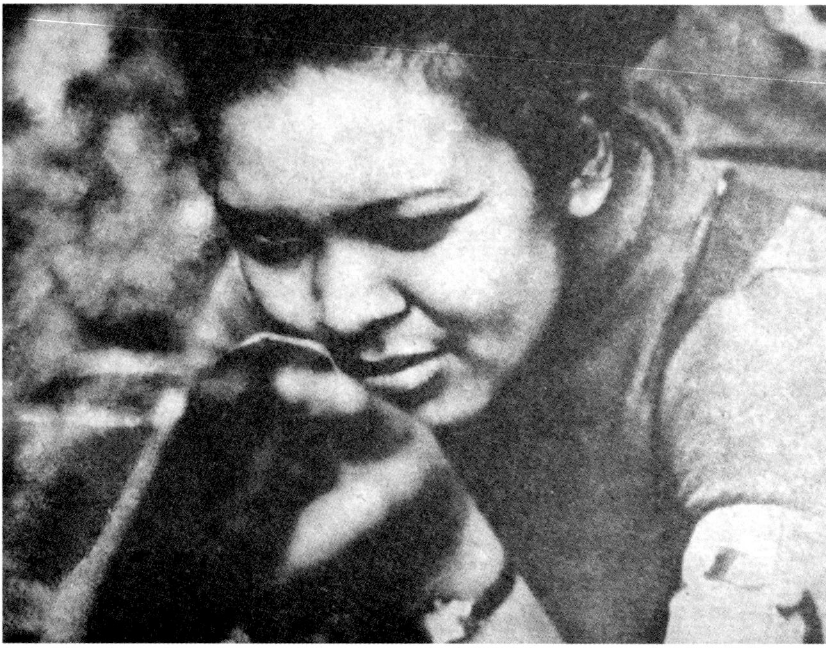

period featured at the top: "No revolutionary victory is possible without the active participation of women" (figure 2.13).

The images in this literature are strikingly devoid of any representation of Vietnamese women outside fields of combat (figures 2.14 and 2.15), echoing much of the official rhetoric in the Vietnamese liberation movement itself about the martial skills, courage, and heroism of these "long-haired warriors." The OIPFG report details how the Vietnamese struggle unleashed the military, political, and intellectual capacities of women, particularly their tenacity in guerrilla warfare alongside their male comrades.[60] An extensive first-hand account from the ROTPI also addresses Vietnamese women's military expertise. Based on a 1965 delegation visit to the People's Liberation Armed Forces—communist guerrillas who had infiltrated South Vietnam to oppose the Diệm administration and its American allies—the report remarks on the substantial number of women engaged in direct combat, the command of military units, the maintenance of security in liberated villages, the organization of the peasantry, and education and training.[61] It also speaks at length about the displays of self-sacrifice, revolutionary faith, and emotional and physical strength by Vietnamese women on front lines and in prisons alike.

At first glance, visual representations of Vietnamese women in this literature appear not only to correspond to the image crafted and propagated by

**Figure 2.14.** (*opposite*) Photograph of woman demonstrating her martial skill. From *Women in Vietnam*, a pamphlet of essays published in 1967 by the Revolutionary Organization of the Tudeh Party of Iran. Courtesy Archiv für Forschung und Dokumentation Iran (AFDI).

**Figure 2.15.** (*below*) The Iranian Left's depiction of revolutionary Vietnamese women highlighted their military capacities, particularly their tenacity in guerrilla warfare. From *Women in Vietnam*, a pamphlet of essays published in 1967 by the Revolutionary Organization of the Tudeh Party of Iran. Courtesy Archiv für Forschung und Dokumentation Iran (AFDI).

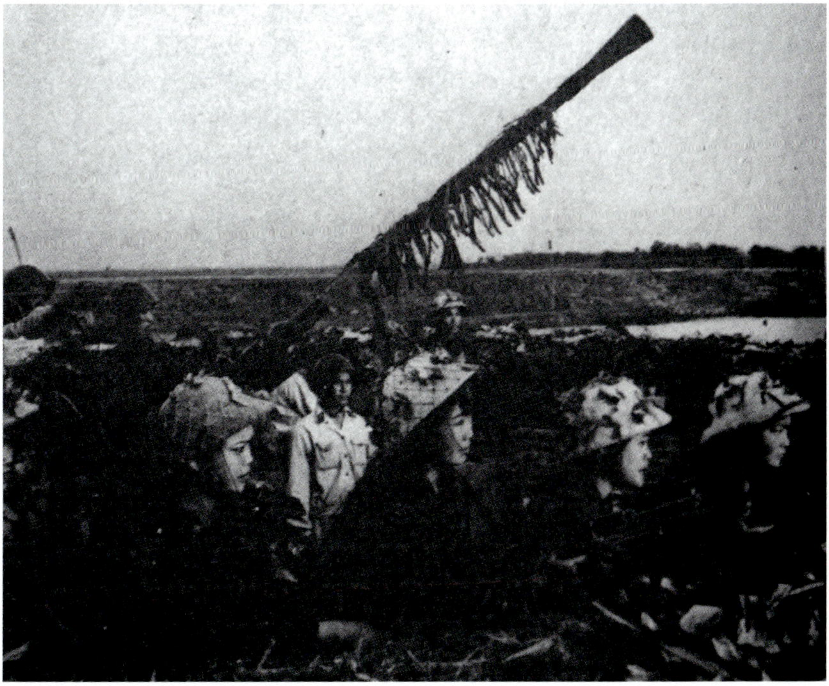

the socialist-aligned Vietnamese national liberation struggle itself but also to provide a promising display of internationalist solidarity. Yet, a closer examination reveals the failure of these representations to reflect the complex and multilayered strategies and subjectivities of Vietnamese women.

The male-dominated Leftist leadership in Iran reduced Vietnamese women's quest for liberation to anti-imperialist struggle alone and muted their efforts at mobilizing women on their own behalf. The revolutionary Vietnamese woman came to stand in as the archetype for a desexualized female revolutionary, whose liberation lay in her fierce and undivided dedication to the national struggle alone. This process of remediation simply reinforced the Iranian Left's tendency to give short shrift to the issue of male domination. Instead, the icon of the revolutionary Vietnamese woman was conjured in ways that ended up bolstering these organizations' overall blindness to or passivity toward women's attempts at addressing the specificity of their gendered experiences as part of the larger revolutionary struggle. It also distorted the image that Vietnamese revolutionaries, at least among the Vietnam Women's Union, held of themselves. This, in turn, significantly hindered the capacity of the Iranian Left to articulate genuine solidarity with Vietnamese women.

This schism between socialist and feminist concerns is by no means limited to the revolutionary Iranian context. However, it takes shape in ways tied to the nation's particular history. The Left's attempts to fold women's issues into other political and economic grievances, along with a generalized skepticism toward autonomous and rights-based approaches to the woman question, were, at least in part, a response to gender reforms undertaken by the Shah. By the late 1970s, the limits of these reforms had become increasingly clear. While allowing for significant improvements in women's legal status, they had also exacerbated the state's regulation of women's bodies, labor, and sexuality. These reforms required greater attention to broader politico-economic crises and a move away from the articulation of women's liberation through the prism of individual rights and freedoms. Yet rather than meaningfully accommodate this necessary paradigmatic shift, the discourses of the revolutionary Iranian Left instead largely subsumed gender-based concerns under class and national struggles altogether, expressing an overall hostility toward autonomous feminist contestation.[62]

Similarly, in their representations of revolutionary Vietnamese women, Leftist organizations actively downplayed discussions within the Vietnamese women's movement about the merits of independent organizing. While cognizant of the necessity of understanding women's emancipation in conjunction with class-based and national struggles, socialist female leaders in Vietnam nevertheless maintained the need to create autonomous spaces within which women could develop a critique of patriarchy and articulate their own needs and experiences. As such, the experiment in Vietnam entailed efforts to implement an organizational separation that allowed for women's mobilization within the broader national struggle on behalf of their own liberation. Yet, the Iranian Left's depiction of the Vietnamese revolution mutes such efforts. Instead, visual representations of revolutionary Vietnamese women seemed to suggest that these women were dedicated exclusively to armed struggle and military-based national liberation strategies.

In its writings, the OIPFG suggests that experiments within Vietnam present a direct challenge to feminist ideas that attempt to sever women's struggles from revolutionary action. Questioning the basis for solidarity among women of different classes, the OIPFG points to the Vietnamese revolution to argue for the necessity of women fighting alongside men of their own class to eliminate the roots of their oppression through socialist and anti-imperialist struggle.[63] The ROTPI similarly draws on the Vietnamese experience to suggest that what is needed is a "proletarian ideology of women's rights" that rejects bourgeois legal frameworks in favor of armed struggle.[64] Praising the Vietnamese revolution, it writes further that "women's struggles take place in factories, rice fields, prisons, trenches, and the dark hearts of the enemy," with their freedom only possible through the violent seizure of power away from imperialists and their appointed leaders.[65]

In tandem with this theoretical deficiency, the Left also imagined the revolutionary woman as a committed guerrilla fighter who is "desexed."[66] This desexualization of the revolutionary woman was a function of the Left's profound hostility toward the dominant cultural values promulgated by the Shah, seen to represent the influences of an imported "imperialist culture." In responding to the Shah's sexualized feminine ideal, Leftist discourse worked to promote a "tacit *denial* of female sexuality," deeming concerns with sexual expression and aesthetic markers of femininity as bourgeois deviations.[67] This cultural response was perhaps most obvious in the unwritten uniform and code of conduct that had become prototypical among women on the Left. In fact, these activists came to be known for their so-called modest behavior and desexualized appearance, typically expressed in plain and loose clothing and the absence of cosmetics, in a manner that calls to mind the marked differences between the gendered public performances of Madame Bình and Madame Nhu.[68]

At the same time, the figure of the desexualized, toiling militant woman was promoted on the Left as a result of the prevailing guerrilla culture. A blend of asceticism and qualities traditionally associated with masculine behavior, this culture reified values such as physical strength, emotional restraint, courage, self-discipline, and the rejection of any personal pleasure or self-fulfillment, all in the name of "serving the masses."[69] Sexual discipline, in particular, constituted a critical component of the practices of the guerrilla organizations on the Left, with expressions of love and sexuality—particularly, though not exclusively, those outside marriage—chastised as distractions and, worse yet, as symptoms of a bourgeois morality.[70] Some organizations that considered even marriage and family commitments to detract from revolutionary obligations opted to promote—at times with detailed protocols—specific forms of acceptable proletarian or revolutionary love and marriage.[71]

Here, the Iranian Left diverges significantly from the Vietnamese national liberation movement in its representation of the iconic revolutionary woman. Similar to insurgent movements elsewhere in the Third World, a common trope associated with the militant woman in Vietnam was of a "tough yet tender" female guerrilla fighter, often visualized by the image of a woman holding a baby in one arm and carrying a rifle on the other.[72] Yet, the Iranian Left's imaginary contains little trace of revolutionary women's attachment to family, whether in Iran or Vietnam. Visual representations of revolutionary Vietnamese women here, for instance, do not contain a single image signaling these women's dual roles as mothers and fighters. Instead, this literature highlights their martial and leadership skills, depicting them as devoid of any familial bonds and responsibilities. While motherhood appears as a common framing device in women's struggles, nationalist movements, revolutions, and state-building projects across the globe,[73] the Iranian Left does not appear to invoke maternal identities or deploy maternal frames in its discussion of women's roles in revolution.

The tendency of the Iranian Left to tone down gendered identities brought mixed and contradictory results. On the one hand, the incorporation of women into militant struggle as ostensibly equal participants—rather than as women—departs considerably from traditional gender roles and the commonplace association of women with pacifism and passivity. It recognizes women's capacities as agents of political and social change and has the potential to enhance self-esteem and a sense of empowerment. In fact, Leftist organizations were exceptional in Iran in the number of women they attracted among their ranks—as sympathizers, members, or guerrilla activists. At the same time, however, such attempts to "mute gender"[74] do not, and cannot, do away with gender as a category that structures and gives meaning to subjective experiences. While they may provide an opening for male-female bonding beyond traditional constraints, these spaces ultimately do little to disrupt gender binaries.[75] Nor do such efforts decenter masculine privilege.[76] Indeed, rather than placing femininity on an equal footing, they promote the devaluation or overall denial of womanhood—with the ideal revolutionary figure still defined in reference to typically masculine traits. What is more, in the absence of spaces to articulate specifically gendered concerns, the mobilization of activists as desexualized participants significantly hindered the development of gendered consciousness.

In these ways, the Left's crafting of the female revolutionary revealed key ideological blind spots relating to gender politics and women's emancipation. The pamphlets produced by the ROTPI and OIPFG are marked by a discernible silence on the distinct needs, interests, and challenges of women in the Vietnamese liberation struggle. Although these documents assign great importance to women's participation and highlight the remarkable martial skill of Vietnamese women, they remain shortsighted. Not only do they reflect a theoretical vacuum in their understandings of Iranian women's emancipation, they are also strikingly devoid of any analysis of how gender may have, as a category of its own, shaped revolutionary processes and outcomes in Vietnam.

Iranian women refused to remain passive in the face of this male-defined revolutionary movement. On March 8, 1979, only a short few weeks after the Pahlavi monarchy was toppled, they took to the streets of Tehran in massive and unprecedented numbers. Responding to statements made by leader Ayatollah Khomeini about the need for mandatory hejab (veiling) and occupational gender segregation, and commemorating International Women's Day, they poured out in the hundreds of thousands to register their discontent and disillusionment with the fruits of the revolution. While these women were united by their opposition to mandatory veiling, the struggle for many activists went much further. For these women, this was a movement not only to protect their individual rights and freedoms but also to safeguard the revolution's egalitarian spirit and promises of liberation. Unhappy that their concerns were overshadowed by other political and economic grievances, scores of women took advantage of the brief political opening that had emerged with the fall of the Shah to compose and articulate their own demands and to make a case for the primacy of their rights. In their contestations, they created a new and now iconic image of womanhood—one that to this day still sees broad circulation as a symbol of the revolution's failings. The image features the scores of women on the streets of Tehran in March 1979 (figure 2.16). It offers not only a bold new vision of revolutionary woman-

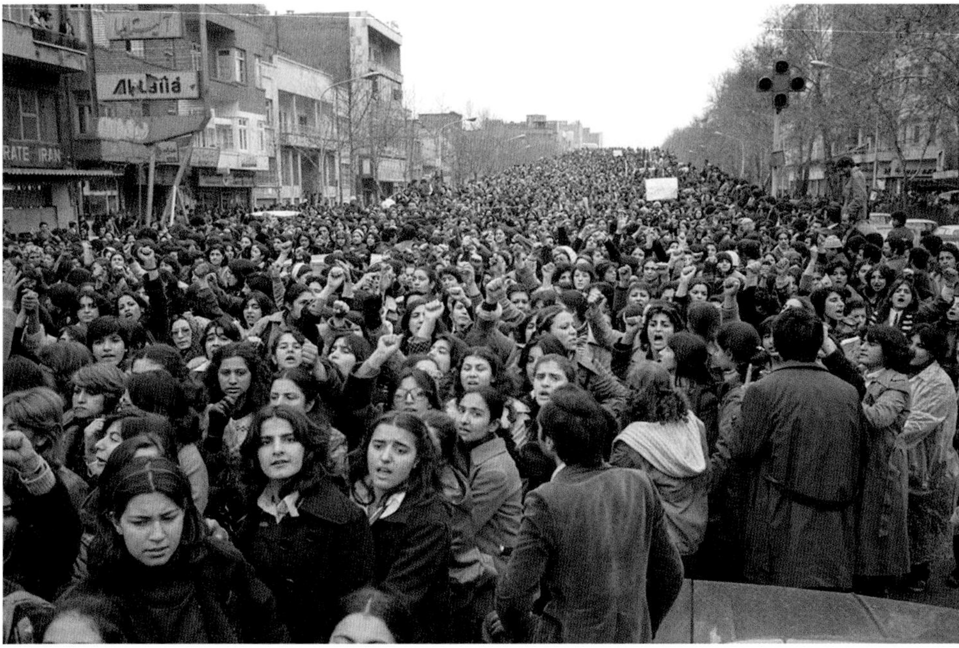

hood but also a resolute disavowal of any revolutionary politics that fails to center women's liberation as a primary site of struggle.

## POLITICIZED ICONS

Critics often consider Vietnam's war for national liberation as a watershed in visual history. Not only did this conflict herald the ascendance of television; just as importantly it marked the last great gasp of photojournalism.[77] As photographer Jorge Lewinski wistfully remarked, "So far as photographic coverage is concerned, there never was, and probably will never be, another war like Vietnam. . . . Vietnam was a big production number, a big sell."[78] While critics have written extensively about photographs of this war, their analyses focus mainly on photographs disseminated by a Western press, which disproportionately covered American experiences of the war while giving short shrift to Vietnamese perspectives and their significance for the expression and dissemination of alternative ideological positions. With a few notable exceptions, scholars have overlooked the work of numerous uncred-

Figure 2.16. Hengameh Golestan, Untitled (Witness '79 series) Enghelab Avenue, Tehran. Photograph, March 8, 1979 (printed 2014). Digital print on Hahnemuhle Fine Art Pearl Paper; 45.1 × 30.1 cm (48.5 × 33 cm paper); © Hengameh Golestan, Courtesy Archaeology of the Final Decade.

ited photographers working beyond the auspices of the Western press; they have ignored the ways that Vietnamese photographers and viewers attempted to advance their own agenda; and they have underappreciated the potential impact of this work on other resistance movements in the Global South.[79] Addressing this gap in scholarship, this chapter has attended to the multiple significations of the figure of the revolutionary Vietnamese woman in Vietnam, Palestine, and Iran. We analyzed how this figure was contested in a politically divided Vietnam prior to 1975, and how the northern Vietnamese version of this figure then became iconic, circulating in the visual rhetoric of revolutionary movements in Palestine and Iran during the 1960s–70s.

In Vietnam, Palestine, and Iran, the icon of the revolutionary Vietnamese woman helped focalize and complicate the relationship between national liberation, Leftist revolution, and women's emancipation. In Vietnam, the North and South vied for political control over the icon of the revolutionary Vietnamese woman, contesting who would wrest moral authority over the question of female liberation and national independence. In Palestine, the icon of the revolutionary Vietnamese woman drew international attention to the relatively overlooked Palestinian national liberation struggle and paralleled Palestinian leaders' attempts to theorize the entanglement of national liberation with women's emancipation. In Iran, women protested against the Leftist Movement's remediation of the icon of the revolutionary Vietnamese woman as a desexualized guerrilla fighter, expressing demands for gender-specific rights and freedoms. What brings these sites together, then, is not a unified understanding of the meaning of this icon; on the contrary, in drawing attention to its varied interpretations, we have sought to explain the complex processes through which this icon was resignified and rearticulated at disparate sites of revolution.

During the 1960s–70s, the figure of the revolutionary Vietnamese woman exerted influence *as* an icon. This iconization was potent not because it attested to an essential core of Vietnamese womanhood but rather because it resonated in different iterations across disparate sites, forging a sense of solidarity that was not always met, even as it remained idealized. By emphasizing women as icons, we do not mean to diminish their political efficacy, nor do we wish to dismiss the substantial contributions and sacrifices of Vietnamese women during the war. On the contrary, we contend that iconization became a pivotal tactic for asserting transnational influence. Indeed, the "revolutionary Vietnamese woman" was a multiform category, whose meanings morphed as the icon traveled along asymmetrical circuits of Third World revolution.

### *Notes*

1 The Young Pioneers was a communist youth organization.

2 Odd Arne Westad, *The Global Cold War.*

3 On the role of women in the Vietnamese revolution, see Turner-Gottschang with Ho, *Even the Women Must Fight*; and S. Taylor, *Vietnamese Women at War*; and S. Taylor, *Vietnamese Women, Vietnam Studies.*

4 Sandra Taylor surmises that the term was first used to describe Madam Nguyễn Thị Định. See "The Long-Haired Warriors," 187n22; 182. Another reference to the origin of the term can be found in Định's memoir, *No Other Road to Take*. However, Mary Ann Tétreault writes that the Diệm regime coined the term *the long-haired Army*. See Tétreault, *Women and Revolution in Africa, Asia, and the New World*, 121.

5 Nail, *The Figure of the Migrant.*

6 Armstrong and Prashad, "Solidarity: War Rites and Women's Rights," 222.

7 Tétreault, *Women and Revolution in Africa, Asia, and the New World.*

8 Despite the persistence of problematic claims about the "transhistorical" nature of visual culture, we should resist assuming that the revolutionary woman is universal. See Mirzoeff, *An Introduction to Visual Culture*. Critiques of this claim about visual culture's transhistorical qualities can be found in Tang, *Visual Culture in Contemporary China*; and Noble, "Visual Culture and Latin American Studies."

9 Cumings, *Parallax Visions.*

10 For more on Vietnamese-US solidarities with antiwar activists, see Wu, *Radicals on the Road.*

11 Bình, *Family, Friends, and Country*, 154.

12 Honig, “Maoist Mappings of Gender”; Salaff and Merkle, “Women in Revolution,” 182.

13 Fall, *Ho Chi Minh on Revolution*, 336.

14 Transcript of Ho Chi Minh’s address to the VWU Meeting, October 1966.

15 See, for example, a well-known *Life* magazine cover (August 9, 1963) featuring Madame Nhu. http://content.time.com/time/covers/0,16641,19630809,00.html (accessed January 11, 2022).

16 Lieu, “Remembering ‘The Nation’”; Leshkowich, “The Ao Dai Goes Global.”

17 Phu, *Warring Visions*. See also Beins, “Radical Others.”

18 Madame Ngô Đinh Nhu, “In the Face of Hate,” March 21, 1963, Vietnam Archives, Lubbock, Texas.

19 Nhu, “In the Face of Hate.”

20 There is no question that this number is inflated. Ambassador Joseph A. Mendenhall noted, “While there is . . . a theoretical possibility of a Woman’s Paramilitary Force of 216,000, practical difficulties will probably prevent there being more than a few thousand in existence by the end of 1962.” US Department of State, Foreign Dispatch #346, February 23, 1962. In “Stimulated Apostles of Peace,” Madame Nhu claimed that there were 1,127,000 active members, “in addition to an infinite number of associate members” (March 1963).

21 Leshkowich, “Wandering Ghosts of Late Socialism.”

22 Gresh, “Reflections on the Meaning of Palestine,” 68.

23 Kim, *Ends of Empire*, 9; Klinghoffer, *Vietnam, Jews and the Middle East*; Bass, *Support Any Friend*; Khalidi, “The United States and Palestine.”

24 Bard, “U.S. Israel Strategic Cooperation.”

25 For more on connections between Vietnam and Palestine during this period, see Gandhi, *Archipelago of Resettlement*, 30–34.

26 Fateh is the romanized reverse acronym of the Arabic حركة التحرير الوطني الفلسطيني *ḥarakat al taḥrīr al-wuṭunī al-Filasṭīnī*, which means “Palestinian National Liberation Movement.” Fatah means “opening,” “conquering,” or “victory.” Sometimes the Anglicized spelling appears as “Fatah” or “FATAH.” For more of Fateh’s ideology and structure, see Y. Sayigh, *Armed Struggle and the Search for State*; and Said, *The Question of Palestine*.

27 Fatah (Palestine National Liberation Movement), “Toward a Democratic State in Palestine,” pamphlet presented to the 2nd World Conference on Palestine held in Amman, September 2–6, 1970.

28 Many Palestinian archives have been destroyed by Israeli forces. The Palestinian Poster Archive, featured online, is one digital archive that seeks to organize, research, and preserve images of Palestine. See https://www.palestineposterproject.org for more information. Compared to the other six posters in the series preserved in the Palestinian Poster Archives (https://www.palestineposterproject.org/special-collection/fatah-5-series), this poster is the only artifact to draw explicit

comparisons with another liberation struggle, and one of two that feature women. The other image featuring a Palestinian woman draws a comparison between Golda Meir, an older Jewish woman who was born in the USSR, raised in the United States, and elected Prime Minister of Israel on March 17, 1969, and Ayesha Audi, a young woman born and raised in Palestine. Beneath their photographs and a description of their national origin, black text in capital letters asks, "TO WHOM DOES PALESTINE BELONG?"

29 Though we can only speculate on the intended audience of this poster, the use of English instead of Arabic suggests an international viewership. One intended audience, for example, may have been activists in the United States, where large-scale anti-Vietnam War protests critiqued American imperial aggression in Southeast Asian and expressed sympathy for the northern Vietnamese national liberation struggle. In contrast, few Americans actively supported or even knew about the Palestinian cause during the 1970s. For an Arabic version of this poster, see https://www.palestineposterproject.org/poster/vietnam-palestine-arabic.

30 For more on this history, see Espiritu, "Cold War Entanglements."

31 "Fateh Men in China, Vietnam," *Fateh* 2, no. 6 (April 2, 1970), IPS; Iyad, *My Home, My Land*, 67–69; T. Smith, "Enemy in Vietnam Opens Wide Drive," quoted in Chamberlin, *The Global Offensive*, 1. "In pictures: General Vo Nguyen Giap and world leaders," Vietnam.net, October 7, 2013, http://english.vietnamnet.vn/fms/government/86140/in-pictures—general-vo-nguyen-giap-and-world-leaders.html.

32 PFLP, "Palestine Resistance Rejects Settlement," *Al-Tali'ah* (Kuwait), October 30, 1968, reproduced and translated in *Selected Arab Documents on the Palestinian Fedayeen*, July 1968–February 1969 (Beirut: IPS, 1969). PFLP, *Military Strategy of the P.F.L.P.* (Beirut: Information Department, PFLIP, 1970), 65. Quoted in Chamberlin, *The Global Offensive*, 26.

33 "Hadith Sahafi khas Sayyid Yasir Arafat, Rayiss al-Lajanah al-Tanafithiyah al-Munathamah al-Tahir al-Filastiniyah Huwal Qadaya al-Sa'ah," November 28, 1973, WFA, 473; Craig R. Whitney, "East Berlin Festival Week Ends," *New York Times*, August 6, 1973, quoted in Chamberlin, *The Global Offensive*, 175.

34 It is important to note that other posters drawing connections between Vietnam and Palestine using the figure of the male revolutionary fighter exist. See for example the 1972 PLO poster designed by Ismail Shamout, entitled "Victory: Vietnam—Palestine," that can be found in the Palestinian Poster Project archives: https://www.palestineposterproject.org/poster/al-nasr.

35 The first usage of the keffiyeh as a symbol of Palestinian national identity can be traced to the 1936 Palestinian revolt against the British during the British Mandate. Prior to 1936, the cotton and usually all-white headdress was part of a complex sartorial code differentiating people by rank, region, sect, age, gender, and hometown. In comparison to the fez (tarbush) or Western hat, this headdress marked its wearer as a rural man of lower-class status. During the early twentieth century,

the keffiyeh began to be associated with "Arab" nationalism, in contrast to the fez of the "Ottoman" Turks. Then, in 1936, the hierarchical class connotations of the keffiyeh were overturned. Although the official political leaders of the independence struggle hailed from the urban upper and middle classes, the armed guerrilla fighters were almost exclusively rural peasants, who used the headdress to hide their identities from British spies. In 1938, the rebel leadership commanded all Palestinian Arab townsmen to don the keffiyeh as a gesture of solidarity. It thus was taken up as a national symbol of Palestinian independence. In the mid-sixties, the Palestinian fedayeen, the militant resistance fighters, reanimated the keffiyeh as a uniting symbol of national struggle. They chose the black-and-white checkered keffiyeh in particular, given that in the 1950s it was used to distinguish the Palestinian soldiers from Jordanian soldiers, who wore red-and-white ones. Interestingly, the black-and-white keffiyeh first began to circulate in the United States in association with the anti-Vietnam war protests of the 1960s and 1970s, offering another point of connection between Vietnam, Palestine, and the United States. For more about the history of the keffiyeh as a symbol of Palestinian nationalism and its uptake in the United States, see Swedenburg, *Memories of Revolt*, and Swedenburg, "Seeing Double."

36 Before Israel's declaration of statehood in 1948, Palestine was part of the British Mandate. The British supported the notion of a Jewish homeland, as evidenced by the Balfour Declaration of 1917.

37 Jammal, *Contributions by Palestinian Women*, 32.

38 For more on the history of Palestinian women's role in the national liberation movement, see Antonius, "Fighting on Two Fronts"; Sharoni, "Palestinian Women's Resistance"; Kazi, "Palestinian Women and the National Liberation Movement"; Abdulhadi, *The Political Role of Palestinian Women*; Kawar, *Daughters of Palestine*; Sayigh, "Encounters with Palestinian Women"; and Sayigh and Peteet, "Between Two Fires." For more on Palestinian women's participation in the First Intifada and afterward, see for example Sabbagh, *Palestinian Women of Gaza and the West Bank*; Holt, *Women and Conflict in the Middle East*; and Kuttab, "Palestinian Women in the *Intifada*."

39 In 1968, the PLO National Charter declared that armed struggle is "the only way to liberate Palestine." See Kawar, *Daughters of Palestine*, 34.

40 Kazi, "Palestinian Women and the National Liberation Movement," 29.

41 PFLP also diverged with Fateh in critiquing Arafat's 1974 decision to acknowledge Israel's 1948 borders and settle for a Palestinian state in the occupied territories of Gaza and the West Bank. For more on the differences between Fateh and the PFLP, see Kawar, *Daughters of Palestine*, 18.

42 Kawar, *Daughters of Palestine*, 19, 26, 36.

43 Viner, "I Made the Ring from a Bullet."

44 For a more complete biography of Leila Khaled, see Irving, *Leila Khaled*.

45 Khaled, *My People Shall Live*, 88.

46 Khaled, *My People Shall Live*, 89, 178. Khaled repeats this sentiment in the book's conclusion: "Since most resistance movements have either been defeated, undermined or contained, with the exception of the Vietnamese nationalists, it was imperative that the voices of the revolution be stilled, or at least weakened in Palestine. Thus came the June War of 1967 that was intended as the grand finale in America's attempt to restores 'sanity and order' in the world and rid mankind of the contagious virus of liberty and revolution" (220).

47 Khaled, *My People Shall Live*, 154.

48 "Ying Nol Tsnu" is the name that appears in the archive, so it is reproduced it here. However, this is not a Vietnamese name. This misspelling most likely evidences an inaccurate phonetic interpretation of the Vietnamese name into Arabic, which was then retranslated inaccurately from Arabic into English for this publication. The name might refer to Nguyễn Ngọc Dũng, who participated in several important international meetings during the 1960s–70s. Phonetically, this seems like a close match. Alternatively, the name might refer to Nguyễn Thị Định, the cofounder and chair of the Women's Union for the Liberation of South Vietnam, or Nguyễn Thị Bình, the vice chair. Thanks to Frank Proschan and Nhan Nho for these insights.

49 "Woman-as-Revolutionary," 170. This quote, reprinted in the *Journal of Palestine Studies*, was originally printed in *Al-Hadaf* (August 17, 1974). *Al-Hadaf* conducted the interview with Madame Ying No Tsnu.

50 The section above details how Phan Thi An of the Vietnamese Women's Union sought to merge the concepts of women's liberation and national liberation. The passage here concentrates on similar sentiments expressed by the GUPW.

51 "Woman-as-Revolutionary," 170–71. Abu Ayyad's words first appeared in *Wafa* (August 5, 1974) and were reprinted in this issue of the *Journal of Palestine Studies*.

52 "Woman-as-Revolutionary," 171. Ellipses in original.

53 Fathi Arafat, *Majallat al-Hilal al-Ahmar al-Filastini*, no. 50 (January 1978): 18, cited in Antonius, "Fighting on Two Fronts."

54 Kuttab, "Palestinian Women in the *Intifada*," 71.

55 Kuttab, "Palestinian Women in the *Intifada*," 73.

56 Antonius, "Fighting on Two Fronts," 26–45; Kawar, *Daughters of Palestine*, 22.

57 For a historical overview of Iran's encounter with the Cold War, see Chubin, "Iran"; Keddie and Gasiorowski, *Neither East nor West*; Cottam, *Iran and the Unites States*; and Bill, *The Eagle and the Lion*.

58 With its main leaders based outside of Iran, and given the success of the SAVAK in crushing the organization's multiple attempts at staging armed rural uprisings in the 1960s, the ROTPI would ultimately fail to establish a durable network inside the country. Nevertheless, its reports from Vietnam provide important insights into dominant conceptualizations on the Left about the role of women in armed

struggles. For more about the organization, see Behrooz, "Iranian Revolution," 193–95.

59 For a comprehensive history of the rise and fall of the Fedaii Guerrillas in Iran, see Vahabzadeh, *A Guerrilla Odyssey*.

60 OIPFG, *Zan-e Baluch* [Baluch Women], Women's Committee of Supporters of the OIPFG in Sistan-Baluchestan, 1985.

61 The authors also provide detailed accounts of the conduct of female prison guards toward captured American soldiers. Commenting on the petite size and stature of these women—with guns "larger than their torsos" flung from their shoulders, and face to face with male Yankee officers who "appeared taller even when sitting down"—they express a particular fascination with the fear that these fierce women managed to instill in their captives. See ROTPI, *Zanan*.

62 Shahidian, *Women in Iran*, 129.

63 OIPFG, *Zan-e Baluch* [Baluch Women] (Women's Committee of Supporters of the OIPFG in Sistan-Baluchestan, 1985).

64 ROTPI, *Zanan*.

65 ROTPI, *Zanan*.

66 Shahidian, *Women in Iran*, 146.

67 Shahidian, *Women in Iran*, 141.

68 Shahidian, *Women in Iran*, 145.

69 Moghissi, "Troubled Relationships," 220.

70 Indeed, the ideal female militant on the Left was an asexual or desexed revolutionary "whose love for the masses left no room for carnal love" (Shahidian, *Women in Iran*, 144).

71 Shahidian, *Women in Iran*, 144.

72 Carreon and Moghadam, "Resistance Is Fertile," 24. This "tough yet tender" trope is reproduced in the GUPW poster (see figure 2.11).

73 Carreon and Moghadam, "Resistance Is Fertile," 19–30.

74 Ortega, "Looking Beyond Violent Militarized Masculinities," 490.

75 Ortega, "Looking Beyond Violent Militarized Masculinities," 503.

76 Volo, "A Revolution in the Binary?"

77 On the role of the US media in covering Vietnam, see Hammond, *Reporting Vietnam*; Hallin, *The Uncensored War*; Hagopian, "Vietnam War Photography as a Locus of Memory."

78 Lewinsky, *The Camera at War*, 197.

79 Since the late 1990s, a handful of exhibitions, photo books, and documentary films have examined Vietnamese photography, but primarily configured as works from the "other" side. These include: Emering, *Viet Cong*; Page and Faas, *Requiem*; Page and Niven, *Another Vietnam*; *Vietnam's Unseen War: Pictures from the Other Side* [documentary] (New York: National Geographic Television, 2002); Chauvel, *Ceux du Nord*. Writers who have Vietnamese photographers have also published books

that feature their works from the war. See Tính, *Khoảnh Khắc*; and Mai Nam, *Một Thời Hào Hùng*. The few scholarly studies of Vietnamese photography, include Christina Schwenkel's brilliant analysis of the *Requiem* exhibition and the museum as sites where memory is negotiated transnationally, and Nina Hien's research on photography in late socialist Vietnam. See Schwenkel, "Exhibiting War, Reconciling Pasts"; and Hien, "Reanimating Vietnam." In addition to exhibitions on photography, curators have examined propaganda posters from the other side, including Heather, *Vietnam Posters*.

# 3

ERINA DUGANNE

# Group Material's "Art for the Future"

## VISUALIZING TRANSNATIONAL SOLIDARITY AT THE END OF THE GLOBAL COLD WAR

In June 1982, Group Material, a collective of young activist artists based in New York City, organized a groundbreaking exhibition titled *¡LUCHAR! An Exhibition for the People of Central America*. Held at 19 West 21st Street in Manhattan, the exhibition was a collaboration with the community center El Taller Latino Americano and a number of other likeminded Central American solidarity organizations that occupied the second floor of that address.[1] Composed of contemporary US and Latin American artworks and artifacts, *¡LUCHAR!* made a political statement against the Reagan administration's interventionist policies in the region. It also recognized and supported the culture and art making practices of Central Americans.[2] In so doing, the exhibition not only contested the Reagan administration's efforts to position the conflicts in Central America as proxies for the Cold War rivalry between the United States and the USSR. *¡LUCHAR!* also provided a significant, though now largely forgotten, model of transnational solidarity between the Americas.

A photograph that accompanies a short review of the exhibition in New York City's oldest Spanish language newspaper, *El Diario La Prensa*, clarifies this aim. In the image, Group Material's Doug Ashford and exiled Salvadoran artist Daniel Flores y Ascencio stand next to a pair of photographs taken by Ecuadorian native Bolívar Arellano.[3] Like many photographs taken at art exhibition openings, the image seems to serve a referential function in its documentation of individuals posing next to artworks. Upon closer inspection, however, the meaning of this image exceeds this evidentiary purpose. Through its assemblage of geographically distinct artistic nationalities culled from across the Western Hemisphere alongside its circulation within *El Diario La Prensa*, the photograph imagines the prospect of Latin American cultural and artistic agency as well as transnational collaboration and support.

The transnational solidarity suggested in this photograph was not new to the 1980s. Rather, this kind of "extra-national political activism" has a long genealogy that extends back, as historians Christine Hatzky and Jessica Stites Mor note, to "two interconnected historical moments . . . both of which addressed the evils of imperialism and the expansion of transnational capitalism."[4] They included nineteenth-century anti-slavery societies in Europe as well as the United States and early twentieth-century international working-class movements, which grew out of the success of the Russian Revolution and led to the development of organizations such as the Communist International or Comintern. Both movements provide historical examples of efforts to form international alliances and exchanges across the globe. Yet, the problem with this historical understanding of transnational solidarity is that it fails, as Hatzky and Mor crucially point out with respect to Latin America, to "[reflect] on the very different dynamics of solidarity that emerged from the global South" and thereby situates "this activism as between First World humanitarians and their unequal Third World counterparts."[5] To counter this asymmetrical tendency in scholarship on transnational solidarity, scholars such as Hatzky and Mor have sought to realign discussions, especially those within a Latin American context, from a North-South to a South-North and a South-South vantage point, with the hopes of "[uncovering] nuances of understanding that can be gained from focusing on reciprocities and contingencies within solidarity networks and between partners in struggle."[6] This chapter on Group Material's *¡LUCHAR!* owes much to this growing body of scholarship. At the same time, it departs from these studies in its consideration of the visual. That is, rather than focus on transnational political action in the Americas broadly conceived, I consider the complex and ever-changing relationships between aesthetic experience and activist practices produced in the first half of the 1980s.[7]

My interest in transnational visual practices, or what I call *visual solidarities*, hinges on two propositions. First, I use this concept not to address the ways in which aesthetic practices can build commonalities or forge identifications. Rather, I consider the kinds of misrecognitions or contingencies that they also create. Second, I argue that to understand the political possibilities opened up by transnational visual solidarities, one must situate these practices in time. To address these two interrelated aspects of visual solidarity—its contingency and its temporal framings—I begin this chapter by first establishing the aesthetic and political parameters—in this case, postmodernism and the global Cold War—under which Group Material organized *¡LUCHAR!* as well as the doubt and fear they produced. I then move on to consider how members of Group Material attempted to use *¡LUCHAR!* to overcome the logic of this art/politics binary as well as some of the contingencies that resulted. I conclude by turning to Group Material's subsequent 1984 exhibition *Timeline: A Chronicle of U.S. Intervention in Central and Latin America*. I use the *Timeline* exhibition to suggest how members of Group Material, building upon instances of misrecognition within *¡LUCHAR!*, understood the necessity of constructing transnational visual solidarity within the ensuing exhibition not just in terms of futurity but through a critical engagement with the past. And, specifically, a past that included the hemisphere's broader histories, multiple temporalities, and vexed geographies that had been ignored and even suppressed through the Reagan administration's and the mainstream news media's polarizing discourse of Cold War–era communist aggression in the region. It is this effort by Group Material, then, to use their exhibitions to empower viewers to think differently about the present, the past, and, by extension, the future that serves as the basis for my exploration of the political possibilities as well as the limitations of transnational visual solidarities at the end of the global Cold War.

In 1982, when Group Material organized *¡LUCHAR!*, many practitioners of a politically informed art were experimenting with techniques that Hal Foster defined as an "oppositional" or a "resistant" postmodernism. Critics like Foster, defined this so-called political postmodernism, in terms of contingency, or its ability to "question rather than exploit cultural codes, to explore rather than conceal social and political affiliations." In short, for Foster and critics such as Douglas Crimp and Craig Owens, among others, a postmodernism of "resistance" or an "oppositional" postmodernism instilled in viewers a sense of doubt about "the world as it is."[8] Nevertheless, these critics disagreed on how to frame postmodernism's politics: whether it should be in terms of a "resistance" to modernist aesthetics or sexual difference, or whether, as Crimp suggested, some forms should be characterized as "regressive" and others as "progressive."[9] Evidence of the inadequacies of postmodernism's politics also extended beyond the art world. In the mainstream news media, for instance, postmodernist strategies of doubt were used to challenge, or even unmask, the ideological nature of the Reagan administration's foreign policies in Central America and thereby counter the fear used to justify these policies. Yet, as I will suggest below, despite the efforts of the news media to harness postmodernism's politics of resistance against the Reagan administration's Cold War interventionist policies, in the end such oppositional tactics only served to perpetuate the very ideological terms that news media initially attempted to deconstruct.[10] It was within and against this framework of a "resistant" postmodernism and the global Cold War that Group Material first developed the visual terms of a transnational solidarity.

When Ronald Reagan took office on January 20, 1981, he immediately began to implement his foreign policy of combating the spread of so-called Soviet-backed communism across the globe. Central America occupied a central position in this foreign policy, which would later be known as the Reagan Doctrine. In Central America, Reagan adopted a dual policy of military support. In El Salvador, his administration provided aid against the Farabundo Martí National Liberation Front (FMLN) rebels. In Nicaragua, meanwhile, his administration backed the Contra war against the Sandinistas. To gain public acceptance for these interventionist policies, Reagan sought to convince the US public that the FMLN rebels and Sandinistas were working together as part of a larger global communist scheme—fronted by the USSR via Cuba—that posed a significant threat to US national security.[11]

The ideological terms of this Cold War propaganda campaign were thus set in motion almost immediately after Reagan took office. As Reagan's newly appointed secretary of state, General Alexander M. Haig Jr., famously declared, within a month of Reagan taking the oath: Central America and, more specifically El Salvador, was "'the place to draw the line' against communist influence."[12]

Besides preserving the imaginary geopolitical boundaries of the global Cold War, Haig's "line against communism" and, by extension, the United States' intervention in Central America, more broadly, was also meant to instill fear in the US public about what might happen if communism were not contained. This fear of an unknown future, as anthropologist Joseph Masco has recently argued, was not new to the US public but is one whose "origins reside in the logics and lessons of the Cold War" and especially the "nuclear war machine . . . designed first and foremost to produce fear of the near future in adversaries and to harness that fear to produce a stable bipolar world."[13] Like the affective politics of the Cold War nuclear war project, which, as Masco continues, "was fought incessantly at the level of the imagination," Haig's invented "line against communism" likewise provided the Reagan administration with a means to harness US public sentiment so as to uphold their Cold War rhetoric of containment.

The Reagan administration also perpetuated the politics of the "nuclear war machine" in Central America through their use of "secret information" to shape public fears about the threat of communism in the region.[14] On February 23, 1981, Haig released an eight-page State Department white paper titled *Communist Interference in El Salvador* that outlined "the central role played by Cuba and other Communist countries . . . in the political unification, military direction, and arming of insurgent forces in El Salvador."[15] For Haig and the State Department, however, it was not enough to simply activate these Cold War fears verbally; they also sought to stimulate them visually. To that end, the white paper—purportedly drawn from hundreds of pages of confiscated "secret" insurgent documents—also included a map detailing the arms flow to El Salvador, a copy of a list of weapon commitments from Vietnam, and two sets of photographs of captured weapons. Together these documents, as was detailed in the white paper itself, provided "definitive evidence of the clandestine military support given by the Soviet Union, Cuba, and their Communist allies to Marxist-Leninist guerrillas now fighting to overthrow the established Government of El Salvador."[16]

When the white paper was first released on February 23, 1981, the mainstream news media largely accepted it at face value. Less than a month later,

**Figure 3.1.** Pages from US Department of State, *Communist Interferences in El Salvador: Documents Demonstrating Communist Support of the Salvadoran Insurgency* (Washington, DC: US Department of State, 1981).

however, some journalists and other individuals already critical of US interventionist policies in Central America began to challenge its accuracy. And, by June 1981, even conservative leaning newspapers such as the *Wall Street Journal* began to dispute its truthfulness, judging that its conclusions were "flawed by errors and guesses."[17] Much of this criticism was based on close analysis between the white paper itself and the hundreds of pages of "secret" classified insurgent documents that the State Department released with it, which were said to provide "incontrovertible" proof of the participation of communist countries in the Salvadoran civil war. But, when critics analyzed these supporting documents, they found that they failed to "substantiate the massive tonnages of arms allegedly shipped by communist countries to El Salvador" or demonstrate any credible link between "the Soviet and Cuban role."[18]

The white paper was mired not only with textual discrepancies but also with visual problems. Within the white paper, the State Department presented photographs as transparent, unmediated documents. The captions, which serve to fix what each image depicted, reinforced their seeming truthfulness and objectivity. Yet, as in similar debates widely taking place within postmodernist criticism at this time, photography's truthfulness and objectivity, especially documentary photography's, was far more contingent and mutable than generally acknowledged.[19] The postmodern instability of photographic meaning, or the incongruence between what images depict and what they mean, extends to photographs in the white paper. Several of the images were not newly discovered. They had instead been in the government's possession since the Carter administration—although the Reagan administration failed to disclose this information. Moreover, though these intelligence photographs had influenced Carter's decision to resume aid to the Salvadoran government, which he had briefly suspended in the wake of the

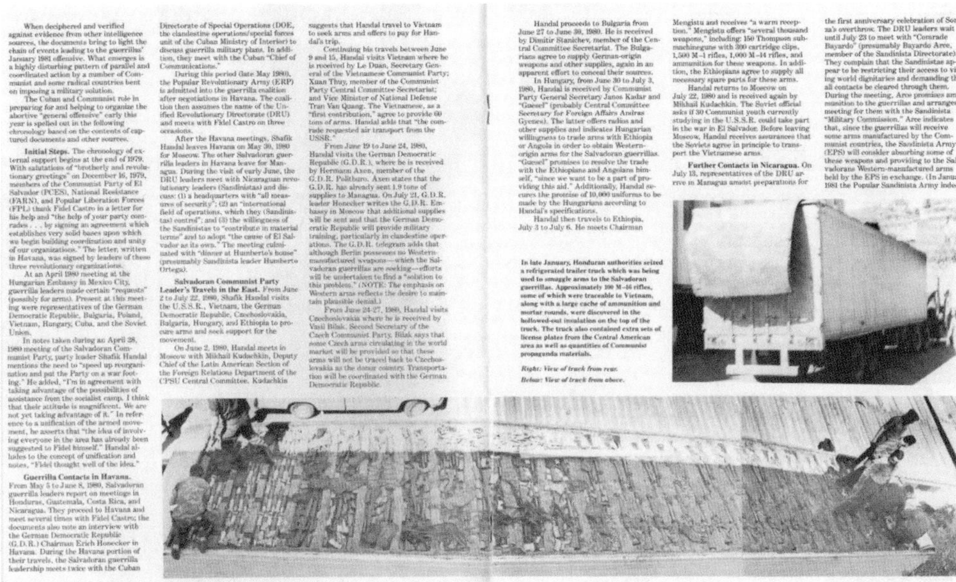


widely publicized human rights abuses represented by the murder of four American churchwomen in El Salvador in December 1980, they by no means had convinced his administration that the leftist Salvadoran insurgents were part of a larger communist takeover in the region.[20] The inclusion in the white paper of a bird's-eye view of a trailer truck seized in Honduras further underscores the contingency of these photographs. In this image—which purportedly depicts 100 M-16 rifles, some of which, as the caption notes, were supposedly traceable to Vietnam—the top right side of the truck has been noticeably montaged to make it appear longer and hence to make the weapons cache seem more expansive than it actually was (figure 3.1).[21]

In response to these textual and visual inconsistencies, the State Department issued a rebuttal defending the conclusions of the white paper on the basis that its claims originated in "additional still-secret intelligence reports."[22] Here, the members of the State Department imply "*the idea* of secret knowledge" in which, as Masco explains of the Cold War nuclear war project, "the secret thus becomes a means of claiming greater knowledge, expertise, and understanding than is in fact possible."[23] But, whereas the deployment of "secret knowledge" in the nuclear age and, more recently, in the counterterrorism state has mostly provided a means to dispel doubt, the Reagan administration never mobilized secrecy and deception to eradicate the possibility of doubt completely. Instead, the Reagan administration sought to manage doubt so as to uphold existing power structures. Put differently, the Reagan administration used "*the idea* of secret information" in terms of Central America to construct an environment in which the claims and assertions put forth about the spread of communism in the region could be called into question without having "the underlying hegemonic assumptions or the overarching Cold War ideological framework,"[24] as historian Roger Peace describes them, disrupted.

The cover story "Taking Aim at Nicaragua," published in the March 22, 1982, issue of *Newsweek*, clarifies this point.[25] The article begins with a description of a press briefing orchestrated by the Reagan administration on March 9, 1982. For this "media campaign," the government's so-called premier photo interpreter, John T. Hughes, turned to blown-up aerial reconnaissance photographs, as he had done twenty years earlier during the Cuban missile crisis under the Kennedy administration (see figure I.5). But, this time, Hughes used reconnaissance photographs to demonstrate that Nicaragua, via the Soviet Union and Cuba, was supplying arms to the Salvadoran leftist guerrillas.[26] To further uphold the Nicaragua-Salvador connection upon which their interventionist policies in the region depended, the *Newsweek* editors also reported that the Reagan administration relied on the eyewitness account of Orlando José Tardencilla Espinosa, a Nicaraguan whom Salvadoran troops had captured in 1981, while he was fighting with the guerrillas.

At the same time that the *Newsweek* special report details what transpired during the State Department's press briefing, it instilled in readers doubt about the purported truthfulness of many of its claims. This uncertainty is evident in the editors' discussion of the grainy aerial reconnaissance photographs used by Hughes. The authors agree, for instance, that these images "[demonstrate] that the Sandinistas had been far from candid about the size of their military buildup." But the authors also point out, "nothing in the declassified material showed a direct conduit of arms into El Salvador."[27] In short, like the photographs in the white paper, what the images depict and what they are said to mean is incongruent. The *Newsweek* special report also emphasized important discrepancies in the eyewitness account of Tardencilla.[28] The editors elucidate, for instance, that when brought before reporters, Tardencilla, rather than specify how he had been sent to El Salvador by the Sandinistas, "confessed" that he had been "tortured and beaten into collaborating with El Salvador and Washington."[29] By calling attention to this confession, the authors again emphasize how, like the meanings of the reconnaissance photographs, Tardencilla's eyewitness account was far more open-ended and uncertain than the Reagan administration let on.

A political cartoon by Don Wright that accompanies the *Newsweek* special report casts further doubt on the evidence that the Reagan administration supplied to justify their interventionist policies. For this cartoon, Wright eschewed his usual medium of drawing for a photograph to which he appended the following caption: "Evidence just released by Secretary of State Alexander Haig includes this actual unretouched photograph taken by Spy Satellite showing group of Nicaraguans directing guerrilla war in El Salvador." As the nineteenth-century attire and hairstyles of the subjects substantiate, the photographic proof that Wright supplies in his political satire is not an "actual unretouched photograph taken by Spy Satellite" of "Nicaraguans directing guerrilla war in El Salvador." Instead, as baseball aficionados might recognize, Wright appropriated a woodcut reproduction of a photograph of the 1882 New York Mets baseball team initially published in the August 5, 1882, issue of *Harper's Weekly*. Although not all *Newsweek* readers may have been familiar with the specific baseball reference included in Wright's cartoon, the incongruity between what the image depicts and what the caption states would have been immediately clear. Moreover, in including Wright's political satire as part of their special report on what they call Reagan's "Propaganda Blitz," the editors at *Newsweek* again called into doubt the current administration's efforts to use photography to establish a causal link between the leftist insurgents in El Salvador and communist governments worldwide. On another level, the inclusion of Wright's cartoon also highlighted the malleability and contingency of photographic meaning. For a news publication, this seemingly postmodernist approach was especially noteworthy given that, as communication studies scholar Barbie Zelizer more recently has noted, "the fact and actuality of photographic depiction has [*sic*] been so central to supporting the journalistic record."[30] It would seem, then, that the inclusion of Wright's political satire enabled the editors at *Newsweek* to encourage readers to doubt the truthfulness of photography as a medium.

Given the tendency of the Reagan administration to use any means necessary to establish its interventionist agenda in Central America, including outright deceit, the news media's "postmodern" criticality was especially needed. The problem was that, while the *Newsweek* editors used Wright's cartoon to question the transparency and seeming objectivity of photography and thereby unmask the ideological nature of the Reagan administration's foreign policy strategies in the region, they did little to expand the Cold War debate beyond whether or not a communist threat in fact existed in Central America. Put simply, the press's postmodernist hermeneutics of suspicion did not achieve its desired political objectives. This is because the public doubt

Figure 3.2. Bolívar Arellano, *Bodies of Dutch Journalists Murdered in El Salvador*, 1982. © Bolívar Arellano. Courtesy of the artist.

that Wright's cartoon raised about the validity (or not) of communist aggression affirmed rather than dislodged the ideological framework already put in place by the Reagan administration's propaganda machine. In this way, it became impossible to consider, for instance, how the administration's decision to turn to "premier photo interpreter" John T. Hughes might inextricably link the Reagan's administration's current interventionist policies in Central America to a much larger and more complex history of US–Latin American relations. In the United States, these relations extended back to the New Left's support of international solidarity with the Cuban Revolution.[31] It was against this polarizing logic of the global Cold War that Group Material sought to use their 1982 exhibition *¡LUCHAR!* to envision an alternative visual solidarity between the Americas that would begin to address the limitations of an "oppositional" postmodernism and its methodology of a hermeneutics of suspicion to unmask ideology.

## ART AND POLITICS

On view at El Taller Latino Americano in New York City from June 19 to July 9, 1982, *¡LUCHAR!* included a constellation of objects: FMLN demonstration banners; posters by the Cuban political movement Organization of Solidarity of the People of Asia, Africa and Latin America (OSPAAAL); paintings by Nicaraguan schoolchildren; works from such US artists as Mike Glier, Anne Pitrone, and Martha Rosler; and material by Latin American artists such as Daniel Flores, Catalina Para, and Jesús Romeo Galdámez, among others.[32] Through juxtapositions of cultural practices—art and politics—as well as regions—North and South—in *¡LUCHAR!*, Group Material attempted to foster, as Doug Ashford explains, "a sense of shared destiny essential to aesthetic experience and political emancipation."[33] The aim of Group Material, in other words, was to forge transnational solidarities through the visual.

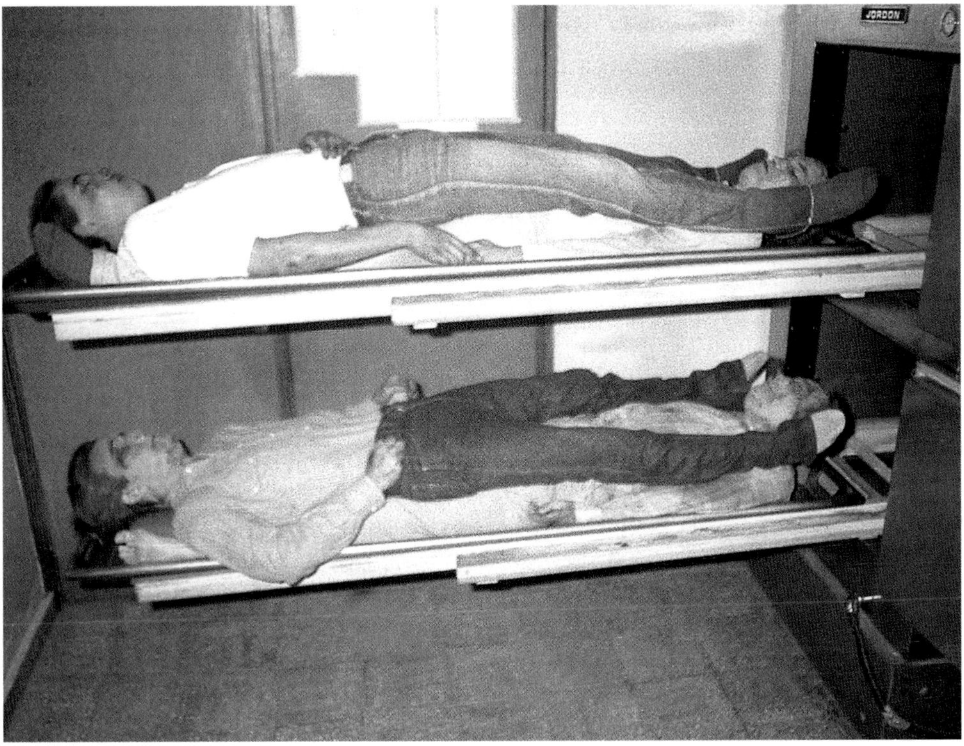

To build a framework for understanding how transnational activism might work in visual terms, next to the exhibition's title on the entry wall, Group Material prominently displayed the pair of photographs by Arellano discussed at the beginning of this chapter. Arellano took these images while working for the Associated Press in Central America in the early 1980s. The top photograph depicts the corpses of four Dutch journalists who had been murdered in El Salvador only three months prior to the exhibition's opening (figure 3.2). In the image, the journalists are stacked by twos, head to toe, on morgue refrigerator drawers in the capital city of San Salvador, some 30 miles south of where they had been killed. Within *¡LUCHAR!*, this photograph seems to function primarily as objective, even factual information. It provides historical evidence of state-sponsored atrocities in El Salvador that the Reagan administration continued to deny in their effort to link the oppositional movement in El Salvador with the Soviet Union. According to a report by the Salvadoran government, which at the time the Reagan administration found no evidence to "contradict,"[34] the journalists were accidentally killed in cross fire between the Salvadoran guerrillas and a group of government

**Figure 3.3.** Bolívar Arellano, ***Hands of Dutch Journalists Murdered in El Salvador***, 1982. © Bolívar Arellano. Courtesy of the artist.

soldiers on a routine patrol. The Dutch government, however, vehemently denied this official account, insisting instead that government soldiers, who had trailed the journalists to an interview with Salvadoran guerrilla leaders, deliberately killed them.[35] In addition to spurring solidarity protests across Europe against US interventionist policies in Central America, the controversy over these murders also caused several members of Congress to publicly question whether the United States should continue providing foreign aid to El Salvador's government if they continued to commit such human rights violations.

While Arellano's photograph clearly references these contemporary Cold War debates over the humanitarian crisis in Central America, Group Material did not use this image to prove that the death of these journalists was real or even to cast doubt on the truthfulness of the Reagan administration's position regarding these murders. Given the coercive tactics of the Reagan administration's propaganda machine, in which even doubt could be used to uphold their interventionist policies, Group Material needed a different visual strategy, one that did not fall back on either the fear produced by the truth claims of a documentary practice or the doubt of the deconstructivist tendencies of postmodernism. To overcome this art/politics binary, Group Material turned to a second photograph by Arellano. Mounted directly below his first, this image—a close-up of the top two deceased journalists' right hands, poignantly clasped together—did more than visualize the human dimension of the journalists' deaths, which was often marginalized or ignored. They also offered the possibility of a "third meaning" (figure 3.3).

In his 1970 essay, "The Third Meaning," Roland Barthes distinguishes between an image's "obvious" and "obtuse" meanings. According to Barthes, an "obvious" meaning is that "'which presents itself quite naturally to the mind,'" while an "obtuse" or "third" meaning is that which exceeds signification and is "at once persistent and fleeting, smooth and evasive."[36] For Barthes, in other words, an image's third meaning is that which disrupts or alters the image's obvious or cultural meaning. Barthes would go on to expand these

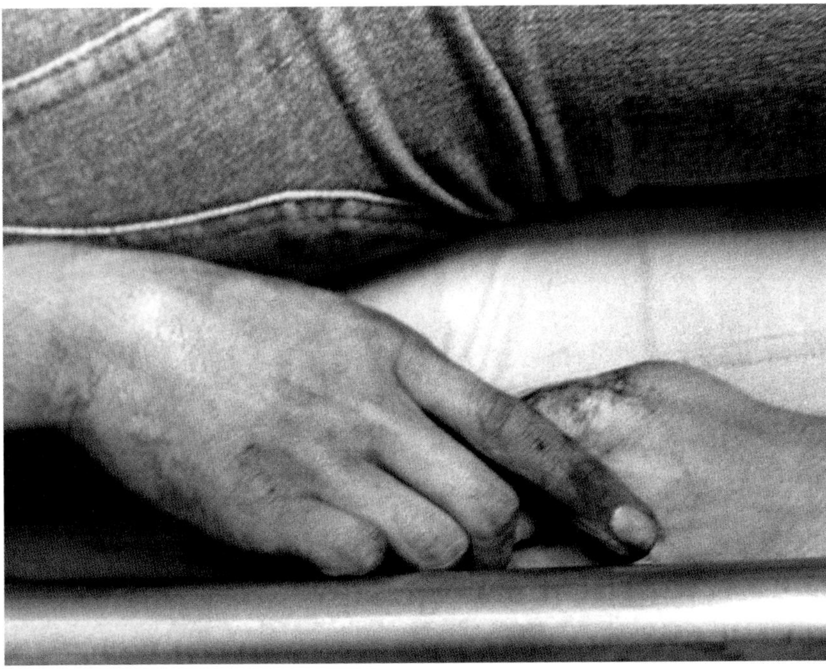

notions in *Camera Lucida* (originally published in French in 1979 and translated into English in 1981), in which an image's obvious and obtuse meanings become the basis for his terms *studium* and *punctum*. While these terms have been well rehearsed within the discourse of photography and visual studies, more generally, what remains under-discussed is their formulation in relation to photographs from Central America and, more specifically, photographs that photojournalist Koen Wessing took in Nicaragua.[37] It is the implications of these Central American photographs that is also central to my concept of visual solidarity.

In formulating his notions of studium and punctum in *Camera Lucida*, Barthes turns to a portrait by James Van Der Zee of an African American family. When Barthes first discusses this photograph, he evokes his concept of punctum in terms of the strapped pumps worn by one of the women in the image. A few pages later, however, he changes his mind and states that "the real punctum was the necklace she was wearing; for (no doubt) it was this same necklace (a slender ribbon of braided gold) which I had seen worn by someone in my own family."[38] This shift in Barthes's conceptualization of punctum is important because, as Margaret Olin notes, Barthes's description does not align with what is actually depicted in Van Der Zee's photograph.

Barthes misrecognizes the pearl necklace that the woman wears for a gold one.[39] Likewise, Barthes also makes a similar slip in his reading of Wessing's photograph from Nicaragua (see figure I.2). Although Barthes claims that the image was taken in 1979, it was actually shot in 1978 as part of a series that Wessing made "about the city of Estelí in Nicaragua, which had been bombed by President Somoza's army in an attempt to put a stop to the Sandinista offensive."[40] Though slight, this slip is significant because it foregrounds the extent to which the affective potential of this photograph, or its punctum, is predicated in terms of misrecognition or contingency. This misrecognition or contingency is also central to my concept of visual solidarity, a point to which I return shortly.

Besides this misrecognition, Barthes also discusses Wessing's Nicaragua photograph in terms of time. In *Camera Lucida*, Barthes writes about his first encounter with one of Wessing's photographs from Nicaragua in an illustrated magazine. What gives Barthes "pause" about this image, and even causes him to seek out additional photographs by Wessing from Nicaragua, is "the co-presence of two discontinuous elements, heterogeneous in that they did not belong to the same world (no need to proceed to the point of contrast): the nuns and the soldiers." It is from this duality, or the sense that certain of Wessing's photographs at once document the revolution in Nicaragua but also point to something beyond it, that Barthes goes on to theorize his ideas about studium and punctum. While Barthes ultimately uses these terms to reflect upon the relationship between photography and death, it is telling, maybe even fortuitous, that Barthes initially formulates his ideas about the role of contingency in photography in terms of images from the Nicaraguan revolution taken by, as Barthes points out, "the Dutchman Koen Wessing."[41] Wessing's nationality is important here because, even though his photographs from Nicaragua—as well as images that he took of the 1973 military coup in Chile—do not document transnational solidarity between Europeans and Latin Americans, they nonetheless imagine the possibility of transnational collaboration and support through their making and subsequent viewing, including by the Frenchman Roland Barthes in a news magazine in Europe, and then through their later reproduction in *Camera Lucida*. In short, Wessing's photographs are not only about, as Barthes initially proposes, "*that-has-been.*" They are also about "*this will be.*" And, while Barthes understands "*this will be*" primarily in terms of death, or "*he is going to die,*"[42] the transnational terms of their making and viewing also renders Wessing's photographs from Nicaragua about an as yet unrealized transnational solidarity. It is this future potential imagined by Wessing's photographs that connects them to

Arellano's images in *¡LUCHAR!* as well as to my conceptualization of visual solidarity.

Whereas in Arellano's first photograph, the stacked, laid out bodies encourage a reading of the image in terms of studium, or its cultural meaning, the second image features a close-up of the hands of the two deceased journalists. The latter image accordingly not only proffers a greater emotional response, or punctum, but also asks for a different kind of reading of the photographic signifier. By unsettling the explicit referentiality of the atrocities represented in the first photograph, the punctum, or second image, transforms the studium reading of Arellano's first photograph into "something more than blood, something more than inert matter, something," as Cuban writer Edmundo Desnoes would later note about Susan Meiselas's photographs of the dead in Central America, "that transcends horror and calls for solidarity and a future."[43] In other words, within *¡LUCHAR!*, this second close-up image of the slain journalists' interlocked hands dislodges the referentiality of the first photograph and opens it up to the prospect of transnational solidarity. Together, Arellano's photographs not only documented contemporary historical atrocities. More importantly, they visually activated the possibility of a larger, global community in solidarity against US-backed repression in Central America.

This reading of *¡LUCHAR!* is echoed by critic and activist Lucy Lippard, who, in her speech at the exhibition's opening, passionately described *¡LUCHAR!* as an "art for the future." But did the exhibition, in fact, result in broader hemispheric exchanges and encounters? Did it begin to break down the East-West binary that dominated so much of the Reagan administration's and the mainstream media's discussions of the communist-inspired conflicts in Central America? In a contemporary *Village Voice* article, Lippard mentions the "apprehensive phone calls" that Ashford received just prior to the opening of *¡LUCHAR!*, in which so-called art world artists fretted that their works "would be seen as naïve and politically incorrect," while those working "in left organizations worried that their contributions would be seen as 'too dogmatic' and not artful enough."[44] Such circumstantial evidence suggests that ideological debates over art and politics, which tended to pit these practices as diametrically opposed to one another, remained a major deterrent. The antagonistic reactions of visitors and staff members associated with the Central American solidarity organizations housed at El Taller, where *¡LUCHAR!* was installed, as well as Group Material member Tim Rollins's own ambivalence about the exhibition, further substantiate the entrenched nature of the art/politics binary at this time.[45]

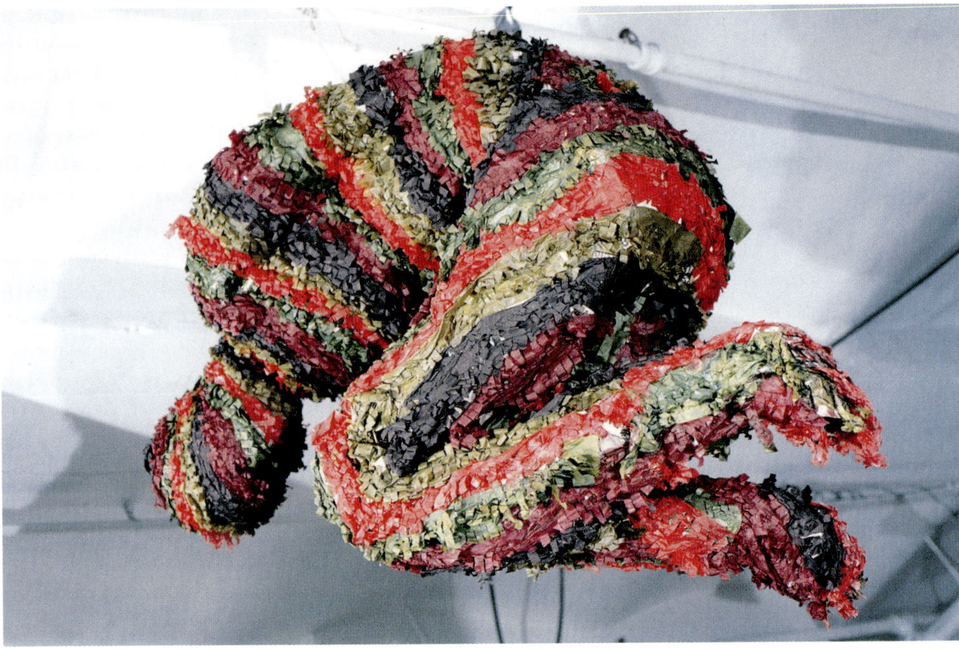

What most troubled the exhibition's Latin American public was Group Material's prominent display of US artist Anne Pitrone's colorful life-size papier-mâché piñata entitled *What's in the Campesino? Homage to the Dismembered* (figure 3.4). For many Latin American visitors and staff members, who had little to no familiarity with Euro-American contemporary art making practices, Pitrone's suspended piñata, a human figure bent over as if gagged and bound, disturbingly recalled actual torture experiences that they or others whom they knew had personally experienced.[46] For them, Pitrone's ironic artistic engagement with issues around human rights abuses in Central America was simply not comparable to a Sandinista banner or paintings of the revolution by Nicaraguan school children—produced in a seemingly more accessible visual language—also on view in the exhibition (figure 3.5). In short, their expectations of what a revolutionary art should look like did not align to what Pitrone, a US artist, envisioned, supposedly in solidarity with them.

This misrecognition speaks to the difficulties of constructing transnational solidarity within the Americas in visual terms. Though Pitrone and, by extension, many of the other US artists in *¡LUCHAR!* sought to make art in visual solidarity with artists from Central America, they struggled with

**Figure 3.4.** (*opposite*) Anne Pitrone, ***What's in the Campesino? Homage to the Dismembered.*** Installation view, ***¡LUCHAR! An Exhibition for the People of Central America***, El Taller Latino Americano, New York, 1982. Courtesy Group Material.

**Figure 3.5.** (*below*) Work by Nicaraguan schoolchildren. Installation view, ***¡LUCHAR! An Exhibition for the People of Central America***, El Taller Latino Americano, New York, 1982. Courtesy Group Material and Fales Library and Special Collections, New York University Libraries.

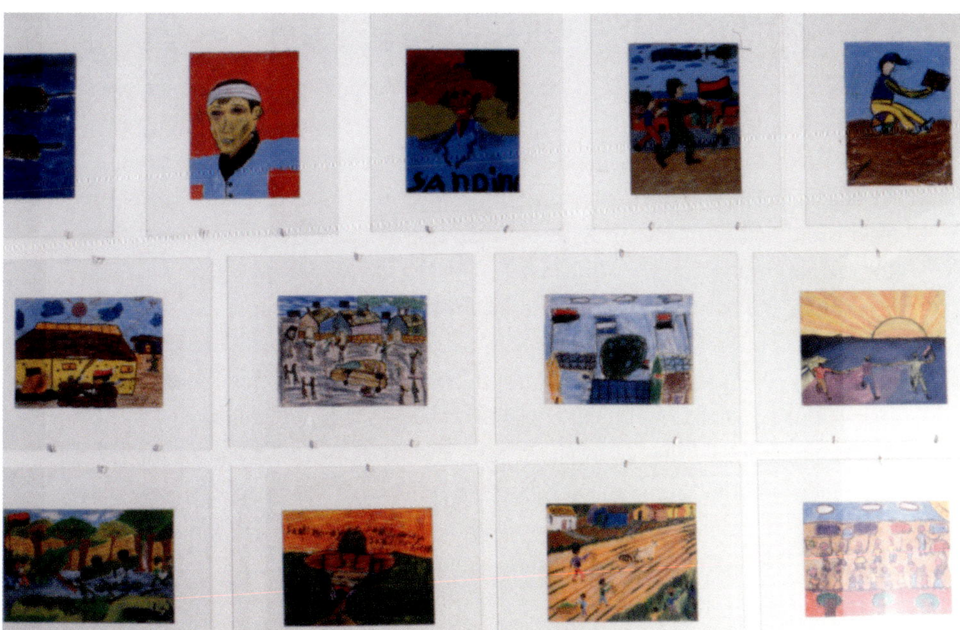

the commonly held belief that explicitly political art was "aesthetically uninteresting" and should rather be infused with "irony, subtlety, wit, and calculated ambiguity." Yet, in so doing, as Lucy Lippard explains in her essay "Too Political? Forget It," these artists "often labored under the illusion that [they] could make 'the people's' art for them."[47] Conversely, the responses of the Latin American visitors to *¡LUCHAR!* were also the product of narrowly conceived ideas about what revolutionary art should look like. They exemplified "the trap," as Nicaraguan Comandante Bayardo Arce noted, "in order to make revolutionary painting, we must paint *compañeros* in green with rifles in hand, or barefoot children in the *barrios*." This assumption was equally problematic, most especially since it failed to consider current revolutionary cultural expressions being developed in Central America, particularly in Nicaragua, where, as director of the Sandinista Association of Cultural Workers (ASTC) Rosario Murillo explains, "When we talk about revolutionary art we are not talking about pamphlets—the clenched fist or the raised gun. We are talking about art of quality, which expresses insights into the reality of life."[48]

It was precisely this kind of "art of quality" that Group Material's Tim Rollins hoped to include in *¡LUCHAR!*. In a quasi-fictional essay written for *Real Life* magazine, Rollins describes how, while preparing for *¡LUCHAR!*, he and Ashford eagerly awaited the arrival of a crate in the mail, containing actual artifacts from the civil wars in Nicaragua and El Salvador. Their excitement about the contents of this box, however, was quickly "crushed" when upon its opening, as Rollins reflects, they found "nothing but little images of the usual self-consciously crude renderings of erect muscular arms holding rifles, drawings of revolutionary heroes by schoolchildren, some poorly designed flyers and pamphlets." At the same time that Rollins and Ashford felt "disappointed" with what they found within the box of revolutionary artifacts, Rollins maintains that they likewise felt "guilty for not 'liking' what was sent." After all, as Rollins continues, "These are objects from a *real* revolution. People have been shot for producing this art that falls so short of our aesthetic standards." Still, these feelings of guilt did not stop him from lamenting, "We don't know what to do with the things."[49] Though these reflections by Rollins may not be entirely historically accurate, alongside the reactions of the Latin American visitors and staff members, they nevertheless attend to the difficulty of fostering a transnational as well as transcultural dialogue regarding aesthetic experience, solidarity, and the global Cold War.[50]

The question remained, then, how to navigate these constricting binaries of art and politics. For Rollins, it was a recent issue of *People* magazine that provided him one answer. In his *Real Life* essay, Rollins also wrote that on the same day that he and Ashford received the seemingly disappointing box of revolutionary artifacts in the mail, he later encountered, while flipping through a recent issue of *People* magazine, a photograph of Salvadoran President José Napoleón Duarte painting in his home studio.[51] From the article that accompanied this photograph, Rollins learned that on Sundays, Duarte would shut himself off from "rampaging guerrillas or stiff-necked generals" to paint "a still-life bowl of lilies" or "sun-drenched buildings and idyllic landscapes." According to the article, these paintings allowed Duarte "to relax from the pressures. . . . Instead of thinking of all the problems, I have to think what color to use."[52] Upon reading this personality profile about Duarte on the eve of what would be a "phony and disastrous election" in El Salvador, Rollins supposedly had a revelation about what was missing from *¡LUCHAR!*: "It's *that* painting of lily-pads that we need for our solidarity exhibition, for more than anything we've received from the revolutionary front, it is in that painting of waterlilies [*sic*] that one can best discern the real basis for the misery, genocide and fascism now inflicted on the majority in Central America." In this passage, Rollins suggests that what makes Duarte's painting so important is not its aesthetic form or political content but its "social function." He continues, "The more bogged-down we get in aesthetic evaluation, the more the social function, the uses, the practical, human meanings of the artworks are disregarded. A truly democratic art is going to be the strangest thing the world has ever seen."[53] In short, for Rollins, constructing transnational visual solidarity depended on the social work that aesthetic practices do in the world.

But the problem remained of how to activate in aesthetic terms such "human meanings" without, at the same time, disregarding the very real cultural and humanitarian concerns specific to Central America and US involvement in the region. For Rollins, at least, Duarte's still-life painting of water lilies seemed to provide a model for addressing this problem. The position of still-life painting within El Salvador and Duarte's complicity with this European art making practice is key to understanding Rollins's reasoning. Introduced in El Salvador during the Spanish colonial period, still-life painting was an elitist and paternalistic tradition often used to suppress Indigenous interests, rights, and culture.[54] In turning to this practice as a means to "relax," Duarte was not only ignoring the present humanitarian crisis taking place within El Salvador, more critically, he implicated himself as part of a longer history of oppression and subjugation. This realization of the ways in which aesthetic practices might evoke the past in a manner that connected them to the present, as well as to the future, became the basis for Group Material's subsequent exploration of the visual *and* temporal dimensions of transnational solidarity in their exhibition *Timeline: A Chronicle of U.S. Intervention in Central and Latin America.*

## PAST, PRESENT, AND FUTURE

On view from January 22 to March 18, 1984, as part of the activist campaign Artists Call Against US Intervention in Central America, *Timeline* filled four walls at P.S. 1 Contemporary Art Center in Queens, New York, with a disparate group of objects that ranged from cultural artifacts and documentary materials to contemporary and historical works of art. Among these items was propaganda from the insurrections in Nicaragua and El Salvador, including a Sandinista National Liberation Front (FSLN) banner and a FMLN scarf, in addition to commodities—bananas, coffee grinds, tobacco leaves, cotton, and copper—that directly referenced long-standing US imperialist interests in the region, as well as newspaper clippings and press photographs.[55] Interspersed alongside these cultural artifacts were works of art made by some forty contemporary artists, most from the United States, including Richard Prince and Barbara Kruger, among others, as well as by such historical figures such as Tina Modotti and John Heartfield. In addition, at the center of the room, Group Material installed a large red sculptural navigational buoy that US artists Barbara Westermann, William Allen, and Ann Messner had made for the November 12, 1983, march against US intervention in Central America in Washington, DC.[56]

As in *¡LUCHAR!*, Group Material displayed these objects in a collage-like array on the walls, with relatively little explanatory material. What differed in this exhibition, however, was the relationship of the works on display not just to a potential future, but also to the past. Whereas in *¡LUCHAR!*, Group Material had used contemporary US and Latin American artworks and artifacts as well as transnational collaborations to envision a revolutionary future, in *Timeline*, they used predominantly, though not exclusively, US contemporary artworks to situate the idea of transnational visual solidarity not only in terms of the present moment and a potential future, but also in terms of the historical past. To this end, Group Material hung all of the items in the exhibition either above or below a three-inch red-painted timeline that extended horizontally across all four walls of the room. Spanning the years 1823 to 1984, the dates marked off in black on the timeline correlated approximately to a chronology that had been prepared by members of the Committee in Solidarity with the People of El Salvador (CISPES) and mounted on the installation's entry wall. The chronology listed US interventions in Central and South America as well as the Caribbean.[57] Yet, as artist and critic Thomas Lawson notes in his *Artforum* review of *Timeline*: "Those seeking exact correspondences between dates and display items would have been disappointed for the evidence was put to a different use."[58] Here Lawson refers to the fact that, though many of the works in the exhibition were made in the 1970s and 1980s, their placement along the red-painted timeline did not necessarily synchronize with these time frames.

Arellano's photographs of the murdered Dutch journalists are cases in point. Within *¡LUCHAR!*, Group Material used these photographs, alongside the other US and Latin American art and artifacts, to activate the possibility of transnational visual solidarity against US-backed repression in Central America. Within *Timeline*, however, Group Material shifted the visual terms of this transnational exchange to emphasize its relationship to the past and the ways in which the vexed geographies of the global Cold War were also entangled within overlapping and conflicting temporalities. To this end, Group Material mounted Arellano's photographs, which he had taken in March 1982, just below the date "1984" on the red-painted timeline (figure 3.6). Though placed at the conclusion rather than at the beginning of the exhibition, this positioning likewise emphasized that the meaning of these photographs exceeded their referential function. As in *¡LUCHAR!*, their asynchronous placement within *Timeline* underscored that the meaning of these photographs was not closed and completed but instead continues to inform the present moment of 1984, when viewers would have initially encountered the exhibition at P.S. 1.

At the same time that Group Material linked Arellano's 1982 photographs to the present moment, their spatial placement directly across from another photograph of dead bodies that Arellano also took in 1982 while working for the Associated Press, likewise links them to the historical past. In this image, the mangled corpses of recently killed Salvadoran guerrillas are piled haphazardly onto the flatbed of a military truck. Like the image of the Dutch journalists, this photograph also references recent events in El Salvador, specifically fighting in an impoverished suburb of San Salvador between military forces and rebel insurgents that resulted in these killings as well as in the horrific dragging of three guerrilla rebels through the streets behind a pickup truck. Yet, rather than report on this fighting directly or comment on the scant coverage that it received in the US print media, within *Timeline*, Group

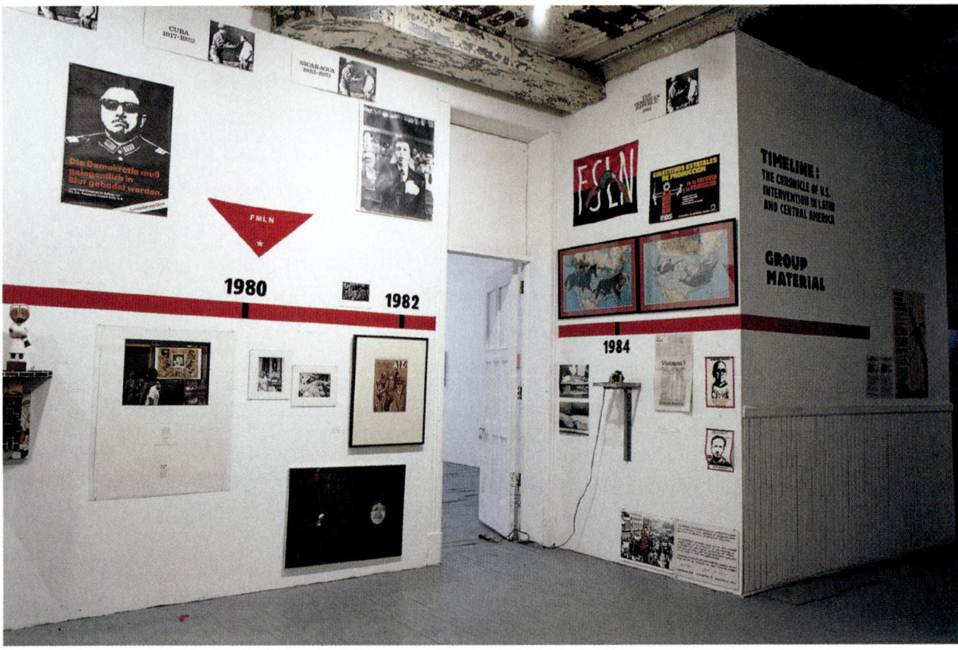


Material placed Arellano's photograph just to the right of "1932," the year of the Salvadoran peasant massacre or "Matanza"—in which around 30,000 civilians (mostly Indigenous people) were brutally killed by the Salvadoran military—that is listed as part of the chronology put together by members of CISPES (figure 3.7).

Group Material's asynchronous placement of Arellano's third image may again appear contradictory. Displaying this photograph from 1982 in reference to a massacre from 1932, which is not even depicted in the image itself, might appear to denigrate both sets of killings. Such an understanding, however, assumes that the value of Arellano's photograph lies in its "factuality" and "actuality." However, as in Arellano's photographs of the murdered Dutch journalists, that is not the case. Though Arellano's photograph does not in fact depict the 1932 massacre, through its asynchronous placement on the red-painted timeline, viewers are encouraged to read the violence that it depicts no longer exclusively with respect to the present humanitarian crisis, but rather in terms of the past and, more specifically, the larger history of state-sponsored inequity and subjugation in El Salvador that was closely intertwined with US interventions in that region.

As the chronology prepared by members of CISPES notes, the year "1932" was not just the date of the 1932 peasant massacre, it was also the year in

**Figure 3.6.** ***(opposite)*** **Installation view, *Timeline: A Chronicle of U.S. Intervention in Central and Latin America*, P.S. 1, New York, 1984, with Arellano's photographs just below the date "1984" on the red-painted timeline. Photograph by Dorothy Zeidman. Courtesy of Group Material.**

**Figure 3.7.** ***(below)*** **Installation view, *Timeline: A Chronicle of U.S. Intervention in Central and Latin America*, P.S. 1, New York, 1984, with Arellano's photograph just to the right of the date "1932" on the red-painted timeline. Photograph by Dorothy Zeidman. Courtesy of Group Material.**

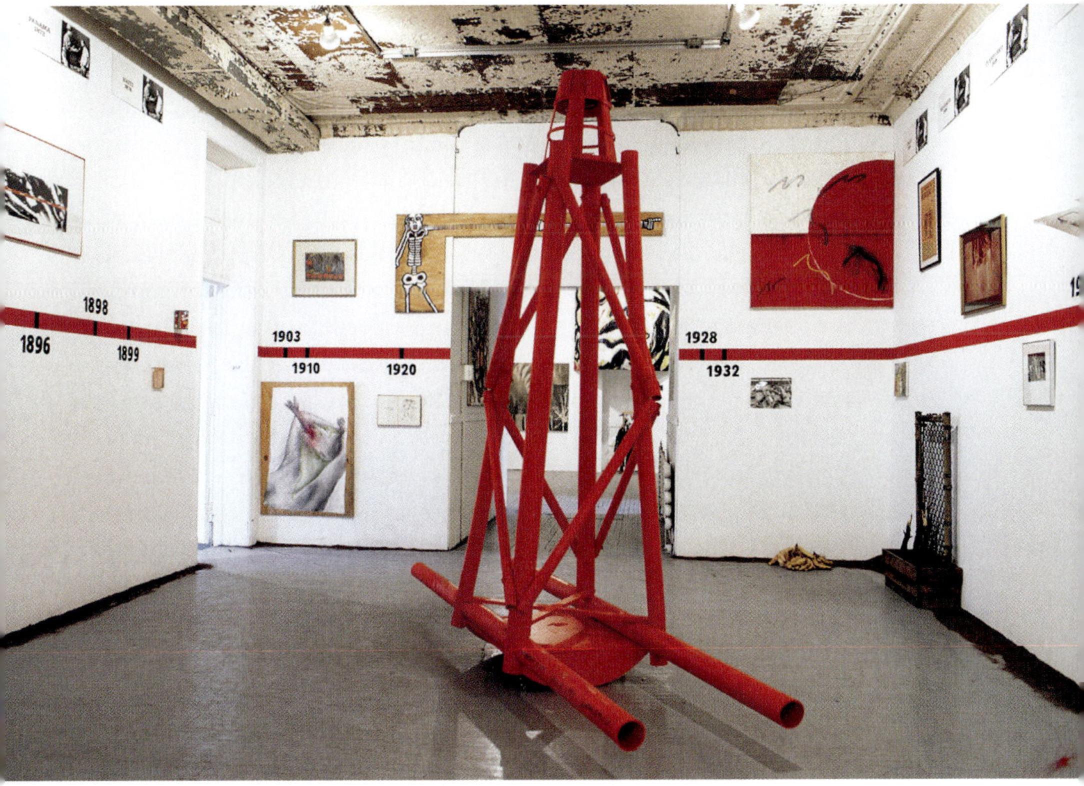

which five US and British/Canadian warships were sent to El Salvador out of fear "that the revolt was being backed by Moscow,"[59] as one commanding officer reported in a confidential telegram. Given the Reagan administration's efforts to justify US intervention in El Salvador through its own Cold War agenda, the link between the present and past via Arellano's photograph and its placement in the exhibition would have been critical to redescribing how US public sentiment related to and concerning the history of US intervention in Central America could be deployed. Rather than ask viewers to doubt the accuracy of Reagan's fear-inducing assertions of Soviet expansionism in the region, the placement of Arellano's photograph within *Timeline* encouraged them to consider the larger history of US interventions in the region and the ways in which communist aggression was repeatedly used as a smokescreen for imperialist objectives. The heap of rotting bananas placed on the floor below Arellano's photograph would have further encouraged this kind of embodied reflection. Mirroring the pile of bodies, the rotting fruit shared not only formal parallels with the decimated corpses but also ideological affinities, since bananas were one of the very commodities upon which US economic interests and, by extension, US-backed repression in the region depended.[60]

The significance of the 1932 peasant massacre in the present moment was also reiterated through the date of the exhibition's opening, January 22, 1984, which was the fifty-second anniversary of the 1932 massacre. Objects on display on the wall directly across from Arellano's 1982 photograph of the slain guerrillas and the heap of rotting bananas also relate to the 1932 massacre. There, just below and to the right of "1984," the year when *Timeline* was on view at P.S. 1, Group Material hung a silkscreen print of Agustin Farabundo Martí, the legendary revolutionary leader who helped to instigate the peasant uprising in 1932 and who was subsequently executed by the Salvadoran military after they massacred up to 30,000 Indigenous insurgents. In honor of his memory, the 1980s Salvadoran revolutionaries called their organization the Farabundo Martí National Liberation Front, or FMLN, which is referenced through a scarf bearing their name that Group Material placed just above "1980," the year of the group's founding. Through these numerous references to the 1932 peasant massacre, Group Material linked the past to the present and thereby highlighted the ways in which the Reagan administration as well as the mainstream news media attempted to ignore and even suppress this larger history in order to uphold the ideological framework of Cold War–era communist aggression in Central America.[61] At the same time, however, for Group Material, such redescription of the current humanitarian crisis in El Salvador was not an end in itself. Taken together, Arellano's photographs documenting atrocities in the Salvadoran civil war were not just objective historical documents that belonged to the past. Instead, on the walls of *Timeline*, they became dynamic objects, whose mobility and contingency could empower viewers to think differently about the present, the past, and, by extension, the future. One could even call them "conversations," as Ashford would later aptly describe his own art making practice, "that can move groups from history to a future."[62]

More recently, however, *Timeline* has been criticized for its lack of Latin American agency. Curators Shoair Mavlian and Inti Guerrero, who organized *A Chronicle of Interventions* at the Tate Modern in 2014 in response to Group Material's 1984 *Timeline*, contend that the exhibition "may well speak more about American anti-establishment and leftist anti-war generations rather than voice, or properly represent, the true context of Central America." In making this critique, the curators based their appraisal largely on the fact that, though *Timeline* included exiled Latin American artists, "due to the socio-political complexities and limited means of communication of the time," the exhibition failed to include "artistic and intellectual production from the region itself."[63] This assessment is mostly accurate. Beyond Arellano, *Timeline*, in fact, included no exiled Latin American artists whatsoever. It was, rather, *¡LUCHAR!* and Artists Call, more broadly, that integrated these voices. It would seem, then, that Group Material's omission of an autonomous Latin American point of view from *Timeline* not only reflects a Euro-American-centrism but also implicates the exhibition within a larger global Cold War narrative of the United States once again speaking on behalf of the interests and wishes of its neighbors to the south.

The authority of this argument, however, begins to break down if we take into account not just which artists were included in *Timeline* but also who collaborated with Group Material on its making. Even though the exhibition may not have included works by artists in exile from Latin America, it was conceived, as members of Group Material reiterated in a 1988 interview, in collaboration with "the Committee of International Solidarity of the People of El Salvador, El Taller Latino Americano, Casa Nicaragua, and others who brought information from sources radically different from the dominant media." Moreover, as they continued, "Without them and chance meetings with artists and intellectuals who were here in exile from Central America, our work wouldn't have been possible."[64] Still, as the contingencies of *¡LUCHAR!* so poignantly revealed, developing such transnational and transcultural solidarities were not ends in themselves. It was also necessary to situate these affiliations in terms of the complexities of the region's historical past. The potential of transnational visual solidarity, in other words, could not be severed from the hemisphere's broader histories, multiple temporalities, and vexed geographies. This does not mean that Group Material intended *Timeline* to speak for "the region itself." Rather, they used the visual representations in *Timeline*—many of which had seemingly nothing to do with the history of US oppression and military involvement in the region—to activate and reimagine overlapping and multifaceted narratives, time periods, and spaces. Largely forgotten today, these transnational solidarity-raising activities by Group Material attest to the complex, shifting, and even fraught ways in which aesthetic experience and activist practices were inescapably intertwined within and against the intricate histories and temporalities of the global Cold War.

### *Notes*

1 The cultural institutions included Casa Nicaragua, Committee in Solidarity with the People of El Salvador (CISPES), Puerto Rican Solidarity Committee, and Committee in Solidarity with the People of Guatemala (NISGUA), among others. For more information about *¡LUCHAR!*, see Ault, *Show and Tell*, 74–76; and Group Material Archive, MSS 215, box 1, folder 36, Fales Library and Special Collections, New York University Libraries.

2 See Press Release for *¡LUCHAR!*, May 25, 1982, in Group Material Archive, MSS 215, box 1, folder 36.

3 See "*¡LUCHAR!* Exposición conjunta," *El Diario La Prensa*, 1982, in Group Material Archive, MSS 215, box 1, folder 36.

4 Hatzky and Mor, "Latin American Transnational Solidarities," 128–29.

5 Hatzky and Mor, "Latin American Transnational Solidarities," 132.

6 Hatzky and Mor, "Latin American Transnational Solidarities," 129. The authors further contend that a network of international, anti-imperialist activities in Latin America likewise helped to shape what transnational solidarity could mean. These include transborder solidarity campaigns around Cuban independence, the Mexican Revolution, the national liberation struggle led by Augusto C. Sandino in Nicaragua, and the Cuban Revolution, among others.

7 While the transnational dimension of the Central American Peace and Solidarity Movement (CAPSM) has recently received increased attention from scholars, considerations of the visual remain largely absent from these discussions. See, for instance, Perla Jr., "Si Nicaragua Vencío, El Salvador Vencerá," 136–58; Perla Jr., "Heirs of Sandino," 80–100; and Perla Jr. and Coutin, "Legacies and Origins," 7–19. One notable exception is Stuelke, "The Reparative Politics," 767–90.

8 Foster, "Postmodernism," xii, xv.

9 See Owens, "The Discourse of Others"; and Crimp, "Appropriating Appropriation," 27–34.

10 This problem is also one that occurred within the context of the art world. See Solomon-Godeau's discussion of "postmodernism as style" in "Living with Contradictions," 2–23.

11 For a further discussion of Reagan's media campaign as well as opposition to it, see, Perla Jr., "Media Framing and Opposition," 158–203.

12 Chairman Charles H. Percy, quoted in Oberdorfer, "Salvador Is 'the Place to Draw the Line' on Communism," A20.

13 Masco, *The Theater of Operations*, 15.

14 Masco addresses the effects of "secret information" in both the nuclear war project of the Cold War and the counterterror state of today in his chapter "Sensitive but Unclassified: Secrecy and the Counterterror State." See Masco, *The Theater of Operations*, 113–44.

15 US Department of State, *Communist Interference in El Salvador*, 1.

16 US Department of State, *Communist Interference in El Salvador*, 1 and 8.

17 Kwitny, "Tarnished Report?," 33. See also Dinges, "White Paper or Blank Paper," C7; McGehee, "The CIA and the White Paper on El Salvador," 423–25; Kaiser, "White Paper on El Salvador Is Faulty," A1; and Poelchau, *White Paper Whitewash*.

18 Dinges, "Chilling Accusation," F11.

19 Beginning in the late 1970s and continuing through the 1980s, critics such as Martha Rosler, Allan Sekula, Abigail Solomon-Godeau, and others, building largely on the theories of Roland Barthes and Walter Benjamin, offered trenchant critiques of documentary photography's supposed truth value. See, in particular, the essays included in Rosler, *3 Works*; Sekula, *Photography against the Grain*; and Solomon-Godeau, *Photography at the Dock*.

20 See the discussion of the white paper in Grande, *Our Own Backyard*, 86–89.

21 The State Department's photograph of the trailer truck is also reproduced in "The U.S. Gets Tougher," 37–39. Its montaged construction is noted in Maslow and Arana, "Operation El Salvador," 55.

22 Dinges, "Chilling Accusation," F11.

23 Masco, *The Theater of Operations*, 138.

24 Peace, *A Call to Conscience*, 51.

25 In 1984, the cover of this issue of *Newsweek* was on view at the New Museum of Contemporary Art in New York City as part of the exhibition *The Nicaragua Media Project*. There it was used as part of the section titled "Rhetoric of the Image," which paired captioned and uncaptioned photographs and newspaper tear sheets to unmask ideologies related to the Reagan administration's Cold War agenda. For more about this exhibition, see Duganne, "*The Nicaragua Media Project* and the Limits of Postmodernism," 146–68.

26 See Taubman, "U.S. Offers Photos of Bases," A1.

27 "Taking Aim at Nicaragua," 20.

28 This account was also spoofed in a sketch on *Saturday Night Live* in which representatives from the CIA and the militaries of El Salvador and Nicaragua have trouble identifying Orlando José Tardencilla Espinosa, who was played by Tim Kazurinsky. Some of their guesses include Jane Fonda and Ed Asner. See *Saturday Night Live*, March 20, 1982.

29 "Taking Aim at Nicaragua," 20.

30 Zelizer, *About to Die*, 6.

31 See Van Gosse, *Where the Boys Are*.

32 The full list of participating artists can be found in Ault, *Show and Tell*, 258; as well as in Group Material Archive, MSS 215, box 1, folder 36.

33 Ashford, "Aesthetic Insurgency," 116.

34 "U.S. Accepts the Account by Salvador on 4 Newsmen," 6.

35 "Story of Newsmen's Slaying is Reconstructed in Salvador," 22.

36 Barthes, "The Third Meaning," 54.

37 For one notable exception, see Selejan, "Postmodern Warfare in Images," 77–88.

38 Barthes, *Camera Lucida*, 53.

39 See Olin, "Touching Photographs," 99–118.

40 See "Koen Wessing: Nicaragua, 1978," Stedelijk Museum (1988.1.0028), accessed January 11, 2022, https://www.stedelijk.nl/en/collection/43665-koen-wessing-nicaragua?page=1.

41 Barthes, *Camera Lucida*, 23.

42 Barthes, *Camera Lucida*, 96.

43 Desnoes, "The Death System," 40. This essay was notably published in an anthology on rethinking the cultural value of semiotics.

44 Lippard, "Revolting Issues," 75.

45 For an overview of the art/politics debate, see Lippard, "Too Political?," 38–61.

46 See Ault, *Show and Tell*, 74–75.

47 Lippard, "Too Political? Forget It," 56–57.

48 Quoted in Lippard, "Hotter Than July"; reprinted in Lippard, *Get the Message*, 294–98.

49 Rollins, "Particles, 1980–83," 8.

50 Artifacts from the conflicts in Central America also appeared in Group Material's 1982 exhibition *Primer (for Raymond Williams)*, held at Artists Space just prior to and concurrently with *¡LUCHAR!* and were likely sent to Ashford as part of a mail correspondence he had started with Ernesto Cardenal in relation to work he was doing as a public high school teacher in Bedford Stuyvesant on Cardenal's liberation theology and Solentiname community. For more information on *Primer*, see Ault, *Show and Tell*, 70–73 and 258; and Group Material Archive, MSS 215, box 1, folder 35.

51 See Saar, "Of Bullets and Ballots," 24–29.

52 Saar, "Of Bullets and Ballots," 26.

53 Rollins, "Particles," 8.

54 See Magana, *Gods, Spirits and Legends*; Kirking and Sullivan, *Latin American Still Life*; and *Two Visions of El Salvador*.

55 An overview of the activist campaign Artists Call can be found in Ashford, "Aesthetic Insurgency," 100–119. See also the special issue of *Art and Artists* 14, no. 4 (January 1984) devoted to Artists Call; and Duganne and Satinsky, *Art for the Future*.

56 The full list of participating artists can be found in Ault, *Show and Tell*, 258; as well as in Group Material Archive, MSS 215, box 1, folder 41. For critical overviews of the *Timeline* exhibition, see Grace, "Counter-Time"; and Diack, "Hand over Fist."

57 The CISPES chronology was also reproduced in the exhibition's catalog, a copy of which can be found in the Group Material Archive, MSS 215, box 1, folder 41.

58 Lawson, "Group Material, Timeline, P.S. 1," 83. *Timeline*'s asynchronicity, and especially the art historical antecedents that informed it, is also taken up by Claire Grace in her "Counter-Time."

59 Confidential telegram from Commanding Officer of USS *Wickers*, January 25, 1932, quoted in Lindo-Fuentes, Chang, and Lara-Martínez, *Remembering a Massacre in El Salvador*, 65.

60 For an example of how photography was used in Honduras to contest the imperial model of a "banana republic" put forth by the Boston-based United Fruit Company, see Coleman, *A Camera in the Garden of Eden*.

61 For more information on the 1932 massacre, see Lindo-Fuentes, Chang, and Lara-Martínez, *Remembering a Massacre in El Salvador*.

62 Ashford et al., "A Conversation on Social Collaboration," 70.

63 Inti Guerrero and Shoair Mavlian, "A Chronicle of Interventions," text accompanying exhibition at Tate Modern's Project Space, London, May 2–July 13, 2014; and TEOR/eTica art space in San José, Costa Rica, October 9, 2014–February 22, 2015.

64 Group Material, Interview with Critical Ensemble, *Art Papers* (September/October 1988): 25.

ÁNGELES DONOSO MACAYA

# 4

# Interrogating the Cold War's Geo-Politics from Down South

## *CHILE FROM WITHIN* (1990) AND THE CONSTRUCTION OF A SITUATED VISUALITY

**The Western eye has fundamentally been a wandering eye, a travelling lens. These peregrinations have often been violent and insistent on mirrors for a conquering self—but not always. Western feminists also *inherit* some skill in learning to participate in revisualizing worlds turned upside down in earth-transforming challenges to the views of the masters. All is not to be done from scratch. —Donna Haraway**

---

**There's a certain way in which we understood photography historically—the idea that you go out and picture the "other," come to know the "other," and bring back their image. We understand how the subjective first-person narrative works, and the traditional equation of**

**author, subject, and viewer. But how do the medium and the meaning change, when the so-called "other" participates and shapes the end result? And how does that change the reading or the experience for the viewer? —Susan Meiselas**

In September 1989, almost a year after the majority of Chilean people in a national referendum said "No" to more than sixteen years of dictatorship by voting against the military rule of General Augusto Pinochet, and around the same time that East and West Germans began to cross over—and demolish, bit by bit—the Berlin Wall, in what would mark the beginning of the end of the Cold War, the traveling exhibition *Chile from Within* opened at the Mandeville Gallery at University of California, San Diego. It was organized to accompany the release of *Chile from Within*, a book edited by a group of Chilean photographers in collaboration with Magnum photographer Susan Meiselas who had traveled to Santiago, Chile, to cover the referendum that would end the dictatorship.[1] While in Santiago, Meiselas came into contact with local photographers. She spent time with them and had the opportunity to witness the work they had been doing for more than a decade. The idea of editing a book of photographs about life under the dictatorship emerged from their conversations.

The book was published in October 1990.[2] The book showcases seventy-five black-and-white photographs taken between 1970 and 1988, by photographers who lived in Chile during the military dictatorship;[3] it includes texts by Marco Antonio De La Parra and Ariel Dorfman, two renowned Chilean writers; provides a selected chronology of the period; and offers notes about the plates written by the photographers themselves. With the exception of a few images, the book centers on anonymous individuals in public and private spaces, in everyday situations. Commenting on the show, most US reviewers emphasized the variety of situations and themes it portrayed. One critic underscored that the show offered an "account of Chile that is not exactly documentary, but illustrates the heated confrontations between the military and the public over the past two decades."[4] This critic's oscillation between "not exactly documentary" and "documents nonetheless" is telling. While the review takes note of the evidentiary status of the photographs, the statement "not exactly documentary" indicates certain presumptions about what photojournalism (or documentary photography) produced in "areas of conflict" should look like. Indeed, to critics in the United States, the most remarkable aspect was that the photographs had been produced "from within"; in other words, its images had been "taken by insiders—Chileans, not American journalists on assignment."[5]

This chapter seeks to foreground the hemispheric significance of *Chile from Within*. My analysis emphasizes the book's situated perspective and heterogeneous visuality about the military dictatorship period. Particularly important to my argument are Donna Haraway's formulations about "situated knowledges"[6] and Sara Ahmed's phenomenological account of the notion of "orientations."[7] I argue that the situated view constructed by *Chile from Within*—a view from/of the "southernmost" nation—agitates and interrogates traditional narratives about the temporality and geo-politics of the Cold War. As Sarah Bassnett, Andrea Noble, and Thy Phu argue in the introduction to their special issue of *Visual Studies*, "Cold War Visual Alliances": "the workings of power are palpable in what is summarily disregarded and outside the field of vision altogether, through obscuring and even erasing evidence of proxy violence that erupted in sites beyond the framework of this bipolarity, namely the global South."[8] My reading likewise illuminates the geo-politics implicit in studies about photojournalism during the global Cold War.[9]

*Chile from Within*'s distinctive perspective is related to the situated visuality the book formulates about the period of the Chilean military dictatorship and to structures of seeing from areas "foreign" to a US perspective.[10] Yet, what are the characteristics of "seeing from within"? What is and is not privileged in the look "from within"? And does the concept of "within" dismantle binaries, of, say, insider/outsider and, if we follow this logic, Global North and Global South? While the concept "from within," as formulated in the book, does not necessarily undo these binaries, it calls upon us to examine and interrogate these structures of seeing. *Chile from Within* unveils and disseminates other ways of looking (at) and of documenting conflict. In this account, the daily life, the waiting and the wanting, are given as much relevance—and more visual currency—as more "news-like" events, such as massive protests or instances of police repression. "From within" is thus a declaration, an affirmation of another way of looking. It is a way of looking that witnesses, accompanies, attends, waits, affects, and is affected by what it sees. The look from within offers a "more real" account, in the sense that it is an "intimate" view.[11] At the same time, the perspective is not a warrant for authenticity or veracity. Instead, the "look from within" reveals itself in the speed of the take, in the out of focus or the partial blur that obfuscate some images, in the close-ups of faces screaming, crying, and singing. It is heterogeneous, fragmentary, incomplete, and partial. It is also a formulation, an elaboration; a crafted visuality, composed in the selection and sequencing of images.[12]

*Chile from Within* is also noteworthy for what it tells us about the lasting effects of the military dictatorship and, more broadly, the Cold War. The book was published after the end of the Chilean military dictatorship and at the assumed twilight of the Cold War. At the time of publication, the book evoked a present haunted by a traumatic past and—despite the hopeful outcome of the plebiscite—imagined the future as an uncertain time, where the shadows of violence and repression loomed. In 1989, US critics did not fail to notice the haunting aspect of the book: "Many pictures show signs that violence continues. Too many show funerals. [ . . . ] Too many show the wounded, the fights and—most frightening—police carting away the arrested. You wonder, will they ever return?"[13] We now know there are thousands of people who never returned.[14] Because of the critical orientation that the book adopts with regard to temporality—the unresolved aspect of state violence and military repression—the book not only frames and talks about Chile's past but also speaks about and to the present.

Despite the book's telling temporality, despite its collaborative, transnational, and hemispheric foundation,[15] and also despite Meiselas's own sustained effort to keep disseminating, expanding, and recontextualizing the book (an effort evident, for instance, in the 2013 publication of a digital bilingual edition),[16] *Chile from Within*, until this day, remains unstudied.[17] Unlike other documentary projects edited by Meiselas, with the exception of a handful of reviews the project received at the time of its publication, the book has received little critical attention in the United States,[18] a neglect that speaks volumes about the geo-politics of visuality, wherein the culture industries of the Global North exert a determining influence in shaping what gets to be seen and what remains unseen and unrecognized.

## CRITICAL ORIENTATIONS: WAYS OF SEEING—AND NOT SEEING—CHILE

The critical neglect of *Chile from Within* symptomatizes the geo-politics implicit in the historiography of photography. Because of the geopolitical orientation of disciplinary writing, the history of photography has produced and perpetuated certain narratives and ideas, leaving out (because they are "out of sight," or not in one's "line" of inquiry) heterogeneous photographic practices. According to Gearóid Ó Tuathail in *Critical Geopolitics* (1996), a hierarchical way of seeing the world has enabled not only particular global actions—from the British Empire onward—but also the writing of geo-politics itself. For Ó Tuathail, the exclusion of certain geographical areas is the disavowed cornerstone of geopolitical writing.[19] Indeed, Latin America is one such area that has been excluded. Photography critics replicate these geopolitical orientations and their hegemonic positions when they overlook the work of photographers from the Global South. For example, commenting on the development of photojournalism in Latin America in the seventies and eighties, one critic explains: "Much of the memorable reporting was done by outsiders, like Susan Meiselas, who were able to publish their work in Europe and the United States. For those who stayed, *publication was often impossible*, or required brave and creative remedies—as in 1988 when one group of Chilean photographers made themselves into a 'living newspaper,' demonstrating against General Pinochet by carrying their work through the street."[20] While it is undeniable that publishing high-quality photographic books was difficult during the dictatorship years, the publication of photographs was not *impossible*. In fact, I would go as far as saying that under the dictatorship, photojournalism *flourished* in Chile. Meiselas was able to *see* this. As she later reflected, she "felt it was important that the world see Chile through their eyes, rather than those of us who had come from afar."[21]

The South-to-North trajectory that produced *Chile from Within* as well as the multifaceted viewpoints displayed in the book vis-à-vis the period of the military dictatorship in Chile invite us to reconsider the visuality and temporality traditionally associated with the Cold War. Perhaps, more pressingly, it also allows us to question the geo-politics of photography and photojournalism in the second half of the twentieth century. Like various fields of knowledge, occupations, and industries, photojournalism has been, historically, a male-dominated industry, and, to a certain extent, it continues to be so. This photographic activity, moreover, has been predominantly considered and studied in close connection with the foreign policy of the United States and its allies in the Global North. Because of this critical orientation, photojournalism has been commonly framed as a photographic practice that takes place in "other" or "foreign" spaces.[22] However, I contend that the practice of photojournalism is always already a "global" practice that takes place "outside" the boundaries of the nation-state. This geopolitical orientation, to evoke Meiselas's quote in the epigraph, replicates (neo)colonial power dynamics—for instance, the notion that photography and other forms of knowledge are produced in the Global North, relegating the people and the places in/of the Global South to the position of object of study or theme.[23]

Undoubtedly, the Cold War framework is far-reaching, and its dominant representation has been the polarizing opposition between the United States and the USSR.[24] This framework has been used to study a set of violent conflicts, all very different from each other.[25] Despite its shortcomings, the concept carries important weight. With regard to twentieth-century Latin America, the Cold War framework helps to illuminate the perpetuation of colonial power dynamics, as Odd Arne Westad suggests in *The Global Cold War*.[26] Indeed, the Cold War that the United States waged in Latin America, as Stephen Rabe observes, was multifaceted in accordance with varied political and social contexts.[27] Centering the Latin American Cold War thus allows us to interrogate the chronological arc within which the Cold War is traditionally framed as well as appreciate the multifaceted aspect of this conflict.

When it comes to Chile, the priority of the United States was to avoid, at whatever the cost, Salvador Allende's rise to power and the fulfillment of his socialist agenda. Threatened by the prospect that Allende would become president in 1964, the Kennedy administration (through the CIA) devised and financed a ferocious propaganda campaign in 1962 to secure the victory of a different candidate, the Christian Democrat Eduardo Frei Montalva.[28] The intervention was effective: Frei won the 1964 election by a landslide, with 56.1 percent of the votes. While US involvement continued throughout Frei Montalva's term (1964–70), it became critical during the 1970 presidential elections—which Allende won, despite the intervention—and was extreme during Allende's interrupted term as president. The United States deployed different methods to "generate political warfare and economic chaos in Chile"[29] because both President Nixon and his national security advisor Henry Kissinger viewed Allende's election and his presidency as a symbolic affront to US influence not just in the region but also globally.

The US-backed civic-military coup that ousted the government of Allende in 1973 and instituted one of the most infamous dictatorships in the history of Latin America dramatically changed the course Chilean society followed during the second half of the twentieth century. Seventeen years of brutal state persecutions, killings, torture, and political imprisonment, alongside major neoliberal reforms and censorship, radically altered forms of social cohesion, political expression, and the ways subjects and events became (in)visible in public space. This extreme situation pressed political and cultural actors to create different discursive and representational strategies in order not only to counter and resist the visibility practices of the repressive regime, but also to maintain an active cultural arena.[30] Photography played a crucial role in this regard.

September 11, 1973—the day of the coup—also marked the start of the effort to silence the independent press through the suspension of freedom of speech. In 1974, the military instituted the National Directorate of Social Communication (DINACOS), which resorted to various legal and administrative measures to further restrict these rights. Thereafter, and until March 1978, when the State of Emergency was lifted, these freedom of speech rights were curtailed by successive decrees. Yet despite these numerous and varying restrictions, the independent press, which began circulating in 1976, became the voice of opposition forces. The magazines *Solidaridad*, *Análisis*, *Hoy*, *Apsi*, and *Cauce*, and the newspapers *Fortín Mapocho* and *La Época* became effective sources of counter-information and were instrumental in denouncing human rights violations in the public space. Chilean photographers and photojournalists often worked under dangerous circumstances and risked arrest, kidnapping, and even torture for doing their jobs. In 1981, the Independent Photographers Association (AFI) was established so that photographers would have an identification card to protect themselves and their work.[31] Some AFI photographers worked freelance, supplying their images to different media aligned with the opposition; others worked for specific media outlets.[32] Besides working as photojournalists, many AFI photographers also developed their own documentary work and strove to facilitate spaces and venues for the dissemination of this work.

This is the background of *Chile from Within*, a book that grapples with the complexities of life under dictatorship. The timing of the book's publication is significant, for the Latin American chapter of the Cold War did not close in 1989, or even in 1991. In the 1990s, Chile had to reckon with lingering Cold War legacies, that is, with a past that was still very much present. In June 1990, the first mass grave was found in Pisagua. The excavation there was followed by more gruesome discoveries. Subsequently, torture victims and relatives of the disappeared stepped forward to provide testimonies. Meanwhile, Pinochet refused to step down; instead, he continued to dominate political life, first as commander-in-chief of the army (a position he held until 1998), and then as a member of Congress (the 1980 Constitution granted him and his acolytes lifelong seats in the legislature). The aftershocks of Pinochet's dictatorship are a lasting consequence of US involvement in the country. Despite the discoveries of mass graves and despite the detailed and horrific testimonies given by the victims of torture, Pinochet "denounced the Rettig commission as a 'sewer' and boasted that the armed forces took pride in saving the country from terrorism and international communism."[33] How could Chileans and, above all, the victims of the dictatorship come to terms with the nation's traumatic past under these circumstances, when none of those responsible for these crimes of atrocity was held accountable?[34]

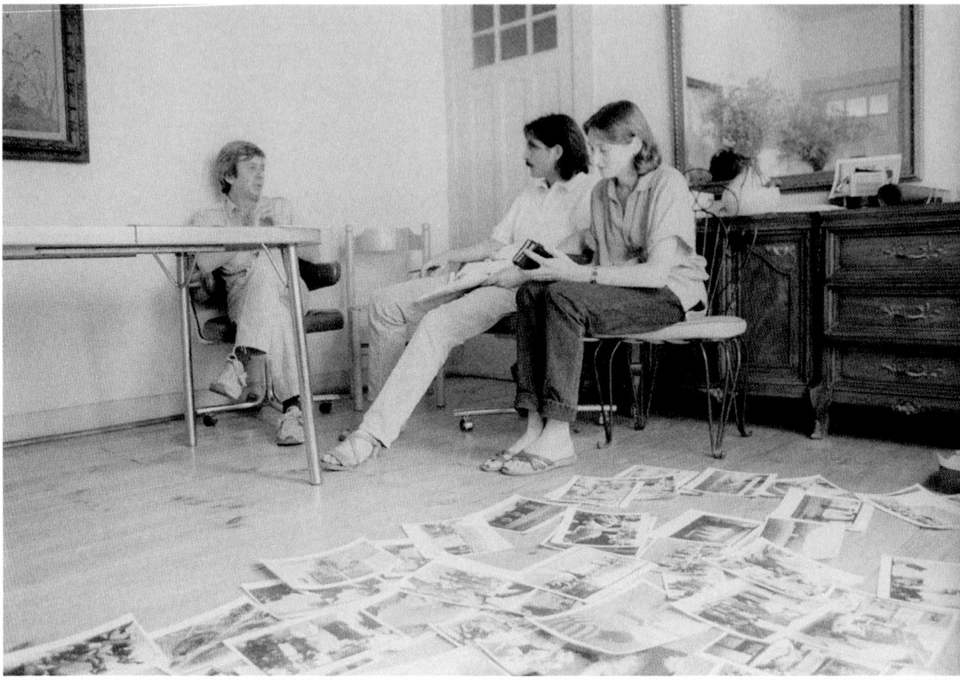

# THE SITUATED VISUALITY OF *CHILE FROM WITHIN*

*Chile from Within* centers diverse groups and communities, including high school students, old and young women, protesters, *pobladores*, policemen, "Yes" and "No" supporters, ecclesiastical authorities, military authorities, human rights workers, Mapuche people, and *campesinos*. The book also situates (and is situated in) different spaces such as churches, land takes, beauty contests, funerals, vigils, private homes, schools, streets, and parks. This situated and heterogeneous visuality is the result of collaborative work and begins with a peculiar methodology: countless photographs scattered over the floor (figure 4.1). "I had never seen so many photos thrown onto the floor. It was new to me, and practical, there was no table that could hold all the photos. We also walked around barefoot."[35] Thus Alejandro Hoppe recounts one of the first meetings with Susan Meiselas, held at Helen Hughes's home, in Santiago, Chile.[36] The practice of scattering, however, did not imply randomness. Rather, it served as a form of preliminary visualization.

Numerous photographers with different styles and bodies of work had taken thousands of photographs over the years. For this to be a truly collab-

**Figure 4.1.** Marcelo Montecino, Álvaro Hoppe, and Susan Meiselas at Helen Hughes's house in Santiago, Chile, 1988. Photograph by Alejandro Hoppe. Courtesy of the artist.

orative project, the selection process had to be collaborative and collective as well. Scattering, then, was an alternative form of organization. Seeing all the photos together, disseminated on the floor, allowed the photographers to have an overall sense of the span of the materials, to gain a better grasp of the different aesthetic and thematic proposals and of the distinct places, subjects, experiences, and situations recorded. It also gave them a better sense of the repetitions and of what was missing. In the course of looking at the scattered photographs, a good deal of reminiscing took place. Studying the photos, the photographers wondered about what people abroad (in the United States) knew about Chile and about the dictatorship, more specifically. They also imagined the different types of stories they could plot: "This can go together, or this can go here. . . . Here is the fear, the fear and Pinochet. This is the anguish, then we see the despair, this whole series is like . . . Ah! Like from within."[37] From the hundreds of prints that lay scattered on the floor in Hughes's room that day, about a hundred passed the first round of selection. The process continued for a few days, as getting to the final count of less than a hundred prints was not easy.

The Chilean photographers believed it was pivotal to include images that directly framed military repression. At the same time, they agreed with Meiselas that the book could not focus exclusively on episodes of violence or protest scenes. The possibilities were, in this respect, multiple. What should be shown of Chile and the dictatorship and how? What episodes or moments should have greater centrality? What sensations, what affects should prevail in the story: fear, waiting, anguish, anger, hope? The photographers collaborated and worked together on the final selection and sequencing of the images. Meiselas actively participated in the conversations, offering suggestions and ideas regarding their questions. On one occasion, for example, she suggested: "At the level of the images, I am seeing something pretty heavy-duty. . . . I think there is an intimate story here. It's impressions of how someone lives

**Figure 4.2.** Military Tribunal, downtown Santiago, 1987. Photograph by Alejandro Hoppe. Courtesy of the artist.

in Chile. Let's say, how a photographer lives in Chile, something that goes beyond the sense of a guy who comes here to hunt down news."[38] The result of this photographic collaboration is an intimate yet heterogeneous narrative.

De La Parra evokes some of the affects that traverse these images in his introduction, in which he suggests a closeness to the events as a key aspect of the visual story:

> Unlike many books of photography that arise out of journalistic interest in a nation torn by conflict (violence is always irresistibly exotic), this volume has been created entirely from within, by witnesses who lived what the images focus on, in some ways like fragments of a self-portrait, avoiding any contact with curiosity, mere information, or aesthetic contemplation of any kind. [ . . . ] These images had to be taken by people who *lived* in Chile, from within, developed within the deafening din of an unending time, through the very same habits photography was trying to break. These images are confessional, suicidal: it hurt to take them.[39]

Here De La Parra seems to posit *Chile from Within* as a more authentic view of the period. Yet his claim does more than emphasize closeness as a guarantor of authenticity; it underscores the intricacies of the look from within. These intricacies are an effect of the book's situatedness, of its coming from "inside." De La Parra continues, "These photos were taken on the run, riding the waves of the suffering of those years, a sort of defense against the atmosphere of war that floated for a time, always so much longer than what one would have wanted."[40] In this statement, De La Parra emphasizes the intimate connection between the images and the experiences lived by the photographers so as to acknowledge the book's irredeemably situated and partial quality. At the same time, he also assumes a contradictory and, at times, even a chagrined stance when he states, "Implicit in these photos are the barricades of burning tires, the books slipped by contraband, the photos we did not take: going to work as if it were nothing, or crying out in a stadium filled with ghosts, visiting a friend held prisoner in an abandoned beach resort, the pho-

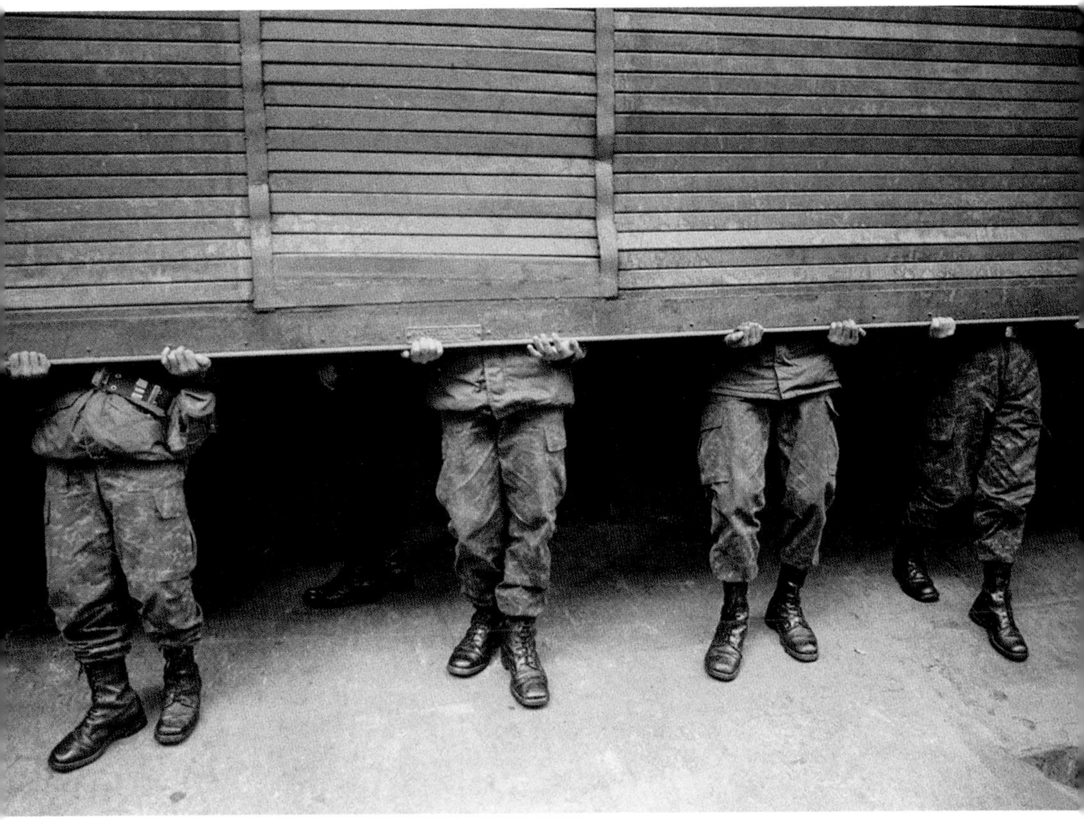

tos we refused to look at, those we found intolerable to remember."[41] In referencing "the photos we did not take," De La Parra speaks to how *Chile from Within* likewise evokes the many absent, impossible to make, images, including those of the disappeared and of the clandestine torture centers.

The jacket photograph, by Alejandro Hoppe, further advances the concept of a situated visuality (figure 4.2). The photograph frames four soldiers lifting a heavy metal roll-up door; only their legs peek out from under the door, their hands firmly gripped to the bottom of it. The frontal light coming from outside is not enough to illuminate what remains hidden inside (or "within"), behind their backs. The images broach, in particular, the problem of a partial vision: what is seen and what is not seen, what must remain invisible or hidden because of censorship, and what cannot be seen because it has already been annihilated or disappeared.

The idea of a situated—and in this case, interrupted—vision is also suggested in the initial sequence of the book. The three photos by Luis Poirot that

**Figure 4.3.** Shortly before the curfew, Santiago, 1981. Photograph by Helen Hughes. Courtesy of the artist.

make up this sequence serve as the anteroom, or the frame for the story, which begins after the acknowledgments section and De La Parra's introduction. The first photograph transports the audience to the time of Salvador Allende's Popular Unity. The image, taken in 1970, centers on Salvador Allende, who stands next to first lady Hortencia Bucci, greeting the crowds from the presidential balcony of the Palacio de La Moneda. But because of the consequence of US involvement in Chile's political life, "it rather seems," as De La Parra notes, "that Allende and his wife are saying goodbye. We will not see them again in the book. The photograph proves painful beyond any ideology."[42]

The impact of US intervention in Chile is further visualized in the photograph that follows. Taken in 1973, in the days after the coup, the image frames the exact site—the presidential balcony—from the same angle. But, unlike the previous photograph, the balcony is empty and in ruins. No victorious greeting here. Everything in this picture indicates destruction and erasure: the windows without glass, the crooked pieces of iron that loom, the traces of bullets pockmarking the walls, and the dark residue of the fire that decimated the Palace after the bombing. Paired with this image is Proclamation No. 7, a brief warning published by the Military Junta on the same day of the coup, which demanded that the population submit to the military. The third photograph, which appears on the following page, also frames the government Palace, but this time, we see a general view of the destroyed building taken at the moment when hundreds of people approached the downtown area to view the destruction of La Moneda, in ruins. While it is not possible to see the facial expressions of the people pictured, one can imagine their reactions: astonished, terrified, worried, incredulous, and, perhaps even, satisfied. The contrast suggested by the imposing view of La Moneda, in ruins, and the hundreds of people observing, who look, in comparison, insignificant, offers a gloss on the threatening warning reproduced on the previous page: "If public order is in any way disrupted by disobedience to its decrees, it will not hesitate to act with the same energy and decision which the citizenry has already had the occasion to observe." As César Barros A. argues, the military wanted people to see La Moneda Palace in ruins, they wanted people to per-

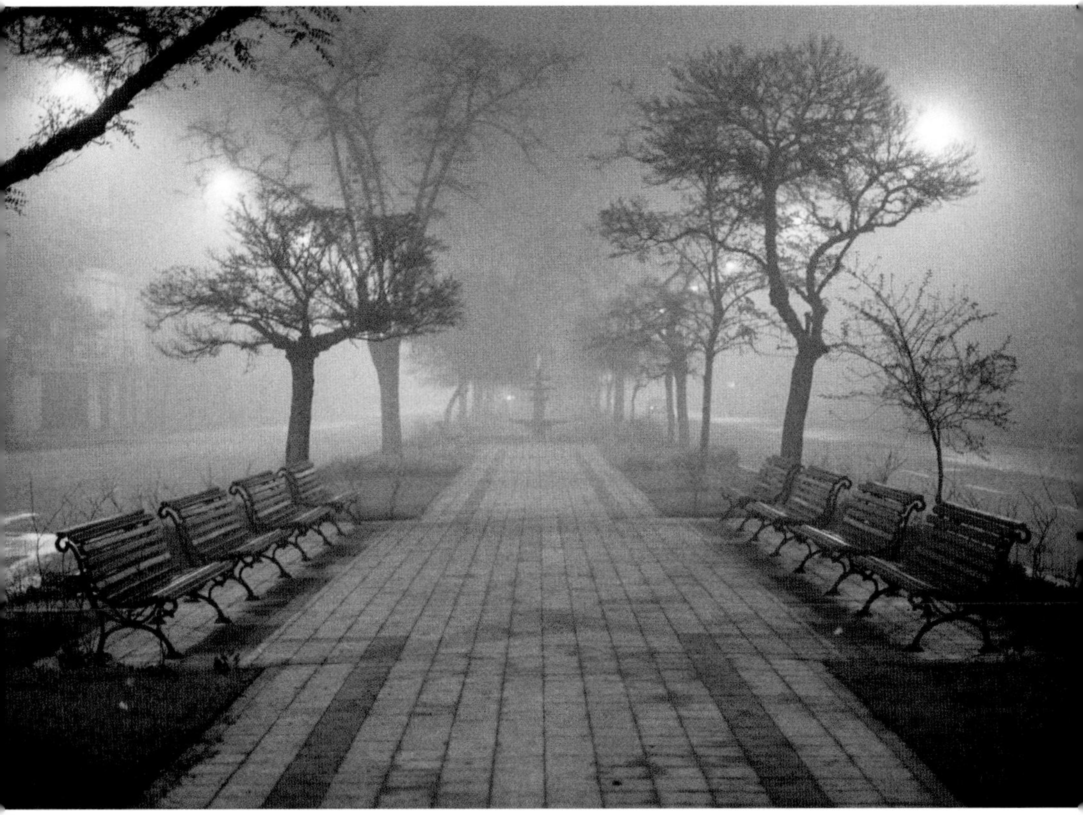

ceive (and fear) the capacity of their destructive power: "One could think of the palace and its surrounding area as a space turned into a sound stage, and of the State terrorists as television producers, conscious that the bombardment's image and sound would profusely circulate, and that it would have a powerful effect on the material and ideological future of the newly constituted dictatorship."[43]

After these introductory images, the narrative begins in earnest with more quotidian spaces: family rooms, empty squares, tango clubs, street corners that do not frame violence or repression but rather indirectly evoke it. The prompt establishment of a curfew forced people to stay in their homes at night. Héctor López's photograph thus frames a daily scene: a television lit in the main room of a house, projecting the image of Pinochet addressing the country in a national broadcast. The images that follow this daily scene evoke the curfew in other ways: a photograph by Helen Hughes (figure 4.3) frames a desolate square, covered with mist "shortly before the curfew," while

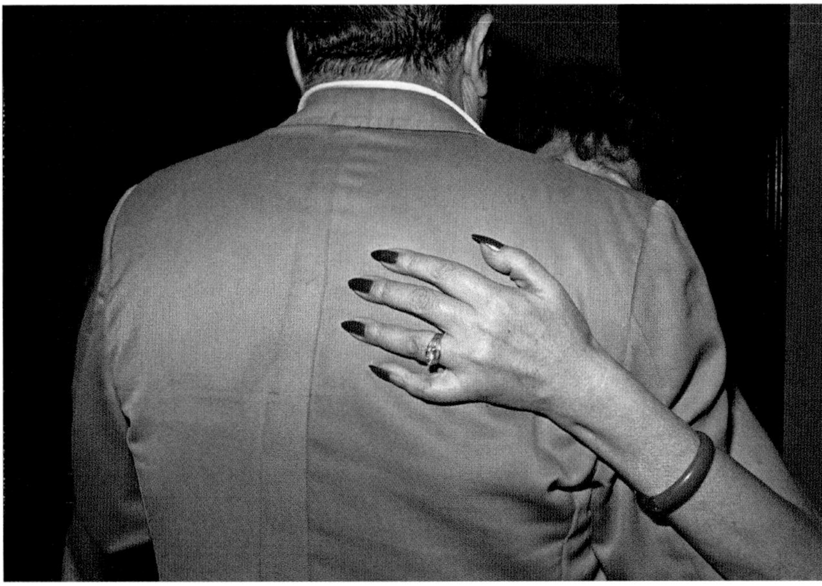

the one by Paz Errázuriz depicts a clandestine tango club, where people spent the night dancing to resist (and survive) the curfew (figure 4.4). The view displayed in these first scenes is also situated, partial, incomplete: Errázuriz's camera, for example, focuses on the hand of a woman who holds the back of her dance partner. The back occupies almost the entire frame. Like the photograph on the book's cover, everything in the background is covered in complete darkness. These initial photographs suggest the frailty of this quietude, in a sense evoking the calm before the storm, which is soon interrupted by an image of a detention (figure 4.5). In this photograph, Hughes shows the precise moment an individual is arrested and forcibly taken into a police car. The almost total black that dominates the frame—the silhouettes of the policemen barely stand out against the darkness of the night—and the partial blur of the shot denote the speed with which the photograph was taken, suggesting that there was not supposed to be a photographer documenting this moment.

The partial blur and the extreme angles of the camera are more frequent in photographs of confrontations between protesters and the police that follow. Some focus on young people and children injured as a result of bullets or blows perpetrated by police officers. As in Hughes's photograph, the blurring of the focus reveals the urgency of the situation, that strain is also seen in the faces of those who carry the wounded bodies. One of these photographs,

**Figure 4.4.** (*opposite*) Bar in Santiago, 1987. Photograph by Paz Errázuriz. Courtesy of the artist.

**Figure 4.5.** (*below*) May 1st Detainee, Santiago, 1979. Photograph by Helen Hughes. Courtesy of the artist.

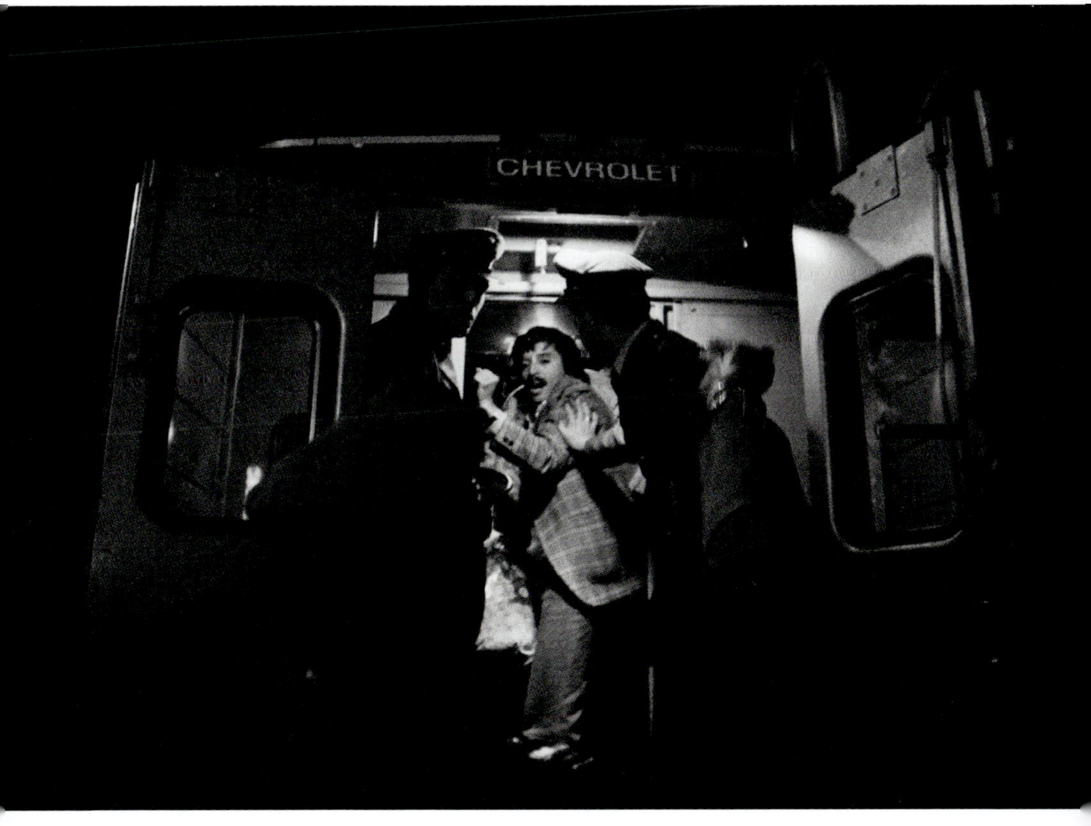

**Figure 4.6.** Outside O'Higgins Park, Santiago, 1985. Photograph by Héctor López. Courtesy of the artist.

taken by Claudio Pérez during a confrontation in La Victoria neighborhood in 1984, focuses on four men who run in a hurry, carrying in their arms the body of a wounded child. The child's face conveys pain. Several people can be seen escorting the men who run, as if tagging along, including another photographer, Pérez's colleague. For the residents of La Victoria, a neighborhood located in a peripheral district of Santiago, the presence of photographers in these situations was critical. The images taken in La Victoria during confrontations with the military or the police and then published in opposition magazines were the only records of the repression perpetrated against the residents.

*Chile from Within* contrasts moments such as these, in which the camera acts quickly, constrained by the agitated rhythm of violence and repression, with other moments in which time—and the eye—seems to pause. Several photographs suggest this change of pace. An image by Juan Domingo Marinello taken in 1973, for example, focuses on an elderly man on a desolate street. The man, with his back to the camera, is in the process of dragging a liquid gas tank placed on an improvised rolling board. His slow gait contrasts with the speed of the car that appears, out of focus, in the upper left of the frame, crossing the street.

While the photos in *Chile from Within* cover the entire period of the dictatorship, it is important to note that they are not organized chronologically. Although the story has a temporal sequence, this temporality marks affects and rhythms—urgency, expectation, fear, sorrow, joy, doubt, rage, and so forth—instead of historical milestones. These affects are suggested by the varied situations, experiences, and episodes that are documented: we see people crying and chanting at funerals and vigils; we see people yelling, fighting, and resisting the military forces at street protests; we see friends smiling and chatting at a wedding celebration; we also see people running on the streets, indicating celebration, jumping and hugging each other after the triumph of the "No." The book's asynchronicity becomes even more pronounced toward the end of the story. The last part includes at least ten photographs that depict different demonstrations prior to the referendum as well as spontaneous

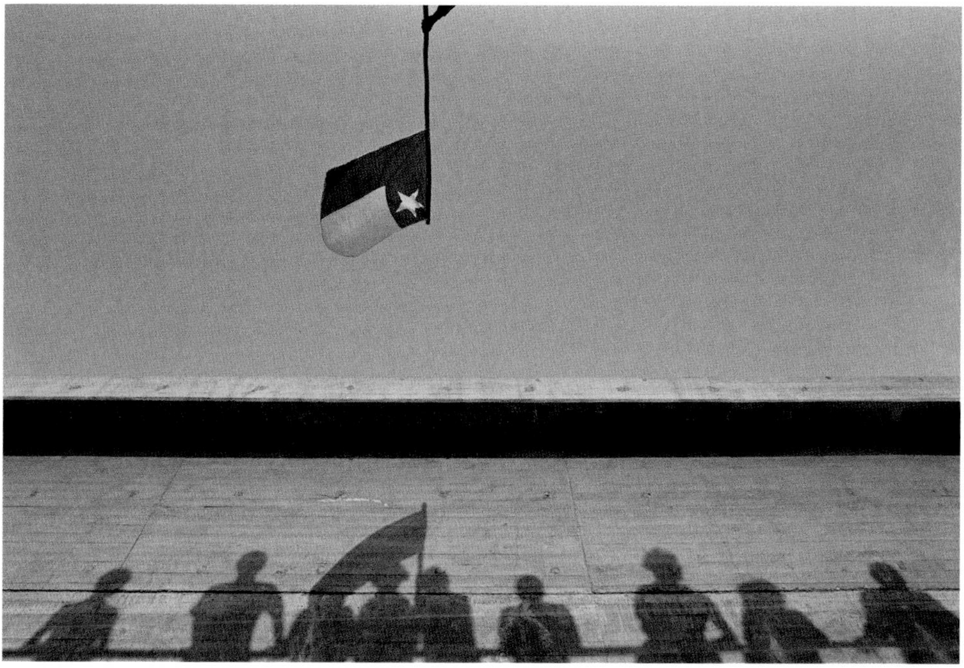

celebrations after the triumph of the "No" vote. All these images, taken by different photographers, were taken in 1988, the year of the plebiscite. However, the last two photographs go backward—they were taken in previous years—and they do not evoke the celebratory tone of the other pictures. The penultimate image in the narrative, taken in 1987, is the same one that appears on the book's cover. Framing a closed and dark space opening up (or closing down), the photograph's placement both at the opening and at the end of the book evokes the idea of a past that is still there, unresolved, half-open, haunting the present and the future.

The last photograph in the book also takes up questions of the past, but this time through the lens of historical reckoning and transitional justice (figure 4.6). Taken by Héctor López outside O'Higgins Park in 1985, the image is split into two halves. The top half centers on the Chilean flag, the main national symbol, but turned upside down, its star pointing downward, while the lower half frames the shadow of a group of people. One member of this group holds the flag visible in the top half. *Chile from Within*, published in the year that marked the end of the military dictatorship in Chile, and at the beginning of an era that allegedly marked the end of the Cold War, does not close, then, with a triumphant vision of the whole process. On the contrary,

López's photograph could have been taken twenty years ago, ten years ago, or even today. Indeed, the apparent timelessness of the photograph hints at the extent to which the "legacies of those brutal decades are with us still," as Gilbert Joseph offers with regard to the lasting effects of the Cold War in Latin America.[44] The image of the flag turned upside down alludes to the ongoing debt, moral and material, of the Chilean state to the families, who were victims of state terrorism during the dictatorship[45] and thereby urges us to reconsider the lasting effects of the Chilean military dictatorship and, by extension, the spatiality and the temporality in which the Cold War has been traditionally framed.

## CONCLUSION

*Chile from Within* asks us, then, not only to subvert the geo-politics implicit in the historiography of Cold War photojournalism but also to reconsider the link between the topography of vision and the geo-politics of visuality. As I have argued, the insiders' view that the book reveals does not elevate it as a more trustworthy one with regard to the events portrayed. Instead, *Chile from Within* declares, from its very title, a situated, unfailingly partial, incomplete, and emotionally charged view. This structure of seeing is not univocal or homogeneous but rather multiple, fragmented, and contradictory. More than a look, it is a constellation of looks—a mode of heterogeneous visuality.

This type of seeing offers a rejoinder to the geo-politics of visuality with its colonial and imperial orientation of North-South and West-East. Its collaborative process of producing a visuality from within also contests the erasure of photographic practices from the Global South. But, if looking "from within" is a form of critical orientation, a way of enacting situatedness, how, then, should we read Meiselas's own involvement and participation in the process of formulating this look "from within"? Surely, Meiselas's photographic practice is groundbreaking in many fronts, and *Chile from Within* is an example of Meiselas's feminist and collaborative approach to the practice of photography. Since very early on, she challenged the gender bias implicit in the practice of photojournalism.[46] When she joined Magnum Photos in 1976, there were very few women photographers in the agency. When she traveled to Nicaragua two years later, in 1978, she became the first woman photographer to document the Sandinista insurrection.[47] Furthermore, throughout her career, Meiselas has devised different ways to interrogate and dismantle the imperial and colonial features that haunt the medium and the practice of photography. Meiselas has said, "Sometimes I think that a photograph is instead of a relationship, and yet a photograph *is* a relationship."[48] If this is so—if a photograph *is* a relationship—then even if there are no photographs by Meiselas inside the book, *Chile from Within* can be seen as *the photograph* that Meiselas took in Chile.

Thus, while the book does not include any photograph taken by Meiselas, her view is certainly present. This is apparent in the sequencing of the photographs as well as in the images' contextualization. Her photographic practice is already proof of this stance: she always stays, looks, and listens. Such an approach, which Ariella Azoulay describes as unlearning the position of the photographer as expert, is an eminently feminist and situated practice, one that reroutes the channels through which knowledge (and images) are circulated (South-North) and thereby broaches a form of a temporality different from that of "global" photojournalism.[49] Part of this unlearning entails not taking photos and instead facilitating other forms of photographic exchange. The shifting of roles, from image producer to facilitator and editor, generates an opening that allows "others"—mostly photographed subjects, and in the case of *Chile from Within*, fellow photographers—to construct and narrate visual stories in their own terms. Chilean ways of looking—denoted by the project's directional marker, "within"—provides a guide for US viewers to see, witness, and grasp the consequences of US intervention in Latin America during the global Cold War. The situated, collective, and heterogeneous visuality of *Chile from Within* frames different situations, individuals, communities, and places; the narrative includes a few happy moments and many heartbreaking ones. Situatedness transpires from the images and lends strength to the narrative. This complex, variegated, demanding, critical, and alert body, this multimembered photography book from within, continues to reveal what remains unaddressed. It insists on a democracy to come.

## *Notes*

Support for this project was provided by a PSC-CUNY Award, jointly funded by The Professional Staff Congress and The City University of New York. In writing about *Chile from Within*, I commemorate the late Andrea Noble, who shed light on the effects of Eurocentric prejudices vis-à-vis the study of photography of and from Latin America. Her research in Mexico and Guatemala not only reoriented the focus toward visual practices deemed peripheral, but also centered photography produced in Latin America within the history of photography. This chapter is dedicated to the memory of Andrea—a remarkable female scholar whose research underscored the ties between photography, affects, gender, and memory.

*Epigraphs*: Donna Haraway, "Situated Knowledges: The Science Question in Feminism and the Privilege of Partial Perspective," in *Simians, Cyborgs and Women: The Reinvention of Nature* (1991), 192; Susan Meiselas, "Photography, Expanded: Conversation with Chris Boot." *Aperture Magazine*, no. 214 (Spring 2014), https://aperture.org/blog/photography-expanded-conversation-chris-boot/.

1 About the Latin American Cold War, see Grandin, *The Last Colonial Massacre*; Joseph and Spenser, *In from the Cold*; Rabe, *The Killing Zone*; Darnton, *Rivalry and Alliance Politics*; Bassnett, Noble, and Phu, eds., "Cold War Visual Alliances."

2 I am extremely grateful to Susan Meiselas, for answering my questions and granting me access to her archive and to Paz Errázuriz, Alvaro Hoppe, Alejandro Hoppe, Helen Hughes, Héctor López, Susan Meiselas, James Nubile, Luis Weinstein, and Óscar Wittke for the information they provided me while researching this chapter.

3 The photographers who participated were Paz Errázuriz, Alejandro Hoppe, Álvaro Hoppe, Helen Hughes, Jorge Ianiszewski, Héctor López, Kena Lorenzini, J. D. Marinello, Christian Montecino, Marcelo Montecino, Óscar Navarro, Claudio Pérez, Luis Poirot, Paulo Slachevsky, Luis Weinstein, and Óscar Wittke. The Visual Studies Workshop of Rochester was in charge of promoting and selling the photographic exhibit of *Chile from Within*. This exhibit also traveled to Toronto, Canada, and Perpignan, France.

4 Susan Freudenheim, "Chilean Photos, Folk Art, Document Rage, Passion," in the (San Diego) *Tribune*, September 22, 1989, C-1. Filed in Meiselas's *Chile from Within* project archive.

5 Judith Reynolds, "City Life: Diving into the Pool of Art," date and source illegible. Filed in Meiselas's *Chile from Within* project archive.

6 Haraway reconsiders vision as a partial sense; it is historically situated, "always constructed and stitched together imperfectly, and *therefore* able to join with another, *to see together* "topographies": "The topography of subjectivity is multidimensional; so, therefore, is *without claiming to be another*" (193). Vision, according to Haraway, is incomplete and imperfect. It is situated at the same level of the bodies—below or on the margins—and therefore open to possible (joint, contiguous, collaborative) visions. Haraway thus counters and even queers the modality of vision that has prevailed since the Cartesian revolution—i.e., vision as a sense first and foremost linked to a (master, human, male) sovereign subject, to an abstract and not situated point of view, and therefore to the rationality of war and to logics of appropriation, domination, exploitation, and extraction of human and nonhuman resources, characteristics of the capitalist mode of production. Har-

away's formulation evokes the geo-politics of visuality and highlights the "Western eye," a modality without geographic location, detached from all topography. See Haraway, "Situated Knowledges," in *Simians, Cyborgs and Women*, 183–201.

7 In Sarah Ahmed's formulation, orientations refer to the lines or directions that bodies follow in a given space or field and to the relationships that bodies thereby establish with objects deemed "available" in such a space or field. Bodies neither choose nor decide which orientations to follow; on the contrary, "'orientations' depend on taking points of view as given." Ahmed, *Queer Phenomenology*, 14.

8 Bassnett, Noble and Phu, "Introduction: Cold War Visual Alliances," 119.

9 The notion of geo-politics delineates the original exclusion of geographical areas—an exclusion that constitutes the foundation of the writing and the discipline of geopolitics. In Gearóid Ó Tuathail's words, "[o]fficial articulations of geopolitics attempt to dissimulate the geo-politics that makes them possible, to repress their conditions of (im)possibility." Ó Tuathail, *Critical Geopolitics*, 67. Kennedy's orientation in *Afterimages*—which emphasizes what he describes as an "American worldview" and gives short shrift to other perspectives, indeed relegating *Chile from Within* to a footnote—is a telling example of the geo-politics implicit in the historiographies of photography.

10 In *Afterimages*, Liam Kennedy focuses on the particular ways in which US global actions have been captured, framed, and mediated by photography, and on the extent to which visualizing techniques have been instrumental in producing the "framings of war." See Kennedy, *Afterimages*, 4. See also Panzer, "Introduction," in *Things as They Are*, 9–33.

11 Discussing possible titles for the book, Meiselas offered: "It's important to grab a hold of Chile and put something in the title that says this is not a tourist's Chile. Something more intimate." See "Fragments from a Conversation: Making of This Book. Spring / Summer, 1989. Exchanges between Susan and Chilean Photographers: Alejandro, Álvaro, Claudio, Héctor, Helen, Marcelo, Óscar, and Paz, edited by Lee E. Douglas," in Meiselas, *Chile from Within* [ebook]. Unfortunately, the eBook, published by MAPP in 2013 to commemorate the 40th anniversary of the coup, is no longer available for purchase. This digital version included material not included in the 1990 printed edition—videos, contact sheets, and transcriptions of the conversations between the photographers who coedited the book, including the quoted passage.

12 The photographs were also exhibited in Chile on a number of occasions in the 2000s, serving each time as a "mirror" that reflected—and instigated audiences to reflect on—the country's recent past. In fact, this book became so relevant "within" the country, that in 2015—in the year of the twenty-fifth anniversary of the English publication—it was translated into Spanish and published in Chile. *Chile desde adentro* reactivated debates about the historical memory of the period of the dictatorship and about political reparations, highlighting the key

role photography played and play still within these processes. The book sold out, and over thirty thousand people visited the accompanying exhibition—a record number for a photographic exhibition in Chile. The photographers gave guided tours and visits. See Macaya, "A Little History of Photographic Displacements."

13 Freudenheim, "Chilean Photos, Folk art, Document Rage, Passion."

14 Since 1990, four commissions have been established by the Chilean State to recognize the victims of the military dictatorship and give them reparation: the 1990 Comisión Nacional de Verdad y Reconciliación (known as "Rettig Commission"); the 1992 Corporación Nacional de Reparación y Reconciliación; the 2010 Comisión Asesora para la Calificación de Detenidos Desaparecidos y Ejecutados Políticos y Víctimas de Prisión Política y Tortura; and the 2003 Comisión Nacional sobre Prisión Política y Tortura (known as Valech Commission). According to the numbers given by the second report of the Valech Commission ("Valech II," published in 2011), the number of victims exceeds 40,000, of whom 3,065 are dead or disappeared. This approximate figure takes into consideration people disappeared, executed, tortured, and recognized political prisoners, but it does not include exiles or the families of the victims. To see the complete reports (Valech I and Valech II), see "Información Comisión Valech," Instituto Nacional de Derechos Humanos, accessed January 4, 2022, https://www.indh.cl/destacados-2/comision-valech/.

15 *Chile from Within* should certainly be read within the series of transnational artistic solidarity endeavors that emerged in various countries during the seventies and eighties. See Mor, *Human Rights and Transnational Solidarity*.

16 The 2013 edition was published in commemoration of the 40 years of the civic-military coup. Meiselas coproduced it with Luis Weinstein, Helen Hughes, and Lee E. Douglas. This expanded version includes contact sheets; color photographs; audio-visual and bibliographic material; and declassified National Security Archives documents.

17 For example, Kennedy evokes the *Chile from Within* project in a footnote, in the following terms: "In 1990, she helped to edit a book of images by Chilean photographers covering conflicts in that country" (196).

18 Critical studies, publications, and retrospective exhibitions of Meiselas's work so far have only briefly referenced *Chile from Within*—if they reference it at all. The essays included in Kristen Lubben's *Susan Meiselas: In History*, focus on projects authored by Meiselas. In the interview that frames the volume, *Chile from Within* is touched upon briefly in the section titled "Beyond Nicaragua and El Salvador." See Lubben, *Susan Meiselas*, 118–21.

19 As Matthew Sparke explains, the hyphenation of geo-politics "serves as a running reminder of the disciplinary exclusions through which geopolitical truths have been fashioned." Matthew Sparke, "Graphing the Geo in Geo-Political," 376.

20 Panzer, "Introduction," 27; emphasis added.

21 Heatwole and Mourelo, "Extending the Frame."

22 See, for instance, Sontag, *Regarding the Pain of Others*; Mirzoeff, *How to See the World*, in particular 97–124.

23 Thy Phu's reading of the revolutionary look present in Vietnamese photography during the war in Vietnam also underscores this issue. Phu's study illuminates (and incites us to interrogate) the geo-politics implicit in photography criticism. A revolutionary look, according to the Western photography criticism produced in the 1970s and 1980s, was impossible: (dis)oriented by the humanitarian lookout deemed characteristic of *all* documentary photography and by the spectacle of violence deemed pervasive in photojournalism, Susan Sontag and others decried photography altogether. Photography could not be used for revolutionary purposes. Phu turns to Vietnamese photographers to explore a revolutionary way of looking—and she finds it. See Phu, "Vietnamese Photography and the Look of Revolution," 286–320.

24 For a reconsideration that links the problem of perspective and the geopolitical imagination see Agnew, *Geopolitics*.

25 See McPherson, "The Paradox of Latin American Cold War Studies," 307–19.

26 See Westad, *The Global Cold War*, 396–97.

27 Rabe, *The Killing Zone*, 194.

28 Much of the material Rabe quotes comes from the "Chile Declassification Project" (1999–2000), which consists of more than twenty-four thousand documents released by the Clinton administration. See also Taffet, *Foreign Aid as Foreign Policy*, 67–93.

29 Rabe, *The Killing Zone*, 133.

30 See Richard, "Margins and Institutions: Art in Chile Since 1973."

31 See Macaya, "Arte, documento y fotografía," 407–24.

32 See Macaya, *The Insubordination of Photography*.

33 Rabe, *The Killing Zone*, 181.

34 About the "Aftermath" of the Latin American Cold War, see Rabe, *The Killing Zone*, 175–96. About the politics of memory in the post-dictatorship period, see Richard, *Utopías*.

35 "Hoja de contacto. Alejandro Hoppe. Summer 1990," in Meiselas, *Chile from Within*.

36 In that first meeting were present Alejandro and Álvaro Hoppe, Paz Errázuriz, Helen Hughes, Marcelo Montecino, and Susan Meiselas. Óscar Wittke and Claudio Pérez, not present on that occasion, also collaborated in the book edition.

37 "Fragments from a conversation."

38 "Fragments from a conversation."

39 Marco Antonio De La Parra, "Fragments of a Self-Portrait," 15.

40 De La Parra, "Fragments of a Self-Portrait," 15.

41 De La Parra, "Fragments of a Self-Portrait," 15.

42 De La Parra, "Fragments of a Self-Portrait," 14.

43 Barros, "Declassifying the Archive," 127.

44 Joseph, Gilbert M., "Latin America's Long Cold War," 403.

45 This reading is similar to Andrea Noble's interpretation of Mexico's official response to the disappearance of the 43 normalistas in Ayotzinapa in 2014, a violent act, which she reads as part of a broader regional history that encompasses the Tlatelolco massacre in 1968 and the contemporary war on drugs, of which the misrecognition of the forty-three normalistas is one macabre chapter. See Andrea Noble, "Introduction: Visual Culture and Violence in Contemporary Mexico," 417–33.

46 The photographers Eve Arnold and Inge Morath joined Magnum in the 1950s. Marilyn Silverstone, Mary Ellen Mark, and Martine Franck joined at about the same time as Meiselas did.

47 At the time, there were only a handful of writers and television producers working in Nicaragua. A few women photographers started to document the conflict in the next few years, including two Nicaraguan photographers, Margarita Montealegre and Claudia Gordillo. See James Estrin, "Susan Meiselas: Breaching Boundaries in Photography."

48 Meiselas, *Susan Meiselas: On the Frontline*, 94.

49 Ariella Azoulay defines such position as "a set of imperial assumptions shared with many other professional positions that under the imperial condition were institutionalized with regard to particular objects innate to certain fields of knowledge, endowing them with a certain authority and right to exercise violence against others." Ariella Azoulay, "Unlearning the Position of the Photographer as Expert," 103.

5

JENNIFER BAJOREK

# Decolonization and Nonalignment

## AFRICAN FUTURES, LOST AND FOUND

What can photographs "of" or associated with the emergence of the postcolonial state in Africa show or tell us that other images or documents cannot? If we construe photographs chronicling the emergence of these states as living images or documents bearing material traces of anticolonial and decolonial imagination, how do we remain faithful to them and to the larger historical and theoretical questions they open up?[1] These questions become all the more vexing in the case of photographs documenting the shifting affinities and processes of realignment facilitated or exemplified by the Cold

War, the Non-Aligned Movement, and related expressions of pan-African solidarity. For such photographs occupy a troubled and troubling position in postcolonial archives, many of which are descended, physically and in their archival protocols, from institutions that were established by Europeans and that played an integral role in cultivating colonial bureaucracy and attendant colonial infrastructures. This trouble is often magnified in the case of formally state-sponsored archives, given the visible or palpable investments of so many of these images in nonstate and nonterritorial forms of sovereignty. Over nearly two decades, scholars working in an array of disciplines in diverse contexts in postcolonial Africa have subjected the archival logics and infrastructures that were imposed through the projects of European colonialism to heightened critical scrutiny.[2] This vital work of decolonizing the archive must, I argue, grapple not only with colonial archival legacies but with visions of African liberation that contest or complicate these legacies. This chapter explores these questions and the allure of these visions of liberation through readings of two distinct sets of photographs connected with decolonization and the emergence of Cold War–era solidarities in west Africa.[3] Each of these archives contests, in its way, the constituted logics of the state form.

Globally, decolonization and the Cold War were contemporary processes of systematic political realignment that entailed seismic economic, technological, and aesthetic shifts in the experience of people living in the colonial world. In the territories of l'Afrique occidentale française (the AOF), the Cold War was one of many drivers of decolonization, as local political parties embraced either communism or socialism—first, in the image of their metropolitan counterparts, the French Socialist Party (under the aegis of the Section française de l'internationale ouvrière [SFIO]) and the French Communist Party (Parti communiste français [PCF]), which had risen to dominance with the founding of the Fourth Republic, in 1946, in France, and later, as the reigning political ideologies of the emergent postcolonial states. At the same time, both African peoples and African political leaders seized on and actively exploited opportunities for strategic maneuvering opened by the pull of US-Soviet polarities in particular spheres of influence, as anticolonial insurgencies and wars for liberation in the Congo, Guinea-Bissau, Angola, Mozambique, South Africa, and elsewhere became proxy wars fought or backed by American, Soviet, and Cuban troops and agents. Perhaps most crucial to emphasize in this context is the importance, after the Bandung conference in 1955, of the Non-Aligned Movement in west Africa.[4] With the coming of independence, many west African states saw nonalignment as a powerful tool for reimagining the postcolonial world order, and they vigorously took up the framework of nonalignment. Ghana, under Kwame Nkrumah, led the charge when, in 1958 (one year after Ghanaian independence), he began to articulate his vision for a nonaligned Ghana. The bulk of AOF territories followed suit after they opted for independence in 1960 (Guinea-Conakry, led by Sékou Touré, was the only territory of the AOF to be an exception to this rule, having chosen independence during the 1958 referendum on the French Community), and, at two successive conferences in 1961 and 1964, the majority of ex-AOF territories formally joined the Non-Aligned Movement.

Despite important local and regional differences, in most postcolonial African contexts, nonalignment was seen as consistent with the new forms of African unity that would displace European rule. By the early 1960s, nonalignment had become a watchword for all those who were imagining new forms of African unity, federation, and solidarity, and nonalignment was ultimately adopted as an official position by every single country in Africa, with Western Sahara and South Sudan being the only two exceptions.[5] The Cold War and decolonization were, in other words, two sides of the same coin across Africa, given not just their coordinated timing but the shaping of key dimensions of the latter in response to the former.

At the same time, there were many contradictions inherent in the word and concept of "decolonization" in west Africa, not all of which can be explained within the Cold War frame. These contradictions were already apparent in the 1950s, and they became particularly pronounced in 1958, the year that gave us Charles de Gaulle's infamous referendum on the "French Community," which inadvertently hastened the coming of independence to the AOF. The September referendum was preceded by de Gaulle's equally infamous address, of July 13, 1958, known as the "Message of Friendship and Hope," in which he announced the dissolution of the existing system of political organization in favor of "A vast and free Community."[6] This community, which would henceforth be known as the "French Community," would be "a great political, economic, and cultural group established in the mode of federation."[7] In the speech, de Gaulle spoke explicitly for the first time of "décolonisation": the name that he would give to France's new, neocolonial policy.[8] These contradictions played out in many scenes, one of which was the struggle for African unity in the name of "federation," understood by many as a viable *alternative* to independence.

The first series of photographs of interest to us, which I saw in several different archives in Senegal (both state-sponsored and community-based), is associated precisely with this African vision of federation. These are photographs connected with the formation and aftermath of the Mali Federation, an ill-fated union of what are today two, independent African states (Mali and Senegal), which existed for a few fleeting months in 1959, immediately prior to independence. The second set of photographs, located in a state-sponsored archive in Benin, depicts a series of military exercises in Western Sahara and related shows of support from nonstate entities, including the member states of the Non-Aligned Movement and the United Nations. Western Sahara is a territory whose sovereignty is to this day disputed. It is also home to the people of Western Sahara or the Sahrawi people, who have been engaged in an armed revolutionary struggle against Morocco since 1975, when Spain lost control of the territory.

Thematically, both archives confront us with the forceful solidarities that were articulated by people living in west Africa and across the Sahel in the 1960s and 1970s, as they fought for alternatives to colonial forms of social and political organization, free market capitalism, and emergent Cold War polarities. On a more theoretical level, both archives offer insight into the nonlinear, layered, and open-ended temporalities that photographs can engender. Through my readings of particular photographs and their visual and historiographic logics, I suggest that these temporalities are part of what allowed people living in west Africa to articulate these solidarities. At the same time, I demonstrate that traces of these solidarities *survive*, that they remain not just visible but also *active* in photographs dating from this period, and that this survival contributes to these images' value as tools for decolonial research. Finally, both of the archives in question exist in institutionally fractured spaces. They linger between public and private, or official and unofficial, archives, or they are located in institutional contexts that are more dynamic than we might at first assume. These fractures, I wish ultimately to suggest, amplify their potential for reactivation and, therefore, their decolonial potential.

## ENVISIONING AFRICAN UNITY

While doing research in Senegal, in 2007 and 2008, I noticed that there were a surprising number of photographs of Modibo Keïta, the first president of the Republic of Mali, housed in public, state-sponsored, and private, community-based collections or collections held by families in both Saint-Louis and Dakar. Given that a particular focus of my research has been on documentary photography, reportage, and photography of political events by African photographers in the 1960s and 1970s in Francophone west Africa, I was, on the one hand, not surprised to find these photographs of Keïta. They belong to the larger genre of what photographers in the region refer to as "political photography."[9] At the same time, there was clearly something special about these photographs—many of which depict Keïta in the company of Léopold Sédar Senghor—and they often elicited a sentimental response from local interlocutors. This response is much less typical of the genre, and it stemmed from the ideas that these photographs convey about African unity and friendship between African nations—ideas that were already powerfully evoked by the Malian leader's presence in Senegal. The archival situation of these photographs is also significant to their contemporary interpretation. The fact that some of them were in state-sponsored or institutional collections (such as that of the Centre de Recherches et de Documentation du Sénégal, or CRDS, in Saint-Louis, Senegal—the former Saint-Louis IFAN)[10] and others were in privately held collections, amassed by independence-era politicians or by independence-era photographers, raises important questions about their "proper" place in the archive of the postcolonial state.

In an image that has come, for me, to be paradigmatic of this larger archive of images (figure 5.1), Keïta walks out in front of an entourage of well-dressed men and women. The majority of the figures visible in the photograph—there are at least a dozen—are walking in concert with Keïta, with his left foot (in babouches, a slipper originating in the Maghreb and ubiquitous in the Sahel), and, by extension, their left feet, forward. The length of his stride is amplified by the flowing line of his boubou, with this line accentuated still further by his choice of a fabric in a vertical stripe pattern. While most of his compatriots appear to be looking straight ahead or toward the ground, Keïta himself looks boldly up and at a point just behind the camera, conveying his confidence and poise as a leader. As if to further underscore this confidence and poise, Keïta's face is dramatically lit, with the right half of his face in shadow and the left half illuminated by the afternoon sun. The vertical line, dividing light from darkness and the Malian president's face into perfect halves, echoes the rectilinear form of the train tracks, which we see running from left to right at a slight diagonal angle, in the bottom third of the frame. The vertical line also bisects at right angles the line of Keïta's arm, held cocked at the elbow as he holds his hands clasped, casually yet seemingly deliberately, in front of his body. Other elements of the composition, particularly the image's framing, which makes masterful use of the rule of thirds, underscore Keïta's dominant placement in the group.

A fuller discussion of the visual and iconographic elements of these images of Keïta would necessarily devote time and attention to Keïta's and Seng-

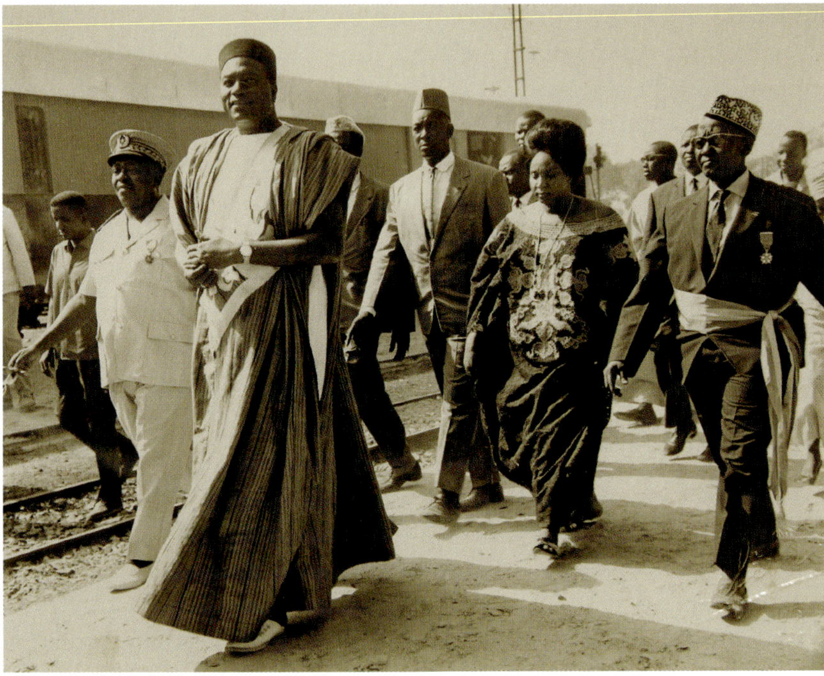

hor's different styles of public and photographic self-presentation, including their different approaches to posing, bodily comportment, and dress. Keïta was tall, particularly in comparison with Senghor, and the Malian president was frequently photographed striding, waving, and flashing a smile (figures 5.2 and 5.3)—a fact that is all the more striking because Senghor seems never to have smiled for the camera. Similarly, in many of the photographs, Keïta appeared at official state functions in "traditional" African dress (see figure 5.1). Senghor, ever the urbane agrégé, was almost invariably photographed wearing European dress (figure 5.4).[11] Keïta's long, flowing boubous would have embodied, then as now, west African ideals of masculinity, beauty, and power. As such, these visual elements can be read as a sartorial expression of a process of Africanization that was also going on in the political arena. Building on but perhaps also extending beyond these elements connoting an ascendant "Africanness," these photographs often evoked an aesthetic response grounded in affective experience. El Hadj Adama Sylla, a photographer, amateur photography collector, and retired museum curator (who had been on staff at the Saint-Louis IFAN, later the CRDS, since 1956), has explained that the Senegalese have always been fond of Keïta, due to the close trade relations shared between the Malians and the Senegalese as well

**Figure 5.1.** (*opposite*) Modibo Keïta in boubou, walking along railroad tracks on a state visit to Senegal. The reopening of the Dakar-Niger Railway remains, today, closely associated with the renewal of diplomatic ties between Mali and Senegal, which had been cut with the dissolution of the Mali Federation. Near Kaolack, Senegal, c. 1966. Photograph by Lefèvre. Collection of Ibrahima Faye and Khady Ndoye. Courtesy Gnilane Ly Faye.

**Figure 5.2.** (*below*) Modibo Keïta (*left*) and Léopold Sédar Senghor (*right*) riding in a motorcade near the port of Kaolack, Senegal, c. 1966. Photographer unknown. Collection of Ibrahima Faye and Khady Ndoye. Courtesy Gnilane Ly Faye.

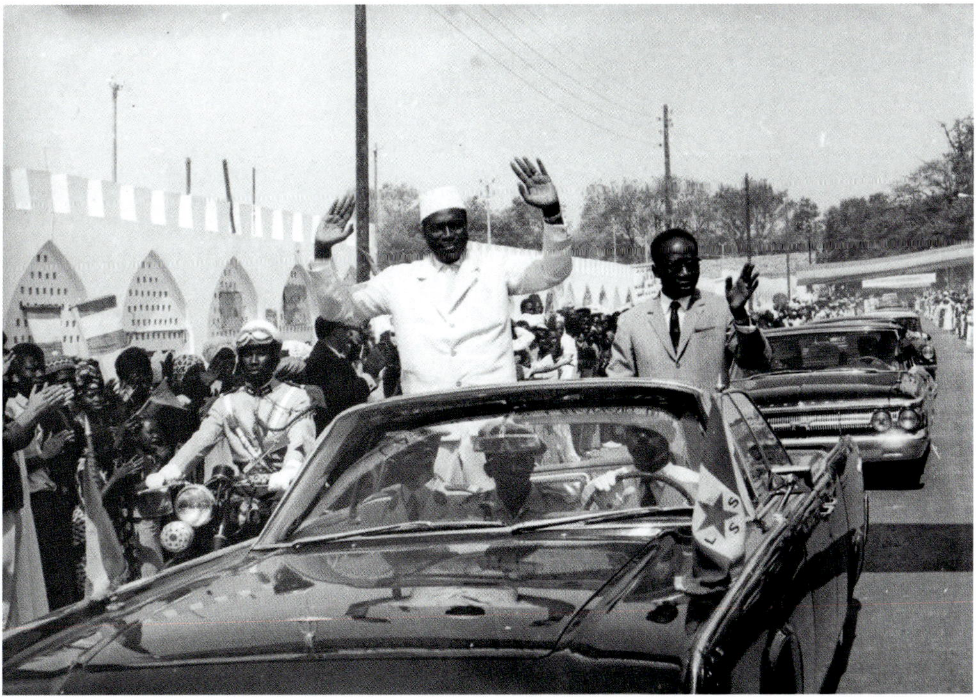

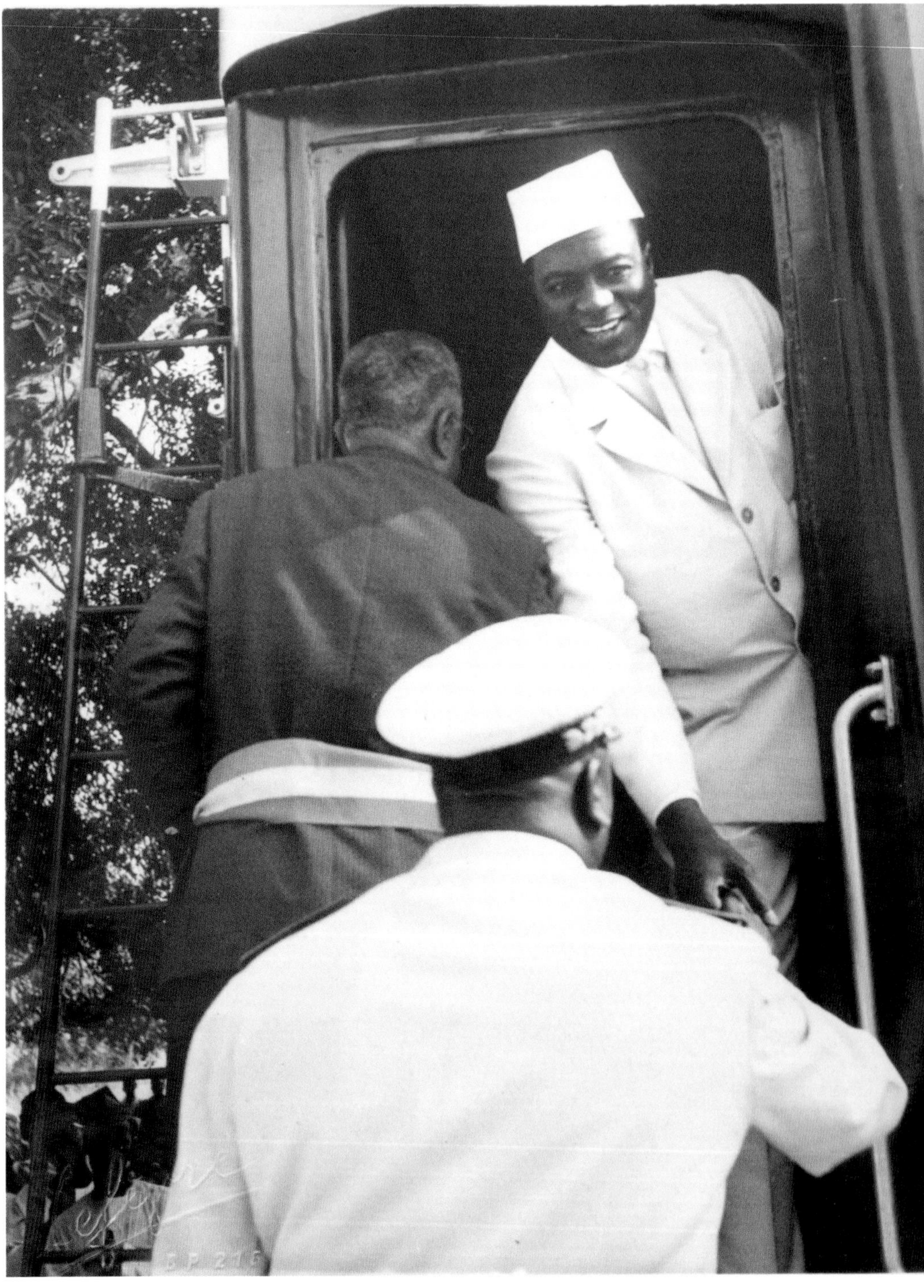

**Figure 5.3.** (*opposite*) Modibo Keïta in white suit, leaning out of a railroad car. Near Kaolack, Senegal, c. 1966. Photograph by Lefèvre. Collection of Ibrahima Faye and Khady Ndoye. Courtesy Gnilane Ly Faye.

**Figure 5.4.** (*below*) Modibo Keïta (*left*) and Léopold Sédar Senghor (*right*) crossing the tracks of the Dakar-Niger Railway. Near Kaolack, Senegal, c. 1966. Photograph by Lefèvre. Collection of Ibrahima Faye and Khady Ndoye. Courtesy Gnilane Ly Faye.

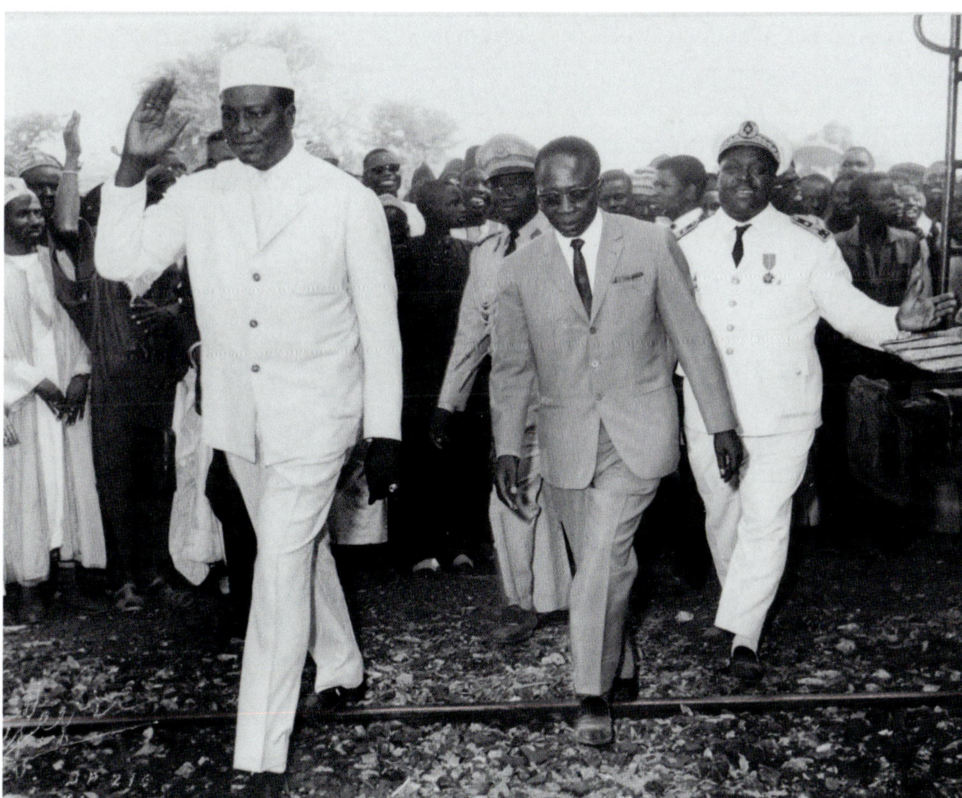

as to close family ties spanning ethnic and language groups and colonial borders.[12] Even in Dakar, where one is much farther from the border with Mali, the responses elicited by photographs of Keïta were characterized by statements of admiration, nostalgia, and ebullient affection.

While these and other aesthetic factors (visual, iconographic, affective) undoubtedly play an important role in contemporary responses to these photographs, my interpretation of these images follows a different path. Rather than focusing on visual or iconographic elements (which can be traced at least in part to Keïta's savvy management of his image, as well as to the skill of the photographer), I propose that these images derive their special interest and power from their connection with an alternative to independence that was envisioned by African activists, intellectuals, and political leaders in the late 1950s: that of a union or federation of African states. This is the alternative that was instantiated in the symbolically potent but practically fleeting creation, by Keïta and Senghor, of the Mali Federation.[13] Against the backdrop of this richer and more complex history—in which African liberation was not primarily bound to the state form and the paths leading to decolonization were still open to debate—seemingly superficial aesthetic differences, visible or legible in a smile or a boubou, take on deeper meanings.

The Mali Federation was created, on April 4, 1959, as a union of what were, at the time of its formation, still two colonial territories: French Soudan (Mali) and Senegal. It was dissolved barely four months after its creation—and approximately two months after the coming of independence to the bulk of AOF territories in 1960. The union's dissolution under threat of violence, in August 1960, marked the beginning of a period of deep estrangement between its two member states. Seen from one angle, the Federation was little more than a federalist experiment that ended badly. In the context of the larger political zeitgeist, however, it was an attempt to realize a more radical political vision that would soon be eclipsed by independence. For the Mali Federation was founded on an underlying political conviction that France's west African territories would emerge victorious from the struggle against colonialism if, and only if, they could work cooperatively and replace the system of colonial "dependency."[14] In other words, in contradistinction to the atomistic arrangement of autonomous states denoted by the term *independence*, proponents of the Mali Federation hoped to establish an interterritorial system of political and economic collaboration within Africa. The Mali Federation was not just a federalist experiment but an experiment in a more radical approach to decolonization, one that stood at an oblique angle to independence per se. Starting with the 1944 Brazzaville conference, federation in west Africa came to be particularly closely associated with the Left, and both Communists and Socialists embraced the term. At the same time, this vision of an African federation was framed in explicit opposition to a competing federation that was being articulated under the banner of the French Republic: a federation of African territories that would remain, in essence, part of France.[15]

There is little consensus as to the causes of the Mali Federation's failure, but it is widely accepted that, with this failure, both leaders were badly burned.[16] Senghor, despite his deep investments in an ideological and cultural pan-Africanism (in the form of Négritude), remained wary of collaboration with other African countries for the duration of his presidency, which ended in 1980.[17] The Federation's dissolution left Keïta so embittered that he refused all diplomatic relations with Senegal until June 22, 1963. Dramatically, at the moment of dissolution in August 1960, Keïta was escorted from Dakar, where the official administrative apparatus of the Federation had been located, to the Senegal-Mali border. Thus it was, once again and no less dramatically, to the border that the two presidents went, finally, to greet each other when they commenced the period of the "thaw," which lasted from 1963 to 1966, and announced the renewal of diplomatic ties. These photographs of Keïta in Senegal (see figures 5.2, 5.3, and 5.4), which seemed so special to me and to local interlocutors, and which elicited such a strong response, almost certainly commemorate an official visit that he made to Senegal in December 1966.[18] The timing of this visit is, in fact, crucial, for in 1966, Keïta came to Senegal in order to mark the formal renewal of diplomatic relations—the end of the "thaw."[19] Hence, the central role played, in this particular series of photographs commemorating Keïta's official visit, by the Dakar-Niger Railway, whose tracks feature centrally in them (see figures 5.1, 5.3, and 5.4). The railway, which linked the two countries economically above all, symbolically represented the renewal of diplomatic relations, and the photographs both illustrate and help us to grasp the significance of this 1966 encounter.

The Dakar-Niger Railway was, for the first half of the twentieth century, the jewel in the crown of France's plans to industrialize its colonial territories in Africa. A large-scale and vital piece of colonial infrastructure consisting of about 1,287 km (or approximately 800 miles) of rail line, the railway linked Dakar, a major port city, with inland Bamako.[20] Although construction of the railway actually began in the nineteenth century, the final section of track did not open until 1924. After the foundering of the Mali Federation, when diplomatic relations between Mali and Senegal were severed, trains did not cross the border between the two countries. So closely identified was the renewal of diplomatic relations between the two countries with the reopening of the railroad for local interlocutors that, in Saint-Louis in 2008, Sylla referred to this renewal simply as the opening of the railroad.

In fact, this was not the first time that, in the run-up to independence, west African political leaders sought to articulate a shared project of political and economic liberation that would not be orchestrated from Paris. The Mali Federation was already a citation, and a strategic *recuperation*, of an earlier vision of interterritorial collaboration in west Africa, toward which local political leaders had been working energetically under the Fourth Republic. In more ways than one, then, Keïta's and Senghor's formation of the Federation can be interpreted as a rejoinder to earlier French efforts to balkanize African states on the eve of decolonization, perhaps most famously in the form of de Gaulle's 1958 referendum, which I mentioned earlier. The referendum, held in September of that year, completely dashed earlier visions of interterritorial collaboration in west Africa. Infamously, the referendum's "either/or" structure forced African political leaders to choose between two untenable alternatives: membership in the "French Community," proffered as an antidote to the existing colonial system, and "independence" (construed as total autonomy). Given this patently false choice, de Gaulle's "invitation" to act collectively within and as the so-called French Community—an invitation that was issued in the wake of the Fourth Republic's foundering, precipitated by the revolt of the French Army in Algeria, in May 1958—rang hollow in the ears of African activists, intellectuals, and political leaders.

It is in response to this explicit French agenda of African balkanization, promoted by de Gaulle's referendum and *in the name of decolonization*, that Senghor's and Keïta's efforts to create a viable African federation must ultimately be understood. Doubtless, their vision for federation had its limitations, at least as they sought to realize it practically. For example, both accepted that postcolonial African states should take the form of sovereign nation-states in the image of Europe, and both leaders trafficked in nationalism, despite their misgivings about the state form. And yet, by working together to create an African federation, and by doing so at the very moment that de Gaulle was attempting to *eradicate* the very possibility of interterritorial collaboration in Africa, Senghor and Keïta came together in a potent demonstration of anticolonial, pan-African political will.

It is a strange and slightly disconcerting moment when the Dakar-Niger Railway comes to stand for a visionary attempt at African federation, and when a railroad, more generally, becomes a visual metaphor for African unity. Not only was the railroad a colonial infrastructure project, but its initial construction was closely associated with the brutality of forced labor and other colonial abuses of African labor.[21] No doubt many of the contradictions inherent in this visual metaphor of federation and of unity can be attributed to the internalization of colonial ideologies of modernization. But the more interesting contradictions stem from the fact that these images depict not a single moment in west African history but the interplay of several different moments, as well as the rapid succession of different political projects, each one connected with a different vision of interterritorial collaboration, federation, and solidarity. Although the shifting relationships between these different moments and projects are difficult to localize in space and time, all become visible to us in these photographs.

In fact, there are at least three "images" of decolonization and African liberation that are visible in these photographs of Keïta, which feature so prominently in Senegalese archives documenting this period. The first is an image of the Mali Federation's creation in 1959, a visionary attempt at African federation flying in the face of European efforts at balkanization. The second is an image of the Federation's foundering and of the bittersweet consolidation of Mali and Senegal as independent nation-states in the wake of decolonization. The third is an image of the reconciliation of Senghor and Keïta, in 1966, after this balkanization was complete. Each image is written over an earlier image of liberation or, alternatively, each predicts and promises the image yet to come. A fuller understanding of these photographs documenting the "re-opening of the railroad" and the renewal of diplomatic ties between Senegal and Mali, and the special quality that these particular images have for Senegalese interlocutors, requires that we see these images, likely taken in 1966, as citing all of these other earlier historical events and moments and as renewing their promise in the present.

Keïta maintained his reputation as a popular, and populist, leader and as a committed socialist throughout his career. He is widely remembered as a founding figure in the Rassemblement démocratique africain (RDA), a monumentally important interterritorial political party that articulated ambitions for African unity in the late colonial period.[22] Despite the psychological devastation that ensued with the failure of the Federation, Keïta remained strongly identified with the populist and pan-African politics of the RDA, and he became an outspoken proponent of the Non-Aligned Movement. Not only was Mali an early member of the nonaligned states, but Keïta represented Mali at the second conference of nonaligned states, held in Belgrade in 1961 (where Senegal was not represented, becoming a member only later, in 1964). Keïta also participated in drafting the first charter of the Organization of African Unity in 1963. A testament to Keïta's close identification with nonalignment in the popular political imagination, another photograph that I saw in a Senegalese collection shows a crowd of people that has gathered, according to convention, to dance and sing and greet the Malian leader. We see them holding a sign bearing the word, in French: *non-alignement* (see figure 5.8).[23] To the right of the sign, in the image's rear plane, we see that someone is holding aloft a framed photographic portrait of Keïta.

The public display of a photograph in the streets during such an event is, on the one hand, unremarkable: it is a convention of public gatherings celebrating the arrival (or departure, in the case of funeral processions) of prominent individuals across the region. And yet, in other respects, this photograph of a portrait of Keïta held aloft is remarkable, in that it distinguishes this photograph from those in which African unity is made visible or legible by the railroad. For this photograph knits together "traditional" African approaches to public commemoration and celebration, such as singing and dancing, with a decidedly "modern" approach, such as nonalignment, presenting us with yet another example of photography's nonlinear, layered, and open-ended temporalities.

## AFRICAN FUTURES: SPARKED, LOST, AND FOUND

The complexly layered temporalities and plural and shifting histories that move through archival photographs from this era become similarly apparent through a series of photographs that I saw in the national archives in Ouando, a suburb of Porto-Novo, Benin. Working in those archives in 2009, I came across, by chance, a box of photographs that had been deposited by president Mathieu Kérékou, sometime during his first presidency (Benin was then the Republic of Dahomey), which began in 1972.[24] It interested me that the president of a newly independent west African state had taken an interest in collecting photographs of any sort. My curiosity was fanned still further when, after I had spent a few hours rifling through the box, it was made to disappear and I was told I "should not ask about those photographs anymore."

The disappearance of these images was, on the first and most immediate level, mystifying. The principal object of my research in Benin was in fact the police files of the Sûreté coloniale française, or colonial security service, in Dahomey, which contained criminological photographs. It is difficult to imagine a more brutal and violent series of images than these criminological photographs, most of which were mug shots of convicts who had escaped during penal labor, a direct descendant of the colonial forced labor requirement, or corvée. By contrast, the photographs in the mysterious box seemed uncontroversial, calculated to cultivate patriotic or pan-African sentiment, and therefore open to readings likely approved by the state: monuments to martyrs decked with bouquets, evidence of coup plots put down by the regime then in power, the military exercises of other people's revolutionary parties. Even when photographs depicted military exercises or marching troops, they were not documents of violence. The fact that this particular box was made to disappear, its contents judged by someone to be menacing enough to censor forty or even fifty years after they had been taken, lends support to the hypothesis that the histories conjured by photographs associated with the formation of postcolonial states in Africa are powerful enough to be or to become a threat. These alternatives trouble the official version of these histories, even fifty years later. The solidarities that circulate through these photographs are not relegated to the past but are still able, at least potentially, to be reactivated. Otherwise, why else would they have been taken away?

Before this box was made to disappear, a bolder hypothesis about their origin had been proposed to me by Grégoire, a member of the archives staff.[25] He intimated that rather than merely being collected by president Kérékou, the photographs had been *commissioned* by him. Grégoire made this assertion about a specific series of photographs documenting military exercises or troops passing in review in Western Sahara (figures 5.5, 5.6, and 5.7).[26] Based both on ethnographic interviews with local photographers who were engaged in political work and research undertaken in their archives, I believe it is highly implausible that Kérékou sent a photographer to Western Sahara to photograph military exercises connected with a nascent revolution there. Some of these photographers worked for their presidents or for other politicians as early as the mid-1950s. Zinsou Cosme Dossa, whom I interviewed in Porto-Novo at length in 2009, was, when he was hired by the colonial administration of Dahomey in 1957, the first African photographer to have been hired in an official capacity by the French colonial administration in the AOF; Félix DeMesse, whom I also interviewed in 2009, was the first official state photographer of the independent Republic of Dahomey (later the Republic of Benin). Both men worked closely with high-ranking officials and politicians, and DeMesse was the head of the photographic section of the ministry of propaganda and information under Kérékou. Yet neither man was ever, as far as I know, sent on assignment across national or territorial borders. Confirming my own primary research, research by other scholars strongly suggests that the majority of African photographers of the independence generation

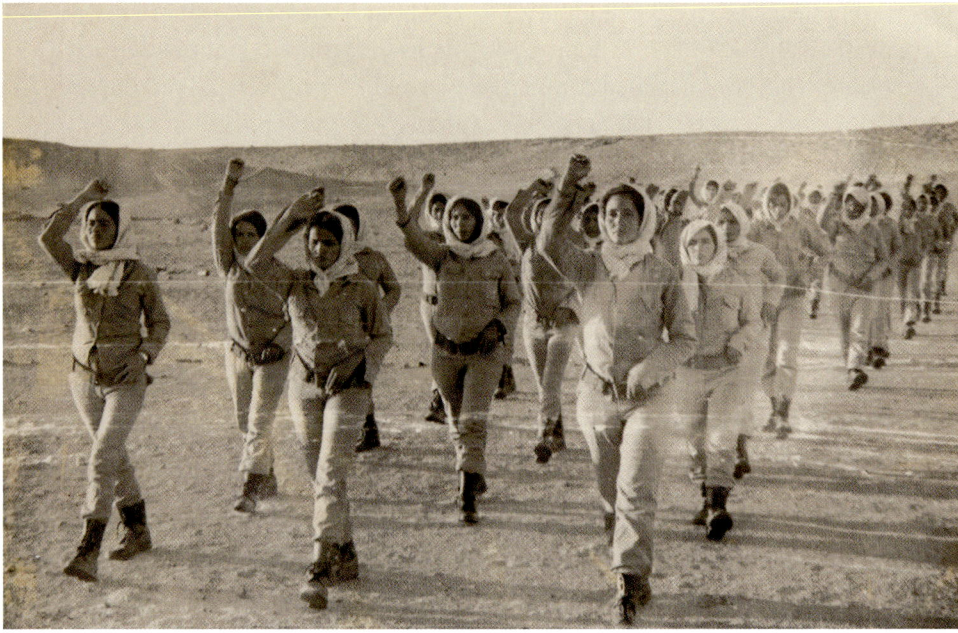

rarely, if ever, traveled outside their home countries on assignment, not even in the years following independence, although they often had opportunities to travel internally.[27] Yet even the most open-ended speculation about this unlikely scenario raises interesting questions about these photographs and the glimpses of solidarity they afford.

This broader context suggests that the photographs from Western Sahara contained in Kérékou's box were likely taken by a local photographer—Spanish, Moroccan, Algerian, or (less likely) Sahrawi—in Western Sahara and only later circulated to Kérékou in Benin. They were probably taken in 1975, on the occasion of a visit by a United Nations envoy to inspect the legitimacy of the Polisario Front's claims to represent the Sahrawi. A 1979 article by Michael M. Gunter describes this May 1975 visit, citing a UN General Assembly report of the "Visiting Mission [of the Special Committee on Decolonization] to Spanish Sahara." The report emphasizes the preponderance of banners declaring independence that were displayed for the occasion: "Everywhere the Mission saw signs displayed demanding total independence of the Territory from Spain and rejecting integration with any neighboring country. Typical of the slogans carried on these signs, which were also repeatedly proclaimed orally to the Mission, were: 'We demand absolute independence,' 'No to Spanish colonialism, no to Morocco and no to Mauritania,' and 'Sahara for the

**Figure 5.5.** ***(opposite)*** **Female troops, possibly Algerian, marching in connection with the struggle for liberation in Western Sahara. By 1975, the war in Western Sahara had become a proxy war between the United States and the Soviet Union. In or near Western Sahara, c. 1975–76. Photographer unknown. Courtesy National Archives of Benin, Porto-Novo, Benin.**

**Figure 5.6.** ***(below)*** **Military exercises related to the struggle for liberation in Western Sahara. A banner visible at the right of the image, beyond the distant crowd, reads "Polisario es una realidad" [Polisario is a reality]. In or near Western Sahara, c. 1975–76. Photographer unknown. Courtesy National Archives of Benin, Porto-Novo, Benin.**

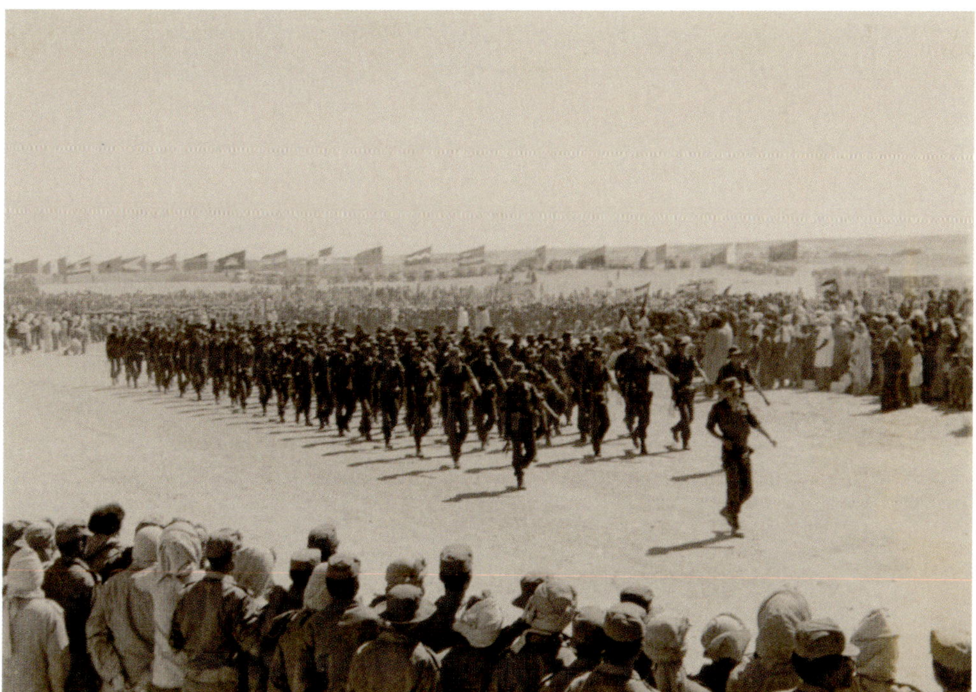

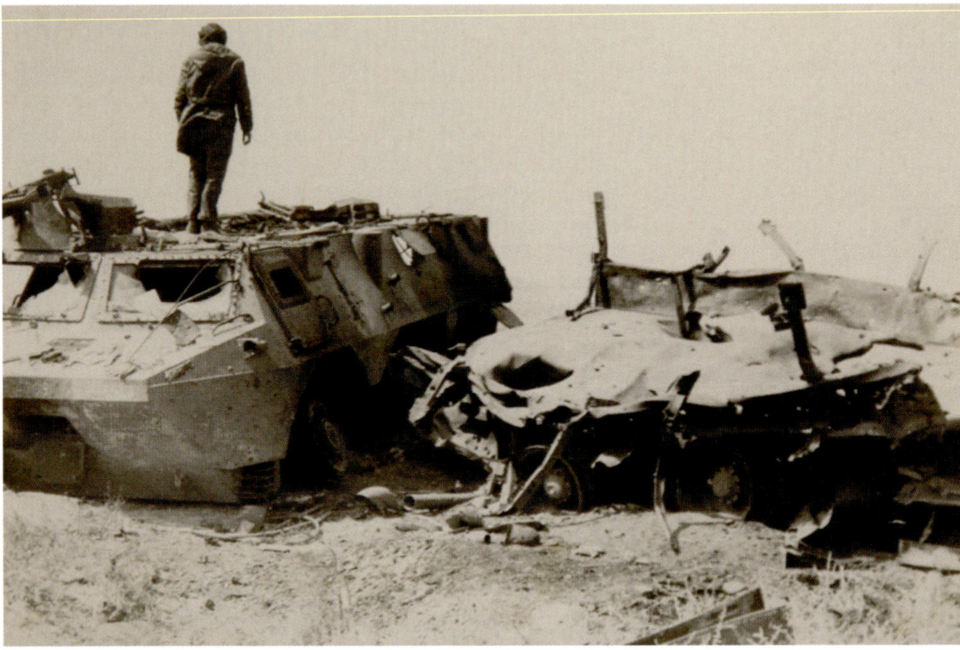

Saharans.'"[28] The report's references to these slogans seem particularly appropriate to the second in this series of photographs (figure 5.6): toward the upper right corner of the image (just beyond the crowd), a banner reads "Polisario es una realidad" (Polisario is a reality). Both the banner and the flags arrayed behind the crowd in the same image strongly suggest that this photograph was taken in connection with a UN visit, or the visit of some other international body such as the Organization of African Unity, the Arab League, or the organization of nonaligned states.[29] Indeed, Grégoire explained that the flags visible in the background are those of the nonaligned states. The Non-Aligned Movement formally recognized the right of the Sahrawi people to seek self-determination in 1973, a decision that undoubtedly raised the profile of their struggle internationally. Historically, there has been significant overlap and cross-pollination between the UN and the nonaligned states, and, in 1975, the member states of both organizations would have been virtually identical.

It is also possible, however, that these photographs document a later chain of events, starting in November or December 1975, when Morocco moved to occupy the north of Western Sahara, in direct contravention of a UN vote to form a plebiscite, co-organized by Morocco, Spain, and Mauritania (Western Sahara's neighbor to the south) about the territory's future, even before the full withdrawal of the Spanish authorities.[30] Two other photographs from the

**Figure 5.7.** (*opposite*) Damaged tanks photographed as evidence of armed conflict in connection with the struggle for liberation in Western Sahara. In or near Western Sahara, c. 1975–76. Photographer unknown. Courtesy National Archives of Benin, Porto-Novo, Benin.

**Figure 5.8.** (*below*) Senegalese citizens gather to celebrate a state visit by Modibo Keïta. In addition to marking the occasion with traditional singing and dancing, the crowd holds aloft a sign reading "Non-Alignement" and a photographic portrait of Keïta. Senegal, c. 1966. Photographer unknown. Collection of Ibrahima Faye and Khady Ndoye. Courtesy Gnilane Ly Faye.

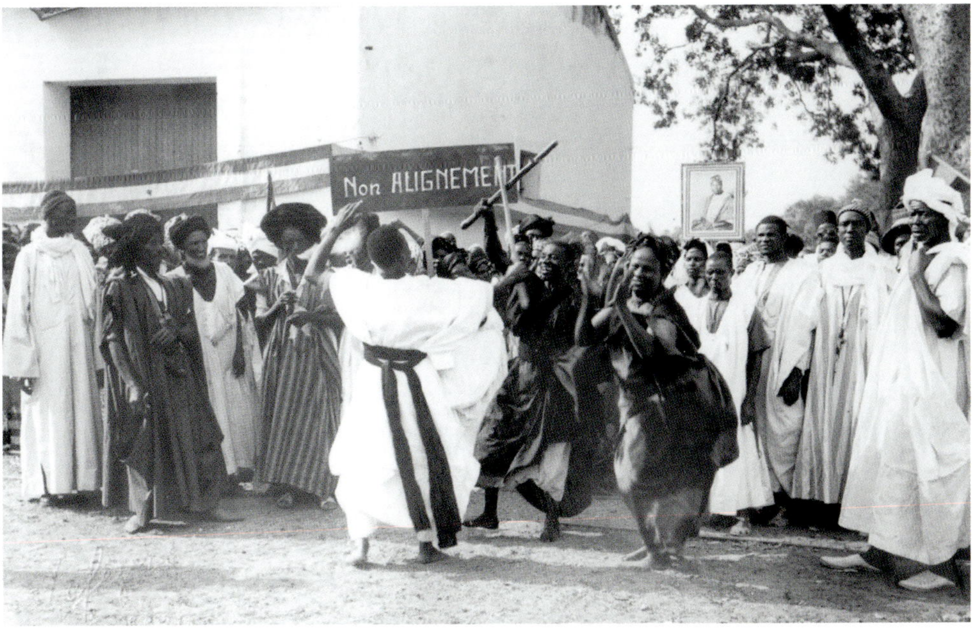

same series, depicting parading female troops and a damaged tank (see figures 5.5 and 5.7), lend credence to this interpretation. The period spanning late 1975 and early 1976 was one of escalating military tension in the region: in January 1976, there was a serious encounter between a Moroccan armored unit, which had ambushed an Algerian company at Amgala in Western Sahara (Algeria was in favor of independence for Western Sahara), and, a few days later, the Algerians wiped out the Moroccan garrison, resulting in five hundred casualties.[31] The war in Western Sahara had, at this point, already become a proxy war between the United States and the Soviet Union: Morocco was supported, albeit largely indirectly, by the United States. Algeria was allied with Moscow. The photograph of the parading female troops could be an Algerian battalion: Algeria's troops were freshly trained and armed to the hilt after the Algerian civil war and were the envy of many an African nation. The tank visible in the third and final photograph could be an Algerian tank.[32] Whether we favor the interpretation privileging the flags (suggesting that the photographs were taken during the May 1975 UN visit) or that privileging the damaged tank (suggesting that the photographs were taken after January 1976), it seems incontestable that these photographs were taken, collected, and circulated by parties wanting to make the case both for the military prowess of Polisario and its allies and for the legitimacy of the Sahrawi people's claims to self-determination.

Despite the relative solidity of these hypotheses, Grégoire's version of events, in which Kérékou *commissioned* these photographs in Western Sahara, remains intriguing. Whether or not it is factually true, this story contains elements of a history inflected by the lived experience of the independence generation. Such an act, the commissioning of a photograph of someone else's revolution, exceeds more familiar gestures of solidarity or of recognition, such as those made when one government recognizes another's sovereignty, or when one state formalizes diplomatic relations with another. To commission a photograph of someone else's revolution is to do more than simply acknowledge this people's right to self-determination, and it is to do more than express solidarity with their liberation movement. It is to document that solidarity—and to archive it. It remains uncertain whether archiving such an event—not just photographing it, but photographing it in order to deposit documentation of that event in the archives of a sovereign state (in this case, Benin)—confers greater legitimacy upon the other's demand for liberation (in this case, the territory of Western Sahara, whose sovereignty remains in dispute). But this act of archiving definitely gives this demand a future, ensuring that it will be handed down to later generations.

I spoke, at the beginning, of the nonlinear, layered, and open-ended temporalities that photographs can engender and of the importance of these temporalities to decolonial research in particular. The word *decolonial*, as I am using it, has gained currency in contemporary theoretical discourse and will be familiar to many readers. Yet it is vital to recall the genealogy established by Walter Mignolo, from whom I borrow the term. Mignolo himself credits Aníbal Quijano with a very particular understanding of the concept, which stems from the very particular relationship that inheres between "modernity" (modernidad) and "coloniality" (in Spanish, colonialidad). According to Mignolo, Quijano underscores that coloniality is not just part of, or contemporaneous with, modernity; it is its condition of possibility: its "invisible and constitutive side."[33] Decolonial thought, Mignolo thus argues, is in its morphological and *conceptual* elaboration a critique not just of modern bodies or archives of knowledge but of modern modes of *knowing*, which have been determined by colonial histories of power.

The question about a decolonial photography and decolonial research *on* photography cannot, in other words, simply be satisfied with the search for a distinctly African image of colonial modernity: photographs of decolonization taken by African photographers. It must also ask after, and attempt to describe, a distinctly African vision, advanced with and through photography, of what had, already in 1966 or 1975, begun to succeed it. This vision, although it may affect or impact what we see or think we see in an image, cannot simply become manifest in a single photograph or even in a multitude of photographs if they are interpreted as referring, purely retrospectively, to events that exist only in the past. Rather, this vision extends to encompass the *future* of a given image, as well as people's desires for that image's future: what it might someday do or show.

What, then, is the status of all these photographs depicting alternative futures for postcolonial Africa? By what methods can we excavate the histories they contain? How, at the same time, can we remain faithful to these histories, without succumbing to the official histories of the states whose archives sometimes house them? This chapter has provided some provisional ways of addressing these questions, on the basis of these two archives of images that I saw in west Africa, by delving into their power to speak to unresolved histories, and their palimpsestic capacity to show multiple images that have been superimposed or written over other images, in which alternative visions of African liberation were being framed.

The photographs taken in Western Sahara, now housed in the national archives in Benin, offer a glimpse of an ambitious vision of revolution and a nonaligned world. Regardless of who took these photographs, the act that led to their deposit in the Beninese national archives converts these images into documents of an actually existing pan-African solidarity. These images, like those chronicling the vision of African unity and, therefore, liberation that was represented by the Mali Federation (the photographs of Keïta discussed in the first half of this chapter), do more than simply give us a faithful image of the past. They offer a vision of alternatives to coloniality that have yet to be fully realized and a glimpse of a history of decolonization that, could it be remembered, would threaten our present—a history that does threaten it, as the disappeared box attests.[34]

## *Notes*

1 The concept of "the decolonial," now familiar in scholarly discourse in multiple disciplines, is frequently thought to have originated in the Latin American context and remains, in Anglophone contexts, closely associated with the work of Walter Mignolo. Mignolo himself gives a double genealogy of decoloniality, tracing it, on the one hand, to discussions taking place in the wake of the 1955 Bandung conference and, alternatively, to the work of Aníbal Quijano, whom he credits with having identified the need to decolonize knowledge in an essay, first published in Spanish in 1992, "Colonialidad y modernidad-racionalidad." See Mignolo, *The Darker Side of Western Modernity*: "Decoloniality originated among Third World countries after the Bandung conference in 1955" (xi–xii), and "in the second half of the 1990s I became aware of Aníbal Quijano's explorations on coloniality" (xx), adding that Quijano was among the first to argue that "coloniality is constitutive of modernity" (xxi). See Quijano, "Colonialidad y modernidad-racionalidad," cited in Mignolo, *The Darker Side of Western Modernity*, xx. (Mignolo also notes that an English translation of Quijano's essay later appeared in *Cultural Studies* 21, nos. 2–3 (2007): 168–78.) Other genealogies of the term trace it to radical black feminist discourse arising in the 1960s and 1970s in the United States; still others claim that decolonial thinking and imagination have been in existence "since the very inception of modern forms of colonization." See Maldonado-Torres, "Thinking through the Decolonial Turn," 1. See also note 32, below, which references Mignolo's well-known article, "Delinking," in which he emphasizes the significance of decoloniality to contemporary research.

2 Scholars to have theorized postcolonial archives in various parts of Africa include Liam Buckley (working in The Gambia), particularly in Buckley, "Objects of Love and Decay"; Annie E. Coombes (working in Kenya and South Africa), in Coombes, *History after Apartheid*; Carolyn Hamilton, Verne Harris, and their many contributors (working in South Africa), in Hamilton et al., *Refiguring the*

*Archive*; Achille Mbembe (working in Cameroon and South Africa), in Mbembe, "The Power of the Archive and Its Limits"; Christopher Morton and Darren Newbury (presenting research from multiple regions of Africa), in Morton and Newbury, *The African Photographic Archive*; and Bhekizizwe Peterson (working in South Africa), in Peterson, "The Archives and the Political Imaginary." The turn of the twenty-first century also saw a surge of large public and collaborative history projects drawing on collections of documents (including photographs). See, for example, South African History Online, founded by Omar Badsha in 2001: https://www.sahistory.org.za/. See also History in Progress Uganda (HiPUganda), founded by Andrea Stultiens and Canon Griffin in 2011: http://www.hipuganda.org/ (accessed August 6, 2018). Equally vital have been the contributions of curators and artists who have mobilized historical and archival photographs drawn from African collections to pose exciting questions about photographic temporalities, postcolonial historiography, and decolonial knowledge production. Among the artists whose work has brought these questions into contemporary museum and gallery contexts are Sammy Baloji (Democratic Republic of Congo and Belgium), Sam Hopkins (Kenya and multiple museum archives in Europe), Maryam Jafri (multiple archives in Africa considered comparatively with Asia), George Mahashe (South Africa), Santu Mofokeng (South Africa), Zineb Sedira (Algeria), Andrea Stultiens (Uganda), and Ibrahima Thiam (Senegal). For my own prior treatment of these questions, see Jennifer Bajorek, "Photography and National Memory," and Bajorek, "Decolonizing the Archive."

3 I write *west Africa* deliberately without an initial capital in order to refer to places and people in the westernmost part of sub-Saharan Africa while simultaneously marking a distinction between this geographic region and the political entity known as l'Afrique occidentale française (henceforth AOF) a federation of French colonial territories that existed from 1895 to 1960, and that is often referred to in English as "French West Africa."

4 The Non-Aligned Movement emerged from the 1955 Bandung conference, which brought together the heads of Asian and African states who did not wish to be aligned with either the rising powers of the Soviet Union and the United States or the former colonial powers in Europe, and which was hosted in Bandung by president Sukharno of Indonesia.

5 Founded in 2011, South Sudan is the youngest country in Africa.

6 Ageron, "Les états africains," 271.

7 Ageron, "Les états africains," 271.

8 See Paul Isoart, "Rapport général" and "Le conseil exécutif de la Communauté."

9 "Political photography," "political photographs," or "photography of political things" (la photographie des choses politiques) are the phrases that were used locally, in west Africa, by photographers and members of the independence generation to refer to photographic images commissioned by the state or its representatives.

10 The Institut Français d'Afrique Noire (or, as it is more commonly known, IFAN) was the collective name given to a network of colonial research institutions in the AOF.

11 Leslie Rabine has explored the complex connections between Senghor's self-presentation in political photography and the ideas expressed in his poetry. See Rabine, "Photography, Poetry, and the Dressed Bodies."

12 Interestingly, Sylla's account contradicts those of Western scholars, who have argued that a lack of friendship between Malians and Senegalese was one of the reasons for the Mali Federation's failure. See, in particular, Foltz, *From French West Africa to the Mali Federation*, 149.

13 Prior to independence, many African activists, intellectuals, and political leaders had hoped to find more radical alternatives to the state form. For a thought-provoking recent treatment of some of these alternatives, including some that were being thought by Senghor, see Wilder, *Freedom Time*.

14 A fuller discussion of dependency theory, a theory of economic development that attributes the "underdevelopment" of certain regions and countries to their location on the periphery of the world economic system, exceeds the space that I have here. Important rejoinders to these theories have been articulated by political theorists writing about the state in Africa, including, most notably, Bayart, *The State in Africa*, 25–26; and Mbembe, *On the Postcolony*, passim. See also Billy Dudley's earlier, and extremely lucid, analysis of these questions in his "Decolonization and the Problems of Independence," in Crowder, *The Cambridge History of Africa*, 52–94.

15 Foltz, *From French West Africa to the Mali Federation*, 63.

16 Economic considerations appear to have been a major factor in the Mali Federation's failure, and, in fact, one of the practical premises of the Federation was that Mali and Senegal had complementary economies, with Mali (then French Soudan) having the raw materials necessary to industrial production and a greater potential market to be realized in the future and Senegal having the existing industrial capacity, including not only manufacturing infrastructure but a deepwater port. Foltz suggests that it proved impossible to realize the benefits of this complementarity without a plan for a federal economy. Foltz, *From French West Africa to the Mali Federation*, 154–56.

17 Early factionalization within Senghor's own party has also been attributed to internal conflicts created by the Mali Federation's break-up, as epitomized by the 1962 coup attempt by Mamadou Dia.

18 Faye served in high-ranking positions both before and after independence, including as the governor of four different regions of Senegal. The fact that he amassed an impressive collection of photographs taken in each of the cities where he lived, starting in the mid-1950s (Mbour, Kaolack, Ziguinchor, Saint-Louis, and Dakar are all represented) is already an index of the importance of photography to Senegalese political life.

19 Mr. Vyau de Lagarde, the French ambassador to Senegal at the time of Keïta's 1966 visit, described this visit in a telegram as being of "extraordinary psychological as well as political significance." Télégrammes nos. 1035–40, du 12 décembre 1966, de M. Vyau de Lagarde, Ambassadeur de France à Dakar, à M. Couve de Murville, Ministre des affaires étrangers," in *Documents diplomatiques françaises, 1966*, vol. 2 (Brussels: Peter Lang P.I.E., 2006): "Le Président de la République du Mali, accompagné d'une nombreuse suite, a effectué une visite officielle au Sénégal du 1er au 7 décembre 1966. La véritable signification de cette visite est d'ordre psychologique et politique" (981).

20 The name *Niger* in the Dakar-Niger Railway refers not to the nation-state of Niger but rather to the Niger River, which runs through Mali and through Bamako.

21 The Dakar-Niger Railway was, from an early date, associated with the brutality of forced labor and with protracted and difficult labor strikes. The most famous depictions of the railway strikes are those found in the 1960 novel by Ousmane Sembène, *Les bouts de bois de dieu* [*God's Bits of Wood*].

22 Senghor was also a socialist, but one whose socialist commitments were eclipsed by his own, highly peculiar brand of nationalism and his reputation for realpolitik.

23 Senghor, too, was a proponent of nonalignment. Yet the fact the *non-alignement* signs and banners appear to have been brought out to celebrate Keïta's visit only highlights the strength of his personal association with the movement.

24 Mathieu Kérékou was thrice president of Benin. He first came to power in a coup d'état in 1972, in what was then the Republic of Dahomey, and stayed in power until 1991; he then ceded power in a democratic election before being re-elected in 1996 and 2006.

25 Grégoire is a pseudonym. I have chosen to use one given the apparently controversial nature of the material we discussed.

26 The Sahrawi are also called the "people of Western Sahara." Their struggle is identified with that of the revolutionary group known as the Polisario Front (or, in Spanish, Frente Polisario), which was founded on May 10, 1973. The full name of the group is Frente Popular de Liberación de Saguía el-Hamra and Río de Oro, and the group is generally considered to be a successor of the earlier Movimiento para la Liberación del Sahara, an anticolonial movement that fought Spanish colonization in Western Sahara in the 1950s and 1960s.

27 See, in particular, Nimis, *Photographes de l'Afrique de l'Ouest*; and Keller, "Visual Griots." The one head of state who, I was told by Sylla in Saint-Louis, routinely traveled with his photographer in the 1960s was Mobutu Sese Seko, whose attention to his image was legendary.

28 Gunter, "Self-Determination or Territorial Integrity."

29 I am grateful to Christopher Lee for his generosity in discussing aspects of this photograph in light of his deep knowledge of the 1955 Bandung conference, the Non-Aligned Movement, and African-Asian relations. I am particularly grateful

to him for his suggestion regarding a possible OAU or Arab League visit. Personal communication with the author, September 18, 2015. I have also benefited from consulting Lee's truly excellent edited volume of essays on the 1955 Bandung conference, Lee, *Making a World after Empire.*

30 Howe, "African Atlantic Chess," 12–14.

31 This was the combined tally on both sides. Howe, "African Atlantic Chess," 13.

32 Howe reports that, at the time of the invasion in 1976, the Algerian army had four hundred heavy and medium and four hundred light tanks. Morocco, by contrast, which was not nearly as well armed, had only a smattering of American tanks, which had been supplied, in direction with the conflict, by Saudi Arabia. Howe, "African Atlantic Chess," 13.

33 Mignolo, "Delinking," 450–51. For a fuller genealogy of "the decolonial" in Mignolo, see note 1, above, referencing Quijano's essay as well as alternative genealogies.

34 I would like to express my deepest thanks to Leslie Rabine, the family of Ibrahima Faye (especially his daughter, Gnilane Ly Faye, and his late wife, Khady Ndoye), El Hadj Adama Sylla, Fatima Fall, AbdouKhadre Sarr, and Karim Fall, with whom I looked at and discussed these photographs in Senegal, and to the staff of the Direction des Archives Nationales du Bénin, in Ouando, especially Grégoire (not his real name), Sonia Mahamé, Mathias Massodé, and Franck Komlan Ogou, for facilitating access to photographs in Benin.

# Photo Essays

Photo Essays

Photo Essays

TONG LAM

# 6

# Bifurcated and Parallel Histories

Three decades after the collapse of the global Cold War order in 1989, the dust is far from settled. The traces left behind by the Cold War, therefore, are not always what the French historian Pierre Nora has termed "sites of memory" (lieux de mémoire) that monumentalize the past. Rather, many of them are little known places with legacies that are still secretly and actively informing our contemporary world. After all, as Walter Benjamin puts it, ruins are allegories of modernity and of historical violence. As such, they represent a history of the present. In this ongoing photographic series, *Bifurcated and*

**Figure 6.1.** ***(top)*** **Tong Lam, *Untitled*, from the series *Bifucated and Parallel Histories*, Hong Kong, 2017. Inkjet print. Courtesy of the artist.**

**Figure 6.2.** ***(bottom)*** **Tong Lam, *Untitled*, from the series *Bifucated and Parallel Histories*, Hebei, 2015. Inkjet print. Courtesy of the artist.**

*Parallel Histories*, I use images of Cold War ruins as physical and cultural registers to construct an alternative history that challenges the conventional view of the Cold War simply as a confrontation between East and West. In particular, I emphasize the multiple ways through which the Cold War can be conceptualized by the pairing of images. Each pair, specifically, narrates an aspect of the multifaceted geopolitical conflicts that spanned the globe. The series ultimately contends that the end of the Cold War did not mark the end of history. Quite the contrary, it has given rise to new agonies, violence, displacement, domination, and exploitation with profound consequences that are still unfolding all around us.

## WALL

The Berlin Wall has been a symbol of the Cold War. But the geopolitical tensions had also resulted in other walls that echoed the endless divisions and hostilities. The tall metal fence of an abandoned Vietnamese refugee camp in Hong Kong was one such example. After the Vietnam War (1955–75), millions of Vietnamese "boat people" fled their home country by sea to nearby countries due to economic and political hardships. Those who survived the high seas often had to wait in closed camps like this for years before their eventual resettlements in the Western world. Meanwhile, on a mountaintop near Beijing, there is also this massive bare concrete wall that points directly to Moscow. This remnant of China's Large Phased-Array Radar for detecting possible incoming ballistic missiles is a testimony that the former Soviet Union, rather than the United States, was considered by China as its primary Cold War threat. The Berlin Wall may have collapsed, but these other walls that are still standing stubbornly are reminders that the Cold War demarcations and conflicts were often local and multidirectional, and that similar political hostilities and population displacements persist to this day.

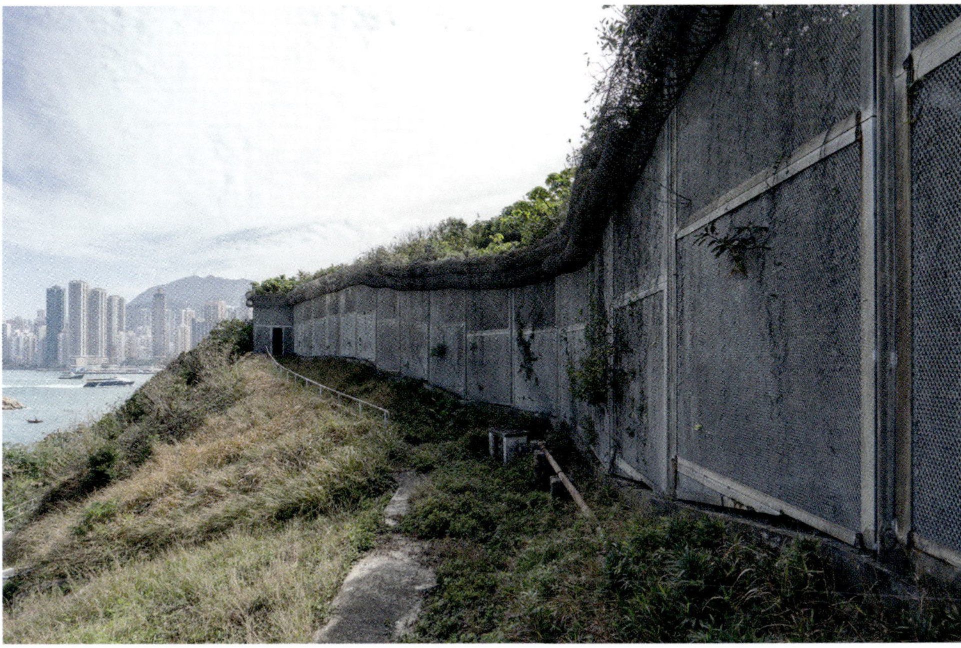

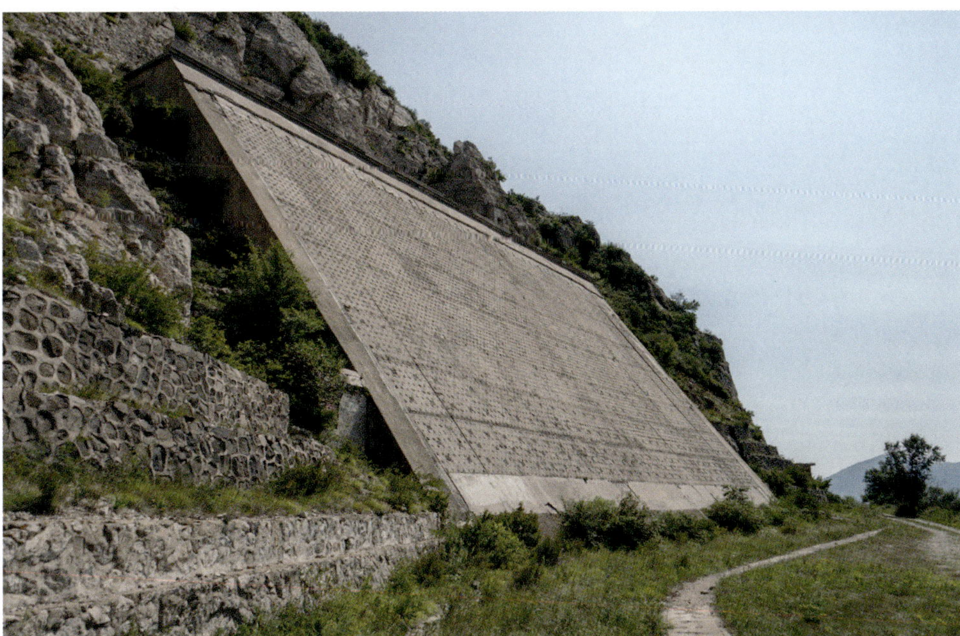

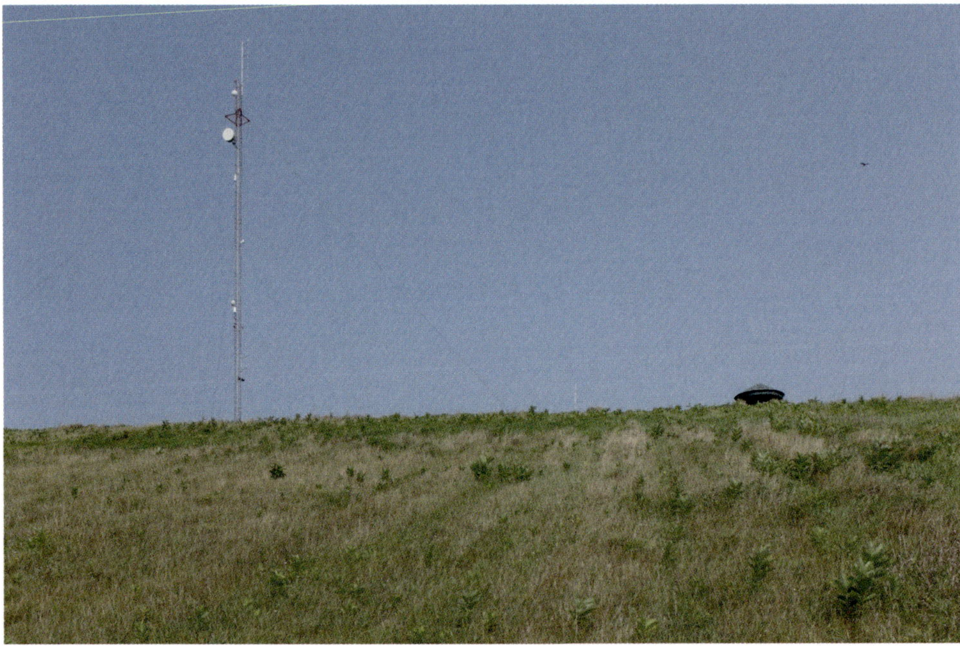

## SIGHT

The Cold War created a geography of fear that involved hide and seek. In Canada, that fear was manifested in the construction of the Emergence Government Headquarters just outside of Ottawa in the late 1950s. The secret bunker complex was designed to ensure the continuation of key governmental institutions in the wake of a nuclear attack. Aside from its antennae and air ventilators, the decommissioned complex remains inconspicuous from the outside even today. The flip side of concealment, meanwhile, was to spy on the enemies. In the early 1960s, the US government began to launch reconnaissance satellites to monitor the Soviet Union and China. In order to see the enemy territories effectively, hundreds of concrete arrows were placed in the Arizona desert for use in calibrating the satellite cameras. This history of the global competition on seeing and not being seen has since led to new infrastructures of surveillance technologies that are used by governments and corporations alike to track our lives and shape our behaviors.

**Figure 6.3.** (*opposite*) Tong Lam, *Untitled*, from the series *Bifucated and Parallel Histories*, Ontario, 2017. Inkjet print. Courtesy of the artist.

**Figure 6.4.** (*below*) Tong Lam, *Untitled*, from the series *Bifucated and Parallel Histories*, Arizona, 2017. Inkjet print. Courtesy of the artist.

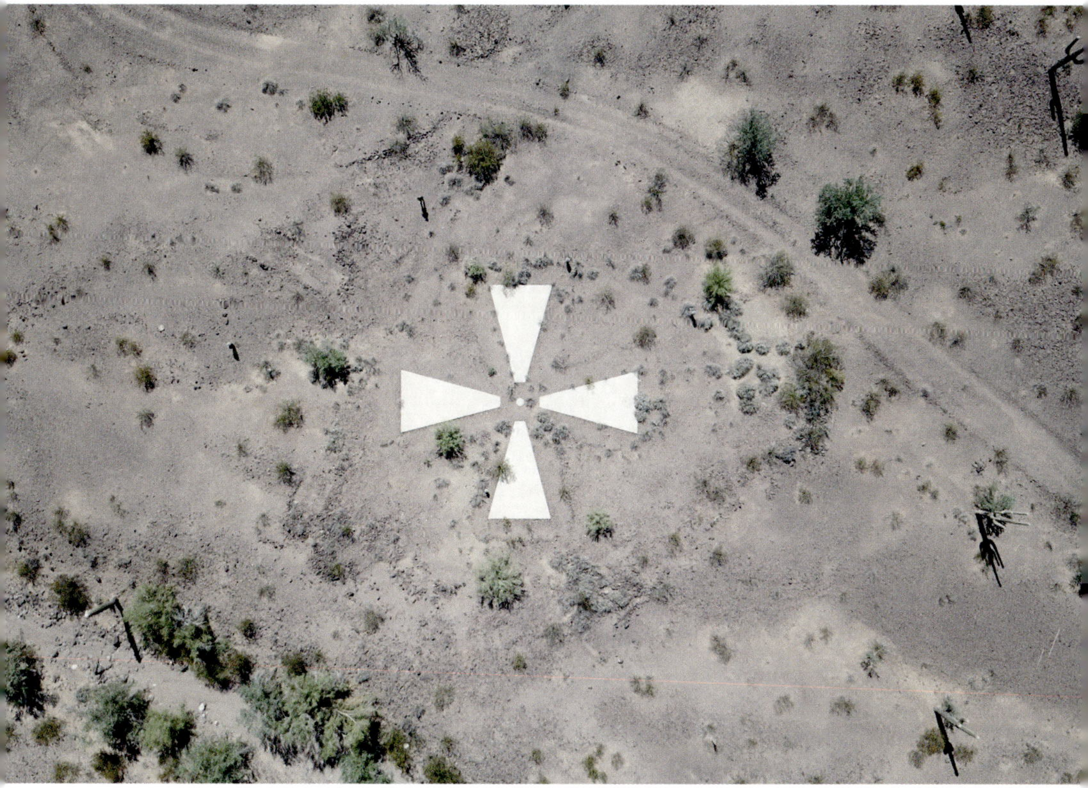

**Figure 6.5.** (*top*) Tong Lam, *Untitled*, from the series *Bifucated and Parallel Histories*, Berlin, 2014. Inkjet print. Courtesy of the artist.

**Figure 6.6.** (*bottom*) Tong Lam, *Untitled*, from the series *Bifucated and Parallel Histories*, Berlin, 2014. Inkjet print. Courtesy of the artist.

## SPEED

The Cold War also involved rapid mobilization. War preparedness required the deployment of large contingents of troops and equipment in strategic locations across the globe. In East Germany, for instance, hundreds of military barracks were built in short order to house Soviet military personnel. These two vertically adjoining rooms, as hinted by the thriving vegetation outside, tell a story of the importance of prefabricated buildings and speed in general for war mobilization. The minor difference in color choice also calls for a reflection on the soldier's everyday life during a long deployment far away from home. Still, nature appears to be indifferent to human endeavors and the numerous wasted lives spent in bunkers and camps. In the end, despite the swift movement of the social and political time of the Cold War, it is the deep time of ecology that prevails.

### *Note*

The idea of this ongoing project was first developed during my residence at the Wissenschaftskolleg zu Berlin in 2013. Some of the still images and videos from the series were subsequently exhibited at the Wissenschaftskolleg zu Berlin in 2014, the Goethe-Institut Toronto in 2016, the Lianzhou Foto Festival in 2018, and the Lishui International Photography Festival in 2019.

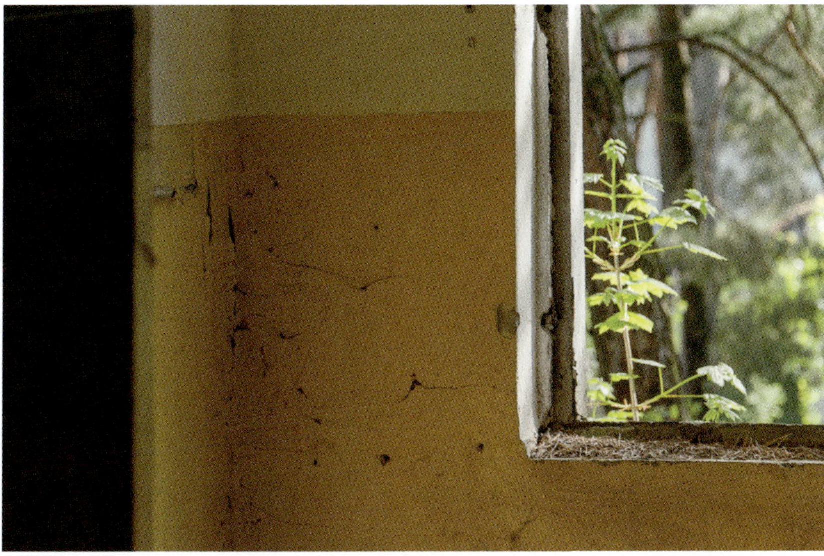

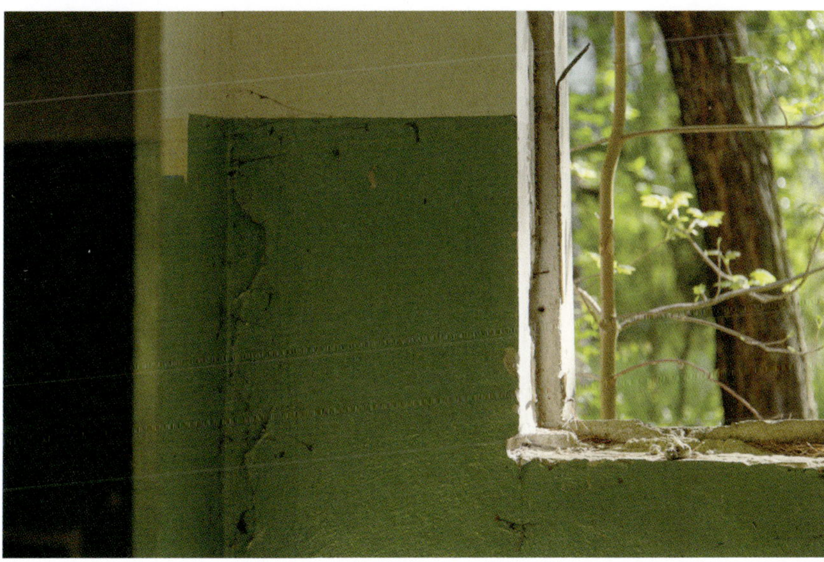

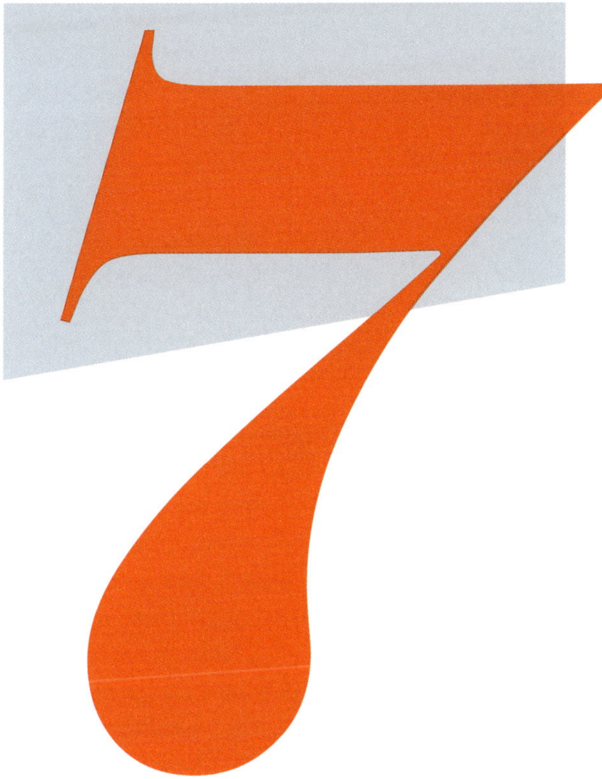

ERIC GOTTESMAN

# Preservation of Terror

In 1974, the international media broadcast news footage of Emperor Haile Selassie, showing him feeding meat to his animals while rural Ethiopians starved. As outrage ensued in response to these images, political factions angled for control. Not coincidentally, it was around this time, specifically in 1977, that the Soviet-supported communist government in Ethiopia (known as the Derg) unofficially banned the use of cameras in public space. The Ethiopian Red Terror (1977–78), or Qey Shibir in Amharic, a period of repression and mass killings, thus also unfolded in the visual field. Derg officials were

**Figure 7.1.** Mother and son reunited, 1978/2002. Rephotographed and degraded, 2006. Toned gelatin silver print (11 × 14 inches). Photograph by Eric Gottesman and unknown studio photographer.

afraid that images might be used to expose their regime's abuses of power. During that time, most Ethiopians had their pictures taken in photography studios. The studios produced small pictures for official documents but, because they were also a refuge from public space, where a fearful regime associated photography with "imperialism" (even though imperialism, understood as American colonialism, had ended), these studios also remained spaces where families could congregate on holidays to record their traditions, and where individuals could safely register their faces on film.

The Derg collapsed in 1987, but its psychological legacy in Ethiopia nearly four decades later continues to mystify identity, impact politics, and terrify those old enough to remember it. Of course, Ethiopians are now permitted to have cameras and, like everywhere else in the world, many people have a camera phone in their pocket. Still, until recently, people continued to visit photography studios and carry around passport photographs of their loved ones.

When I first arrived in Ethiopia in 1999, I saw these images everywhere. The guard of a house I rented in Addis Ababa reached into his pocket one evening and pulled out handfuls of his family members. Stacks of them wrapped tightly in bright yellow rubber bands sat on manila folders in offices around the city. Framed enlargements with decorative markings were framed on the walls of homes I visited. Bank files had these portraits stapled to them. I was new to Ethiopia and these images confronted those that I carried in my head from the international media when I grew up in the 1980s, images that had insisted on displaying the African body as a site of pain inflicted upon it. These subjects, also under siege, were in more control of their images and expressed their subjecthood with purpose. The more I learned about the history of this photographic framework, the more complicated it became.

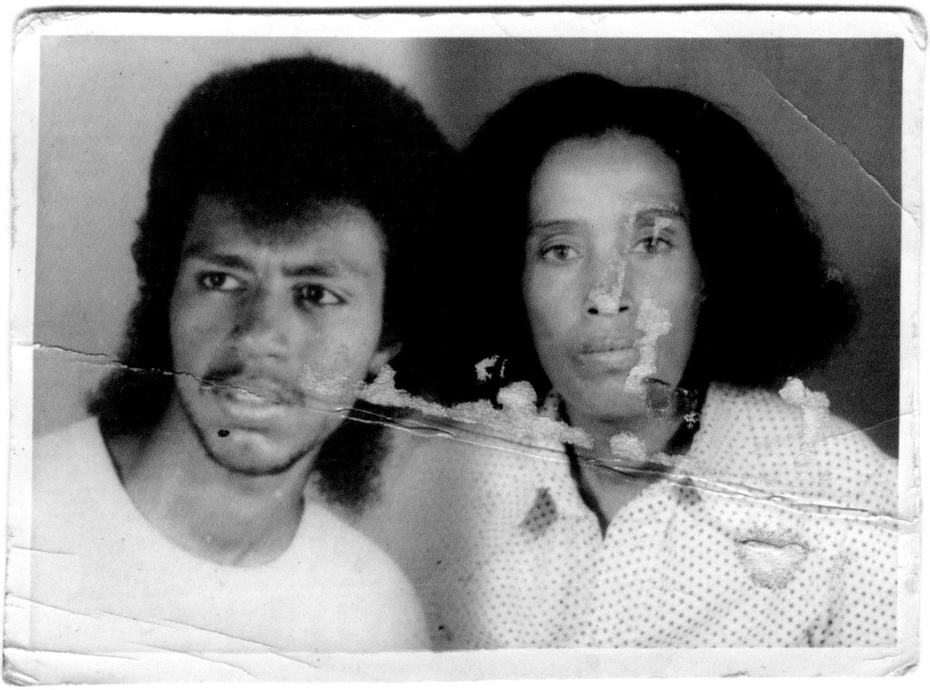

For several years, I visited friends and neighbors in Ethiopia and in the United States and asked to see the images they preserved in their homes, in photo albums, in forgotten boxes, on cluttered desks. I asked these individuals to allow me to re-photograph their images and the marks left on them over the turbulent intervening years. Some of these photographs depict people lost during the Red Terror or in its wake. Some are made more recently with this photographic history in their subconscious. The photograph "Mother and Son Reunited . . ." (figure 7.1) was brought to me by someone who used the darkroom to combine an old image of a boy, missing since 1982, with a new image of his mother who still carries his photograph with her to try to find him.

After I came to understand how the Red Terror was recorded, or not recorded, in studio photographs that specifically excluded imagery of what was happening in public and that were stored in personal archives outside of the public eye, I also understood that there grew a legacy from this form of residual image preservation of terrible events. I went on to explore the pictures

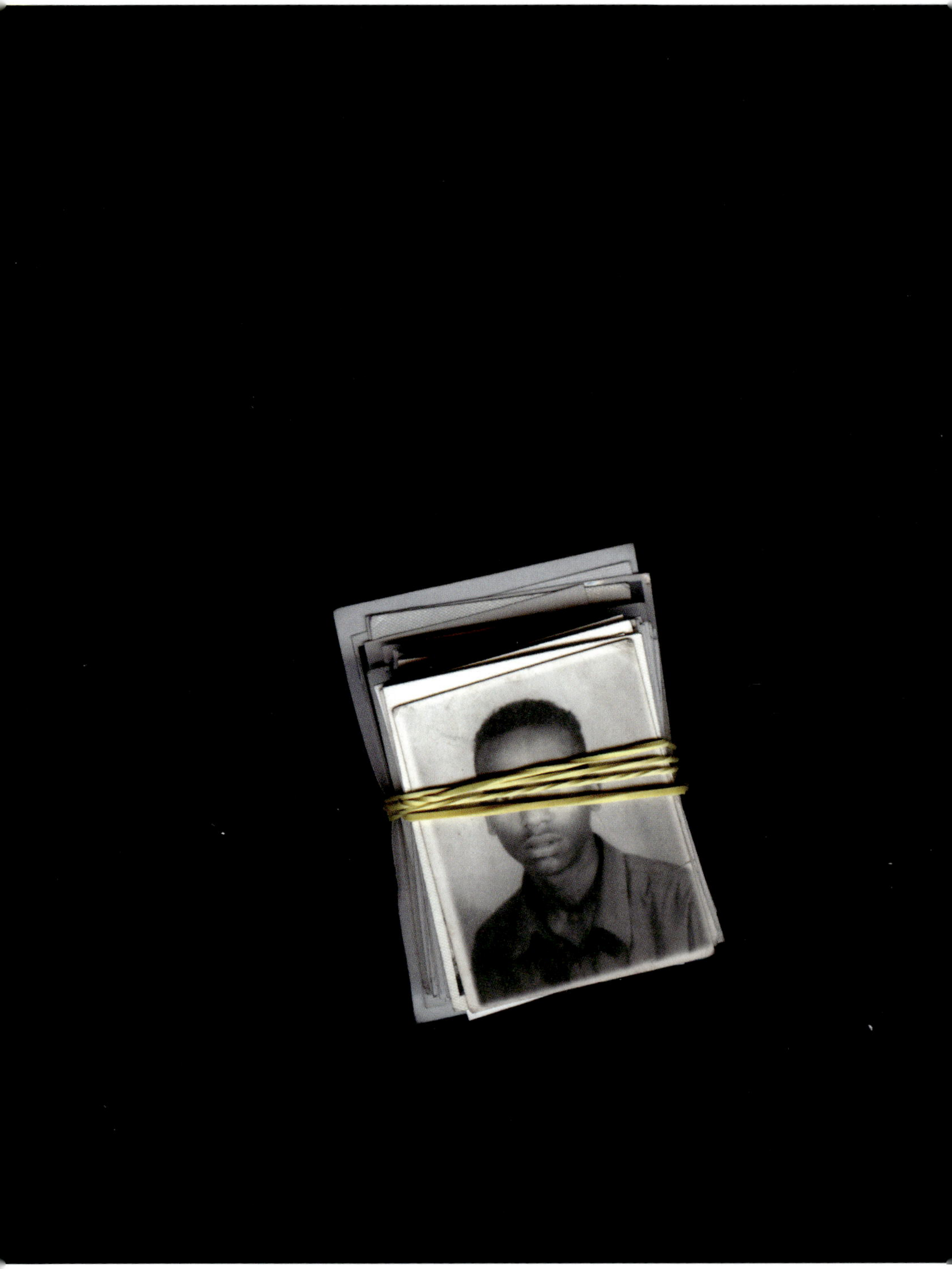

**Figure 7.2.** Banded passport photographs, 2007. C-print (20 × 24 inches). Photograph by Eric Gottesman and unknown studio photographer.

people in the diaspora have carried with them as they fled the Red Terror. I also looked for photographs that Eritrean and Ethiopian refugees remember but, for some reason, had to leave behind. Many of these refugees fled violence in the wake of Eritrea's long war of independence from Ethiopia (1961–91), an event that further complicates this era of the Red Terror, as it was the Derg's overthrow of Emperor Haile Selassie in 1974 that precipitated the Ethiopian Civil War, which lasted until 1991. The refugees' memories of these overlapping wars haunt the photographs that survive and provide the backdrop to those images that did not. The verbal descriptions of these inert photographs (gone, but not forgotten) testify to the power of the printed photograph in a time of digitization.

Sometimes, the physicality of these photographs determines their trajectory in the migrant lives of the people who remember them. One young Eritrean refugee in the United States shared with me the story of a photograph his father found on the body of his slain best friend during the Ethio-Eritrean war. He remembered the photograph and loved it, but his father did not let it leave Eritrea because of the way in which he found it:

> There was a very bitter war. After one particularly bloody battle with the ELF, Dani's father walked along the battlefield and stumbled upon the body of his best friend. In his pocket, he found the picture of the two of them together before the war, both of them looking away, grinning. It was pocket-sized, not a big one. It was stained in blood. And it was the only thing that was left.

These photographs reveal fragments of previously ordinary lives. These nearly two-dimensional rectangular objects seem fleeting, yet they have endured war, ideologies, flight, and physical decay, as well as love and banality. The fear of loss, the terror of violence, or the threat of violence is bound into these photographs both through the images latent in them and through the scratches and tears on their surfaces.

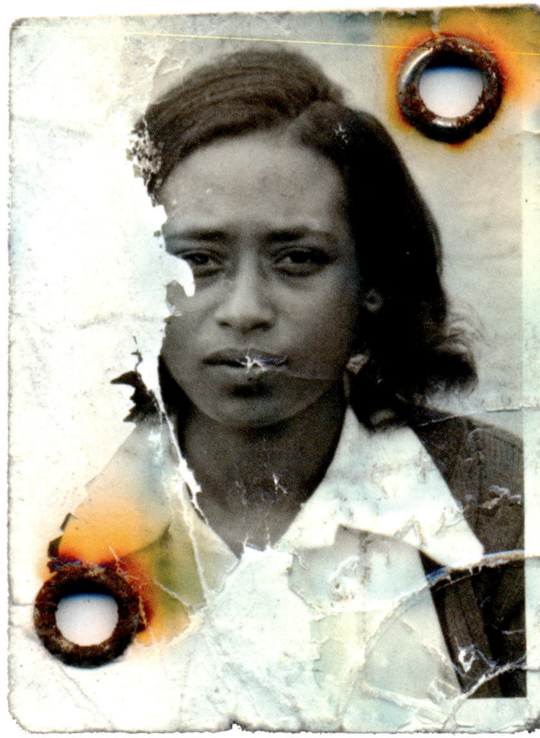

Like seeds sown across the ever-sprawling metropoles consuming the countryside, cement, glass, and steel buildings sprout toward the sky, casting shadows into which memories of the Derg regime recede, even as the influence of a new communist power, China, expands. Ethiopian infrastructure developed over decades as diaspora communities, Europeans, and Americans poured investment into the country through the vehicles of either development aid or private investment. China took a different approach, agreeing to improve infrastructure in part to strengthen relationships with African governments, building roads that connected cities across the country and across the continent (and conveniently opening new markets for Chinese-made goods). Ethiopians themselves, in an ambitious decades-long campaign, contributed funds to construct the Grand Renaissance Dam that will lead the country to greater energy independence. The development, urbanization, and proliferation of technology, including photographic tools and literacy across Ethiopia, shifted political paradigms. Citizens began recording protests on their cell phones. Prime Minister Hailemariam Desalegn stepped down after videos of public protests went viral on social media. The ruling

**Figure 7.3.** (*opposite*) Hanna Mesfin's Mother, 1996/2008. C-print (9 × 12 inches). Photograph by Eric Gottesman and unknown studio photographer.

**Figure 7.4.** (*below*) "If I Could Only Go Back There," 2011. Pigment print (20 × 24 inches). Photograph by Eric Gottesman and unknown studio photographer.

party reshuffled to retain control. Prime Minister Abiy Ahmed inspired a fragile national hope when he began serving in April 2018. Dissidents were released from prison. Major reforms were implemented. Ethiopia and Eritrea signed a peace treaty. That same Eritrean refugee I mentioned above, still barred from visiting his home country, posted pictures on social media with his family in a restaurant in Addis Ababa. After fourteen years of absence, they crossed the border, met him in Ethiopia, and were able to ask the waiter to take a picture of them together.

Prime Minister Ahmed's official photographer opened an Instagram account portraying the daily life of an accessible leader, kissing babies, quietly

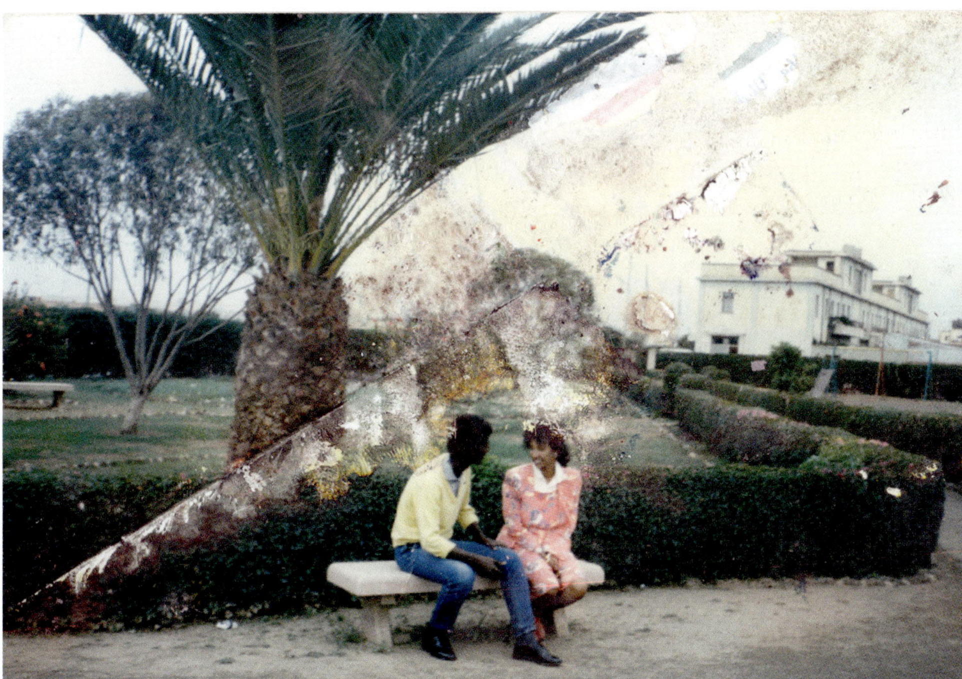

considering consequential decisions, and visiting hospitals to comfort the sick, a humanizing image strategy that diverged from that of previous generations of Ethiopian leaders who had used photographs to assert imperial or military authority. Yet Ahmed's distribution of images depicting him as an accessible, democratic, even vulnerable leader proved an insufficient political tool during the conflict with Tigray that began in 2020. He retreated to tested strategies, assuming the role of a wartime military commander. Local journalists were rearrested. Media was again restricted. While some camera crews were denied access to the conflict, state television broadcast the prime minister's visit to the front lines in full military uniform, reminding viewers old enough to recall Derg leader Mengistu Hailemariam's camouflage. Likewise, Tigrayan forces propagated images of captured Ethiopian prisoners of war to display their military might. Leaders of the TDF remained largely unseen, telephoning in to international news outlets from unknown locations, echoing a tradition of shaping the political narrative through strategic absence.

Despite a dizzying decade and a half of political change, privatization and unimaginable economic growth after the Ethiopian millennium in 2007, one can still find the occasional remnant of the communist period: a rusted hammer and sickle on a decrepit archway, Russian-made Lada taxis chugging up the hills of Addis Ababa, and crumpled black-and-white photographs in the pocket of an old man.

These images attest to the elision of personal and official histories—as well as to the incompleteness of this process. Disintegrating government-sanctioned images provide glimpses of an authoritarian regime's desire to control the visual field, and its failure to do so completely. Old monochromatic images provide a means of recollecting lost subjects and offer a way to remember the privations they endured without relying on the visual association of Africanness (or Blackness) with pain. Just as importantly, these photographs serve as quiet and somber counterpoint to the new, full-color national self-image Ethiopians are busily creating, and questioning, in the contemporary moment.

# Structures of Seeing

Structures of Seeing

Structures of Seeing

ARIELLA AÏSHA AZOULAY

8

# Ending World War II

## THE VISUAL LITERACY CLASS IN COLD WAR HUMAN RIGHTS

The apparent opposition between the two superpowers that defined the Cold War actually masked a disastrous consensus achieved by the Allies. In an era of growing unrest and instability in the territories and colonies that the Allies governed, this consensus was part of the way these powers preserved their imperial enterprise and rights. The Allies, who reaped the rewards of colonial plunder, feared they would lose their power, be held accountable for their past and present crimes, be forced to accept processes of restitution and redistribution of wealth, and make reparations toward millions of people and their offspring. Indeed, World War II was an opportunity for colonial and imperial powers to acquire general amnesty without paying for the racial and colonial crimes of the slave trade, genocides, forced displacements, and the destruction of cultures and arts in colonized places. Fighting against the Nazi and Fascist regimes, the Allies posed as righteous liberators, incapable of committing crimes such as those perpetrated by these regimes, and hence, not accountable for centuries of crimes they had committed as imperial powers.[1] Subsequently, fear of different political principles, modalities, and formations that would revoke their imperial rights prompted the Allies to sign treaties and agreements with their rivals-in-plundering as a means to secure their common form of power and the imperial enterprise. The creation of the UN and its particular idiom of human rights discourse provided the most effective means of assuring their continued domination—and of absolving themselves of complicity in violence. Through a UN-sanctioned idiom of human rights, the Allies presented themselves as providing relief from, rather than perpetrating, violence.

The founding documents of the UN and its rights discourse should be read alongside the mechanisms of pedagogy and violence that were used to obviate other forms of rights claim. The most threatening of these alternative forms were those advocated by colonized people who, despite having served in the Allies' armies, were punished, rather than rewarded, when they claimed their rights at the end of the war. In this context, the massacre in the Thairoye camp in Senegal is emblematic.[2] The degree to which East and West agreed on particular rights included in the UN's Universal Declaration of Human Rights (UDHR) is secondary in this regard. Fundamentally, East and West agreed on their imperial rights to impose a global basic doctrine of human rights, which accelerated and supplemented the creation of numerous, mainly weak nation-states. These nation-states were created through violent processes, embraced and celebrated as part of the UN's advocacy of a doctrine of what could be described as a "liberation-self-determination-national-sovereignty" (which I discuss below), and imposed on new member states as the rule of the game.

In effect, the Allies' agreement to recognize the right to self-determination served to break down the world into small and weak nation-state units. When Franklin Delano Roosevelt and Winston Churchill signed the famous Atlantic Charter on August 14, 1941, they committed to "respect the right of all peoples to choose the form of government under which they will live; and [ . . . ] to see sovereign rights and self-government restored to those who have been forcibly deprived of them." Debates about whether this commitment was fulfilled or broken tacitly assume that this model—self-determination leading to the constitution of a nation-state—is the only desirable political model. Given this context, the UN's founding was instrumental in making the nation-state the preeminently desirable and acceptable political model.

To parcel out the world in this way, the Allies relied on two ultimate tools, which they deployed as justifications: the right to self-determination and the right to safe boundaries, or "dwelling in safety within their own boundaries," as the 1941 Atlantic Charter put it.[3] Reserving for themselves the imperial right to exercise violence in using these tools, they acted as the architects of this operation. The UN promoted a human rights discourse as an efficient mechanism with which to approve imperial violence as legitimate. Thus, imperial violence was exercised rightfully and was distinguished from other types of violence pursued for purposes other than the establishment of nation-states and the preservation of discrete sovereign powers. The imperial powers that promoted this model neither withdrew from centuries of privileges nor did they cease their monopolistic rule over others. Nor did they pay for their genocidal crimes against vast populations on every continent. Rather, from the start, the UN's explicit goal was to ensure that nascent political formations in different places in the world conformed to, and were contained within, its standard model of sovereignty and human rights. Under these circumstances, the promotion of this model as the only acceptable one was yet another way for the Allies to reproduce their global power.

Accordingly, the extension of the principle of self-determination to all peoples—except in the colonies—through the use of "legitimate violence" bridged the gap between "Wilsonian idealism" and Lenin's assumption of "historical progress."[4] The common ground for collaboration between the Allies was their agreement that global imperial power should be retained and shared by them. The question of how to divide the trophy was secondary to this basic agreement. The isolation of Berlin from other areas in East Germany occupied by the USSR and its division (as if to reward each of the four Allies with its share of the trophy), illustrates the effort to secure the Allies' global domination.[5] The legitimization of partition and forced migration ostensibly as a means of effecting justice—but really as an exercise ensuring global control—became inseparable from the process of realizing people's right to self-determination in nation-states.[6]

A structure of a differential body politic and, consequently, a differential sovereignty lies at the heart of this model of self-determination. Put simply, a differential body politic enables, justifies, and legitimates a differential rule of its members. This had substantial consequences not only on the ways violence was orchestrated but also on the ways it had to be perceived, tolerated, and experienced. The discourse of human rights played an essential role in differentiating violence and making it digestible and justified or condemnable and punishable—depending upon who exercised it, against whom, and for which aims. Thus, for example, the Allies' program of partition and organized displacement of populations was to be experienced and approached as a tolerable operation in which people participated for the sake of liberation and the protection of other groups' rights.

I contend that what is known as the "Cold War era" ushered in a form of global visual literacy, whose significance can be grasped through attention to what I call a "curriculum" of human rights literacy, predicated on the differential principle. Even though visual literacy is not just about photographs, nevertheless, photographs—those that were produced, disseminated, and uncensored—were used as the locus of rights' violation par excellence.[7] I focus in particular on the global teaching of "visual literacy," conducted and surveilled by the Allies and implemented through the production and circulation of photographs. Through this visual literacy, violence was to be identified. Moreover, spectators were taught that such violence was utterly justified (in effect to be seen as not violent) and meant to secure world peace.

The "curriculum" of this teaching cannot be reconstructed solely from organized and intentional pedagogical programs, tools, and images.[8] At the same time, direct propaganda was heavily involved, notably in the whitewashing of the liberation of Paris, as reflected in the majority of photographs from which the presence of soldiers from the colonies is absent. I reconstruct this curriculum from what I call the three-dimensional imperial principle, which is important because it facilitated and organized much of the literacy work.

The first dimension of the imperial principle is *temporal*. It entails the imposition of a linear temporality, which enables different peoples and groups of governed peoples with different moments of development—and hence eligible for fewer rights than others—to be associated along a unified narrative of progress. This is essential in both stabilizing imperial achievements as superior and legitimate, and in establishing colonized people as inferior—but with a foreseeable future as recipients of rights at some point, when they could be extended to them. This progressive temporality secures the perseverance of imperial rights, the rights to give—and take—rights from others. This process also required the creation of the past as a discrete tense materialized in and through archives in which imperial crimes belong and where demands for reparations become obsolete. The second dimension is *spatial*.

It entails differentiating between inside and outside, often within one political unit, so as to prevent those constituted as outside from interfering in the benign order of the inside, which is ruled by law and sovereign authority. These two dimensions nurture the third dimension, which is *differential*. This dimension entails maintaining inequality among groups of people in every nation-state, a process that, accordingly, makes the principle of differentiality a matter of fact. In this way, privileged groups experience inequality and the consequent injustices and harms it entails as a given condition rather than as a violent enterprise in which they participate.

Gradual improvements in the condition of colonized people were construed not as a sign of the Allies' cruelty, but as a sign of the colonized peoples' belated maturity, which would eventually allow them to enter the Commonwealth of Nations. The commitment to self-determination and human rights was a means to bind existing or emerging political formations to the three-dimensional imperial principle. Through this means, superpowers were provided the authority to maintain their global rule.

These visual literacy lessons did not consist only of typical human rights photographs, as emblematized in images of the bodies of victims. It includes seemingly unrelated images such as parties with cake in the shape of Hiroshima's mushroom cloud, or "bikinis," the fashion in bathing suits named after nuclear tests. Such images are essential in the orchestration and legitimization of UN-sanctioned violence. In the first section of this chapter, I consider how this three-dimensional imperial principle was enhanced through the classroom of human rights literacy that was pertinent in the transition from one imperial war to another, from World War II to the Cold War. In the second section, I examine the significance of the visual idiom that this classroom produced.

The Allies' curriculum violently enforced lines of division into manifestations of law, order, and regimes of respect for human rights. Moreover, at the core of the Allies' global curriculum were three tenets: the legitimation of their own use of violence and its differentiation from the same use of violence by others; the association of the violence they used with universal ends and purposes, which stood in stark opposition to others' violence, which was defined as evil; and the repression and dispersal of modes of resistance to these norms and regimes.

The visual literacy of human rights had to make these temporal, spatial, and differential divisions operative in a way that guided everyone in the correct interpretation of the overwhelming use of violence, often hardly differentiated. Differences in scale were used to reappraise these divisions. These differences in scale included point of view; platforms of dissemination; degrees of detail; hierarchies of suffering; systems of justification; spectrum of reasons and causes; blurring of magnitude of destruction; views from above and from below; modes of captivity of audiences; narrow and extended contexts; keeping the systemic violence as discrete, etc. However, differences in scale were not invoked to expose and incriminate violence and violent procedures per se, regardless of who exercised them, against whom, under which circumstances, and toward which ends. This violence was exercised in a floodlit arena, that is, it was presented as legitimate action congruent with the protection of human rights.[9] The engineering of an epistemology of human rights, in other words, was not based on the concealment of imperial violence perpetrated by the Allies but rather on its divulgence and exposure along the three-dimensional imperial principle.

## THE COLD WAR CURRICULUM OF HUMAN RIGHTS

There was no end to World War II but rather a process of ending it that consisted of massive campaigns of destruction in the heart of the "old world," as well as in the colonies. Destruction is the familiar imperial way of clearing the way for the *new*. The "new world order" allowed for an unprecedented acceleration of the relegation of existing modes of being into the repertoire of bygone time and their inclusion in "the past." Thus, for example, with the destruction of 97 percent of an ordinary old city like Wesel, Germany, the surviving 3 percent would acquire the status of a rare relic of a long gone past. The new world order was sketched out during a few meetings between three heads of state, Roosevelt, Churchill, and Josef Stalin, who—devoid of constituencies, parliaments, votes, or other political formations and organs—imposed themselves as representatives of the world and decided on the injection of a large dose of the new. A singular vision of the new world order, approved by that new organ, the UN, was meant to stifle competing local and regional models of rule and to suppress imaginative civil exploration of what a better world might look like. This is because alternative models might demand redress of civil rights grossly violated in previous centuries. In short, the formation of a supposedly new world order forbade and marginalized experimentation with different political formations for cohabiting in the world based on the heterogeneous traditions and customs of its inhabitants. In the prevailing historical paradigm, the 1945 transition to a new UN-approved world order marked the *end* of an era dominated by World War II and ushered in a sensation of a "new beginning." But this sensation was not an ephemeral moment of celebration, a swift transition from dark to light. Rather, it was a prolonged and carefully crafted transition, enacted violently using the aforementioned policies.

Several books and exhibitions that appeared in the first decades of the twenty-first century used 1945 in their titles, underscoring that much was left unseen under the prevailing "end of era" paradigm.[10] These books attempt to reconstruct the fabric from which this "end" was manufactured. Many of them discuss the Allies' crimes alongside the exposure of Germans to massive abuse at the end of World War II, in a manner that reveals, if only slightly, the cracks in the opposition between the liberators and the aggressors on which human rights discourse was founded.[11] However, the temporal reconsideration of transition was not accompanied by reevaluation of the spatial division between Europe and its colonies in the Pacific, Africa, and Asia, where destruction, massacres, and oppression persisted. "The ironic contrast," writes Martin Shipway, "between metropolitan Liberation and the deferral of colonial liberation may both illuminate and obscure post-war history of French decolonization."[12] The massacres in Setif and Guelma in Algeria, which started on the day of Germany's unconditional surrender, typify events that the joy of liberation buried. Algerians took to the streets to celebrate Germany's surrender and to advance their anticolonial visions of, and aspirations for, a better world—only to be dispersed violently. Thousands were massacred. Separate accounts of this massacre or other destructive interventions in the colonies did not unsettle the separation between Europe and its offshore territories.

Though some of the books referenced above include a cursory selection of photographs, such images, on the whole, are neither discussed nor analyzed as documents out of which accounts of the violence of the "new world order" might be written. An exception is Dagmar Barnouw's photo-based essay, *1945*, published just before the start of this wave of books.[13] The sections of the book devoted to photography are limited compared to the abundant and varied sights people were exposed to in 1945 as part of the Allies' visual literacy classes. Absent from these sections are images of violence perpetrated by Allies in front of millions of eyes, notably in the colonies or in the mass rape of millions of German women perpetrated in the open. As alumni of the visual literacy class of human rights, we have become world citizens through our inherited experience. We inherited visual schemes, legal discourse, and configurations of knowledge production that shape what can be seen and not seen as violence.

How might we relink images to the catastrophe that has been drained from them? We have a choice: Either we can learn anew to identify in these documents the catastrophes that we were trained not to identify and not to associate with accessible visual manifestations. Or, we can continue to acknowledge or celebrate them as moments of liberation or independence. As part of developing a potential history, we can work toward what I call a "rewind reading," that is, a resistant form of recognition that undoes the pedagogical damage absorbed and handed over through these imperial visual lessons. A rewind reading might allow us to relink images to the violence that was exercised at the sites where they were taken, even if the violence is not immediately legible.[14]

A rewind reading begins with a reminder that the particular discourse of human rights promoted by the UN—an organization that unites states so as to rule differentially over their populations—left millions clamoring for human rights.[15] And yet, forced displacement was carried out as a necessary policy and was not approached as a violation of human rights, even though the displacements were fundamentally unjust and in, many cases, resulted in mass deaths. These events include, for example the transfer of twelve million Germans, who were forced to move from East to West under agreements achieved between the Allies immediately after the end of the war; the orchestrated bi-directional transfer of population to create India and Pakistan in 1947; and the transfer of the majority of the Palestinian population from Palestine as part of the creation of Israel as a nation-state between 1948 and 1950.[16] The fact that these violent mechanisms were also employed by quasi-states granted freedom by colonial powers is not coincidental. Rather, it is symptomatic of the strong link between human rights and the right to self-determination in the post–World War II nation-state model. The founding documents of human rights, drafted during and immediately after this war, were implicated in this massive uprooting of peoples and the legitimization of the global Cold War's new imperial order.

The UN idiom, marred by colonialism and imperialism, depicts the world as a playground for intervention and profit-making and not as a common ground shared by people who care for it without seeking to possess it.[17] The UN rights discourse of the new world order preserved the essence of colonial structures. At the level of the colony, as Frederick Cooper argues, the discourse ensures that others "might try to learn and master the ways of the conqueror but would never quite get there," thereby preventing them from claiming their rights within this discourse.[18] That this is the case is illustrated by the very structure of the UN, expressed in the right to veto, implied in article 27: "Decisions of the Security Council on all other matters shall be made by an affirmative vote of nine members including the concurring votes of the permanent members."[19]

On a global scale, the UN ensured that no political models other than those promoted by the imperial actors would survive, and it did so in a manner that left unquestioned the major political formations, key terms, and models generated by colonialism and imperialism.[20] This common narrative of human rights as a "moral and legal basis" is one of the greatest "achievements" of the new world order's political campaign conducted during and after World War II.[21] In this campaign, the human rights discourse promoted by the UN appears as the only possible discourse of human rights, with the organization depicting itself as an innocuous and neutral instrument for implementing human rights, rather than as a player with a vested interest in a particular discourse surrounding such rights.

In contrast to the dominant UN model built on the eighteenth-century American and French revolutions, alternative human rights idioms received short shrift. These overlooked alternatives were provided by Africans, who revolted against their enslavement; by women, who claimed their right to self-rule or to inherit their husbands' property; by freed slaves, who claimed their right to be paid and have their share in the lands they labored; and by the voices of many others in Asia, the Pacific, Africa, or the Americas, who claimed their right to be equally governed in the empires where a differential form of rule was in effect. Since these other claims insisted that injustices be repaired and compensated as part of this "new world," human rights literacy—intent on perpetuating rather than dismantling the imperial condition—ensured that the clamor of voices would remain unheeded. The foundation of the UN was meant to reassess differential ruling as natural, to render past crimes and achievements a fait accompli, and to parcel out the world into discrete national units, each in which a single people enjoyed self-determination while other inhabitants of the territory could be made superfluous and forcibly deported.

The source of the power and wealth of the principal actors who founded the UN was itself an instance of differential ruling. The UN did not, however, invent this differential ruling, which was a principle imposed and preserved since the founding of the "new world." Its preservation was made possible through what is known as "popular sovereignty," which functioned as differential sovereignty, since it was synonymous with the right to self-determination and understood as a permit to cleanse local populations, thereby destroying their common world for the implementation of a new world and state. And yet, the abundance of refugees, infiltrators, and trafficked people in the world are still not seen today as its immediate product. At the core of this model of sovereignty, which was instituted through the French and American revolutions, is a differential body politic, of which only the group of citizens is recognized by the sovereign, on which it relies for recognition and legitimacy.

A rewind reading requires us to recall the ways in which the group of citizens is mobilized to sustain sovereign institutions through externality, that is, as if they were external to their governed subjects, who take little or no role in shaping them. The first issue at stake is citizenship itself. The fact that some people are citizens and others are not is not seen as something that affects their citizenship. The many, whose lives are affected by a construction of citizenship that depends on the production of noncitizens, play their part, whether invented or improvised, within the three-dimensional imperial condition. The UN, however, was fundamental in *bridging*, to use Frederick Cooper's term, "the classic division [ . . . ] between the 'colonial' and the 'post-colonial.'"[22] No wonder, then, that many of those states created during this transition were poor, weak, and often "quasi-states," as Associate Supreme Court Justice Robert H. Jackson termed them.[23] Thus, to criticize the deprivation of certain populations or nations for not having acquired a full state—those that are only "gate-keepers" (Cooper) or "quasi-states" (Jackson)—affirms a particular political model in which differential rule serves as the only possible form of governance. Differential rule permeates various domains of common life and is the outcome of inequalities and the source of subsequent inequalities. The UN set the standard for differential rule as a fait accompli and made it a condition for nation-states seeking admission into its club. Thus, differential rule, without which colonialism and imperialism would never have materialized and survived, was not construed as an exercise of violence. Instead, it formed part and parcel of the law of nation-states.[24]

## WHAT COULD BE SEEN?

The UN and its five permanent member states (the P5 states) used various platforms to distinguish violence from legitimate state violence. Whereas violence constituted a human rights violation, state violence was rationalized as necessary to secure peace, order, and the rule of law. These platforms for such rationalization included press conferences, photography exhibitions, pamphlets, posters, a ban on cameras, and education programs. Through these varied ways of structuring seeing, the UN sought to instill in the public an internalized, personal sense of human rights, one that would produce widespread respect for, and a commitment to, upholding these human rights, and one that would support institutional responses to their violations. People were surrounded by numerous manifestations of violence, whether imprinted in objects and urban textures or captured in images or continuously circulated. They were also compelled or driven to partake in inflicting some of this violence. In this economy of violence, visual literacy classes functioned preeminently as a kind of first aid, a salve to any anxieties that instability would provoke. For those with the need, or for those who were lost and wanted to act as good citizens, the classes provided assurance that authorities could be entrusted to decide between right and wrong.

Consider the work of Magnum photographer Robert Capa, as emblematized in his well-known image, taken in Chartres on August 18, 1944, of French women whose hair had just been shorn as punishment for collaborating with the enemy. Though many people surround and follow these shorn women in the street, the presence of several official agents in uniforms and hats in the public parade—one of them certainly part of the Forces françaises de l'intérieur (French Forces of the Interior [FFI])—deserves our attention. Their uniformed presence endows the scene with a certain sense of acceptability. Indeed, their proximity to the two women (the second can be seen in other frames from the series) is meant to protect them, or to lead them to prison. Yet, the overt smile they exchange with others in the crowd calls into question the kind of protection they provide. Moreover, as many of these situations occurred with the participation of mayors, soldiers, former resistance fighters, or policemen and in public venues like town halls, they functioned in liberated France as occasions for inscribing lines of division so as to restore sovereignty.[25] To claim, as Fabrice Virgili and others do, that these performances of violence helped renew patriotism through unification procedures, is an understatement, however.[26] In fact, these performances accelerate an unstoppable imperial movement. That is, they impose a new world in accordance with the three imperial lines of division, namely, the temporal, spatial, and differential. People had to be both differentiated *and* included; some forms of violence could be celebrated as over, while some populations were still vulnerable to violence; some grievances were to be amplified and construed as unprecedented, and therefore deserving of immediate assistance; meanwhile others were foreclosed, or simply neglected, to the degree that, once they surfaced as grievances, they carried the stamp of a long forgotten past. Violence did not feature in public life as something to be objected to and therefore criminalized, regardless against whom and by whom it was exercised. Indeed, integral to the teaching of visual literacy was the power to state that it was others who exercised violence. This power to condemn certain types of violence was intertwined with the power to inflict violence as a legitimate policy for the common good. The daily teaching, which relied on accessible images, ensured that spectators correctly identified "legitimate" violations of human rights—and subsequently were able to distinguish human rights violators from its guardians.

In short, the teaching of visual literacy was less about particular types of violence that were to be consolidated publicly as categorically intolerable. Rather, this teaching focused on the *contexts* in which violent action was to be recognized as (il)legitimate, depending on where and when and by whom and against whom it was perpetrated. At given moments, certain types of violence ceased, without their perpetrators being incriminated or punished and without their victims being compensated. The impunity of the former group, and the denial of the latter's grievances comprised the terrain on which differential sovereignty was restored. Thus, rape, deportation, and physical abuse of particular groups could be perpetrated as legitimate tools in the constitution of a specific form of sovereignty, that is, *imperial sovereignty.*

In 1945, the pursuit of liberation produced major catastrophes in different places around the world, notwithstanding the celebration by the Allies for the end they brought to the Nazi and Fascist regimes. Although these major catastrophes differed in duration, means, target, justification, casualties, and consequences, they nevertheless shared common features. On the one hand, they were not construed as catastrophes that should be condemned and stopped. On the other hand, they served as the ground on which political sovereignties were imposed or restored. Due to space constraints, I refer here to three major catastrophes: the annihilation of Hiroshima and Nagasaki; the forced migrations of many millions of people; and the rape of millions of German women.

The disaster in Hiroshima and Nagasaki was geographically bounded, so the management of its containment and representation as a non-disaster was relatively easy.[27] As research on this catastrophe has noted, the military occupation of Japan by the United States included censorship, confiscation of films, and other blue-pencil procedures.[28] However, in no sense did these measures entail an effort to conceal the catastrophe; on the contrary, information about it was widely disseminated, in a manner, however, that denied its meaning as a catastrophe. It is only as alumni of these literacy lessons that the emblematic form of the mushroom cloud could be celebrated as it was. That is, these literacy lessons ensured that the mushroom cloud not be perceived as an image of catastrophe, since bodies were absent; thus it could not be perceived as the index of the genocide of several hundreds of thousands of people. Since the crime was perpetrated in plain view, censorship, camera confiscations, and the obscuring of knowledge could not be used to cover up violence. Indeed, the iconic image of the mushroom cloud, or images of scorched earth from across the world, were and are images of catastrophe but are still not widely viewed and recognized as such.[29] That is, the widespread dissemination of such images in the media constituted a visual literacy class wherein people were taught to see them as images of acceptable revenge. Again, this class also entailed that spectators *not* see in these images of catastrophe the catastrophe itself, which is to say, its linkages to power and policy. Spectators were instead trained to picture themselves on the side of the instructors, those able to judge the violation of rights as necessary. As sovereign citizens, spectators were enjoined to comply with authorized power to pursue ultimate justice in the world.[30] Accordingly, although images of destroyed and erased cities were published in many military and victory books printed early in 1945, they provided scant facts regarding victims despite being full of technical details.[31] Moreover, even though the literacy lesson of rights included rather than omitted the destruction of cities in Japan, Germany, Africa, Asia, or the Philippines, this inclusion was differential, based on lines drawn between recognized and unrecognized human rights.

The class's goal was not to develop universal civil skills for recognizing when human rights were violated, regardless of the identity of victims or perpetrators and the justifications provided. Rather, the aim was to emphasize distance, that is, to recognize the distance between actors depicted in a given image, and to appreciate our role as caring, but still distant, spectators. Censorship was used, then, in a nuanced way, as a dynamic line of distribution between the visible and the invisible, and as one mechanism among others. Visual literacy did not entail the repression of violence but rather produced opportunities to talk about violence, analogous to Michel Foucault's account of the repressive hypothesis in the context of the discourse of sexuality.

The displacement of approximately twenty million people, the second catastrophe, which resulted from the implementation of the postwar policy of self-determination, was not contained within a delineated and distant geographical space as was the case with the bombings of Hiroshima and Nagasaki. This phenomenon also occurred simultaneously in different places and continued on a massive scale until the end of the 1940s. In 1945, this displacement was enacted as part of the "solution" to the "problem" posed by "minorities" to the stabilization of a new world order. Forced displacement also continued, masquerading in India and Palestine as an accepted policy for self-determination. In South Africa and other places, forced displacement was pursued as a simple matter of fact, without need for justification. Refugees were viewed in international law, UN conventions, and public debates as either a "problem" or a "solution." However, they were perceived neither as the consequence of abusive power by sovereign regimes nor as the result of a violation of human rights.[32] The literacy classes lay the foundations for the imperial human rights discourse that, to this day, shapes the imaginary of much human rights discourse. Running parallel to this discourse, people continued to claim their rights individually and in tandem with others. In all these disaster zones, the civil performance of rights took place at the moment of disaster. At the same time, this performance persisted in the way that archives were researched and invented. The imperial condition lures us into assessing the distance between these moments and to position ourselves always in the role of discoverers and rescuers.

We can bridge this temporal gap, however, if we rewind the data and revive it at the moment of its occurrence. Allow me to exemplify this through discussion of the third catastrophe: mass rape. So far, images related to the rape of German women in Berlin remain inaccessible; this does not mean that they do not exist. In fact, archives are full of images that were taken in the very places where these rapes occurred. The category of the "untaken photograph" that I theorize elsewhere, in order to make rape present in photographic archives, has become productive once again in my study of the rape of German women on a massive scale by Red Army, American, and French soldiers at the end of World War II.[33] By "untaken photograph," I refer to the construction of a scene, regardless of whether an image was produced. In this account, I provide a radical definition of photography, which is an event that sets in motion a dynamic encounter between different actors as it unfolds in the presence of a camera, even if an image does not appear. The presumed presence of a camera—real or imagined, which is sometimes perceived as a threat (as in, "we are photographing you!")—suffices to create a photographic event. In other words, the lack of photographs cannot cancel out the photographic event that was set in motion by the presence of the camera, nor can it prevent participants from interacting with what the event of photography generated.

With the help of "untaken photographs" of the phenomenon of mass rape in a city where cameras were numerous, we can question the limits of our phenomenological field and, in the process, make available other elements in the archive to be seen differently. What I am suggesting is that each and every camera present in Berlin during those weeks, when rape was a widespread occurrence, stands in for the untaken photographs of this crime. From the moment this untaken photograph occupies its place in the archive, other items in these archives are necessarily reconfigured. For example, the untaken photograph can take the form of a verbal description, a testimony, a drawing, or a photograph produced following the visual description of one of the participants in the event of photography.

The postwar displacement of populations was not criminalized but was instead made into a required condition to become a successful sovereign regime. This, in turn, was a required condition to gain recognition—and consequently aid and access to foreign markets—by other UN members. Those orchestrating the massive waves of forced migration as a way to end the war were also those running the class in human rights literacy and thus the ultimate arbiters of what constituted human rights violations. These displacements, however, should not be studied solely as affecting their victims. Rather, they shaped the civil skills of millions of people—those who perpetrated them, those who were their victims, and those who bore witness to them—thereby creating the conditions for the archival acceptability of this crime. It is only when these different positions in the occurrence of disaster are assembled to form a whole that we can start to see the scope of the "visual literacy class" in human rights. It is important to emphasize that the primary aim of this class curriculum was to shatter the possibility of assembling such a whole, that is, the whole out of which a catastrophe can be seen for what it is. The inculcation of human rights under the principle of differential rule, reproduced through sovereign nation-states that incarnate this principle, has determined the fate of superfluous populations ever since.

Let me reiterate. Censorship mechanisms—confiscation; appropriation; the looting and savaging of books, films, archives, and works of art; the burning of newspapers—should be studied not solely from the point of view of their direct victims nor solely as acts of concealment.[34] They should be understood as forms and modalities constitutive of imperial sovereignties that were promoted on a mass scale at the end of World War II.[35] The combined pursuit of liberation from violence that should be criminalized and the pursuit of violence that should be tolerated was essential to the process of replacing the human condition, as theorized by Hannah Arendt, with the imperial condition. Literacy classes provided a structure of human rights seeing, transforming the distinction between types of violence into a temporal distinction between what the Allies ended and the new era. Had the imperial triple principle not been imposed with such violence as "the *conditio sine qua non* of all political life," the catastrophe of war might have ended differently, leaving in its wake the prospect for people to shape and restore a variety of political formations for sharing the world among themselves—what Arendt, in *The Human Condition*, simply called "politics." The triple imperial principle squandered such prospects, enabling the Allies to rebuild their world by narrowly conforming to notions such as self-determination, liberation, and partition that limited political life to the pursuit of goals construed as historical progress. By rendering violence into acceptable tools for the pursuit of "freedom" and "peace," imperial visual literacy tools hindered its students' capacity to acquire a broader range of civil skills, not to mention their capacity to identify violence in ways separate from the justifications provided by the Allies.[36]

The massive campaign of displaying in the United States and Britain photographic images from the liberation of the death camps, as well as images from the camps themselves, are at the center of Barbie Zelizer's book, *Remembering to Forget*.[37] Zelizer argues that behind this campaign was the conviction that "the record of the camps' liberation was mandated to be seen."[38] These images were shown as an exception, thus preventing the creation of a common ground to identify human rights violations, and commanding that these should not be compared to any other occurrence of mass extermination.[39] The goal of the campaign, Zelizer argues, was to "go beyond the mere authentication of horror and to imply the act of *bearing witness*, by which we assume responsibility for the events of our times."[40] In contrast to Zelizer, I argue that the capacity to identify—and concomitantly the capacity to assume responsibility for—events happening under our watch is damaged when the grounds on which people account for such crimes is not common, and when one crime is differentiated from another in principle, but without the possibility of debating it openly. Zelizer depicts bearing witness "as a type of collective remembering, [that] goes beyond the events it depicts, positioning the atrocity photos as a frame for understanding contemporary instances of atrocity."[41] Zelizer does not question, on the one hand, how the figure of the witness was construed in relation to the phenomenal field of catastrophe that was delineated in these kinds of literacy lessons. Nor, on the other hand, does she examine how the understanding of contemporary instances of atrocity came to be affected by the propagandistic procedures she describes, that included "strategic recycling" of images—namely the omission of others—and "governmental persuasion."

Almost a decade and a half later, Sharon Sliwinski returns to these images of the liberation of the camps and argues that "indeed what these photographs engendered was something more akin to a paradox: the public bore witness in 1945, but they did not know what they had seen."[42] Sliwinski bases her claim on a historical reconstruction of the belated introduction of the term *holocaust* to the discourse: "Despite the profusion of pictures, it took several decades for the idea of 'the Holocaust' to find expression in public discourse."[43] Despite the absence of the idea, Sliwinski relates to these images as phenomenal manifestations of the Holocaust: "Before the idea of the Holocaust entered public imagination, spectators found themselves gazing upon its image."[44] This argument is problematic both historically and theoretically. In the Buchenwald camp, more than thirty thousand people died, non-Jews in addition to Jews. Non-Jewish Poles, Roma people, slaves, the mentally ill, and the disabled, as well POWs, and religious and political prisoners from all over Europe, were among the piles of corpses captured in the photographs taken there. The piles of indistinguishable naked bodies were the ultimate challenge to the differentiation of the catastrophe along any lines of division. The belated and inaccurate association of these images with "the Holocaust"—that is, with the extermination of Jews by the Nazi regime—is not due to the images being images *of* the holocaust. Rather, this association is due to what could be called a "Holocaust campaign," which imposed a political vision upon the photographed catastrophe. The goal of the Holocaust campaign was to single out the extermination of the Jews, to set them apart from the Nazi extermination plans for other peoples, thus making the Jews' extermination (and "the Holocaust") incomparable to other disasters.[45] But even if the corpses recorded in the images were (solely) of Jews, images are never *of* an idea. An image can serve as fertile ground on which political ideas can be planted and grown, giving the illusion that these ideas arise naturally from the mere image.[46] The absence of the meta-signifier, "holocaust," at the moment when people viewed these images for the first time, does not mean that they were incapable of knowing what was in view. It also does not exclude other meta-signifiers from being at play during the viewing, such as "human rights violation."

At stake at the end of World War II was the capacity of citizens to identify and account for what they saw and to develop their civil skills to recognize violations. Hunger, debris, loss, poverty, homelessness, refugees, raped women, torn bodies, and corpses were sights that people encountered everywhere. At the same time, they participated in these sights as actors, extras (in the cinematic sense), or spectators. Many of these catastrophic sights were concrete events and, in fact, were not presented as images. Nor did images depict past events of defeated regimes. The voices of millions of people forced to leave their homes, and the accounts of millions of raped German women were excluded from the curriculum of the human rights literacy class. In Austria and Germany, dozens of press photographers were trained in the photographic "American model" and worked in US "opinion-research institutes," the Information Service Branch (ISB) and the United States Information Agency (USIA) in their countries.[47] These catastrophic situations and sights flashed in front of citizens' eyes, in swift or slow operations carried out by the Allies to end the war, and yet disappeared from the visual literacy curriculum. The organizing ideas of these sights were articulated through key political terms that had to be learned and ingrained: "peace," "human rights," "sovereignty," "democracy," "independence," "war-ending," or "world order." These visual literacy classes encouraged citizen-spectators to view images as emanating from these ideas and to learn to recognize them in the images.

Visual literacy is hence about the skills of the governed population in identifying its role within the political regime and in acknowledging the distinction between legitimate and illegitimate violence and between acceptable measures and their rights, which should not be violated under any circumstances. Classes were conducted wherever the new world order was implemented. In some places, these classes were loosely structured. Sometimes the local population conducted them. In other cases, classes were organized and intense, and photographs and films were used to demonstrate violations of human rights par excellence, thereby endorsing the authority of those showing them as guardians of rights. Photographs used in this way depicted violations that had already taken place, which were crimes caused by "them" not "us." The images of piles of corpses are a paradigmatic example, since the perpetrators were not only identified—"Nazis"—but had also already been defeated by those who presented the photos. Visual literacy was thus, again, about instilling *distance*, the distance between "us" and "them" (identified as perpetrators), as well as the distance between perpetrators, victims, and spectators. Exceptions to this dynamic of distance were Germans, Austrians, and Japanese, who were required to recognize themselves as perpetrators and bear collective guilt for images branded as being "of" human rights violations.

German women were not allowed to talk about their rape, and after a brief lesson given to Germans in the liberated camps, where they were taught to recognize what is a violation of human rights, they were made economic actors in the implementation of the Marshall plan and represented in photos "witnessing the first sounds of the Freedom Bell"; and they were then christened as inhabitants of "Berlin, the bastion of Freedom," with whom trade must be renewed. The voices of millions of people forced to leave their homes, and the accounts of millions of raped German women were excluded from the curriculum of the human rights literacy class.

There always existed the possibility of a different reading of images of violence justified as "policy." Notably, W. J. T. Mitchell proposes a general scheme, which he terms "the dialectics of migration," that provides a model for how to undo the limits of the photographic frame. Wherever a photograph is used to show "exit," read "entrance"; for "departure," read "arrival"; for "nomad," read "settler"; for "expulsion," read "invasion"; or for "refugee," read "detainee."[48] While we do not know how many citizens resisted the wide-reaching literacy class, we must assume their existence as part of the civil resistance to sovereignty that has always been performed.[49] Citizens who did not internalize the lesson were often those uncounted by the differential body politic. Citizens of states who were appointed as guardians of human rights were shaped in the image of the differential sovereign citizen, a subject whose rights—unlike those of noncitizens with whom she is governed—were protected by the nation-state. These "citizen guardians" were often unaware of the role of their citizenship in perpetuating differential rule.

The photographic discourse of human rights shaped during and following World War II positions the *spectator* outside the situation of rights violations and positions the *victim* at the very heart of this discourse by attributing to the victim a place and a distinct voice. The discourse thereby implicitly conflates the subject of human rights with the visibility of the violation of such rights. The *perpetrator* is typically invisible in this configuration and therefore can be selectively abstracted, generalized, or demonized.[50] Perhaps most importantly, this discourse poses a sharp distinction between these three "categories"—the perpetrator, the victim, the spectator—and presents a clear "division of labor" among them. This division of labor positions the spectator outside the situation, disconnected from the perpetrator and the victim, and therefore absolves the spectator of any potential link to the perpetrator.

This is why perpetrators, especially those in positions as statesmen who do not perpetrate violence themselves, tend to position themselves as spectators when an outcry follows the disaster they created. Thus, speaking in the House of Commons on August 16, 1945, Winston Churchill, could state: "With *the reports reaching us* of the conditions under which the expulsion and exodus of Germans from the New Poland are carried out [ . . . ] it is not impossible that tragedy on a prodigious scale is *unfolding itself* behind the iron curtain."[51] That is, he did so as if he were not responsible for helping to decide on what he described as a tragic policy of forced migration. Crucially, the spectator must be a sovereign citizen in order to be absolved from responsibility and enjoy the stamp of "non-perpetrator." In other words, this scheme rewards and reinforces the canonical model of nation-states that differentially offer such benefits to those governed as citizens under their rule.

When citizens are taught to misidentify the forced transfer of people from their homelands, or their incarceration in refugee camps, as part of a legitimate sovereign plan and policy rather than as a violation of human rights by that sovereign policy, their capacity to recognize such violations diminishes. Citizens gradually learn to obey sovereign policy because it is the law, not because that policy is just.

Though the abstention of the USSR and other Soviet Bloc countries from voting on the Universal Declaration of Human Rights in 1948 is often explained as the diverging approaches of the two blocs to the question of human rights, assumed to be an implicit part of the Cold War, they actually shared several pivotal objectives.[52] Historian Petra Goedde adds another incident to this common narrative of opposition that illustrates Cold War polarity: "At the very moment of the adoption of the declaration in New York, the United States brought accusations of human rights violations against the Soviet Union before the United Nations." The reason was the blockade of "all traffic between the Western-controlled parts of Berlin and the Western Zones of Germany in protest over the currency reform implemented by the Western Allies." In this scene of conflict, it is no wonder that the Soviet Union retaliated and exposed "America's dismal human rights record regarding its African American population."[53] Meanwhile, the military occupation of Germany, the forced reeducation of its population, the destruction of its cities, and the killing of hundreds of thousands of civilians beyond clear military aims perpetrated by the Allies are not construed as human rights violations.

Counterexamples to the narrative of opposition between the superpowers are not exceptions to the rule. Paradigmatic in this regard is their agreement on the creation of the state of Israel in 1948. The dominance of this narrative of opposition between the United States and the USSR in part legitimized their status as "superpowers," enabling them to occupy others' states, to draw arbitrary lines within their social and cultural fabrics, to partition territories, and consequently to divide and displace populations. In sum, it gave them carte blanche to subjugate other states to their standards, terminologies, visions, and models. The superpowers used violent mechanisms to divide the world into two blocs that were in turn subdivided into weak sovereign states. These mechanisms enabled the superpowers to enforce their rule across vast populations. The imperial Cold War curriculum, which reinforced a human rights visual literacy, further entrenched this rule.

## *Notes*

1 This opposition was solidified in the 1945 UN charter that designated an "enemy state" and granted the Allies exceptional power toward these states. Forcing Japan and Germany to accept unconditional surrender, rather than negotiating a peace agreement, had already been agreed upon by the early 1940s and involved plans for military occupation, the displacement of populations, and border corrections. For more on these plans in relation to Germany, see Nordbruch, *Bleeding Germany Dry*, 23–86.

2 On November 30 and December 1, 1944, French forces murdered a number of French West African troops who had mutinied because of discriminatory practices, most notably, with respect to pensions. Ousmene Sembène's film, *Camp de Thiaroye* (1988) depicts this case by foregrounding the colonized soldiers' discourse of rights.

3 North Atlantic Treaty Organization, "The Atlantic Charter," NATO/OTAN, August 14, 1941, https://www.nato.int/cps/en/natolive/official_texts_16912.htm.

4 For Lenin, "the multi-national state represents backwardness" and the "national state" was necessary for the development of capitalism. Samuel Moyn argues that it was the anticolonialists in the post–World War II era who "proved to be more interested in the twentieth-century reformulation of that linkage by V. I. Lenin and Woodrow Wilson a 'self-determination of peoples.'" Moyn, *The Last Utopia*, 85.

5 As is well known, one of the goals of dividing Germany in 1945 into zones of control was to obliterate Germany as a superpower, placing its further development under the Allies' control. Germany was not the only state whose growth and empowerment were limited by the two superpowers. Robert Jackson argues that the international coalition "has presided over the birth of numerous marginal entities [ . . . ], guarantees their survival, and seeks at least to compensate them for underdevelopment if not to develop them into substantial independent countries." Jackson, *Quasi-States*, 23.

6 Rosa Luxemburg's prognosis became the reality: "Can one seriously speak about the 'self-determination' of the formally independent Montenegrins, Bulgarians, Rumanians, Serbs, Greeks, partly even the Swiss, whose independence is itself a result of the political struggle and the diplomatic game of the 'concert of Europe'?!" [ . . . ] The state that best suits these conditions is "not a national state, as Kautsky believes, but a predatory one." Luxembourg, quoted in Vladimir Ilyich Lenin, "The Right of Nations to Self-Determination."

7 Gearty Conor asserts this limited understanding of photography qua photographs at the heart of human rights as a visibility project: "Human rights in this sense is a visibility project. Its driving focus is to get us to see the people around us, particularly those who we might otherwise (only slightly metaphorically speaking) not see at all, or those whom we would try to ignore if we would catch a glimpse of them." Conor, *Can Human Rights Survive?*, 5.

8 On the work of the censure in shaping the image of the war, see, for example, Maslowski, *Armed with Cameras*.

9 On the centrality of the mushroom cloud in the Cold War, see Masco, *The Theater of Operations*.

10 Among them are Schumann and Kroh, *Berlin nach dem Krieg*; or Brettin and Kroh, *Berlin 1945*. This interest in 1945 is not unprecedented, but is remarkable for the number of titles that were published in one decade. Already in 1945, some reports on the plight of Germans were published, such as Mosley, *Report from Germany*, or Byford-Jones, *Berlin Twilight*. Scattered oppositional voices to the plight of the Japanese and Germans were already loud back then too.

11 Stafford, *Endgame, 1945*, 580; Dallas, *1945: The War that Never Ended*, 738; Burma, *Year Zero*, 353; Judt, *Post War*, 933. Among the photographic collections and exhibitions, see Schumann and Kroh, *Berlin nach dem Krieg*; and *1945—Defeat. Liberation. New Beginning: Twelve European Countries after the Second World War*, April 24–October 25, 2015, Deutsches Historisches Museum, Berlin.

12 Shipway, *Decolonization and Its Impact*, 139.

13 Barnouw, *1945: Views of War and Violence*.

14 See my discussion of images of rape of German women in Azoulay, *Potential History*.

15 W. E. B. Dubois related "750,000,000 clamoring for human rights," including only those who were not counted politically. Dubois quoted in Moyn, *The Last Utopia*, 265.

16 On forced migration, see Mazower, *No Enchanted Palace*. On their public protest, see Moeller, "War Stories"; Pluhařová, "A National Discovery and Loss of a Landscape."

17 The world in the second sense would be that described by Arendt, in *The Human Condition*, or by Linebauch in *The Magna Carta Manifesto*.

18 Cooper, *Africa since 1940*, 16.

19 See United Nations, "Charter of the United Nations, June 26, 1945," Avalon Project, Yale Law School, https://avalon.law.yale.edu/20th_century/unchart.asp#art27. The right to veto was also part of the logic of the League of Nations.

20 Jackson, *Quasi-States*, 4.

21 See Azoulay, "Palestine as Symptom."

22 Cooper, *Africa since 1940*, 15.

23 On quasi-states, see Jackson, *Quasi-States*.

24 See Noam Chomsky's criticism of the nation-state: "The nation state is pretty much a European invention, I mean there were similar things, but the nation state in the modern form was largely created in Europe over many centuries. It's so unnatural and artificial that it had to be imposed by extreme violence. In fact, that's the primary reason why Europe was the most savage part of the world for centuries. It was due to trying to impose a nation state system on cultures and societies that are varied and if you look at them had no relation to this artificial structure." Chomsky, "State and Corp." I'm grateful to Yarden Katz for this reference.

25 Fabrice Virgilli mentions that the practice took place publicly in at least 322 communes in France. She describes the situation where they occurred as a "climate of patriotism," arguing that "the number of places used and the various processions allowed everyone to have a sight of the women whose heads had been shaved." Virgilli, *Shorn Women*, 229.

26 Virgilli, *Shorn Women*.

27 Contained as the annihilation of Hiroshima and Nagasaki was, the imperial condition responsible for the globalization of catastrophe, rendering belief in the capacity to delineate the consequences of disaster as always temporary, can be read in this testimony of a White House photographer: "After twenty years as a White House photographer, I retired with a medical disability later discovered to be caused by my radiation exposure. While numerous surgeries and treatments helped to ease my physical suffering (which can't be compared to the sufferings of those unfortunate people who survived the bomb) I remained obsessed by what I had seen." O'Donnell, *Japan 1945*, xiii.

28 See Dower, "The Bombed."

29 See Bruning, *Bombs Away!*

30 See Deák, *Europe on Trial*; Deák, Gross, and Judt, *The Politics of Retribution in Europe*.

31 See for example *Battle Stations! Your Navy in Action*.

32 On the millions of Germans, Poles, Slovaks, Albanians, Indians, Palestinians, Chinese, Jews (after World War II), and South Africans, Ukrainians, and others, who were expelled from their homes, see Mazower, *No Enchanted Palace*.

33 On the rape by Red Army soldiers, see *A Woman in Berlin*. In all these books on 1945, the rape is discussed but, as stated, presented without visual reference.

34 On the surface, these procedures were used for pursuing ends such as the de-Nazification of Germany or Austria; but they were also used independently of such ends, for other ends, or often, for their own sake. On the looting by the Allies see, for example, Alford, *Allied Looting in World War II*; Akinsha, Kozlov, and Hochfield, *Beautiful Loot*; on the redistribution of looted books from Jewish communities, to Israel and the US, under the label of salvage and return, see the correspondence between Hannah Arendt and Gershom Scholem, edited by Marie Luise Knott, *Hannah Arendt/Gershom Scholem*.

35 On the way in which the democratic press combined with censorship, see the interview with Robert Lochner who was involved in the "revival of free media" in Germany after World War II. Lochner, "Interview with Robert Lochner."

36 These ideas were articulated in relation to specific historical narratives in each country. Thus, for example, Dallas describes the following: "In France the main subject of polemic and 'historical' court cases has been, over the last thirty years, Vichy administrators and their treatment of the Jews; in Germany, it is the mix of business with the past Nazi crimes; in Italy and Spain it is the 'cover-up' of past membership. . . ." Dallas, *1945: The War That Never Ended*, 512.

37 On these campaigns see also Olick, *In the House of the Hangman.*

38 Zelizer describes how "over a three-week period in April and May 1945, photographs—produced to convince a disbelieving public that what the liberating forces were seeing was real—were splashed in prodigious numbers across the pages of the daily and weekly press in the United States and Britain." Zelizer, *Remembering to Forget*, 11–12.

39 See Grandin, *The Last Colonial Massacre.*

40 Zelizer, *Remembering to Forget*, 10.

41 Zelizer, *Remembering to Forget*, 13.

42 Sliwinski, *Human Rights in Camera*, 83. Inspired by Felman's figure of the witness, Sliwinski also uses the category of the witness in relation to those images but in its psychoanalytic acceptance of a process that "does not offer a complete statement but rather addresses the impact of events that cannot be fully assimilated into cognition, events that exceed the available frames of reference." Sliwinski, *Human Rights in Camera*, 87.

43 Sliwinski, *Human Rights in Camera*, 84. However, the introduction of the term *holocaust*, which had previously designated other genocides like that of the Armenians, entailed the elimination of millions of non-Jewish victims from the term and its transformation into a synonym of the extermination of Jews only. See Teres Pencak Schwarz, "Five Million Forgotten: Non Jewish Victims of the Shoah," remember.org, accessed January 5, 2022, http://remember.org/forgotten.

44 Sliwinski, *Human Rights in Camera*, 83.

45 On the instrumentalization of the holocaust see Zertal, *Israel's Holocaust and the Politics of Nationhood.*

46 Sliwinski's assumption that an idea is at the origin of these images is refuted by her own effort to read images and words from these early encounters as "an optic through which to grasp the shock of confronting the camps." Sliwinski, *Human Rights in Camera*, 87.

47 See Wagnleitner, *Coca-Colonization and the Cold War.*

48 Mitchell, *Seeing through Race.*

49 See Azoulay, "Revolutionary Moments and State Violence."

50 The identity of the photographer and his positioning in relation to the catastrophe

out of which photographs are produced are extremely valuable to their reading. See for example Marianne Hirsch's discussion of photographs taken by perpetrators. Hirsch, "Nazi Photographs in Post-Holocaust Art." The association of certain catastrophes with distinct perpetrators, even if they are rendered anonymous, is relatively easy in certain major disasters that were acknowledged as such under the imperial condition. Because I associate the position of perpetrators with citizens under the imperial condition, this association is more complex, since the fluctuation between positions is more dynamic. See my discussion of the perpetrator in Azoulay, "The Execution Portrait."

51 Quoted in Botting, *Ruins of the Reich*, 189, emphasis added.

52 The USSR's representative participated in the series of meetings that preceded the signature ceremony. On his exchanges with other members of the committee, see Glendon, *A World Made New.*

53 Goedde, *GIs and Germans*, 652–53.

# 9

SARAH PARSONS

# "Planted There Like Human Flags"

## PHOTOGRAPHS OF THE HIGH ARCTIC AND COLD WAR ANXIETY, 1951–1956

On September 2, 1951, Alex Stevenson, administrative officer in charge of the Eastern Canadian Arctic patrol, telegrammed his supervisors at the Department of Resources and Development in Ottawa reporting proudly that, "SERVICE INCLUDED APPROPRIATE ANTHEMS [STOP] SHIP PASSENGERS COMMA ESKIMO FAMILIES IN ATTENDANCE [STOP] SNOW CLAD MOUNTAINS COMMA ICEBERGS COMMA GLACIERS TUNDRA AND WHITE CARIBOU FORMED BACKDROP FOR IMPRESSIVE OCCASION [STOP] FILM BOARD UNIT COVERAGE."[1] This pomp and circumstance heralded the re-

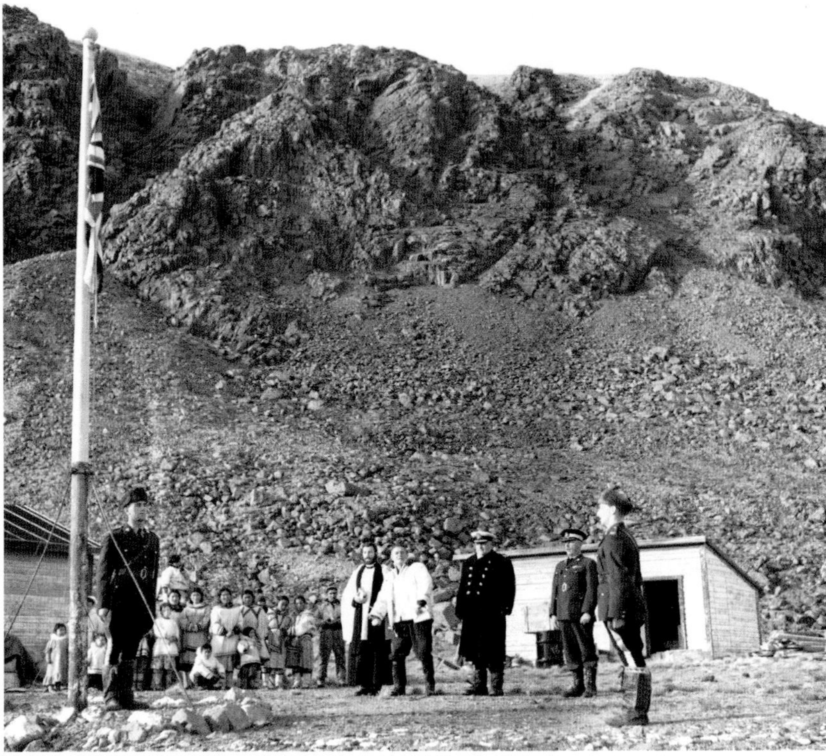

establishment of a tiny Royal Canadian Mounted Police post in Craig Harbour on the southern tip of Ellesmere Island in the High Arctic. Even by Arctic standards, this location is remote. Located seven hundred miles north of the Arctic Circle, Craig Harbour was accessible by government supply ship once a year in summer. Everything seen in this National Film Board photograph (figure 9.1) had to be transported there, and anyone who did not get back on the ship that evening was staying for the year. What prompted the incredible labor, high cost, and elaborate ceremony to reestablish a remote post that had been abandoned years earlier because it was too difficult to maintain and in an area the Inuit had already abandoned in the 1700s? The ambitious final phrase of Stevenson's telegram, carefully left off the official press release the next day, offers a clue. It announced: "SOVEREIGNTY NOW IS A CINCH." The boldness of this claim belies the anxiety it sought to relieve.

In the 1950s, the Canadian concern with state sovereignty amplified to hysterical levels, which can best be understood in the context of Cold War paranoia. Indeed, this was a period when Canada moved out from the shadow of

**Figure 9.1.** **Flag raising at Craig Harbour, Eastern Arctic, 1951. Photograph by Douglas Wilkinson. Courtesy National Film Board of Canada, Still Photography Division, Library and Archives Canada**

mother England (note the flag in the photograph is the Union Jack) only to step into the shadow of its superpower neighbors to the south. During World War II, the US military built airbases in the Canadian Arctic to refuel planes on their way to European theaters of war. One of the largest bases at Frobisher Bay, located on Baffin Island, was constructed in 1942, and by the following year it had a significant population and infrastructure and was not only serving aircraft but also providing crucial long-range weather reports to support European operations.[2] When the war ended, the Canadian government expected the US presence in the Arctic to dissipate. Instead of withdrawing and as Cold War tensions increased, the US government developed a plan in 1946 to build weather stations across this vast zone. Canada balked but, in 1947 negotiated to proceed jointly, albeit to contribute minimally to the costly construction. At the same time, the Canadian government insisted on taking over operations and providing personnel once these stations were completed. Although the five weather stations built by US Air Force and Army engineers between 1947 and 1950 had no official military or industrial mandate, the information they provided was crucial for both realms of activity, especially air travel. They were part of an infrastructure of aerial surveillance connected to war, whether directly or indirectly, according to Caren Caplan.[3] Four of the five stations (Eureka, Isachsen, Mould Bay, and Alert) were located along the coast of the Arctic Ocean, far north of any previous or subsequent settlements. The fifth station was in Resolute, on Cornwallis Island, southwest of Craig Harbour.

Meanwhile, observers in the USSR tracked the tense negotiations concerning Arctic construction. In 1952, a Soviet press report concluded, both prophetically and rather poetically, "Naturally the gaze of the American imperialists has not been attracted by the wild beauty of polar nature . . . or the limitless expanse of snowy tundra in Northern Canada. The eye of the

American businessman notes none of this. . . . In the name of new profits, Wall street [*sic*] carries on feverish preparations for a new world war."[4] Sure enough, a few months later, a group of scientists gathered at MIT to consider the vulnerability of the United States to bombing attacks. When the Truman administration accepted the group's recommendation in December 1952 to proceed with what would become the Distant Early Warning (DEW) line—the US plan to build dozens of stations to create a 9,000-mile radar detection fence along the 69th parallel in the High Arctic, from Alaska to Greenland—Canadian sovereignty panic intensified. When the Canadian cabinet met in January 1953, Prime Minister Louis Saint-Laurent fretted that, "US developments might be just about the only form of human activity in the vast wastelands of the Canadian Arctic."[5] These events, which marked the development of aerial surveillance of northern territory that was becoming increasingly contested, highlight the potential advantage afforded to a vertical vantage point.

The government struggled to gain control over the representation of its vast northern holdings just as it struggled to gain and retain practical control of the scientific, economic, and military operations in the Arctic. In the months leading up to the 1951 photo op in Craig Harbour, internal Canadian government memos expressed two related concerns: first, Thule Inuit hunters from Greenland were crossing the channel to hunt on Ellesmere Island; and second, the United States planned to build a large Air Force base just across the channel at Thule, in Greenland. The presence of anyone—even a few Greenlanders—on Canadian soil posed a threat to national sovereignty, and Canadians feared the United States would take advantage of this vulnerability as they built up their presence in the area as part of their larger plan to gain a strategic advantage in the north. The frozen tundra may not immediately present itself as a theater of the Cold War, but Cold War geopolitics dramatically shaped the Arctic.

Whereas during World War II, US airbases brought people, construction, massive airfields, and jobs to various remote areas so that the whole Arctic region became more visible than it had ever been before, the political climate shifted during the Cold War. A commissioned 1950 *Report on Canadian Sovereignty in the Arctic*, advised that Canadian title to the Arctic must be asserted through "effective occupation alone as the chief and most satisfactory ground of reliance."[6] However, effective occupation had long proved difficult due to the relatively tiny and disparate population in the north.[7] Though the Inuit occupied some of the land in the north, their presence could not easily be seen—as their seminomadic lifestyle left few visible marks on the landscape, making it difficult for the state to establish sovereignty.[8] Within this context of mounting geopolitical pressure, the Canadian government decided to reestablish Craig Harbour as a government outpost. Significantly, Stevenson's telegram links the National Film Board's coverage of Craig Harbour to sovereignty in a way that crucially suggests the potential for visual technologies to recalibrate geopolitical power relations.

This chapter explores how the settler-colonial state enlisted photography to highlight the visual presence of Inuit people as a means by which to establish sovereignty claims in the High Arctic during the global Cold War. The settler-colonial state focused the camera on Inuit people deliberately. The Inuit, because they were indigenous to Canada—even though they did not inhabit the High Arctic (which had been uninhabitable)—enabled the state to stake an autochthonous, that is, an Indigenous, claim to this territory. From their responses to photographs that highlighted problems in the Arctic to the outright government support for photojournalism, the Canadian government was highly attuned to camera diplomacy in this moment. As photo historian Carol Payne notes in her pioneering study of the Still Photographs Division of the National Film Board (NFB) of Canada, the quantity of coverage the NFB directed to the North was disproportionate to its relatively tiny population,[9] but it was crucially in line with intertwined political and economic priorities. Official photos of the Craig Harbour event, accompanied by Stevenson's telegram description, implied that this post and its Royal Canadian Mounted Police (RCMP) officer had been brought to the Inuit families inhabiting Craig Harbour. These accounts, however, obscured the fact that the families did not originally live there, but instead had been relocated to this settlement from Dundas Harbour, an RCMP post farther south that closed in order to reopen Craig Harbour. The official NFB photograph does not convey the full scope of Stevenson's description of the event, but it captures the key combination of state ceremony and naturalized inhabitants. The young RCMP officer stands straight as a rod underneath the towering flagpole. Another uniformed RCMP officer performs the ceremony while being witnessed by a member of the clergy, Alex Stevenson, naval Captain Chouinard, and RCMP Inspector Henry Larsen. The two RCMP officers and Stevenson have adjusted their uniforms in a cultural bridge to Arctic culture by donning traditional kamik boots, and Stevenson also wears a white hide parka. While the Inuit families in traditional clothing are relegated to the background behind the young RCMP officer who dramatically outstrips them in scale, they are arguably the most important aspect of the Craig Harbour flag-raising and its photographic record. The archetypal treeless landscape in the background

**Figure 9.2.** Craig Harbour, Nunavut, 1951. Photograph by Vivian Wilkinson. Courtesy Nunavut Archives, Douglas Wilkinson fonds, N-1979-051: 0070S.

and the flag in the foreground convey a sense of place. And yet place, when unoccupied, does not suffice to establish sovereignty. Clustered as a small yet substantial group in the background and that almost retreats into the intractable landscape—as natural as the rocky terrain that their sheer presence nevertheless has overcome—they symbolically reinforce the central nationalistic message of the foreground. Inuit were the human flagpoles that anchored Canada's northern sovereignty.[10]

I contend that the strategy of photographing Inuit on the ground as a means of asserting settler-colonial authority flips the dynamic that Nicholas Mirzeoff describes in his influential analysis of imperial visual power. In *The Right to Look*, Mirzoeff argues that power asserts itself in geometric terms, with state sovereignty exerted vertically, notably through aerial surveillance, and insurgent power functioning on a horizontal plane. "The place of visualization," he contends, "has literally and metaphorically continued to distance itself from the subject being viewed, intensifying first to that of aerial photography and more recently to that of satellites, practical means of domination and surveillance."[11] Maps could ably represent military and scientific incursions, but a bird's-eye view was unable to fill this apparent terra incognita in Canada, notwithstanding the tensions arising from aerial infrastructures including the weather stations and DEW line briefly outlined above. Instead, the state recognized that the task of claiming this territory by populating the land could be done only through the camera on the ground.

To challenge US encroachment, the Canadian state deployed a horizontal strategy of depicting Inuit people on the ground to justify and authenticate this place as a settlement.[12]

The extent to which the reopening of Craig Harbour was an event enacted for cameras is revealed in an almost simultaneous snapshot by Vivian Wilkinson (figure 9.2). Her color snapshot shows us two camera operators, presumably her husband, Doug Wilkinson, and Jean Roy, who ensured both still and moving coverage of the event. Yet, the snapshot also captures a stage-

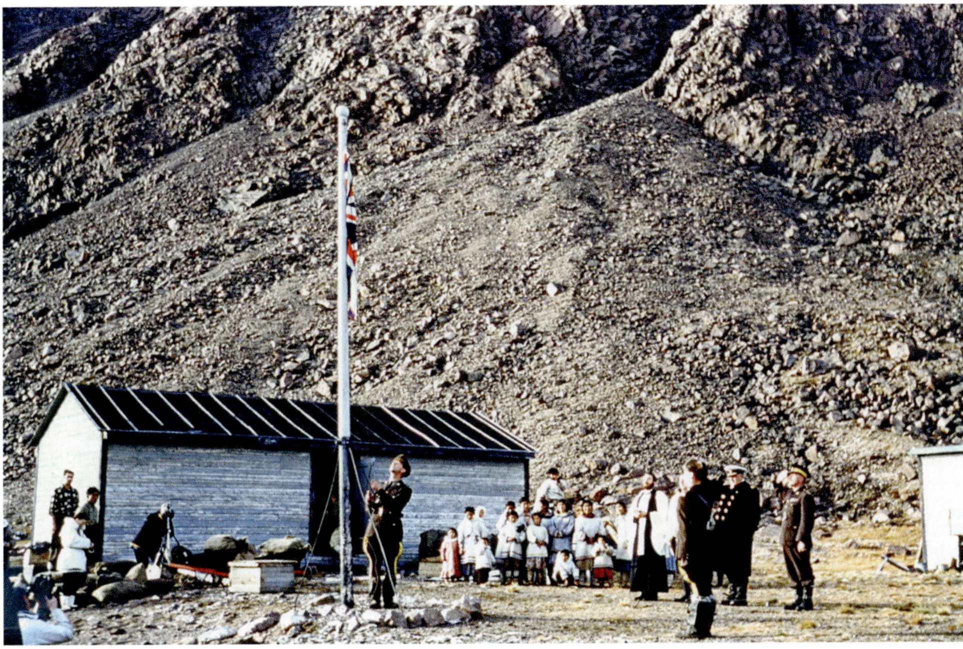

managed set where various people out of costume stay out of the frame, including RCMP Special Inuk Constable Joe Panikpakoochoo who stands to the left of the frame wearing a collared shirt and trousers with suspenders, an outfit distinct from the traditionally dressed Inuit pictured in the official photograph.[13] Careful deployment of photography formed part of a broader Canadian claim to national sovereignty that was, nevertheless inextricably shaped by the context of global Cold War geopolitics as it converged with settler colonialism. At the same time that the Canadian state's visual strategy responded to the potential pressures of competing land claims, this strategy hinged on exploiting the Inuit people who, as I explain below, were forcibly relocated, and on appropriating their indigeneity to wrest control of territory.

## PICTURING INUIT LIFE AND "MODERNIZED" SETTLEMENTS

Photography played a significant role in stoking debates about whether the best future for the Inuit lay in holding onto traditional ways or through assimilation, debates that would acquire greater urgency in the Cold War era. Reflecting on that period in a 1981 documentary, Inuit leader John Amogoalik observed, "The first time I saw a white man, he had a camera and it seems that whenever government officials or tourists came North, they always had cameras and they projected what we considered to [be] the wrong images of the Inuit—the Hollywood image or the stereotype image."[14] Amogoalik suggests the photographers' preconceived notions of Inuit life had a long and storied history. Internationally, the image of the Canadian North and its inhabitants was indelibly shaped by *Nanook of the North: A Story of Life and Love in the Actual Arctic*, a 1922 American silent "documentary" film by Robert J. Flaherty. Filmed entirely in the ethnographic present, Flaherty calls his star (whose real name was Allakariallak), "a kindly, brave, simple Eskimo," and his people (the Inukjuamiut of Northern Quebec) "the fearless, loveable, happy go lucky Eskimo." The NFB image of Craig Harbour captures this way of representing the Inuit. In beautiful, pristine traditional garments, the Inuit families are physically separated from the government and religious officials. In this event, they played the proscribed role of docile witnesses.

The cooperative participation of the Inuit families belied the complexity of Inuit responses to the settler-colonial state, which treated them poorly, to say the least. Indeed, until the large American airbases came to the Arctic in the 1940s, Hudson's Bay Company traders, Royal Canadian Mounted Police, and missionaries provided limited services to the Inuit in their territories. Within the government, there was ongoing debate as to whether the Inuit fell under federal responsibility, as with other Indigenous groups, or under provincial responsibility, since they were not signatories on any treaties. Working from the deep resources and facilities of military bases and joint weather stations, Americans could assist more effectively. From the 1940s on, many Inuit chose to settle near the US facilities, where they took on paid jobs. In so doing, these Inuit set aside hunting and trapping, activities undertaken for subsistence and for trade. American military medics frequently treated ill Inuit not in the military's employ and transported very ill patients quickly to hospitals in the south. The bases also had the best communications systems, allowing for updates on sick relatives down south to be relayed back faster than the Canadians could. This led to growing criticisms by the Americans about the poor care that Canada provided to their citizens, a sentiment the Inuit echoed.[15] A group of elders recalled that, by comparison, the RCMP and other Canadian officials, who already had a strong hand in controlling the daily lives of the Inuit, were "less numerous, less generous, less efficient, their goods were more expensive."[16]

The introduction of Canadian government baby bonuses and old age pensions to the Inuit after World War II confirmed federal government's responsibility, providing some security and shifting family economics in the North; but additional economic challenges arose in the late 1940s and early 1950s. When the fur market went into free fall, those who had prioritized hunting for trade rather than survival found themselves struggling to provide for their families. Groups in different parts of the Arctic, whether the High Arctic or the Barren Lands farther south, were in distress when this dire situation was compounded by changes in the caribou migration. Shortly after the 1951 ceremony at Craig Harbour, Inspector Larsen, the RCMP official in charge of wider Northern operations, wrote to his commissioner, concerned about protecting the traditional way of life in the Far North and providing "humanitarian" justification for relocations. Larsen advised the government to provide supplements rather than major change, advocating that the Inuit, whom he called by the racially charged term *Eskimos*, be broken up from their concentrated settlements so as to "result in a better standard of living . . . in so far as they would have a better chance of obtaining more meat and skin clothing and thereby living more their native way of life."[17]

In 1952, Richard Harrington's book, *The Face of the Arctic: A Cameraman's Story in Words and Pictures of Five Journeys into the Far North*, added ammunition to talks of High Arctic relocations by presenting a dark picture of contemporary life in the lower Arctic, west of Hudson's Bay. Harrington's book featured one long section focused on the Padleimiut people living in starvation, illness, and desperation. In contrast to the picturesque representations favored by the government such as the official NFB photograph of Craig Harbour, Harrington's photographs often showed a much starker vision of beautiful, handmade clothes now completely worn out from life at the edge of survival. Harrington largely presented the struggles as a fact of Inuit life in a remote location and tightly tied to the wavering conditions of the land. However, he captioned a 1950 photograph of an elder, "Near death: Note the Government identification tag."[18] The double indignity for Harrington's Inuk subject resonates loudly. She has been subjected to the government's dehumanizing system of tracking Inuit citizens, and yet the system is revealed as nothing more than an empty trope of modernization since she is starving to death. Harrington hoped "these pictures would . . . show the outside world what real suffering was. They would also show the strength, endurance, courage and ingenuity of an almost exhausted people."[19]

Harrington's book was widely reviewed in the American and Canadian press, fueled in part by the concurrent publication of author Farley Mowat's hugely popular, *People of the Deer*. Although Mowat's original text was not illustrated with photographs, his account also painted a vivid image of the

**Figure 9.3.** Alariak gathering wood, c. 1950. Photograph by Richard Harrington. Although her name was Alariak, everybody called her Alanaaq. © Library and Archives Canada. Reproduced with the permission of Library and Archives Canada. Courtesy Library and Archives Canada, Richard Harrington fonds, a114716.

state of the remote Ahiarmiut people at Ennadai Lake, not far from the Padleimiut; and Mowat placed the blame for their situation clearly on the Canadian government for leaving the administration of the North to the patchwork of religious, commercial, and governmental groups. The public outcry to the revelations in both books was swift, vigorous, and embarrassing to branches of the Canadian government responsible for oversight of the North. The Department of Resources and Development had officials write up rebuttals detailing Mowat's factual errors, which were significant enough to earn him the nickname "Hardly Know It" in the North. However, the authors' revelations were distressing, and the resulting embarrassment helped the US claim that its presence in the Arctic was beneficial. Accordingly, widespread calls for intervention on the part of the Canadian government into the lives of the Inuit turned out to be politically expedient. Both the Ahiarmiut and Padleimiut were subject to "humanitarian" relocations in the late 1950s, and although these moves did not expand the Canadian frontier, active government administration of the Northern Territories supported state sovereignty. In the final analysis, Harrington's and Mowat's accounts added fuel to the changes that were already underway in Ottawa with respect to the North, changes that were designed both to be geopolitically strategic and to publicly trumpet decisive action toward Indigenous welfare.

After decades of justifying threadbare administration and social supports in the North in the name of Inuit cultural preservation, the Canadian federal government profoundly changed course in the early 1950s. In 1953, the Department of Natural Resources and Development, which carried respon-

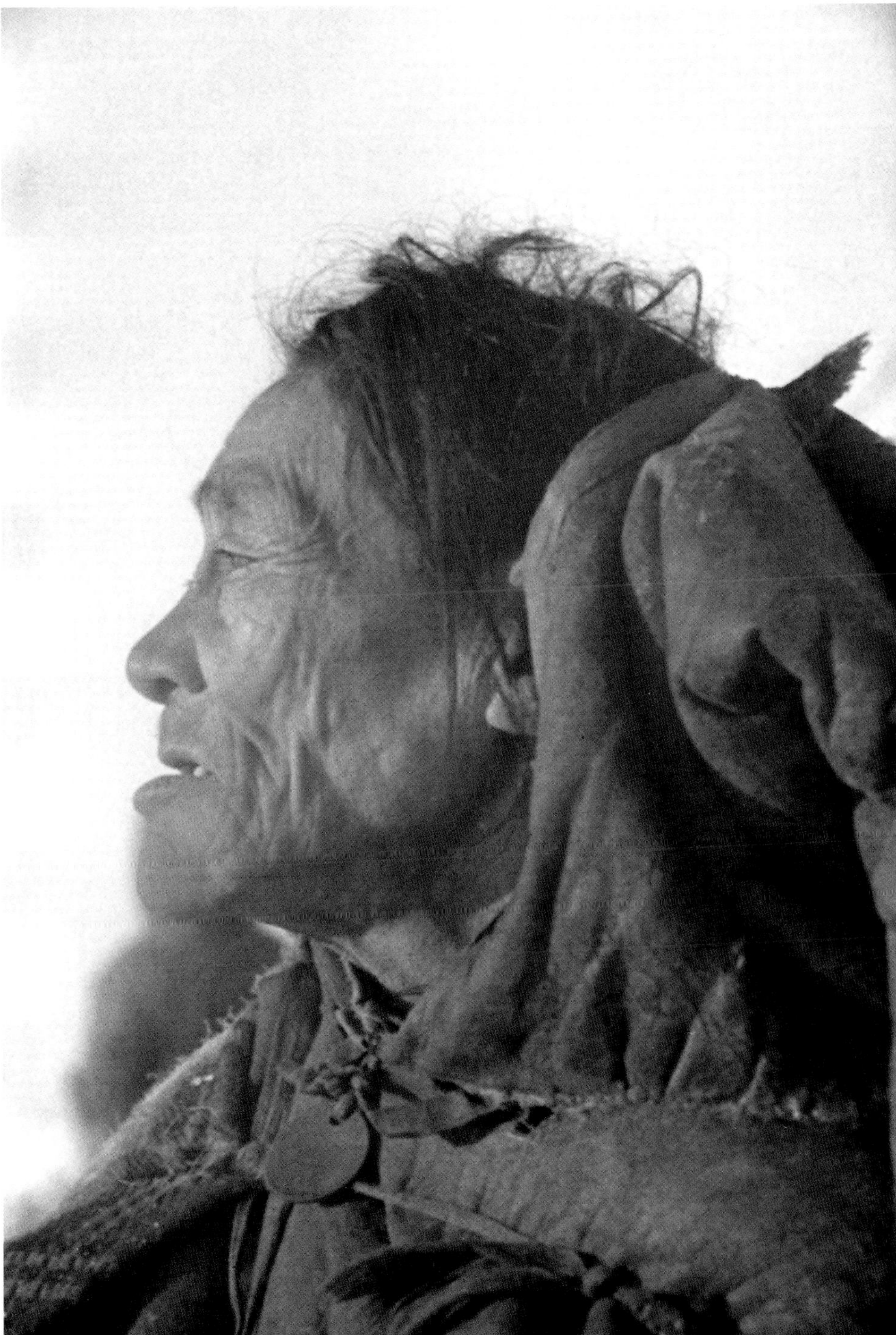

sibility for the North, was renamed the Department of Northern Affairs and Natural Resources (DNANR). This change both signaled the increasing importance of the North and indicated a new strategic direction that addressed the Cold War threats as well as the opportunities offered by natural resources.[20] Shortly after the new Department was created, several key administrators were transferred from the Department of External Affairs. When they took up their new posts in the DNANR, the men transferred had never been to the North nor did they have much, if any, familiarity with Indigenous issues. However, they were trained in diplomacy and strategic operations, expertise that was deemed essential in dealing with the early Cold War Arctic. Within a few short years, it became clear that photography would play a key role in shaping public perception and policy about people and places that almost no southern Canadian or international viewer would ever see for themselves.

## POLITICIZING HIGH ARCTIC PHOTOGRAPHY

In 1956, a high-profile product of the Canadian government's new soft diplomacy hit newsstands and entered living rooms all over North America. The cover of the February 27 issue of *Life* magazine featured a tender photograph of an Ahiarmiut mother, father, and baby with the headline "Stone Age Survivors: Eskimo Family." Inside was a heavily illustrated article with twenty photographs taken by Fritz Goro, *Life*'s science photographer, who had arrived in Ennadai Lake in August 1955 to join the Canadian government's legal anthropologist Geert van den Steenhoven, who was on site conducting research. The article followed an installment on the Mesolithic age in *Life*'s series about prehistoric life, "The Epic of Man."[21] The author concedes that although regular contact with the outside world since 1949 has started to change the Ahiarmiut way of life, it still remained basically unchanged. As one would imagine, the article entitled "Mesolithic Age Today: Caribou Eskimos Illustrate Its Culture" is an ethnographic account of a timeless people, an approach antiquated even by the standards of the mid-1950s.

The ethnographic habit of treating humans as specimens may be worn out, but the pictures themselves would have been a surprise to anyone who read Mowat's and Harrington's books since they show healthy, young people and elders active in fruitful hunting, fishing, gathering and preserving food, and making and using tools. This composite portrait of a self-sufficient and healthy people, by a renowned science photographer no less, stands in stark contrast to the picture Mowat famously painted of the Ahiarmiut just four years earlier, one that had been vigorously challenged by government officials at the time. By withholding the names of those Inuit pictured, the story insists on the fertility and perpetuity of the Inuit as well as their innate claim to the place they inhabit.

At the end of the article, *Life* magazine explicitly thanked DNANR senior administrative officer Ben Sivertz and three other personnel of the newly christened department for their contributions, presumably in the form of access and information provided. Sivertz was one of the experienced officers from Foreign Affairs recently transferred to the DNANR. Viewed through the DNANR lens, the article can be read as a rebuttal to Harrington and others, offering photographic counterevidence to the theme of deprivation they had emphasized. If the Inuit peoples had been in dire straits when Mowat and Harrington visited, this had now been rectified by the government. However, the article and its photographic evidence also served to render visible the Cold War Arctic as a place firmly occupied by generations of Indigenous bodies and timeless ways of life. The fact that the cover image of the Ahiarmiut sits below a headline for an article on long-range missiles is either a helpful coincidence that connects both as part of an early Cold War context or it suggests the DNANR had exceptional influence with the international press.

Although the *Life* article seemed designed to counter the international public image of Inuit desperation, within the government, the newly formed DNANR was simultaneously leveraging stories of struggling Inuit to move forward on the increasingly pressing need to occupy the High Arctic. In early 1953, on the heels of the outcry over Mowat's and Harrington's representations, Sivertz and the other new administrators in the DNANR began to get traction on a plan to move some Inuit groups away from more populated areas. Inukjuat (then called Port Harrison), near where Flaherty had filmed *Nanook*, had grown to be the largest Inuit settlement and developed some challenges in terms of hunting and administration. The Department secured volunteers, including Flaherty's son, Josephie, and his family, with the prospect of rich new hunting lands and a promise that all families would stay together and that they could return home in two years if they wished.[22] In terms of sustainability, there were plenty of other places to which the families could have relocated other than the High Arctic. There were many locations that would have been more fruitful and more in line with their expertise than settlements more than 1500 kilometers to the north (farther north than any Inuit then lived) and, conveniently, just on the northern side of the Northwest Passage, a long-standing claim of the Canadian government and one that had not been agreed to by the Americans. Though these later relocations were as calculated as the flag-raising at Craig Harbour, they were now strategically framed as Inuit settlements rather than as government outposts.

Department officials were pushed to move fast if the relocation was to take place in 1953, given that the transplants could only be taken by summer supply ship. Only once the Inuit transplants were on the *C. D. Howe* heading north were they told that they would be split between two settlements. Photographer Wilfred Doucette, who had been contracted to document the annual journey for the Department of Transportation, said the exact locations were not even finalized until one proposed site turned out to be inaccessible. The chosen locations included Resolute Bay, where the Inuit settlement was to be set apart from the joint US-Canadian weather station and Air Force base built a few years earlier. The second settlement was to be at Cape Herschel on Ellesmere Island, even farther north than Craig Harbour. Doucette recalled that they anchored off Cape Herschel and found themselves surrounded by ice, even at this warmest point of the year. "To the officials in Ottawa," he reflected, "Cape Herschel seemed like a good location. It was at the narrowest point of the Smith Sound, within thirty miles of the Greenland settlement of Etah. The RCMP detachment with a permanent Eskimo settlement would help establish Canadian sovereignty on Ellesmere Island."[23] Reluctantly, the ship sailed back down Ellesmere Island and deposited half of the "exiles," as many called themselves, at Grise Fiord just west of Craig Harbour.

Participants and the descendants of these later relocations have spoken with anger about the lack of consultation, broken promises, and miserable conditions they endured.[24] Descendant Madeleine Allakariallak, who cowrote the song "Kajusita/My Ship Comes In" (1995), echoed many other Inuit voices: "They left us standing on the beach/Planted there like human flags/That winter's fury turned to rags/The hunters showed us empty hands again."[25] Government officials had not taken into consideration the limited snowfall in the High Arctic, which made it hard to build igloos, and left tents as the only housing option, however inadequate, in which to shelter from the frigid temperatures. Adjusting to three months of darkness and their attendant psychological and physical problems proved difficult and strenuous for hunting. Illnesses spread quickly, and the only medical care was provided by the local RCMP constable. Lizzie Amagoalik recalled officials saying, "'Inuit are like dogs. . . . Whatever you tell them to do, they just agree.' They were staring right at us. We were so poor back then. Poor clothing, poor housing. . . . That's how we looked to them. Where could we go? Everything we were promised had disappeared."[26] Unlike many of the other forced migrations during the Cold War era, which Ariella Azoulay discusses in this volume, the High Arctic exiles were not stateless. However, Amagoalik underscores the tenuous access to rights held by Indigenous people conscripted by the state. As Martha Flaherty, a survivor of the relocation to Grise Fiord points out, "If we didn't come here, this would not be part of Canada today. When the Harper [federal] government [2006–15] talks about protecting our northwest passage, defending our Canadian sovereignty, what about us? Isn't that what we did?"[27] Canada's claim to High Arctic sovereignty depended on occupation of this land, but not just by any bodies. Rather, this claim depended on naturalized Inuit bodies. Although the government would not circulate Doucette's images of the High Arctic relocations or any images of the settlements for a few years, it is notable that they prepared to make these Indigenous subjects visible to claim territory.

Canadian Prime Minister Louis Saint-Laurent did not address the relocations or any of the challenges they presented when he spoke to the House of Commons in December 1954 to reassert the importance of actively inhabiting the Far North. But he publicly signaled the shift to make the North a key national priority when he regretted that Canada had "administered these vast territories in the North in an almost continuing state of absence of mind."[28] In the future, he added, "We must leave no doubt about our active occupation and exercise of our sovereignty in these northern lands right up to the Pole." Of the Inuit, even the prime minister had no firsthand knowledge, so he was able only to say he had observed them in representations and was impressed. Shifting away from the protectionist model that had guided most Northern policy in his government, he argued that Inuit Canadians could and would be integrated members of the modern, industrialized, and militarized North he described. He concluded by arguing that the DNANR, its representatives in the North, and its activities, necessarily conveyed through media tools such as photography, will be "symbolic of the actuality of the exercise of Canadian sovereignty."[29]

Officials in Ottawa pushed another round of relocations through in 1955, but field officers had already expressed doubt about the success and sustainability of the whole project. The conditions and morale in Resolute and Grise presented ongoing concerns; however, with the task of High Arctic inhabitation accomplished, St. Laurent's Northern policy shifted toward assimilation. Inuit were encouraged to join larger, modern settlements with access to schools, medical care, and employment. In some places, the DEW line hastened the development of these larger communities. The former US Air Force base in Frobisher Bay (now Iqaluit) became a distribution hub for DEW station construction materials and personnel. Still, the government needed all

**Figure 9.4.** Governor General Vincent Massey aboard a Komatik at Frobisher Bay, N.W.T. [now Iqaluit]. Governor General's Northern Tour. Courtesy Gar Lunney, National Film Board of Canada. Photothèque, Library and Archives Canada, e002265634.

their efforts and expenses in the North to be publicized, and it was not long before the larger Arctic communities and Resolute Bay (Qausuittuq), the tiny northern frontier outpost and joint weather station, became key staging grounds for camera diplomacy.

In stark contrast to the February 1956 *Life* magazine spread on the Ahiarmiut, which could be described as politics disguised as ethnography, there was nothing subtle about the elaborate sovereignty spectacle staged and documented by the state the following month. In March 1956, Vincent Massey, Canada's charismatic governor general, embarked on a 10,000 mile, seventeen-day flying tour of the North that started in the burgeoning Frobisher Bay. The tour featured a flight over the North Pole and managed to link the High Arctic relocations and DEW line construction in a full-blown media blitz. A more perfectly suited star would be hard to find for this ambitious winter undertaking. Not only was Massey the first governor general to visit the High Arctic, he was also the first Queen's representative in Canada to have been born in Canada. He spent years as a civil servant and diplomat and had a long-standing interest and expertise in the development of the North. The final task he completed before taking over the vice-regal post in 1952 was the Massey Report, a hugely influential examination of the arts and culture of Canada in which he staunchly advised the government to develop policies to counter American threats to Canadian cultural sovereignty.

Planning for the tour made full use of Massey's considerable cultural and diplomatic acumen; the resulting coverage within and outside of Canada was extensive and generally cooperative. The carefully assembled press party of nine included reporters from Time-Life, the British United Press, and the North American Newspaper Alliance, as well as two photographers, two film cameramen, and a French language correspondent.[30] The *New York Times* heralded the start of the trip by noting, "The part of the country Mr. Massey will

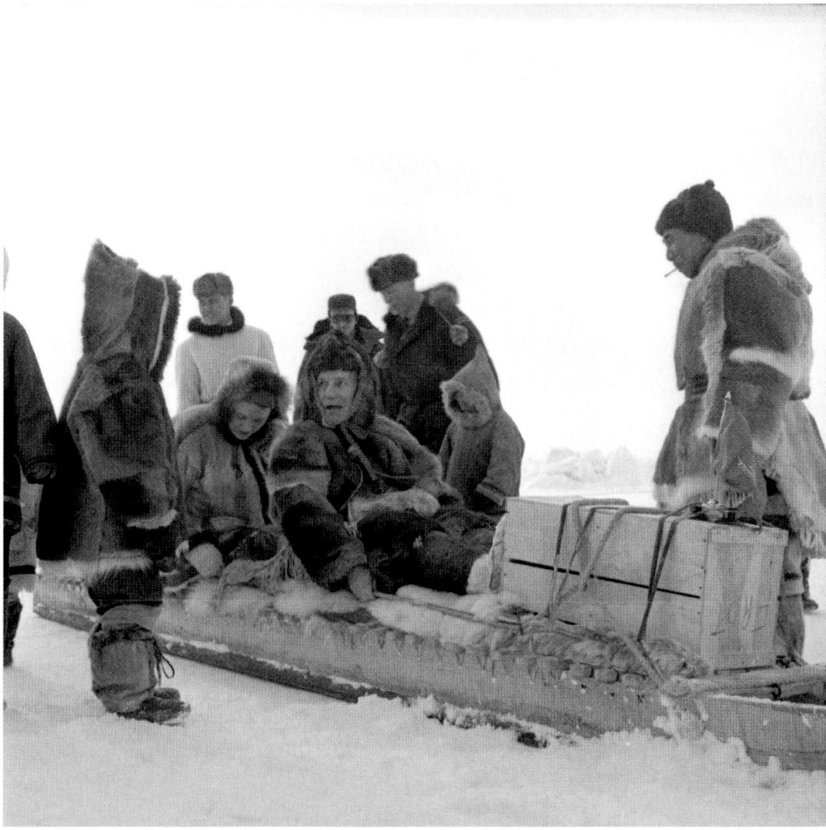

see for the first time is developing rapidly, as a result of measures being taken to defend this continent's northern approaches, and is becoming a vitally strategic zone."[31] Massey would see this development up close when he viewed the construction of the DEW stations "being built by the United States with Canada's cooperation." The article also outlined plans for Massey's flight over the pole, at which point he would drop a flag and a canister filled with records of the flight. As Tania Long, the *New York Times*'s Ottawa correspondent, noted regarding this none-too-subtle stunt, "Canada claims sovereignty over islands and ice masses right up to the North Pole. It is believed here that the Governor General's flight over the Pole is intended to serve a reminder of this fact."[32]

NFB photographer Gar Lunney's photographs of Massey's tour move away from ethnographic models and toward a carefully crafted image of a contemporary and united, if not fully integrated, Canadian North. One of the final images of the trip shows Massey "going native" in Frobisher Bay, dressed in a full fur suit and sitting atop a dogsled fitted with his vice-regal flag (figure 9.4).

This would seem to be in studied contrast to the formal suit and tie worn by the Duke of Edinburg on his visit to the lower Arctic two years earlier. Massey's full suit is also a step beyond the kamik boots worn by the Craig Harbour RCMP officers and the hide parka worn by Alex Stevenson; but in each instance, the choices reflected a carefully calculated effort by the settler-colonial state to adopt and co-opt Indigenous sartorial symbols—moves that replicated, at the level of the government official's body, the larger act of appropriation on the part of the government as a whole. Whether it was in dress, physical position or interpersonal exchanges, Massey dispensed with the traditional formality of his position throughout the trip and chose to present himself as far more assimilated with his Inuit subjects. In this way he visually linked the modern Canadian state to the north, and the modernizing north to Canada.

Lunney's image of three Resolute men posing for his camera as they themselves wait to photograph Massey (figure 9.5) underscore the significance of photography in this modernization, even in a place where the conditions for actually taking pictures were less than congenial. Average March temperatures in Resolute are colder than −30 Celsius. The Brownie cameras the men hold with their thick mitts likely did not work in winter since the film would be too brittle and gears prone to jamming. Nevertheless, the image suggests that a very different set of directions were given for this photographic project than others in the North. A far cry from either the desperation of Harrington's images or the ethnographic present of the *Life* magazine images, Lunney's images go to great lengths to present a more complex and human-centered view of the north. The bulk of the official photographs from the tour do not focus on obvious signs of technical development, such as the DEW line construction or circumpolar flights, but instead they largely map geopolitical concerns onto Inuit bodies and scenes of Inuit life. Here, the subjects are not presented as premodern but rather as modern citizens, as likely to turn their cameras on the governor general as the southerners are to capture them.[33] This was likely both a political and a practical choice, since the epic whiteness of the Arctic winter makes the landscape almost unreadable in photographs, as the background of the image demonstrates.

Journalist Blair Fraser, who accompanied Massey's tour, pointed out that the Inuit were also consuming photography. The inside walls of igloos were traditionally lined with Arctic fox hides to prevent the walls from dripping when the interior warmed up from fire. Significantly, in Resolute, the inside walls of modernized igloos made from wooden houses carefully packed with snow were "lined with old copies of *Life* magazine and *Canadian Aviation*."[34] Ironically, reproduced photographs from an illustrated magazine became one

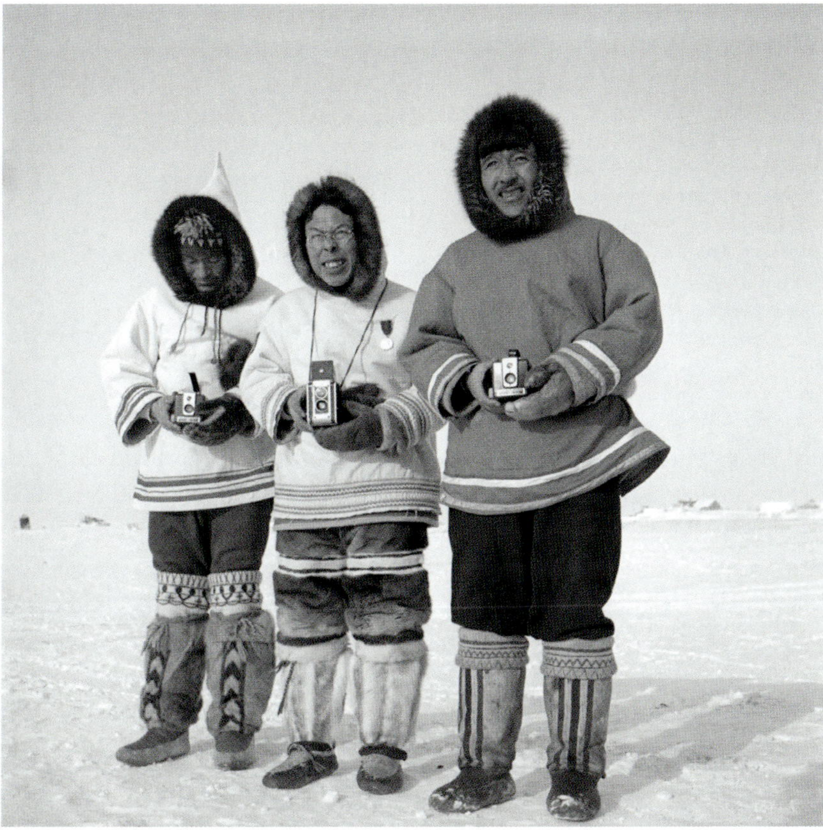

Figure 9.5. Three Inuit men [Daniel N. Salluviniq (Sudlovenick), Joseph Idlout, Zebeddie Amarualik] holding Brownie cameras await the arrival of the Governor General Vincent Massey at Resolute Bay (Qausuittuq), N.W.T [Title updated by Project Naming]. Governor General's Northern Tour. Courtesy Gar Lunney, National Film Board of Canada, Photothèque, Library and Archives Canada, e002265651.

of the materials that would make their lives in this inhospitable place more bearable.

Tania Long completed her first of six *New York Times* articles on Massey's trip by concluding that the chief purpose was to visit the people across these isolated communities and "by doing so, to make them feel a part of Canada." A tightly framed picture of Massey deferentially chatting with an elderly woman in a tidy embroidered parka (figure 9.6) seem designed to sweep away any concerns about the stability and health of this tiny remote frontier community. The Arctic is pictured here as authentically Inuit, and the visual re-

**Figure 9.6.** Governor General Vincent Massey chats with eighty-five-year-old Inuit woman at Resolute Bay (Qausuittuq), N.W.T. Governor General's Northern Tour. Courtesy Gar Lunney, National Film Board of Canada. Photothèque, Library and Archives Canada, e002265650.

cord goes to great lengths to align Massey with Inuit customs and authority despite his role a representative of a settler-colonial government. Note that here Massey dons an elegant, embroidered parka like the woman he stands with, rather than the full fur suit he wore for the photo op on the dogsled in Frobisher Bay. Only a few of these outdoor images appeared in the international press (apparently, in part, because the epic whiteness was even more of a challenge in pixelated print). Those images of the trip that did appear, however, also emphasized the modernity or assimilation of Inuit subjects, such as the image that accompanied one of Long's *New York Times* articles that, rather oddly, featured women and girls bathing in preparation for the governor general's visit. This tour presented the world with many smiling Inuit faces, but as Jasmine Alinder reminds us in the context of the US government documentation of the Japanese Internment Camps during World War II, smiles are ambiguous and often belie unhappy histories.[35]

Sovereignty is never a cinch, which is why Canadian officials drew explicitly and implicitly on photography as a primary tool in the Cold War era. In staking its claim over the High Arctic, the state could not rely on its infrastructure of aerial surveillance but instead deployed cameras on the ground. This chapter situates the production and circulation of images of Inuit peoples in the context of a discourse of modernization versus tradition, which ultimately would take a turn in the 1950s when the settler-colonial state resolved that relocating the Inuit to the High Arctic would highlight a proper course of modernized settlement—in flagrant disregard of Indigenous sovereignty.[36] However, sustained photographic focus on Inuit inhabitation of the North in the Cold War Canada has generated a vast settler-colonial archive of images now being used in efforts at reconciliation. Since 2002, students

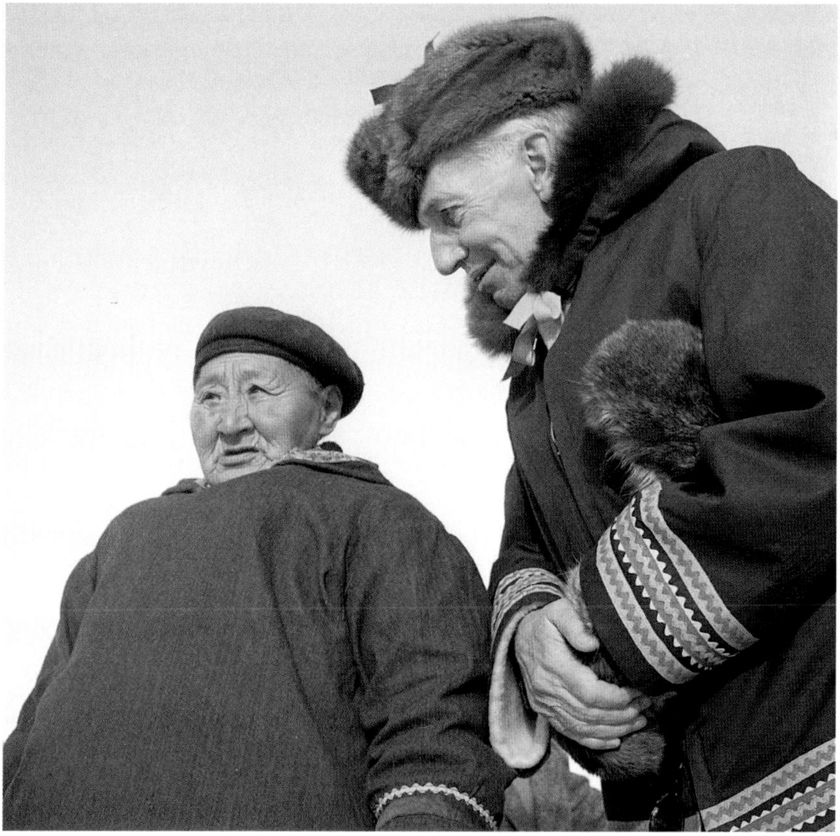

from Nunavut Sivuniksavut College have pioneered the work of *Project Naming*. With training provided by archivists and historians, Inuit students interview elders in Northern communities. Interviews focus on photographs collected by the National Library and Archives, with elders identifying subjects and providing oral histories. As a result of *Project Naming*, the images taken of and from the Northern communities are now being repatriated to those communities. As long-missing Inuit knowledge is added to the central archival records, new possibilities arise to reshape national historical narratives through these photographs. In this way, a reckoning with the consequences of Cold War geopolitics, which drew on indigenous bodies to map out the contours of the state against foreign encroachment, intersects with the ongoing process of reconciliation.

*Notes*

I am grateful for the assistance and advice offered by Edward Atkinson at the Nunavut Archives and for the feedback and insights of colleagues Anna Hudson, Richard Hill, and Carol Payne, the participants in the Mexico City workshop, and the editors and peer reviewers of this volume.

1 Tester and Kulchyski, *Tammarniit (Mistakes)*, 123.
2 FDR's son, US Army Captain Elliott Roosevelt led the 1941 survey for possible airbase sites in the north. In addition to Frobisher Bay (now Iqaluit), other sites included Goose Bay in Labrador and Thule in Greenland. Although selected by the US Air Force, Goose Bay was built in a few months by Canadians to house operations by the United States, Britain, and Canada beginning in December 1941.
3 Caplan, *Aerial Aftermaths*.
4 Galov, "American North in the U.S. Imperialists' Aggressive Plans," 15–16. Original article published in the *Soviet Press* (May 10, 1952): 3.
5 Cited in Lackenbauer, *Human Flagpoles*, 152. *Minutes of a Meeting of the Cabinet in the Privy Council Chamber*, January 19, 1953, Library Archives Canada, Minutes, Cabinet Meeting, 22.1.53. RG 2, vol. 2652, file 07, January 1953–February 26, 1953.
6 Cited in Marcus, *Relocating Eden*, 55. For a compelling account of an earlier sovereignty panic, see Burant, "Using Photography to Assert Canadian Sovereignty in the Arctic."
7 The 1951 census identified the total Inuit population of Canada as 9,493, about half of whom lived in the Eastern Arctic. This paled in comparison to the indigenous population in Alaska (1950) 19,774 and Greenland (1951) 22,890. Canadian Inuit territory in 1950 was about 2.5 million square kilometers, so the density was about 1: 250 square kilometers—or, given the social structures of the communities, 20–30 individuals per 5,000–7,500 sq km concentrated along the vast coasts. See Grygier, *Long Way from Home*, 17.
8 Most Inuit in the 1950s were still fairly mobile, moving within a distinct region between preferred hunting sites where they would set up igloos or tents depending on the latitude and season. Travel was without roads on routes marked by Inukshuk sculptures created from found rocks, a sum of activities that left little imprint on the land.
9 Payne, *The Official Picture*.
10 The term seems to be first used by Tester and Kulchyski, *Tammarniit (Mistakes)*, 114.
11 See Mirzoeff, "Technologies of Oversight," in *The Right to Look*, 17.
12 The modern Canadian Maple Leaf Flag did not become the official flag until 1965. The Red Ensign flag, which had a small Union Jack on a red background and a coat of arms, could be seen as a kind of transitional Canadian flag. That it was not used here but is seen in other Arctic locations in the same period, might be at-

tributable to the fact that the Red Ensign is less graphically striking (and thus less photogenic) than the Union Jack.

13 According to the research conducted by Project Naming, Joe Panikpakoochoo and Panikpak had RCMP appointments to help translate and guide patrols among other tasks. See the NFB photograph taken on the CGS *C. D. Howe* supply ship in July 1951 (Mikan number 3194891, Library and Archives Canada, Ottawa).

14 *The Magic in the Sky*, directed by Peter Raymont (1981).

15 Prior to the Canadian Citizenship Act of 1947, persons born in Canada or those who were naturalized immigrants became British subjects; but this right was not formally extended to indigenous Canadians. Status Indians (First Nations) were considered wards of the state, but after World War II there was significant debate about the status of the Inuit, because no formal treaties existed between the Inuit and the government. Both Status Indians and Inuit were formally granted citizenship in a 1956 addition to the Citizenship Act; however, the Inuit were recognized as citizens in practical terms in 1945, when it was decided that, like all other Canadian citizens, the Inuit were eligible for the new Family Allowance from the federal government.

16 Gagnon and Iqualit Elders, *Inuit Recollections on the Military Presence in Iqaluit*, 327.

17 Cited in Marcus, *Relocating Eden*, 47.

18 Marcus, *Relocating Eden*, 18. For a discussion of the wide circulation of Harrington's Arctic images, see Langford, "Richard Harrington's Guide," 33–56.

19 His wish was fulfilled when Edward Steichen included three of Harrington's photographs of Padleimiut in *Family of Man* (1955), an exhibition sponsored by the US government. Although all pictured starving people, only one was slotted into the section portraying hunger. The others were slotted into the sections on birth and maternal love. From the sovereignty point of view, it is interesting to note that the exhibition and publication listed the national origin of the pictures as "Arctic" and not "Canada."

20 At the 1951 Venice Film Festival, held the same week Stevenson sent his telegram about Craig Harbour, first prize in the Geography division went to an NFB production "Canada's Awakening North." The film portrayed the MacKenzie Delta in the Northwest Territories as a thriving and complex place, ripe with opportunities for economic development.

21 The *Life* series "Epic of Man" debuted in November 1955, months after the *Family of Man* photography exhibition opened at the MoMA. *Life* publisher Andrew Heiskell further highlighted the importance of photography for the "Epic of Man" noting that the series was "re-creating the development of Man himself" and, to this end, "actual photography added a graphic sense of reality to the story of Old Stone Age Man by documenting . . . descendants of Stone Age forbearers living today as their ancestors did more than 10,000 years ago." See "Publisher's Preview," *Life*, December 5, 1955, 153.

22 Melanie McGrath, in *The Long Exile*, provides an account of the relocations by tracing three generations of the Flaherty family. For a comprehensive overview of the organized Inuit campaign for redress and an analysis of commemorative efforts see Wakeham, "At the Intersection of Apology and Sovereignty." It is useful to note that Wakeham reads the 2010 apology as an opportunity for the conservative federal government of Stephen Harper to reassert Canadian sovereignty. This aligns with the problematics analyzed by UBC political science professor and Yellowknives Dene activist Glen Sean Coulthard in *Red Skin, White Masks*.

23 Doucette, "Cape Herschel," 20. Doucette may have received some chastising regarding his openness about the mission. He took a very different stance in a letter to the editor of the *Globe and Mail* and published October 23, 1991.

24 Government documents report Inuit detailing hardships and broken promises from the first months of the relocation. See Dussault and Erasmus, "The High Arctic Relocation." More recent efforts have channeled Inuit voices directly through media. See Nunavut Tunngavik Incorporated, https://tunngavik.com. Another project, Iqqaumavara, launched in 2014. While the videos were no longer accessible when this essay went to print, the Iqqaumavara Facebook page outlines the project.

25 Tudjaat, "Kajusita/My Ship Comes In," lyrics by Madeleine Allakariallak, Jon Park-Wheeler, and Randall Prescott. Allakariallak's family was part of the Resolute relocations.

26 Lizzie Amagoalik speaking, in Kunuk, *Exile* (MPEG video), at 41:40, http://www.isuma.tv/isuma-productions/exile-0.

27 Martha Flaherty speaking, in Kunuk, *Exile* (MPEG video), at 40:09, http://www.isuma.tv/isuma-productions/exile-0.

28 Parliament of Canada, *Debates of the House of Commons* (1954), 696.

29 Parliament of Canada, *Debates of the House of Commons* (1954), 700.

30 Department of Northern Affairs and National Resources, *Visit of His Excellency the Rt. Hon. Vincent Massey, Governor-General*, 4.

31 Long, "Governor-General Starting Tuesday," 17.

32 Long, "Governor-General Starting Tuesday."

33 Lunney's inscription on the back of the photograph notes the camera type: "with their Brownie cameras" (Mikan number 3603875, Library and Archives Canada, Ottawa).

34 Fraser, "The Loneliest Job in the World," 110. In Pond Inlet, photographer Doug Wilkinson reported the same use for the steady flow of picture magazines shipped north. See Wilkinson, *Land of the Long Day*, 15.

35 Alinder, *Moving Images*, 14.

36 See Simpson, *Mohawk Interruptus*; and Coulthard, *Red Skin, White Masks*.

# 10

LAURA WEXLER KARINTHA LOWE & GUIGUI YAO

## Urban Albums, Village Forms

### CHINESE FAMILY PHOTOGRAPHS AND THE COLD WAR

Sitting in her apartment in Tianjin, China, Yang Dazhao described a photograph she took nearly fifty years ago, when she and her family were sent down to the countryside as part of a reeducation program. Yang recalled:

> Our mother got sent down to the countryside—a small village outside of Beijing, very poor—in 1970. Our father didn't think she could survive on her own out there, and didn't they say, "Take your family with you?" So he quit his job and followed my mother. [. . . ] I was the

> one who bought the camera. I saved up for a while. All my sisters and brothers said I was a cheapskate—I only spent 5 fen on meat, but I spent ten or so yuan on a 120 mm camera. You know, it's not that I had any interest in photography or art, but I thought that it was something I should do. Our family had a lot more photos before the Red Guards came and raided our home [*chaojia*] and I was used to seeing photo albums when I was younger.[1]

Yang trailed off there and studiously examined a photograph of her father standing in a field. She said nothing more. But the implications seemed clear: she felt even as a child that she should document what had happened to her family and that it was almost a duty to record their history, more important in some ways than food.

Yang was sharing her family album, and the memories it evoked, with Karintha Lowe, then a first-year graduate student in the American Studies program at Harvard University. Lowe was part of our small research team, and we had been making multiple visits to China from 2007 to 2017 in order to learn more about family photographs taken during the Cold War era.[2] In her field notes from that day, Lowe remarked that "Yang appears unsure of how much more of the story she can share." Here, as with many of the other photographic collections we encountered during our research, the afterlife of the Yang family album did not come easily or clearly into focus.

Interpreting Cold War family photographs takes a particularly complex turn in China today, given ongoing state control of the historical narrative of the Great Leap Forward, the Anti-Rightest Campaign, and especially the decade of the Cultural Revolution (1966–76)—popularly known as the "ten years of chaos." Susie Linfield's account of photography during the Cultural Revolution gestures to the difficulty of gathering material for such analysis: "Mao urged young people to smash the four 'olds'—customs, habits, culture, and thinking—and to cleanse the Party of class enemies, an infinitely expandable category."[3] The paramilitary troupe, the Red Guard, enforced such destruction by conducting periodic raids into the homes of suspected "bad elements." Family photographs, treated by the Party as indexical in nature, were often the first images to be destroyed—either by the Red Guard or by family members in anticipation of such raids. As Robert Bickers describes, "If you were at all savvy, you realised early on that you had to destroy your own private family records, before the Red Guards came and found evidence of your bourgeois, counter-revolutionary past, when you might have drunk coffee in a café bar, à la mode."[4] For many Chinese during the long Cold

War era, to save the family's photographs would have been to precipitate destruction.

But many family photographs, in albums and otherwise, *did* survive, both in China and overseas. As the opening vignette suggests, people also actively documented their lives in the newly formed People's Republic. In a series of essays on "Private Photo Albums" written for the well-known literary journal *Harvest* [*Shouhuo*] between 1986 and 1987, Liu Xinwu encouraged his readers to view family photographs as important artifacts within the narrative of modern Chinese history. Reflecting on the "fatal destruction" of photographs during the mid-twentieth century, Liu posited family albums as providing the possible source material for Ba Jin's well-known proposal for a "museum of the Cultural Revolution."[5] Yet while a small number of private museums—some of them entirely virtual—have since emerged to display such family albums, the exhibitions must negotiate a delicate relationship with the Chinese State. As Jie Li argues in her analysis of virtual museums, the "unofficial status [of these exhibits] has consistently kept the discourse around the 'Cultural Revolution Museum' in the future tense, an unfulfilled but increasingly reiterated wish."[6]

The recent "cultural turn" in Cold War studies has opened up new analytical avenues through which to approach these photographic archives. In *The Other Cold War,* Heonik Kwon traces a new treatment of the Cold War as "both a question of the social order and a question of international order."[7] This framework indicates a revival of historical interest in questions of the everyday, "bringing the milieu of intimate social norms and subtle shifts in the patterns of organizational life during the cold war to the foreground of descriptive and analytical projects focused on the cold war, which have hitherto been narrowly focused on policy documents and profiles."[8] While many popular forms of documentary expression have since been analyzed as part of the Cold War "cultural system"—including on radio, film, and television in Stephen Whitfield's work—we want to note that attention to family photography has only just begun.[9] What critical powers do these family photographs retain as objects of cultural memory? How would domestic visions from Chinese family photographs expand the customary histories of the Cold War? Are there historical perspectives that might be especially advantageous for uncovering meaning in this archive? And what is at stake in attempting to excavate these layers of meaning, and for whom?

Our interviews persuaded us that important documents of China's Cold War history lie virtually untapped by historians in private collections of family photographs and in the stories that family members are able to tell about

**Figure 10.1. On the twenty-first anniversary of the People's Republic of China, October 9, 1970, Chairman Mao Zedong, alongside Vice Chairman Lin Biao, acknowledge the waving of the little Red Books. Photograph Courtesy Getty Images.**

them. We also came to understand that unearthing the meaning of these images will require historians of photography to give much closer consideration than usual to the material forms that such repositories take. In order to begin this exploration, we have found it especially fruitful to juxtapose the photographs of subaltern and privileged makers. This juxtaposition has revealed hidden possibilities of archives, what Ariella Azoulay calls "the undercurrent photographic data," along with some of the unique complexities of assessing Chinese family photographs in historical context.[10] We are interested in exploring ways to untangle some of the ambiguities and ambivalences that exist in and around these objects. Chinese family photographs from the Cold War period can function as a kind of lieu de mémoire, or lieu de contre mémoire of the people, distinct from government-sponsored memory.[11] We aim here to provide some conceptual tools with which to see how they function as "present pasts."[12]

## COLD WAR LEGACIES IN HISTORICAL CONTEXT

On October 1, 1949, Mao Zedong stood on the balcony facing Tiananmen Square and officially proclaimed the founding of the People's Republic of China (PRC). The result of a brutal civil war between the Communist Party and the Nationalists (Guomindang), the newly formed PRC found itself on unsteady ground. While Mao maintained the new nation's roots in an indigenous, popular revolution, the PRC also sought to sustain ideological ties with the USSR, now looking to extend its power in Asia. A few months prior to Mao's October 1st declaration—when the communist victory appeared imminent—the Party's second in command, Liu Shaoqi, had secretly visited Moscow to

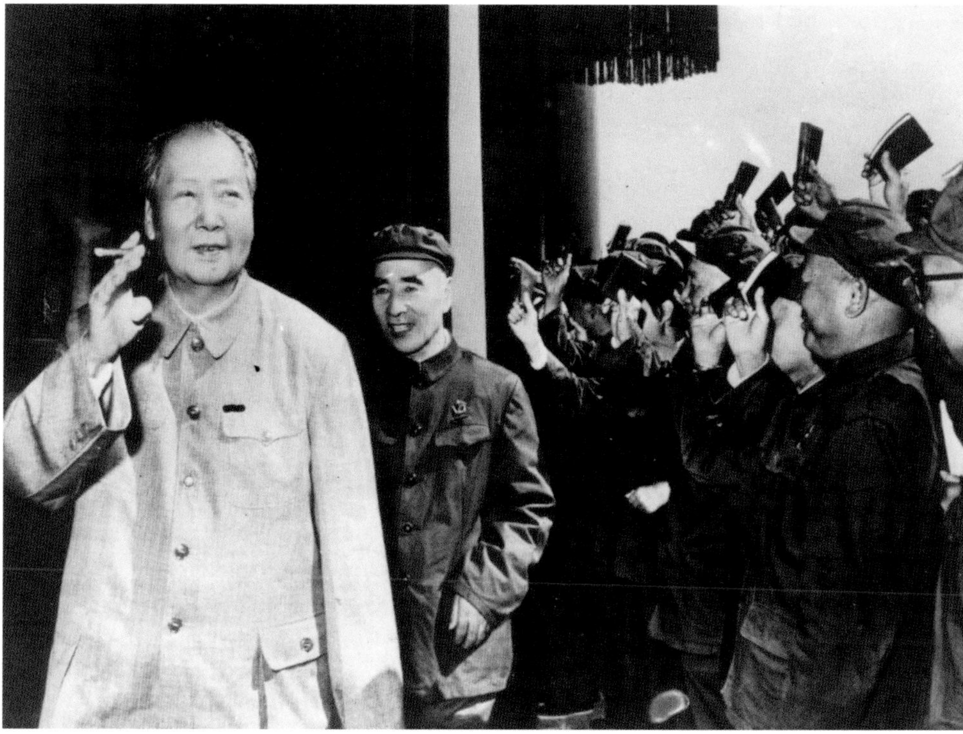

meet with Joseph Stalin. The two leaders confirmed the "revolutionary situation" in East Asia and came to a quiet agreement: while the Soviet Union would continue to forge an international proletarian revolution, China would promote the more localized "Eastern Revolution."[13]

Mao appeared especially concerned with the political use of images in order to advance the proletarian cause. Widely disseminated propaganda posters and photographs from the Cold War era showed ranks upon ranks of uniformed soldiers marching in precisely ordered formations across Tiananmen Square; other images displayed masses of male and female cadets raising their eyes and little Red Books to the painting of the Great Leader. Alongside these monumental designs, popular prints also exhibited joyful laborers tackling agricultural projects or sitting at home, devotedly studying Party precepts. These officially sanctioned images signified the success of the new republic, while subsuming families and individuals into the structure of a profoundly militarized state.

In 1966, aware that he and other founding members of the PRC would eventually retire, and in the shadow of the Sino-Soviet split, Mao attempted an ambitious project to redress the social inequality, the fading of the socialist vision, and the entrenchment of the bureaucratic elite within China. Calling this project the Cultural Revolution, Mao sought to reorganize the entire political and social structure of the nation. In doing so, he wanted to ensure a lasting "spiritual transformation" of the people. He declared:

> China's 600 million people have two remarkable peculiarities; they are, first of all, poor, and secondly blank. That may seem like a bad thing, but it is really a good thing. Poor people want change, want to do things, want revolution. A clean sheet of paper has no blotches, and so the newest and most beautiful words can be written on it, the newest and most beautiful pictures can be painted on it.[14]

Notably, Mao formulated his mission through the metaphor of a blank page, a political canvas upon which he could revise both the text and picture of Chinese national identity. While Mao might not have believed that he could truly erase China's pre-communist history from the nation's collective memory, he disseminated a totalizing view via pamphlets, speeches, photographs, and posters. As Maurice Meisner suggests, "Having rejected the traditional Chinese cultural heritage, Mao attempted to fill the emotional void by an even more iconoclastic proclamation of the non-existence of the past in the present."[15]

Throughout this period, Mao and his advisers also developed a revolutionary foreign policy to match China's domestic transformations. Just one year after Mao's balcony declaration, the CCP began lodging a large-scale military intervention into Korea, in league with the Soviet Union. Adopting a Cold War–era rhetoric, Mao framed his Party as a "front-line soldier" fighting against American imperialists.[16] In a series of private correspondences, Mao argued that if China did not intervene, the global revolution would suffer.[17] Yet the USSR proved an unreliable ally throughout this military foray—failing to provide support to Chinese troops at crucial moments and demanding special rights to operate in China.

State-sponsored editorials from the time period reveal the CCP actively engaging with both the United States and the Soviet Union. A 1968 New Year editorial published simultaneously in the Party's flagship publications read:

> Chairman Mao says: "All reactionary forces will fight to the last gasp at their pending doom." A handful of traitors, spies, and capitalist powerholders in the party, the demons and ghosts (that is, those landlords, rich peasants, counterrevolutionaries, bad elements, and rightists who have not yet been well reformed) in society, and the running dogs of

> the American imperialists and Soviet Revisionists are bound to continue their sabotage and instigation with all possible means, including spreading rumors and planting divisions.[18]

The editorial drew a direct link between the CCP's foreign policy and its local authority. In representing the Chinese state as under ideological attack on all fronts, the CCP appeared to justify its internal project of the Cultural Revolution. As Chen Jian summarizes, "The international aspect of the revolution served as a constant source of domestic mobilization, helping to legitimate the revolution at home and to maintain its momentum."[19] This mutually constitutive relationship was ultimately successful, helping to sustain the Cultural Revolution until Mao's death in 1976.

The Cultural Revolution renders excavating Cold War legacies in family photography a difficult but necessary interpretive task. The domestic, ambitious, and often brutal nature of the Cultural Revolution tends to separate this history from the international geopolitical scene. Generally studied as an upheaval of private life, the "ten years of chaos" appear far removed from the global Cold War. In turn, historians tend to present the Cold War as a contest staged primarily between the United States and the Soviet Union, with China and its concurrent cultural productions featuring as a satellite character. As Rana Mitter puts it, "China played a pivotal role as the third (albeit shorter) leg of a cold war tripod."[20] Characterized by a "certain unsteadiness," China appears in this narrative as pivoting away from the USSR and, consequently, toward the United States.[21]

Assumed to be chiefly supportive, then, the Chinese "shorter leg" of the tripod materializes as a kind of shim in Cold War histories, an instrument for diplomats as they attempted to balance the power between the conflict's primary antagonists. Officially, the state controlled its own image, as is evident in the diplomatic use of propaganda photographs and posters from the Cultural Revolution as instruments to project state power, similar to the visual culture of both the Soviet Union and the United States. Yet there is a dearth of scholarship that chronicles the visual cultural production of Chinese people of, by, and for themselves as nonstate actors in the Cold War drama.

Our ethnographic research in rural areas revealed a differently insular view of the period. In fact, when Guigui Yao mentioned "Cold War" to an informant, Wang Simei, Wang knew nothing of the historical event. As Yao describes in her field notes:

> "Cold War" as a term is far from familiar to the village people, for it is simply not in the news, nor in their everyday vocabulary. Perhaps

it was in the news sometime in the latter half of the 20th century, but most village families didn't own even a radio, and TV didn't become available for most until the early 1990s. When I mentioned "Cold War" to Wang Simei, whose uncle joined the Korean War, she said the term meant that "two people (especially a couple) don't speak to each other and thus is a fight without quarrelling." She knew nothing about such a "war" between countries in the history. Known in China as "the war to resist US aggression and aid Korea," the Korean War constantly reminds people that "the Mei Di" (meaning "the US Imperial," which gives a negative and aggressive image of America) is the biggest enemy of China. Given the degree of scarcity of resources back then in China, any chance of surviving was welcomed by people and some just joined the army when the government called on them (until recently, the possibility of getting a decent job after being enrolled in the army was quite appealing to village families).

Wang Simei's understanding of the term was common in our fieldwork. While people of the Cold War generation in the United States and the Soviet Union knew the term and recognized themselves within it, anecdotal evidence suggests that the precise outlines of the conflict remained unfamiliar to many of the PRC's citizens. As Katherine Verdery suggests, then, studies of the Cold War cannot concentrate solely on the historical event; instead, we must also consider how the Cold War produced "a cognitive organization of the world" that "laid down the coordinates of a conceptual geography grounded in East vs. West."[22] Examined within this frame, we trace how Cold War ideology was filtered through the PRC: while Wang held an apparently ahistorical understanding of the conflict, its "conceptual geography" nevertheless provided her with the domestic language to immediately connect the Korean War with anti-imperialist US rhetoric.

The CCP's treatment of family photography as a form of political testimony —either anti-imperialist or reactionary—further suggests how the Chinese context absorbed these Cold War binarisms. As already delineated, during the Cultural Revolution, Mao encouraged the Red Guard to burn or confiscate family photographs, heirlooms, and furniture that might evidence "reactionary" worldviews. In their study of socialism in Russia, Oksana Sarkisova and Olga Shevchenko describe a political landscape similarly imbricated in the Soviet period where "every chance photograph could all of a sudden become a compromising piece of evidence."[23] As the KGB often presented photographic materials as proof of "subversive activities," individuals began cropping or otherwise destroying their own private archives.[24] During the late 1970s, the Soviet-supported communist government in Ethiopia made a parallel move, linking family photography to political purposes. As Eric Gottesman's contribution to this volume explores, the regime attempted to revise its national history and destroy cultural memory by banning personal photography. Across Cold War geographies, then, familial images offered a plane upon which to realize or contest political ambitions. By reading family photography taken during and around the Chinese Cultural Revolution as part of this more global historical record, we aim here to provide some conceptual tools to begin teasing out the complex narratives that often inform readings of surviving photographs.

## URBAN ALBUMS

The preponderance of surviving Cold War Chinese family photographs currently available to scholars are found in albums of urban people. These albums, often preserved in the collections of antiques dealers, secondhand shops, and paper sellers trading on the "red" nostalgia market, were relatively insulated from the passing of time.[25] The albums are also predominantly "orphaned," accompanied by no one who can speak definitively to the original meanings given to the images. But the spatialization of the images does indicate the presence of surviving meaning—if intact, the organization of the album illuminates something of the maker's original thinking. Or, as we discovered, if the album is no longer intact, the very fact that the photographs are now in disarray can yield surprising new insights.

One of the first orphaned albums we collected speaks *structurally* to the importance of haptic communication in remembering and interpreting experiences of the Cold War era in China. Found in Beijing's *Panjiayuan* Market, this small album features a bright red cover and remains in extremely good condition (figure 10.2). Some studio portraits date images to the 1960s–70s, while other photographs remain undated. But all images feature the same young man and his comrades in uniform. In the series of photographs, the group travels together to see the sacred sites of Mao's China, their uniform poses registering both the depth of their comradery and their collective patriotism. This particular album, however, draws special attention to the presence of information that may not be traceable to the visual images alone. As we soon found in our encounter with the little red album, handling the

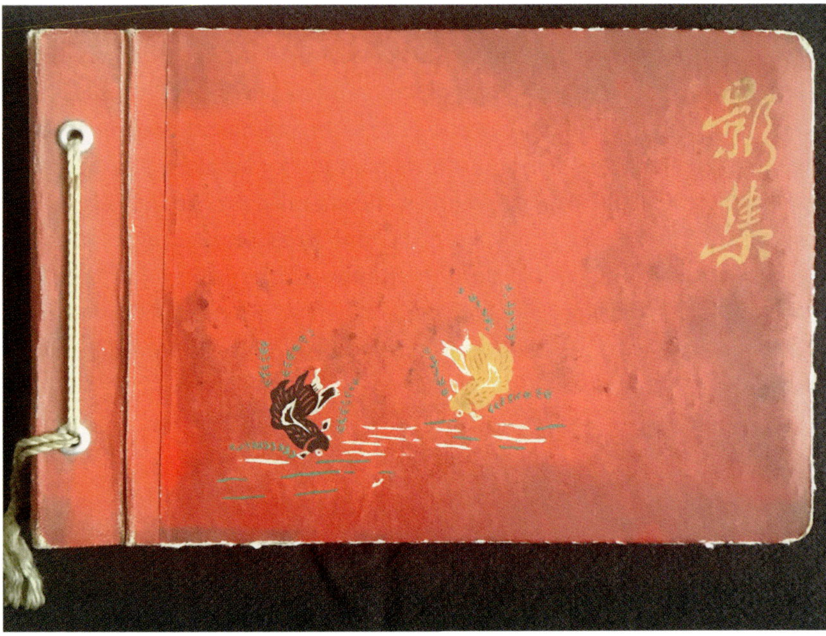


composite images offered an additional way to uncover meaning: turning the pages and flipping over photographs required us to revise and complicate our initial interpretations of the visual record.

At first read, the album appears to feature typical members of the sent-down youth generation. Well-off and well-educated, the sent-down youths could often afford to take and display images of their travels through revolutionary tourist sites. Many of the images in the red album suggest as much; comparatively large, that is to say expensive, the images are examples of the best possibilities of popular photography that existed in China at the time. The photographed youths further evidence their revolutionary fervor through attire: often clad in Mao suits, the men conform to the patriotic dress of the day.[26] One panel of the album in particular vividly displays this revolutionary mode. Comprising two photographs, the diptych shows the young man and his comrades at work. In the first photograph, they are sitting in a field while being lectured to by rural experts. Perhaps the young protagonist paused to take this image himself, or staged the group of laborers to present a tableau. Perhaps he did not take the photograph himself at all, but obtained it from somebody else. In either case, the locals appear chiefly as scenery, their sun hats almost blending into the landscape. In the other work group image, the young men in the group stand assertively together as if in a break from

**Figure 10.2.** ***(opposite)*** **The Red Album, an orphan album purchased at Pan Jia Yuan flea market in Beijing, China. Private Collection, New Haven.**

**Figure 10.3.** ***(below)*** **Interior of the Red Album, featuring group and solo images of a young man's travels throughout China. Private Collection, New Haven.**

their labor. They are subjects in the field. Both of these photographs position all the people in them as willing workers for Mao and echo the ideology that presented the rural countryside as a site of revolutionary exchange. The sent-down youth group, however, had received privileges that most rural people did not, and the album marks their patriotism not only by showing them at work in the fields but also through pictures of vacations to sites of historical significance to the CCP.

A fifth—hidden—photograph ratchets up the contradictions displayed on the page. Tucked behind the image of the four young men on a break from their labor in the field, we discovered a tiny portrait of a young boy who stares

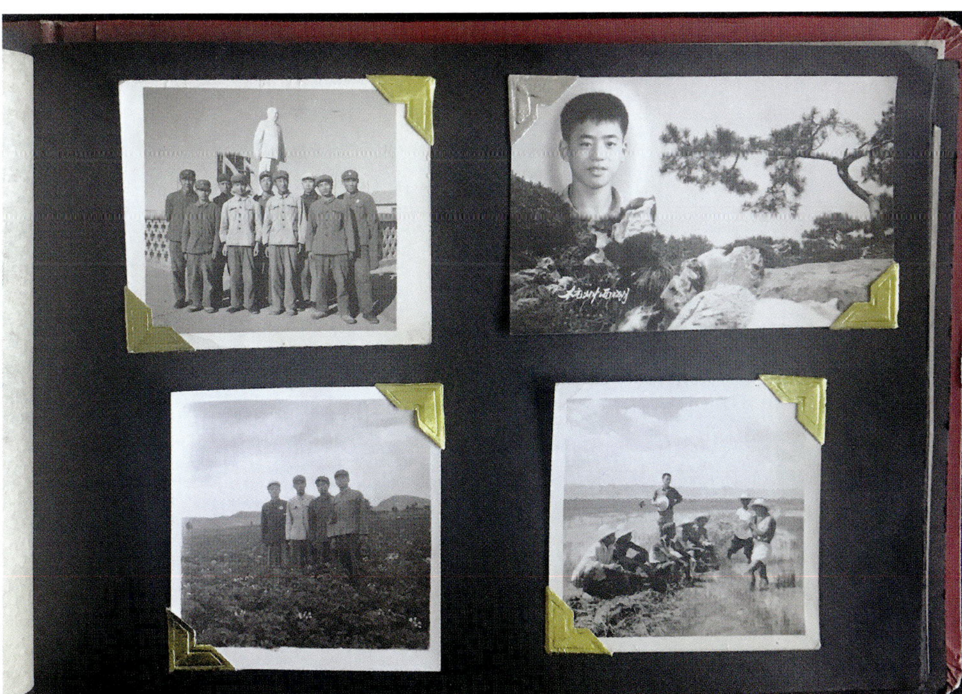

**Figure 10.4.** Tucked behind a group photograph, we found a fifth, hidden photograph of a young boy. Private Collection, New Haven.

directly into the camera. His hair is cropped close to his head, save for a single braid that falls over his left shoulder. This single braid is a "root of life" (ming genzi), or strands of hair grown since infancy to ensure longevity. It indicates the kind of traditional beliefs that Mao was trying to suppress and likely gestures to the album's protagonist's own family, if not to himself at an earlier age. During the Cultural Revolution, if the Red Guard caught a boy wearing his hair in such a braid, they might cut it off.

What should we make of this fifth photograph and its placement, which quite literally hides the picture of a young boy wearing a customary good luck charm behind that of the uniformed youth workers of revolutionary China? At the very least, the secret picture conveys the persistence of traditional family practices during the early years of the PRC and the hidden presence of private meanings in the propaganda images of Mao's massive youth mobilization. The album evidences that certain urban subjects were well aware that the adoption of Mao's style did not necessarily mean consistent adherence to communist precepts, neither with respect to the class privilege that allowed certain sent-down youths to travel in ways unthinkable for the rural population they were supposed to serve, nor with respect to the possibility of preserving tradition. It configures a duality and points ambiguously to the young man's own maintenance and simultaneous distancing of himself from the old ways of his family. As a carefully preserved and inserted artifact of what Marianne Hirsch calls the "familial gaze," the photograph prolongs the aura of kinship in an experience purposely designed to subdue it.[27]

Orphan albums present definite challenges. We cannot ask this young man or his relatives, friends, or neighbors to tell us how he would like his little red album to be handled. We only know that the photographs feature one particular young man in popular revolutionary dress, who posed for revolutionary style photographs in Beijing and Hangzhou, as well as in rural communities during the 1960s and 1970s. But because of the material structure of the album, the album's haptic script is strong. Tucking the portrait of the young boy beneath another image suggests intention, that the album's author rendered one

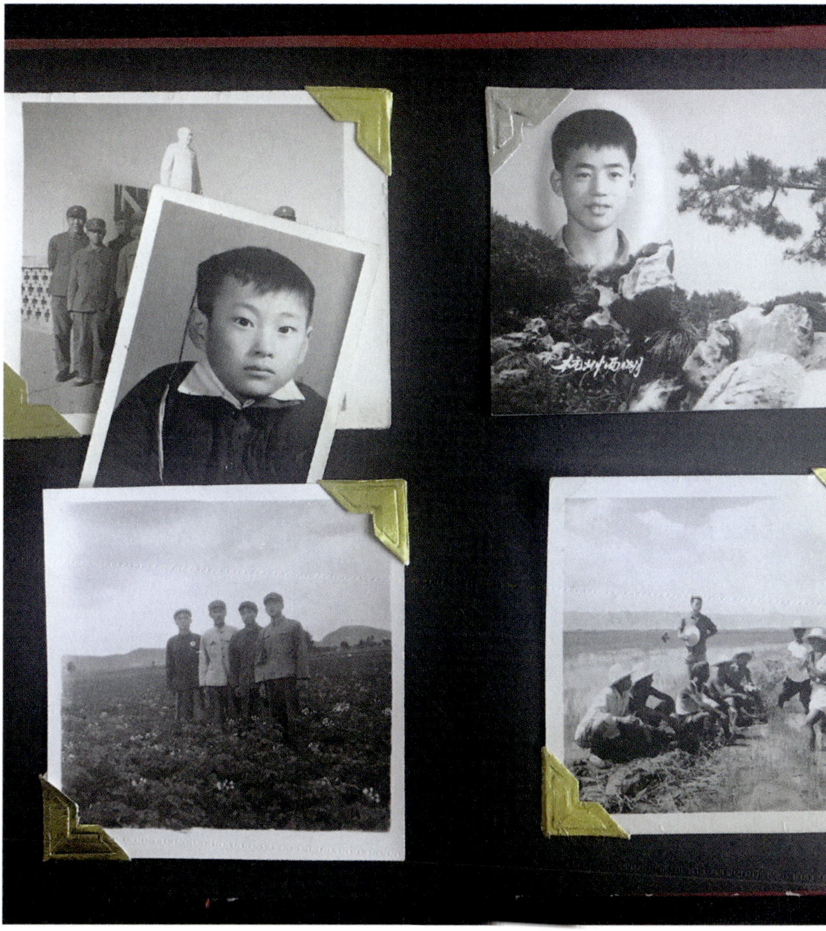

image visible at the expense of another. Discovering it by literally lifting the covering image to find the one below provokes a rich new set of questions. Did the album's author purposefully hide the photograph of the boy, perhaps himself, behind a group photograph? Or did he place the group photograph over the portrait, preferring its orthodoxy to the tiny subversive studio image? Did he intend that others would find it? Or was it to be a purely personal secret? The fifth photograph incites our analytical eye, but it does not answer our analytical questions. Because the album has been orphaned, we cannot unequivocally assert the meaning of this act. Yet because the urban album is impressively intact, we can confidently venture that a meaning exists.

In her encounter with an orphaned album, Catherine Whalen describes her attempts to interpret a series of photographs in the absence of their cre-

**Figure 10.5.** The young boy has a ming genzi or "root of life," strands of hair braided together to ensure longevity. During the Cultural Revolution, if the Red Guard caught a boy wearing this braid, they might have cut it off. Private Collection, New Haven.

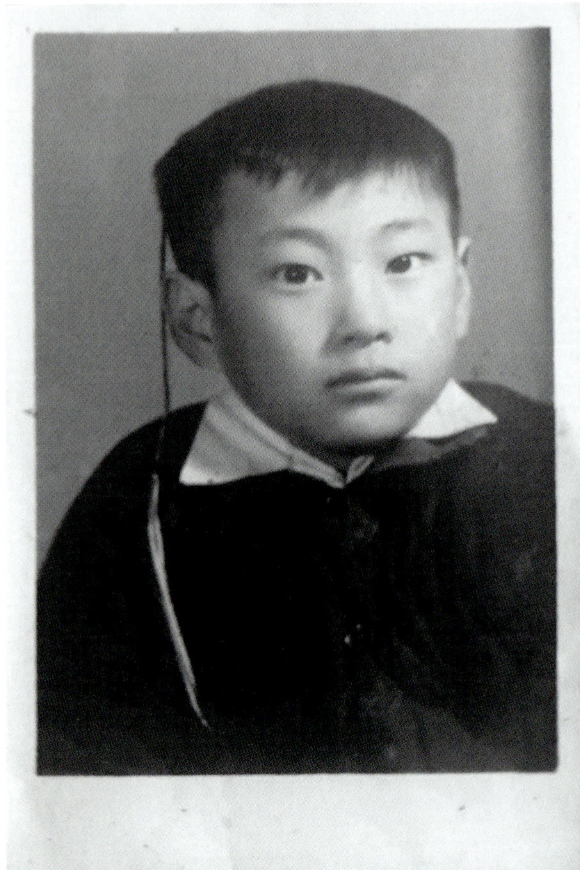

ator. Interweaving her descriptions of the images with her own experiences visiting the photographed locations in real time and space, Whalen makes the case that she and the album's creator become "collaborative narrators; between us, we have still more stories to tell."[28] Much contemporary scholarship on family photography picks up on this thread, emphasizing the importance of material, spatial, narrative, and haptic contact with the objects themselves. Thy Phu and Elspeth Brown made the case in a landmark anthology they edited in 2014, entitled *Feeling Photography*. Likewise, Tina Campt has pointed out that the very creation of family albums as objects functions as "a vernacular practice through which the family constructs and reproduces itself, not necessarily as it is or was, but rather as it would like to be seen."[29] And, Martha Langford argues that "voices must be heard for memories to be preserved, for the album to fulfill its function."[30]

All these vectors of interpretation—space, sound, storage, and touch—bear upon our readings of photographs. Albums can only take on their fullest meaning when we know the "inside stories [that] frame the pictures, animating the most stilted of studio portraits with family secrets and subversive tales."[31] Attending to the materiality of Chinese family photograph albums from the Cold War period thus includes not only locating, reading, or listening to their narratives, but also literally handling them. Through the haptic mode, we can continue untangling how family albums both testify to and resist the government's policy of enforced forgetting, while simultaneously providing images that seem to uphold the master narrative.

Another urban album, this one held by the Wei family in Tianjin, China, helps us trace this dynamic relationship between the records of family photography and the survival of memory. This album documents life during the early twentieth-century, when the Wei family occupied a prominent place in Tianjin society as well-to-do bankers. Several images show the great-grandfather, standing in front of the intricately carved sculptures that formed his rock garden. In other photographs, the great-grandfather is accompanied by his son and his son's chiropractor, a somber-looking gentleman who apparently spent his days caring for the heir to the Wei family fortune. As Wei Wenyi, the album's current owner, explained to Karintha Lowe in an interview, the family's fortunes fell during the Second Sino-Japanese War (1937–45), when the invading Japanese army seized control of the Wei family's banks.

By 1966, the family of six lived in a narrow, two-level apartment in the center of Tianjin proper and kept the album in the drawer of a large desk. During one of the dozens of raids that the Red Guard would conduct into the Wei family home, the guards confiscated this desk, along with other valuable furniture, and stored these items in dedicated warehouses. The desk was returned to the family in the late 1970s, after the Chinese government created offices that sifted through the warehoused goods and sent the items back to their owners, when possible. Wei Wenyi remembers tearing through the red tape affixed to the desk drawers and finding, tucked inside, the preserved photographs of his family's past.

While the desk sat in the warehouse, gathering mold and dust, the photographs themselves had, it seemed, encountered human hands. Certain photographs had gone missing, others had folded corners, and all the photographs had been detached from the album pages and disassembled into an apparently haphazard pile. Someone with legal access to the warehouse—staff, members of the Red Guard, or Communist Party officials—might have rifled

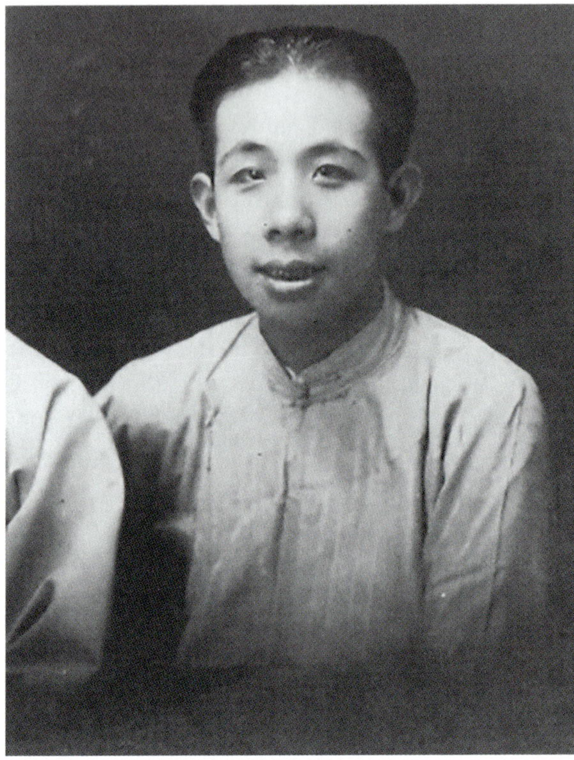

**Figure 10.6.** In anticipation of Red Guard raids, families could elect to disappear "evidence" by cropping out certain portions of their family photographs. Private Collection, Tianjin.

through the photographs. But the warehouses were also relatively unsecured. On occasion, locals would break into the storage units in order to take some of the bounty home for themselves.

Lowe asked Wei how he thought the photographs had survived the Cultural Revolution despite having been gone through by so many human hands. Gesturing to the pile of photographs, Wei shrugged and responded, "Maybe because the photos aren't worth any money, people just looked through them and left them in the desk." Removed from the public sphere, the family photographs seemed to have turned into aesthetic objects. They could be appreciated, perhaps, for their display of intricate rock formations and stylish fashions, or commodified and rejected for their supposed lack of artistic and monetary value. Now, the "album" lives in a shoebox. A graphic designer, Wei has been asked by his family to organize and digitize the images. But he cannot bring himself to do so. The very disorder of the images encodes the history and struggle of his family, and it appears impossible to remedy their losses.

One photograph in this deconstructed album brings us directly to the role of secrecy in preserving family photographs from the Cold War era. In an-

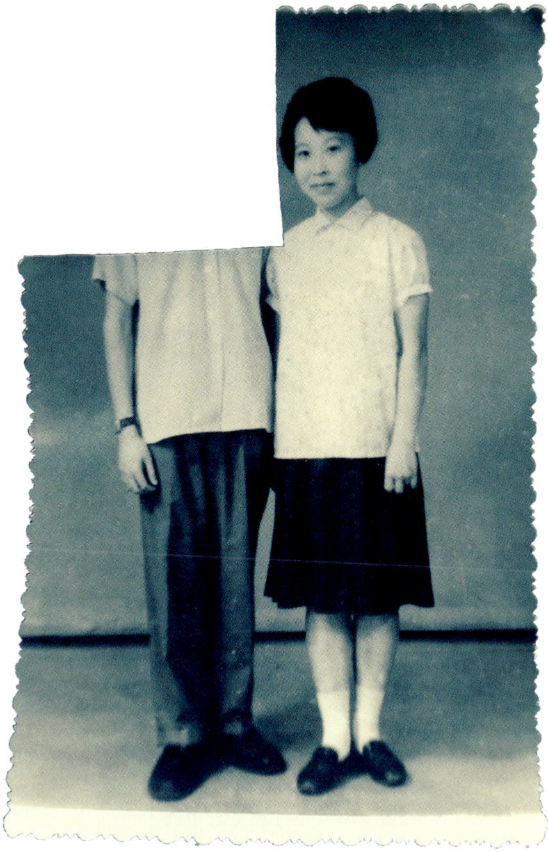

**Figure 10.7.** An image cropped for identification documentation. Private Collection, Wuhan.

ticipation of Red Guard raids, families often burned photographs or threw albums into rivers—but individuals could also elect to disappear "evidence" by cropping out certain portions of their family photographs. Pointing to one image in the shoebox, Wei said, "do you see how it's cropped right here? Why would we cut out a person? [ . . . ] It happened during the Cultural Revolution because this person, I don't know who, must have gotten in a lot of trouble. So, we cut him out so we wouldn't get in trouble, too."

Yet even this strategy of self-preservation through the destruction of family photographs has a counterpoint that renders it ambiguous. Perhaps the cut photograph was not a sign of disfavor at all. During this period, it was expensive and often difficult to get identification photographs that would nonetheless be required for official documents. Families cut the face and shoulders out of regular family portraits and pasted them onto the necessary government forms.

**Figure 10.8.** As we left Yaoji, a man rushed out of his home and showed us a framed photographic collage, normally displayed on his wall. Private Collection, Yaoji. Photographed by Laura Wexler.

In Wuhan in 2014, Guigui Yao and Laura Wexler photographed such an image that was part of the extensive family photograph collection of an urban middle-class family. The owner explained that her relative needed an identification photograph, and so they simply cut one out of another kind of picture. There was no implication here that this particular family might have feared trouble, although such an image found in another collection could have so signified. But the very existence of this practice as a normative approach to identification photographs could also serve as a cover for people who did have something to hide.

Destruction, redeployment, self-censorship, elective ambiguation, and avoidance: these engagements with family photography resulted both directly and indirectly from the instrumental management of images during the Cold War era. Manipulating the image and the album allowed many people to maintain that family photographs were—and were not—what they seemed. Are lost images simply lost, or were they repurposed, or disappeared?

## VILLAGE FORMS

In March 2014, working against the urban current of their photographic archive, Laura Wexler and Guigui Yao arranged formal appointments for a research trip to the farming, in county of Huang Pi, outside the capital city of Wuhan in the province of Hubei, where Yao had been raised. Before going to the village, they stopped to chat with Yao's sister-in-law, who lived in the town of Yaoji, about a twenty-minute walk away from the village. While they were outside saying goodbye, a man rushed out of his house to inquire what they were doing. When they told him, he immediately went back inside and returned with his wife and a framed photographic collage he had just taken off the wall. He was eager to talk.

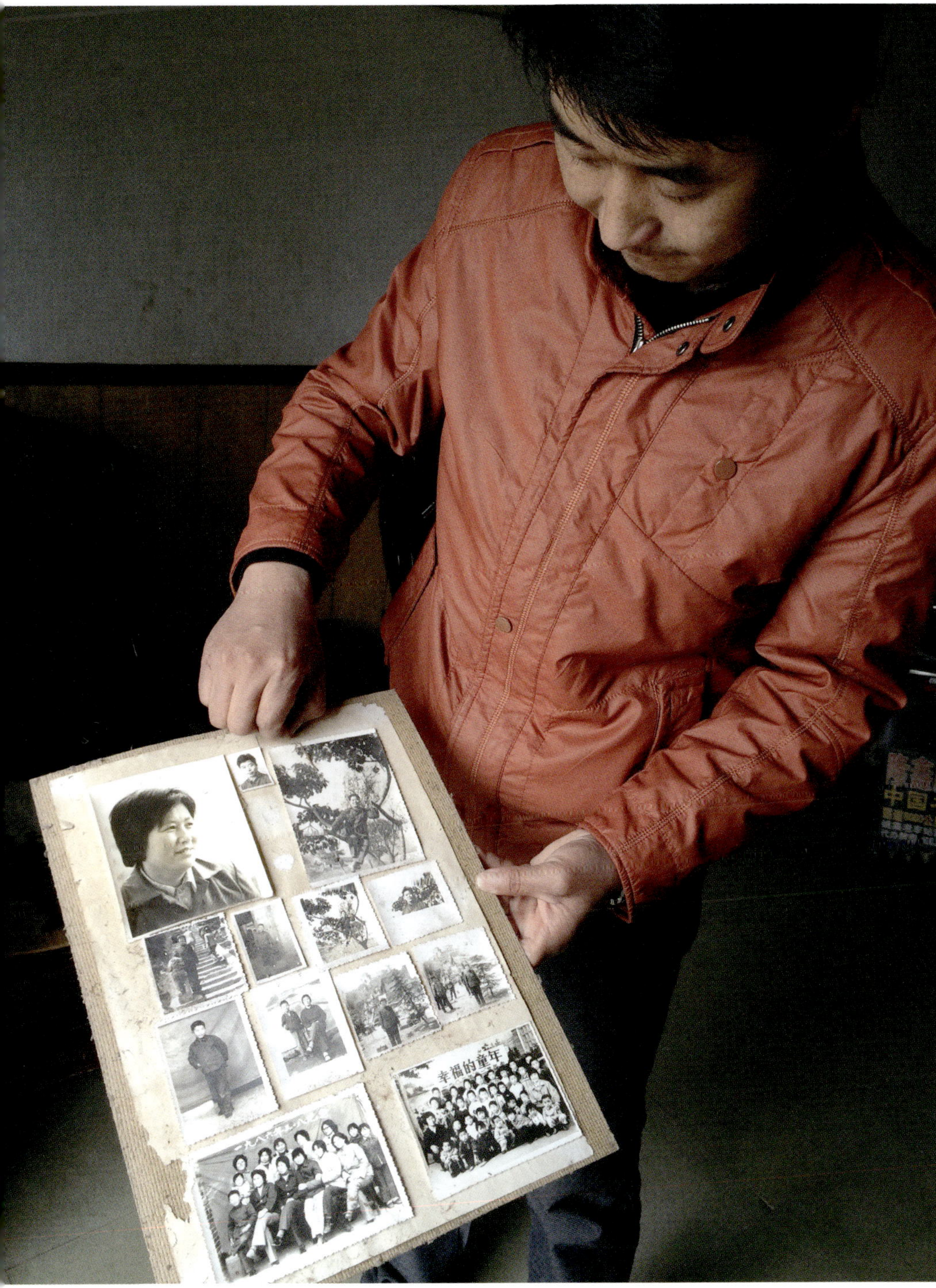
幸福的童年

**Figure 10.9.** A Newspaper "album" of images. Private Collection, Wang Jia Zui. Photographed by Laura Wexler.

A few other neighbors gathered around and everyone went inside the house, where he took the collage out of its frame so that the pictures could be seen more easily. There were photographs of his mother, and one of his father sitting in a tree. There were also several of himself: at five years old in the Happy Childhood Kindergarten, which he told us no longer existed since so many families had moved away from the town; at eight years old in the hospital; at nine, with his mother on a trip. He had a strong memory of getting the photograph made, but was less definite about the trip. There was also a photograph of which he was particularly proud, depicting his mother with a group of women in 1986 at a celebration of International Women's Day. He told us that the photographic collage had been hanging in the living room in his mother's house until she died, after which he began to display the collection in his home.

In the village, another man, also not previously scheduled for an interview, insisted that Wexler and Yao come to his house after he was informed of their project. Several other family members also gathered round. Out of a back room he brought a bundle of newspapers, which he untied while everyone watched. Inside nestled a clutch of photographs from an even earlier time. These included an image of his wife's uncle and a buddy, back from the army; the same uncle with a group of police on Labor Day; a studio portrait of the uncle and his bride upon their marriage; and quite a number of photographs from the factory at Nanjing, where the uncle worked after leaving the Korean War.

This man explained that his uncle had been very lucky. He had joined the army late in the war, as soon as he was old enough to enlist. The third among his brothers to do so, the uncle responded to a call for Chinese volunteers. Since food was scarce at home, this departure helped in his family's survival. But when the uncle returned from war, he found the village in famine. Here, the man explained, was where the uncle's luck came in: he was extremely fortunate at that point to obtain a job in a factory. He continued:

> No one could grow food in the village community. No one could get what they planted. The farms were group owned and the food was sup-

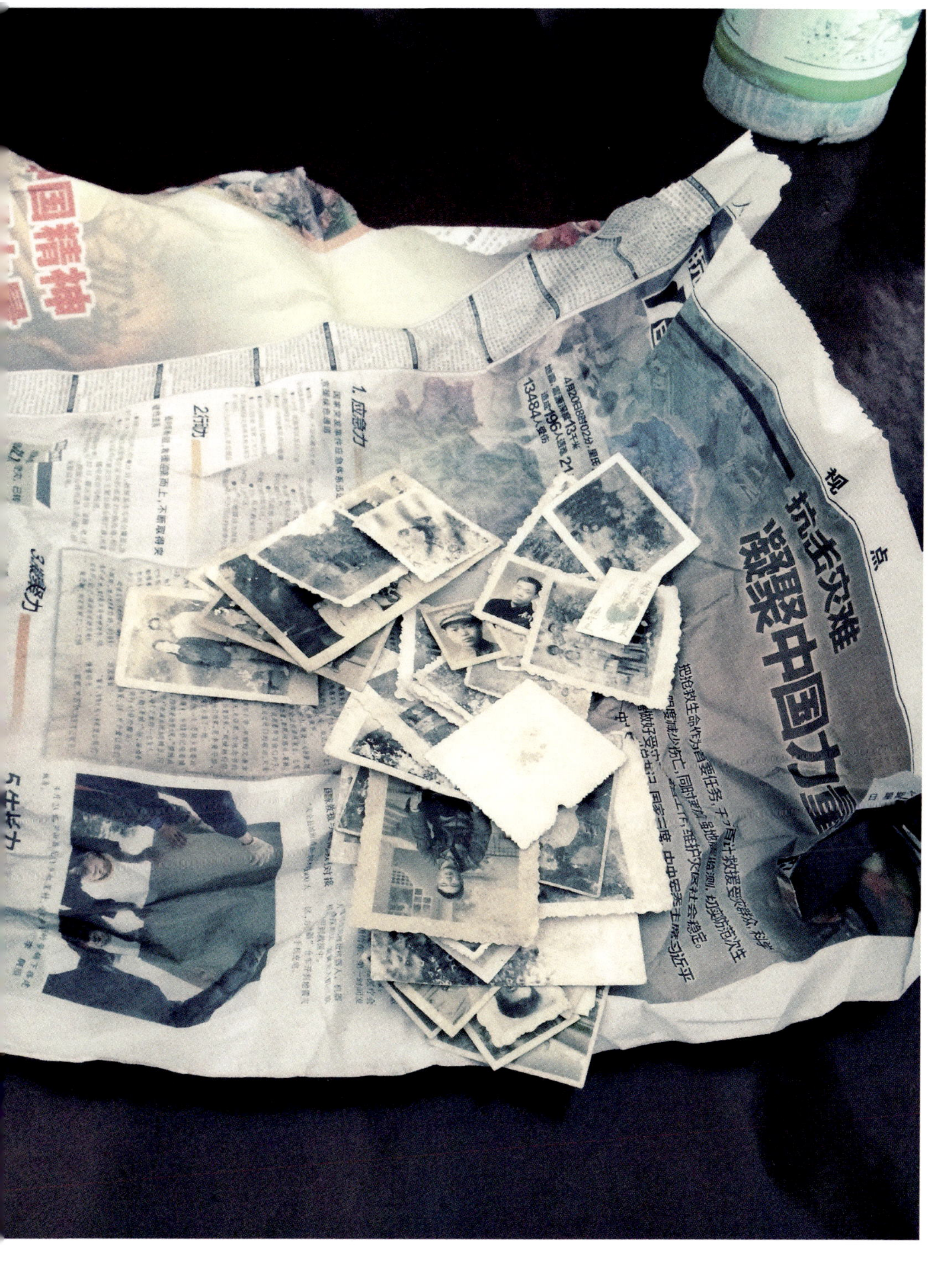
视点
抗击灾难
凝聚中国力量

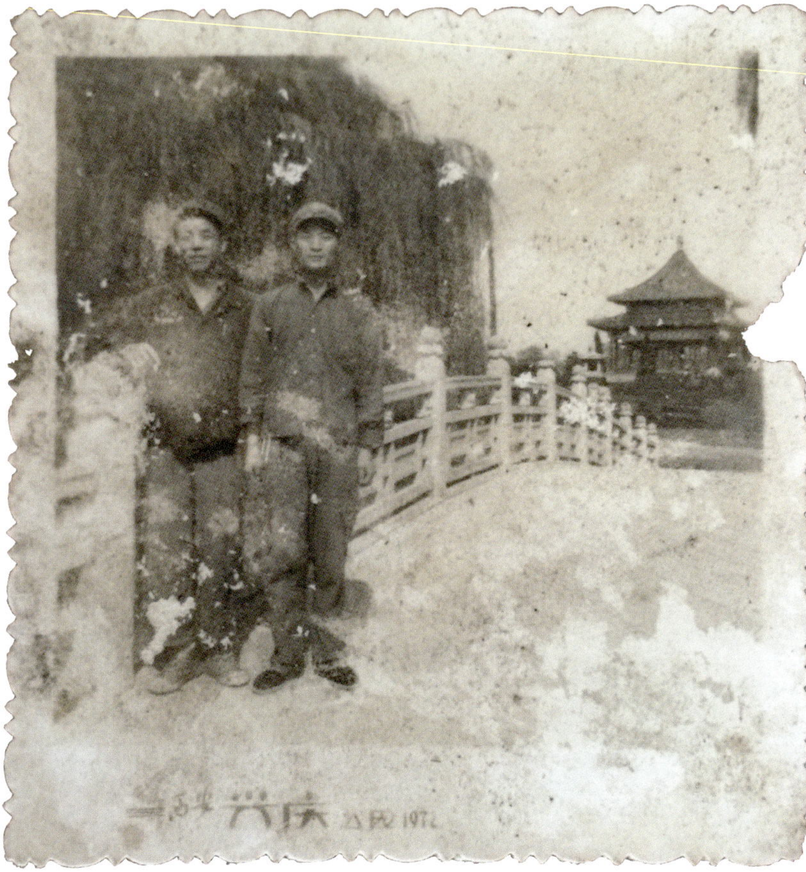

> posed to be distributed, but there was no food to distribute. The volume was not enough. Men and women were working in the fields together, but some were just pretending and did not work hard. There was bad management and competition. Every year we had to send the government a big percentage.

Throughout this story, the man repeated the refrain: "I remember that. I remember that."

This clutch of photographs also contained images from every later phase of the Cold War period. Throughout this period, the uncle had tried to return to the village, but, finding life in the village economically unsustainable, he would be forced to leave again. Finally, he was able to hand his job in Nanjing over to his son and retire back in the village. The collection of photographs, now preserved in newspaper, composed a narrative of his departure and re-

Figure 10.10. (*opposite*)
Family photograph. Private Collection, Wang Jia Zui.

Figure 10.11. (*below*)
For Guigui Yao, a photograph of the fields evokes memories of play and communal labor. Private Collection, Wang Jia Zui.

integration, precious emblems of his constant desire to rejoin the life of the village that had taken so many strategies and so many years to accomplish.

In other houses, often filled with eager neighbors, Wexler and Yao examined more collages, framed and hanging on the walls, as well as images kept in boxes, drawers, and bundles of paper. There was rarely a literal album, but there were plenty of pictures and a multiplicity of stories. Among them was a group of photographs of the entire village taken for a special occasion, and a photograph of women from the village working in the fields. This prompted

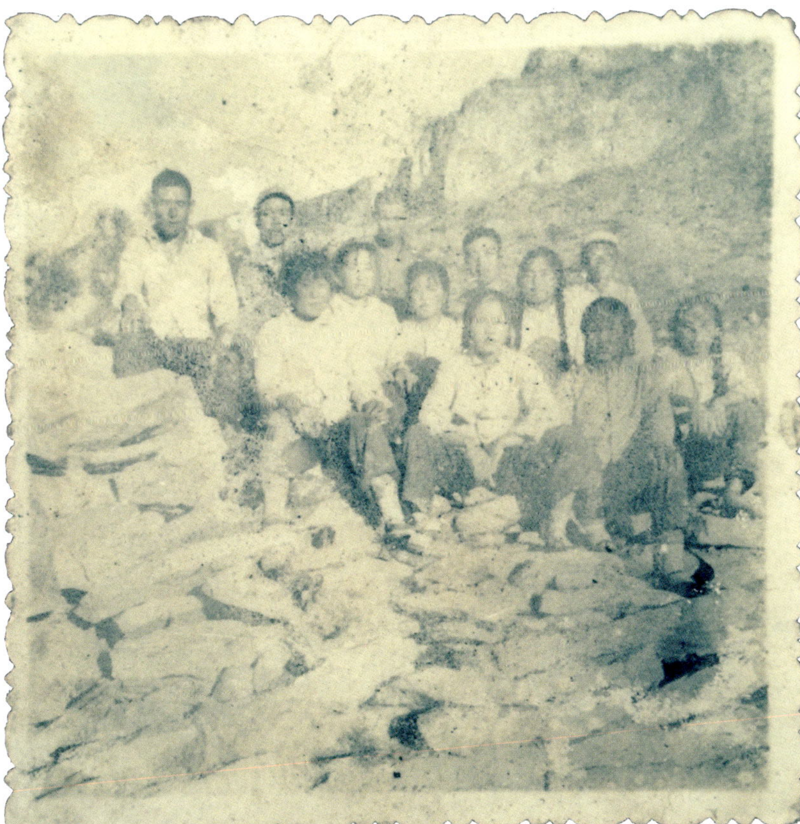

**Figure 10.12.**
**Year after year, the schoolteacher's "family album" recorded the students and teachers of his community, registering the violence sustained by his community during the Cultural Revolution. Private Collection, Wang Jia Zui. Photographed by Laura Wexler.**

Yao to share some of her own memories: "I remember when I was young my mother used to take me to the fields and I would just play there. Sometimes I would help my mother with planting cotton, putting the seeds into the soil with a special tool. I still remember the field over there, just over the hill. My mother with a whole group of women, and I, would just work." Yao's story is exceptional. Impoverished by China's lurching economy, weakened by illness, and shunned by some in the village because of their formerly higher status, Yao's family worked in the fields and survived. Identified as a brilliant student, Yao eventually obtained an education, moved away for high school and college, and now returned to the village as a university professor on a research project. Most of her family had left. The family's house had collapsed. Yet Yao's sense of connection to the village, the photographs, and the stories was unbroken and far from irrelevant. Her PhD dissertation even explored American author Wendell Berry's celebrations of rural life.

Other stories emerged in splinters that were very complicated to interpret. As it happened, when Wexler and Yao first set out for one particular day of fieldwork, they had given a ride to an elderly woman returning to her home in the village from an errand in Wuhan. Yao explained the project to her, and at the end of the trip as she got out of the car, the woman turned back to say something in Mandarin, which Yao paraphrased: "She says that she thinks a lot about the Cultural Revolution. She had been part of a group of students who threw the schoolteacher off the roof of the school. She is wondering now whether that had been a right thing, or a wrong thing, to do." That same afternoon, a woman who now lived in the neighboring town where her son had a small electronics business retrieved a photograph from the back of the shop of herself, her husband, and her sister-in-law, who was her brother's widow.

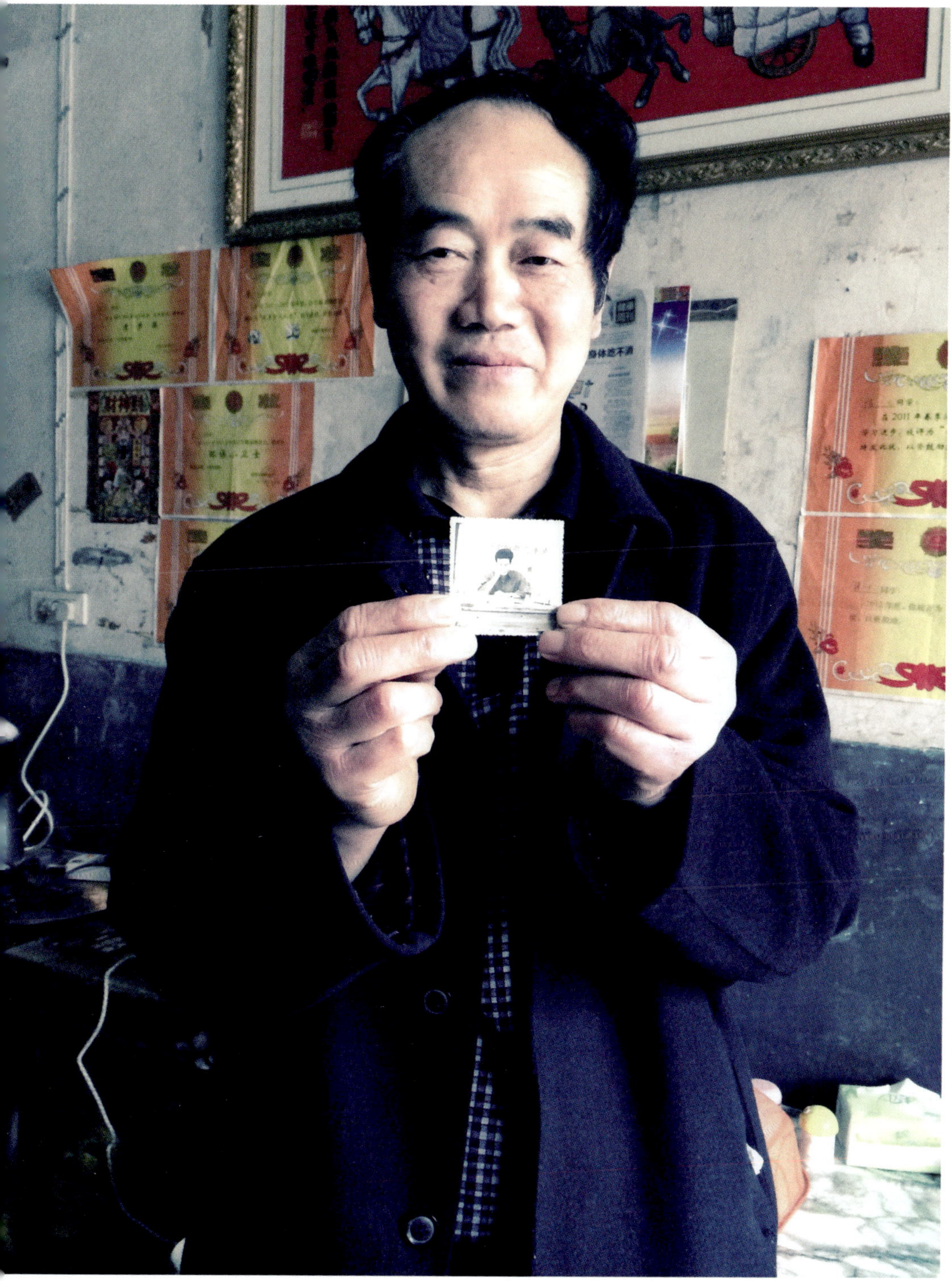

**Figure 10.13.** Yao poses here with an image of Wang Jia Zui. Leaving the village for high school, she now returns as a university professor on a research project. Photographed by Laura Wexler.

She said that her brother "suffered from the Cultural Revolution. Because he suffered a lot, he died young, in 1986. His students came and put him in a bag and dropped him off the roof of the building. Then they went down and got the bag and carried him back up. He was all broken, his bones and his mind." Later, Yao and Wexler visited a schoolteacher who used to live in the village. He said he had been too poor during that time to be able to get any photographs made of himself. But each year, his school would hire a photographer to take a picture of the graduating class, and sometimes one of the parents would buy an extra portrait to give him. Year after year he put these graduation photographs in an album, which he still had and proudly showed us. He said that these images were his family photographs, the only photographic record he had of his youth, about which he assumed we had inquired. It is not an album of his adventures as a young man, like albums of sent-down youths, some of whom had actually been sent to work in the area. It is an album of the labor of his life.

Putting these three anecdotes together, one ultimately recognizes that this schoolteacher, whose family album was literally the same as the record of his school, also appears as a key witness to the violence this community sustained during the Cold War era. His album is important beyond the individual personal story that he traced. What he didn't state was that the album also provided evidence that he had carefully stored and maintained. Year after year, the pictures recorded victims, perpetrators, and onlookers, marking absences and continued presences about which it still remains unadvisable to speak directly. The rumination of the elderly woman in the car—had it had been a right thing or a wrong thing to throw the schoolteacher off the roof?—might someday be publicly acknowledged, but apparently not yet. Multiple individuals held different pieces of a story they shared but would not, or could not, tell. It would have been seriously misguided to inquire throughout the countryside for culminating and directly incriminating privately held images of such horrible events. But the *undercurrent photographic data* of conditions

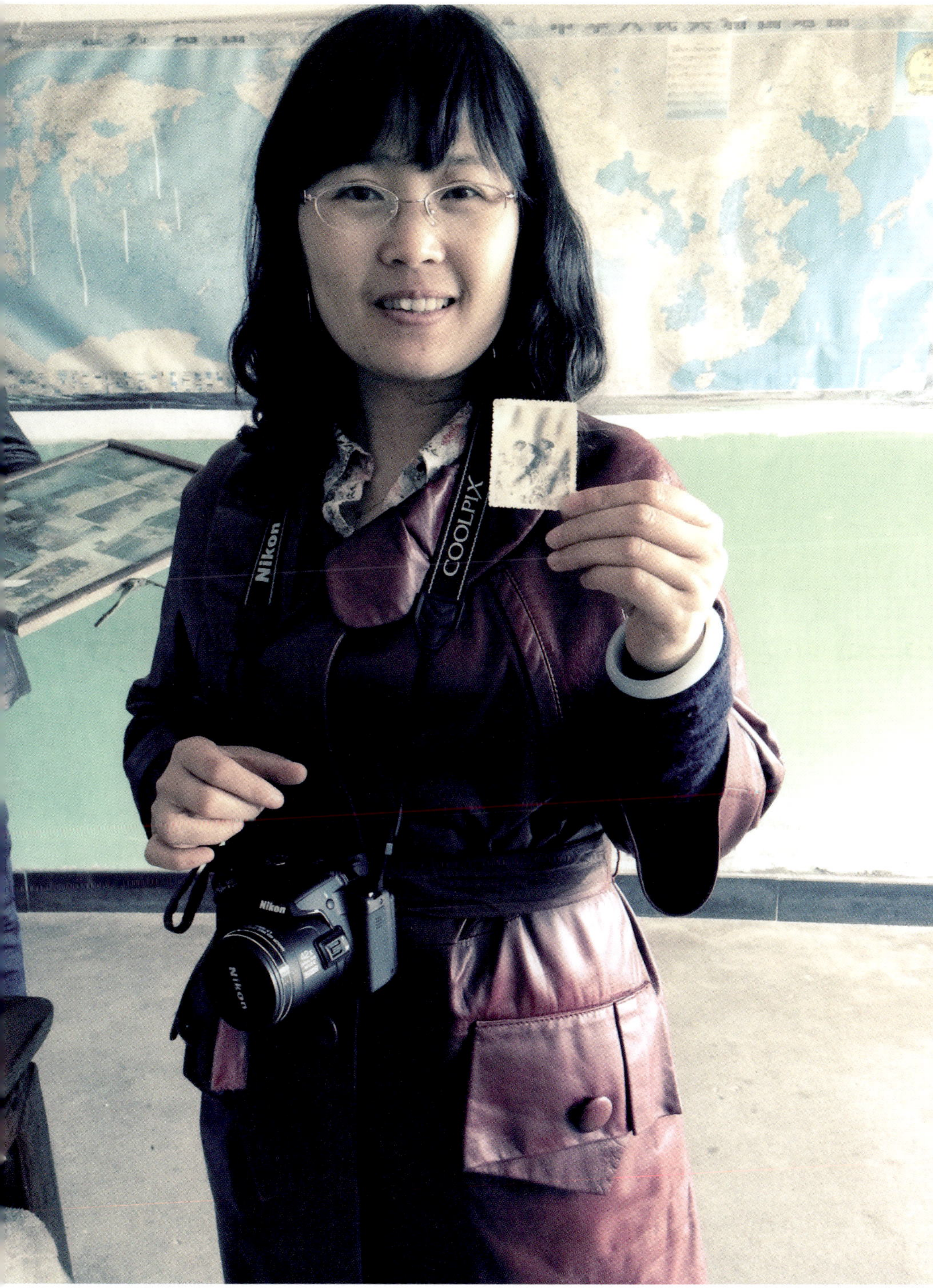
Nikon
COOLPIX
Nikon
Nikon

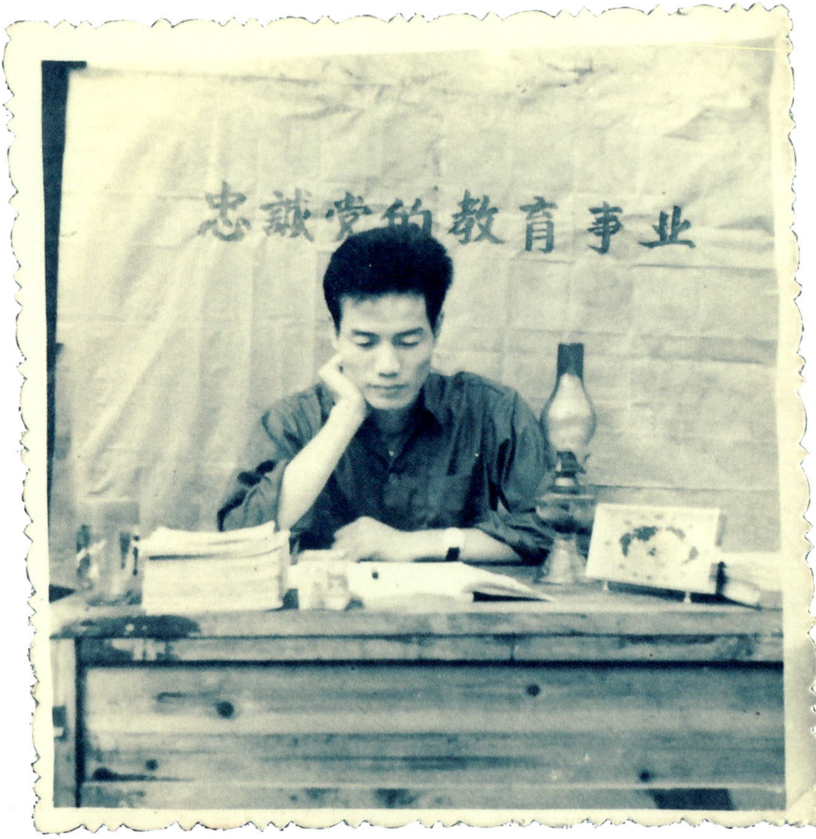

surrounding “the event of photography,” as Azoulay puts it, bring the pieces together. The personal family photographs of the villagers are horizontal, distributed, collective data, arrayed across time and space. Their photographs are a lieu de contre mémoire that they hold in common, a fragmented repository of episodes still officially unmarked and unremembered.

All of these fieldwork anecdotes explode the notion that there is no vernacular photographic record of the Cold War of note in the Chinese countryside. It is true that a vanishingly small number of rural families owned their own cameras. However, even the impoverished were able on occasion to get pictures made, and in the aggregate, many were saved. Two final photographs from Wang Jia Zui, which Yao recalls, illustrate this point:

> Somehow, two photos were taken, one of women working in the fields and the other of both men and women taking a break after working in the fields. Nobody remembers who has taken them. But for the owner,

**Figure 10.14.** This individual image composes a part of the schoolteacher's "family album," a series of photographs commissioned by the parents of students. Private collection, Wang Jia Zui.

> Wang Simei, that was a happy time when all village people worked together in a commune. In the fields, people sometimes made jokes and teased each other. The photos remind her of "a socialist utopia." For her husband, however, these photos convey a false image of the reality—working in a commune was inefficient, because some people simply tried their best to avoid working hard; besides, all families were so trapped in poverty that they had absolutely no way out. The order was that no one should migrate to a town or a city, and everybody should stay and work in the field. After all, when business, even vending, was strictly prohibited, there were no jobs available anywhere else.

As this discussion shows, disagreement exists about the significance of the village archive. The observations of the husband and wife exhibit two distinct reactions to the image as aide-mémoire. The wife sees the successful "socialist utopia" envisioned by the state and even, perhaps, as she experienced it at the time or in retrospect. But to her husband, the two images reveal the forced forgetting of the Cold War era. He details long repressed contradictions: the shared sense of imprisonment; the lack of other jobs; the absence of hope; his anger at those in the commune who, he felt, held back; and the inefficiency of the PRC economy overall. During this time, China's often unstable economic and political situation made open disagreement with state administered policy inadvisable, and it would have muffled disagreement between husband and wife, even this far from Beijing. But confronting this apparently fragmented photographic archive in contemporary discussion allowed these tensions, unforgotten, to spring back to life.

Contemporary photographic theory is ill equipped to take up such liminal, fugitive, and latent archives. According to Jacques Derrida, the archive is an acknowledged institutional space, guarded by powerful figures whose authority is sovereign. Michel Foucault theorizes the archive as a technology of power, while Diana Taylor likens it to a living repertoire of gestures. For Achille Mbembe, on the other hand, the archive is a murderous procedure that attempts to turn the colonized into ghosts. In none of these instances is the archive taken to exist in and as a form of photographic material that is held in common, in suspension, in a virtual space that awaits a new stage of appearance. Yet our fieldwork located the archive form as exactly that, as a chrysalis. That is to say, the archive exists in a potential, transitional state prior to its emergence in the future. Such an archive accumulates meaning as it transacts a communal function, testifying to the promise of further access to a memory of its past that has, for now, only been shared by the community in pieces. In this conceptualization, dispersed meaning is not meaning destroyed but meaning held in abeyance. Such a template almost certainly governed the construction, over and over again during the Cold War, of village archives like the ones we discovered in Wuhan and which remain intact today.

It is difficult to trace the outline of such an archive. This provides one reason why scholars often insist that large numbers of historically significant rural family photographs from the time do not exist. Such an archive is a social contract extended in time and distributed in space. It is not a thing; it is an intelligence that decides whether and when to emerge and for whom, as the aggregation did when Wexler and Yao interviewed the inhabitants of Wang Jia Zui. Nor is it necessarily simple to point out that such an archive has appeared. None of the villagers did. The purpose of such an archive is to store and hide knowledge *in plain sight* by sorting, fragmenting, and distributing it. Exegesis by individuals is not necessarily whole and transparent. In their fieldwork, for instance, Wexler and Yao heard again and again that "nobody remembers" who took the two photographs of the villagers in the field. Within a Cold War geography marked by secrecy, might there be an unstated further reason not to share the memories?

The concept of potential history, as described by Ariella Azoulay in *Potential History: Unlearning Imperialism*, helps illuminate how an archive that exists nowhere and everywhere constitutes the inexhaustible commons of family photographs into the future. Potential history, she writes, "originates from a refusal to accept the outcome of violence as fait accompli and the insistence that there is always something to be done because nothing is over."[32] In *Collaboration: A Potential History of Photography*, Azoulay along with Wendy Ewald, Susan Meiselas, Leigh Raiford, and Laura Wexler remark that "when a community is at stake," all those involved in the event of photography, even after the fact of making the physical artifact itself, participate in remaking its meaning. We might say, for example, that the hidden photograph of the young protagonist of the little red album recodes the propaganda photographs of the CCP. In bringing our attention to the very possibility of a copresent, countervailing image, the photograph helps demonstrate how the gesture of soldiers waving their Little Red Books at Chairman Mao does not necessarily mean that they had subordinated family loyalty into the state apparatus, as was Mao's intention. Possibly, we might locate an opposite meaning behind their gestures: like the Korean War soldier, they were serving their families by serving the state. The photographic legacy of the violence of the Cold War period constitutes a *potential archive*, neither waiting passively to be "discovered" by others who are supposed to know better than its owners its "true" meaning (of which they are themselves often well enough aware), nor acceding to its own destruction in putative self-defense. Rather, the *potential archive* of the Cold War in China awaits opportunities for a collective reinterpretation of the meaning of communal experience, under conditions of its own making, and in its own time.

## *Notes*

1 During the Cultural Revolution, Mao Zedong instituted a "rustication program," resettling around 17 million urban youths to the countryside for manual labor and socialist reeducation. Also known as the "Up to the Mountains and Down to the Countryside" campaign, many of the program's participants are known as the zhiqing, or the "knowledgeable youth." For an informative study of the zhiqing generation, memory, and visual culture, see D. Davies, "Old Zhiqing Photos."

2 Professor Laura Wexler, from Yale University; Professor Guigui Yao, from Jiangnan University; and Karintha Lowe, a graduate student at Harvard University, conducted exploratory fieldwork from 2007 to 2017 on Chinese family photographs during the Cold War era. During multiple research trips to Wuhan, Tianjin, Beijing, and Shanghai spanning that decade, we discussed images and memories with the approximately three dozen people who accepted our invitation to talk about their family photographs. When given permission, we made copies of

these images, some of which appear here. We also collected photographs at urban and rural flea markets, where a demand for twentieth-century memorabilia keeps family albums in circulation, mostly anonymously. In this essay, we share some of the general conclusions of the project, and suggest some principles for further research.

3 Susie Linfield. *The Cruel Radiance*, 103.

4 Robert Bickers, quoted in Ward-Lowery, "The Search for Photos of China's Past."

5 Liu Xinwu, "Yingzi dashu" [Shadow uncle], reprinted in *Siren zhaoxiang bu* [Private photo album] (Shanghai, 1997), 16–17.

6 Jie Li, "Virtual Museums of Forbidden Memories," 540.

7 Kwon, *The Other Cold War*, 140–41. Kwon cites Stephen Whitfield, in particular his *The Culture of the Cold War*, as influential in Kwon's own turn toward social analysis.

8 Kwon, *The Other Cold War*, 140–41.

9 Whitfield, *The Culture of the Cold.*

10 Azoulay, *Potential History*, xvi.

11 Pierre Nora, "Between Memory and History."

12 Huyssen, *Present Pasts.*

13 Shi, "With Mao and Stalin: Liu Shaoqi in Moscow, 84–85; see also discussion in Chen Jian, *Mao's China and the Cold War*, 3.

14 Mao, "Jieshao yige hezuoshe" [Introducing a cooperative]," 3.

15 Meisner, *Mao's China and After*, 316.

16 Chen Jian, *Mao's China and the Cold War*, 7.

17 Chen Jian, *Mao's China and the Cold War*, 7.

18 "The 1968 New Year Editorial," *People's Daily, Liberation Army Daily*, and *Red Flag*, in *Wenhua da geming yanjiu ziliao* [Cultural Revolution research materials] (Beijing: Zhongguo renmin jiefangjun guofang daxue dangshi dangjian zhonggong jiaoyanshi, 1988), vol. 2, page 3.

19 Chen Jian, *Mao's China and the Cold War*, 10.

20 Mitter, "China and the Cold War," 125.

21 Mitter, "China and the Cold War," 125.

22 Verdery, *What Was Socialism, and What Comes Next?*, 4. For an analysis of Verdery in the Soviet context, see Sarkisova and Shevchenko's contribution to this volume (chapter 11).

23 Sarkisova and Shevchenko, "Soviet Past in Domestic Photography: Events, Evidence, Erasure," in Shevchenko, *Double Exposure*, 163.

24 Sarkisova, "Soviet Past in Domestic Photography," 163.

25 Laurence Coderre, "The Curator, the Investor, and the Dupe."

26 First designed as a riposte to the uniforms of the Soviet and Japanese armed forces, the Mao suit indicated both the CCP's early links to the USSR and its concurrent militarization of the Chinese public. As Tina Mai Chen details, "The Mao

suit, because it represented the clothing of the proletariat and the People's Liberation Army, fused the civilian and military traditions of the new modern China. The prevailing vision of the sartorial landscape of China under the leadership of Mao Zedong is one of masses of peasants and workers dressed in Mao suits of navy blue, khaki green, or grey. The uniformity of the clothes and the subdued colors represent an imagined homogeneity across the time and space of the Chinese nation from 1949–1976." See Tina Mai Chen, "Dressing for the Party," 145.

27 Hirsch, *The Familial Gaze.*

28 Whalen, "Interpreting Vernacular Photography," 91.

29 Campt, *Image Matters*, 90.

30 Langford, *Suspended Conversations*, 5.

31 Langford, *Suspended Conversations*, 5.

32 Azoulay, *Potential History*, 291.

# 11

OKSANA SARKISOVA

& OLGA SHEVCHENKO

# Travel, Space, and Belonging in Soviet Domestic Photo Collections of the Cold War Era

Elena is a retired Muscovite and a proud owner of an unusually rich family archive.[1] At the time we met her, she was in her early sixties and did not leave Moscow often; but as a young woman, she traveled all over the former USSR, from Siberia in the East to Estonia in the West, and from Georgia in the South to the Yamal peninsula in the North. Growing up in a communal apartment in Moscow's center, Elena shared a passion for travel with many of her generation. As a child, she would conduct "expeditions" with friends in the neighborhood, exploring back alleys and backdoors, climbing over

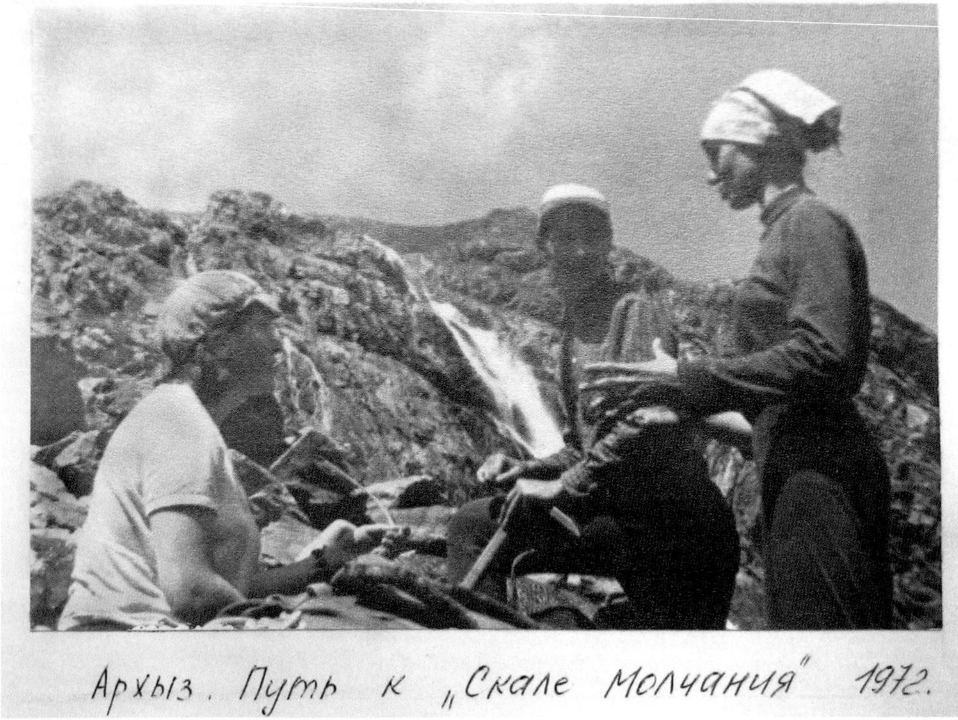


roofs and jumping over fences in order to satisfy her hunger for adventures. "We started from exploring [osvaivat'] the territory right around our building. And after we had it all explored, it became boring, so we moved farther and farther. It was like our personal kind of travel," she reminisced. When she grew older, she found other possibilities for exploration, first becoming a certified trip leader and mountain climbing instructor (a capacity in which she is depicted in figure 11.1), and then finding a job with a research institute that sent her far and wide installing meteorological stations and taking meter readings in various far-flung regions of the Soviet Union.

While few people may be as adventurous as Elena, she belongs to one of several generations of Soviet people who found travel desirable and meaningful, and whose sensibilities were part of a larger cultural and ideological trend. Tourism, or turizm, as it was called in Russian, was not just a way to shake up the drudgery of everyday life in the USSR, nor was it simply a form of leisure. Instead, as historians of Soviet travel and mass culture tell us, state agencies encouraged and directed tourism as "self-improving and socially

**Figure 11.1.** A photograph from a mountaineering expedition to the Arkhyz Gorge in the Caucasus. The caption reads, "Arkhyz. On the way to the Cliff of Silence. 1972." Elena's private collection, Moscow.

constructive: building knowledge, restoring and strengthening the body, encouraging patriotism."[2]

Leisure travel abroad was extremely rare in the USSR. Made officially possible only in 1955, a few years after Stalin's death, it not only required foreign visas but was also closely controlled by the state.[3] By contrast, all through the seven decades of Soviet power, the state actively encouraged leisure travel *within* the country through designated and subsidized tourist networks. Such travel was presented as a way to cultivate the mind and body, and it was promoted as part and parcel of being Soviet. Indeed, in the Soviet Union, a vacation "did not provide an escape from the mobilization of citizens toward the common goal; from its beginning it was a continuation of that mobilization using an alternate setting."[4] In this way, leisure and the ability to travel were simultaneously a duty and a form of entitlement, billed as one of the achievements of the Socialist revolution. Historian of Soviet tourism Diane Koenker calls the annual paid vacation, stipulated in the labor code of 1922, "the most revolutionary contribution of Soviet socialism to promoting the welfare of its work force," and it was certainly celebrated as such.[5]

Opportunities for travel and subsidized leisure within state borders thus made a compelling argument for the superiority of the Soviet system. In the Cold War context, the official rhetoric and the shop-window image of Soviet tourism was promoted not only to the internal audience of Soviet citizens but also to the observers in the capitalist West and the countries of the Third World, for whose loyalty and allegiance the two superpowers competed in their battle for hearts and minds.[6] When addressing foreign readership, the Soviet tourist literature represented the USSR as a cultured and comfortable leisure destination on the map of the world. To the Soviet citizens, the USSR was presented as an entire world unto itself, one in which leisure travel was affordable to all, which helped preempt potential discontents regarding the limitations placed on travel abroad or with relatively modest salaries.

Rather than competing with "the West" in scale or level of service, Soviet tourism claimed a particular experiential quality, positioning itself as markedly different from "bourgeois" travel, which was seen as tainted by colonial legacy. Writing about the early years of "proletarian tourism," Irina Sandomirskaia defined it as "a successful combination of bodily enjoyment, spiritual satisfaction . . . and social joy."[7] Already in the first decades of its existence, the ideological task of Soviet tourism was formulated as no less than to foment a "cultural revolution" in the minds of the new subjects.[8]

Following Stalin's death, the Cold War competition extended from the political to the symbolic sphere, focusing in particular on lifestyle and "quality of life" (as exemplified by the famous "kitchen debate," in 1959, between Khruschev and Nixon).[9] In Katherine Verdery's words, Cold War's binary logic became "a cognitive organization of the world."[10] Along with various forms of social care—from universal access to health care to free education, the postwar Soviet Union heavily invested in an internal tourist infrastructure, creating a vast network of subsidized facilities to demonstrate, in a symbolic competition with capitalism, the accessibility of affordable recreation for all citizens.

Modern touristic experience, as John Urry convincingly argues, has a fundamentally visual nature, and Soviet-era travel was accompanied by active image production, which left traces not only in the publications of the tourism industry but also in people's private archives.[11] And while official rhetoric and representational strategies can be reconstructed from published sources, the popular response to this official discourse is more elusive.[12] To better understand how photographic exploits helped to construct and sustain people's perception of the Soviet project, we turned to family archives, asking a diverse range of families across several regions of Russia to narrate their experiences of travel during the Soviet period drawing on their family photo collections.[13] Approaching tourism as a form of seeing as much as a form of doing, this chapter focuses on the rhetorical representations and photographic traces of private touristic experiences that people shared with us.

Photographic records are important tools of self-presentation. But travel photos from the Soviet period also shaped their owners' sense of Soviet space itself, as well as their imaginary relationship to it. Travel photography thus fulfilled an implicit function: by possessing images of "explored" territories, individual viewers partook in the appropriation of the visited spaces, enhancing the spatial unity of Soviet identity. If ideology, as Louis Althusser maintained, is the representation of "the imaginary relationship of individuals to their real conditions of existence," Soviet travel photographs were quintessentially ideological, in that they gave a palpable visual expression to the unitary notion of the "Soviet people" (sovetskii narod), and to a cohesive spatial imaginary of the "Soviet land" (sovetskaia zemlia) that became essential elements of Soviet self-representation during the Cold War.[14]

Numerous visual scholars have argued that the power of photography lies, among other things, in its ability to naturalize and shroud in an air of innocence and self-evidence the existing social relations.[15] Travel photographs held in Soviet-era domestic archives allow us to see how picture-making is entangled with an individual traveler's imagination of, and relationship to, a place as well as to others in a way that is deeply constitutive of large-scale imaginings of collective communities that transcend a given physical location. In this way, the humble travel photographs in the family albums translate into everyday terms such profoundly ideological constructions as state, nation, and citizenship, serving simultaneously as tools and as constituent expressions of what Michael Billig has termed "banal nationalism."[16] These constructs are not only effective; they also have considerable staying power, as the conversations with our youngest research participants can attest. The younger generation of Russians who grew up after the fall of the USSR often interpreted the photographs of their parents and grandparents in the categories set and transmitted by the older generations. This chapter examines the ways that this ideological work is done by vernacular travel photography, and the relevance these imaginings may have for younger Russians viewing these snapshots in the twenty-first century.

## UNIFICATION OF SPACE

Like their counterparts elsewhere, Soviet-era family archives contain a multitude of photographic genres, from posed studio portraits to informal action shots made and printed by a family member. Though many images depict domestic life, the albums also feature an impressive array of distant locations, represented in a number of formats: from formal group shots of travelers in sanatoriums and resorts to action shots like Elena's, and from amateur snaps to images produced by professional photographers and set in vignettes of architectural landmarks and landscapes.

The geographic scope covered in the family albums is remarkable. Regardless of the family's location or social class, one can usually find at least several photographs taken during a trip to the seaside (either to Crimea or

**Figure 11.2.** Group photograph taken during a package tour to Volgograd. Private collection, late Soviet era, Vladimir.

the Caucasus), a few photographs from Moscow and St. Petersburg (in Soviet times—Leningrad), an array of images from visits to village relatives, and a sampling of the capitals of the Soviet Republics, the most popular being Minsk, Kyiv, and those in the Baltics (Riga, Tallinn, and Vilnius). References to the world outside the boundaries of the USSR are far less frequent, as leisurely travel abroad remained only a distant possibility for most Soviet citizens.[17]

The geographic scope contained in Soviet albums was partly a by-product of the social organization of industrial production that was deliberately dispersed. Just as the chains of connection within Soviet industry spread wide, so did the itineraries of the employees, and, consequently, the visual records of their travels. Photographic collections often blurred the line between work and travel, as in the cases of military families, whose photographic archives feature numerous locations across the republics in which the fathers did their service and in which their family members found temporary homes. But leisure travel offered by far the most numerous photographic opportunities. Such travel was encouraged and heavily subsidized, as tourism was "a means of imaginatively and experientially integrating the Soviet body at the larger, collective level."[18] Indeed, the spread and scope of the family album should not be seen merely as an accidental by-product of the mobile lifestyles led by its owners. Rather, it was a way of advancing, in a visual register, the same politics that justified the mobility of Soviet citizens in the first place, the politics that, from the early years of the USSR, sought to unite, in a web of mutual dependence and interconnectedness, disparate and often quite distant locations.

The unification of space comes across most clearly on a stylistic level in group photographs documenting organized, subsidized enterprise-based tours (figures 11.2 and 11.3). Such package tours were regularly organized to the sites associated with the memory of World War II (referred to as the Great Patriotic War [Velikaia Otechestvennaia voina] in the USSR). Among them, particular prominence was given to the so-called Hero-Cities [goroda-geroi],

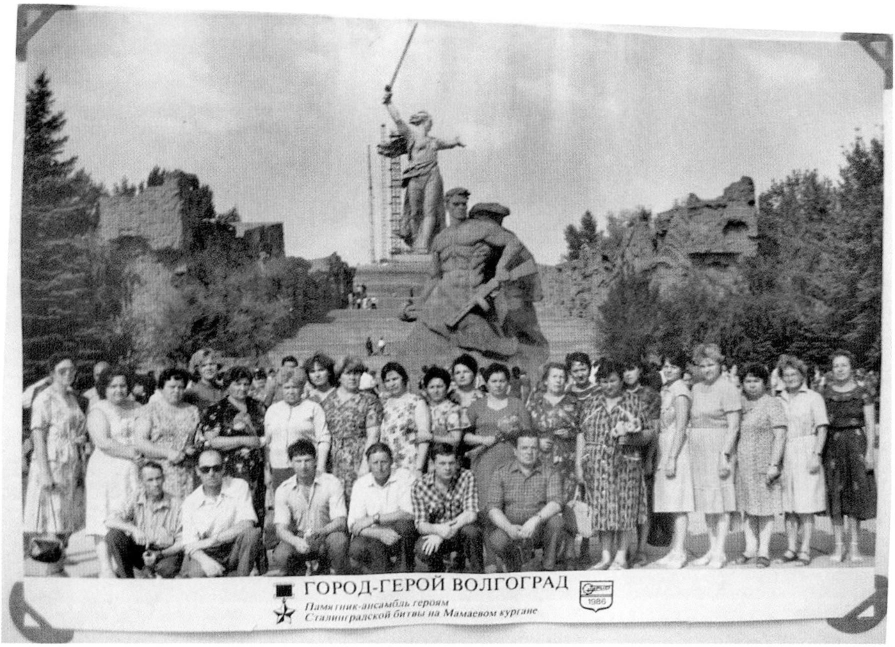


the thirteen Soviet cities and towns that were awarded this special status due to the role their defense played in the course of the war.[19] Other popular destinations were the so-called Golden Ring towns in Central Russia (including the medieval towns of Novgorod and Vladimir), and capitals of the Soviet Republics. This form of domestic travel was described by Gorsuch as "patriotic tourism," whose aim was "to engage [ . . . ] the tourist in rituals of public self-admiration, in which the prestige of the Soviet Union was perpetually re-affirmed."[20]

The visual grammar of snapshots produced in the course of "patriotic tourism" was fairly stable. The composition overall was static and symmetrical, with the group of roughly twenty or more people placed squarely in the middle ground. The people stood (or kneeled, in cases of multirow compositions) frontally, huddled closely together, but without displaying affection or even familiarity with one another. Everyone looked at the camera. The dress was casual, with handbags and briefcases in evidence. The background featured an iconic site associated with the location's claim to glory: monumental sculptures in Brest, Kyiv, or Volgograd; historical old town landmarks in the capitals of the Baltic Republics; medieval cathedrals of the Golden Ring; or the Kremlin and Red Square in Moscow. The people typically were not shown interacting with the landscape but instead posed in a manner quite

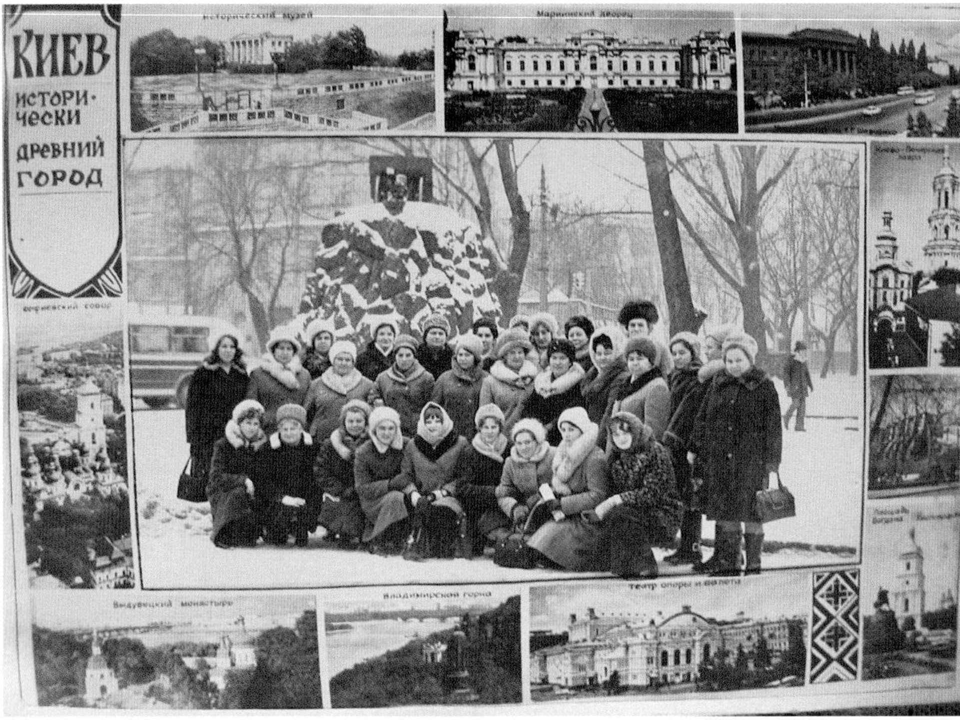


removed from their surroundings, and preserved an air both somber and impenetrable.

The group composition was frequently set in the visual frame with a range of iconic local sights, which inscribed the group experience into the pregiven matrix of the "explored" and clustered spaces. This framing combined the qualities of a photograph with those of a postcard, while also implying a structured, predetermined, and shared travel experience. The captions accompanying the images ("Volgograd—the Hero City," or "Kiev—a Historically Ancient [*sic*] City" in the above examples) further contributed to the overdetermination of the site's meaning. The same stock images were often used in group school photographs and postcards as iconic markers of locality. In other words, both the locals and the visitors were encouraged to see and experience a given site through the prism of the same predetermined iconic sights.

Compositional conventions were strongly imprinted in the late-Soviet photographic practice of group portraits. These conventions included the arrangement of large homogenous groups in several symmetrical rows against the memorial site as a backdrop and showing no signs of intimacy or ex-

**Figure 11.3.** Group photograph taken on a package tour to Kyiv. Private collection, late 1970s, Vladimir.

plicit emotions. Virtually every family archive we saw contained several such group photographs from sanatoriums and images of organized trade-union trips; some participants had entire albums. The rigidity of the photographic conventions of Soviet organized group travels was only further highlighted by the occasional dissonance between the "sitters" and the backdrop, as is the case in figures 11.4 and 11.5.

This visual uniformity of the group travel photographs calls to mind Joseph Brodsky's remark regarding the thin border line gracing the walls of all Soviet public interiors just above the eye level, where the wall color ended and the white stucco of the ceiling began. This was a line "running unfailingly across the whole country," he observed, "like the line of an infinite common denominator," "maddening as it was omnipresent" and effectively unifying the Soviet space.[21] The group photographs of the type described above, like that notorious line, both visually integrated and homogenized the space of the USSR as well as its subjects. The homogenization effect was, indeed, two-fold: not only did disparate albums owned by different families look the same, but so too did the disparate regions of the USSR. The narrow range of "photogenic sites" in which similarly composed groups were inscribed resulted in identical-looking photographs populating millions of family albums. The organized travel formatted the photographic accounts in a way that frequently made it hard for the owners to recognize where a particular image had been taken—because the backdrop (a neoclassical building, a Lenin monument, a fountain) did not have an easily recognizable provenance. A characteristic commentary to such photographs was, "*And this is some memorial in 1958. . . .* [Interviewer: "And where is it?"] *Where is it, this does not say . . .*" For the owner of the image, and for their descendants, the practice of inscribing group photographs with the location and date (and occasionally marking one's place with an arrow) often became the go-to way to identify the photographic occasion and to mark the relevant face in the row of identically posed bodies.

The settings in which these groups pose are now scattered across fifteen nation-states. But the rigid representational conventions of the images make

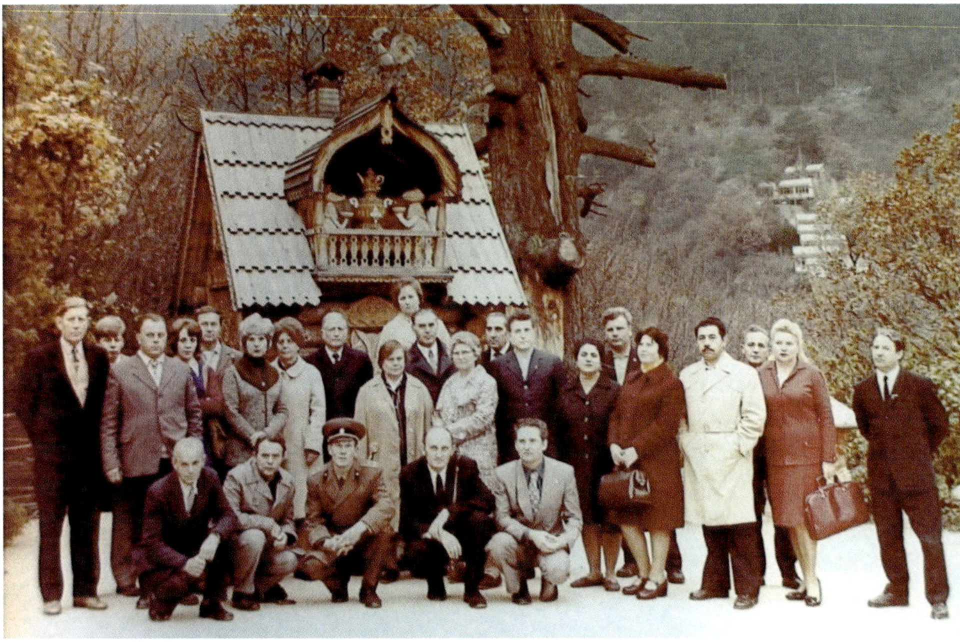

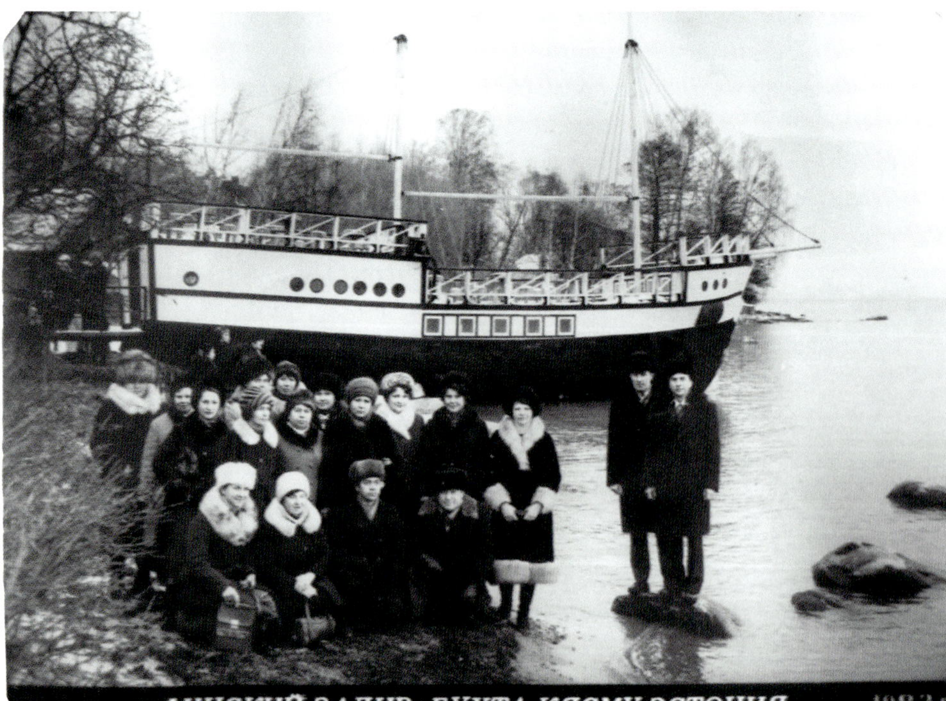
ФИНСКИЙ ЗАЛИВ, БУХТА КЯСМУ ЭСТОНИЯ
1983 г.

**Figure 11.4.** ***(top)*** **Group photograph from a trip to Crimea, which included a visit to the Field of Fairy-Tales, an open-air children's park featuring characters from Russian folktales. Private collection, late 1970s, St. Petersburg.**

**Figure 11.5.** ***(bottom)*** **A group of factory workers from Vladimir posing during an organized trip to Estonia. The caption reads, "The Gulf of Finland, Käsmu Bay, Estonia." Private collection, 1983, Vladimir.**

the places appear reassuringly familiar and ideologically unproblematic, back then as much as today. The habits of seeing that such photographic micro-practices encouraged rested on the assumption that the locations in the photographs were already Soviet, integral elements in the ideological narrative that was shared throughout the USSR. In so doing, these images provided a visual counterpart to the Soviet travel literature, in which "[t]he happy cohesiveness of the Soviet Union was compared to the divisiveness of United States, which was said to be torn apart by class, race and religion."[22]

Indeed, the visual similarity of group travel photos—in clothing, posture, experience, and itineraries—themselves implied a solidarity borne of a shared lifestyle, naturalizing the stretch of Soviet practices and visual conventions both in a geographic and in a cultural sense. An additional element of integration was brought out by the "sitters" (or rather "standers") in the photographs themselves. While some tours were filled with workers from the same enterprise, others brought together workers involved in the same industry, but from different regions of the country. Given the robust photo production that accompanied such travels (in contrast to the often modest photographic output within families, particularly those that did not own a camera), this meant that Soviet domestic archives were to a surprising extent filled by images of people who were *not* family, nor even friends, but whose geographic background and presence in the same visual space of the family album both testified and further contributed to the cultural and physical integration of the Soviet space and its people. At the same time, images made allusions to a metaphorical all-Union family that included, apart from the photographic subjects, the allegorical figures of the Motherland and its heroic defenders, as well as, occasionally, the Party leadership.

Organized package tours to the World War II leiux de mémoire constituted a flourishing subcategory of Soviet patriotic tourism. The visits to the

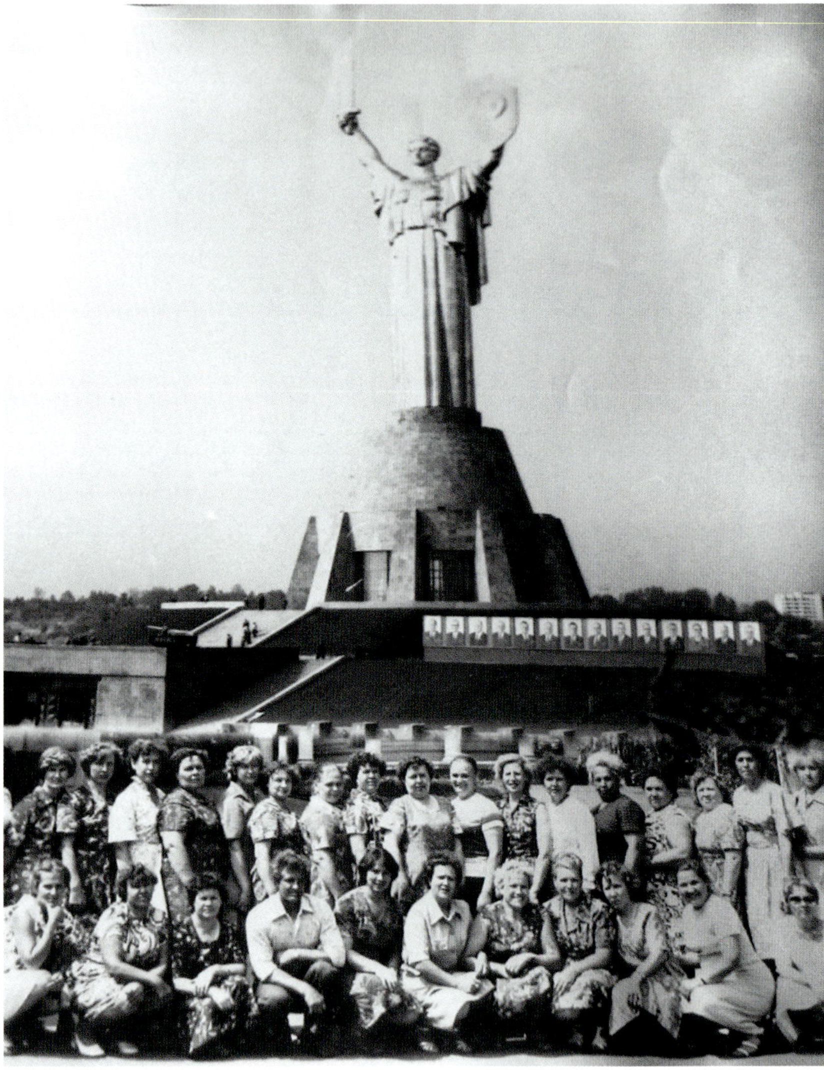

**Figure 11.6.** Group photograph of factory workers from Vladimir taken in Kyiv with the Motherland monument in the background. The monument was opened in 1981 as part of the Great Patriotic War memorial. The row of portraits of the (all-male) members of the Politburo (the Chief Executive Committee of the CPSU) is displayed on the monument's pedestal. Private collection, early 1980s, Vladimir.

World War II memorials had a lasting impact that engrained the war in social memory, defined its visual form, and enhanced its emotional impact. The latter could be easily achieved in the years when many families carried living memories of war traumas. Subsequent generations, too, were instructed in the traditions of what could be called "emotional citizenship," which ensured that certain sites evoked specific, visceral emotions:

> Oh, this is Volgograd, here I am, crying. We got to go on tours for vacation, three days through different towns. Such things are probably not available now . . . It was very affordable. [. . .] Here we are in Brest [present-day Belarus]. Gosh, how many tears we shed there. (F. 79 y.o., Moscow)

On the whole, "patriotic tourism" contributed to the strengthening of the canonized historical narrative of the past, as well as to the selective modalities of looking and seeing that were reinforced by the very process of traveling. The key nodes in this historical narrative transpire in the photographs. The set itineraries and their photographic traces in the albums integrated the prerevolutionary imperial legacy, emphasizing the etatist continuity with special attention to imperial sites as well as marked locations of past military victories. The organized tours seamlessly incorporated imperial palaces and revolutionary hideouts, medieval Orthodox cathedrals and World War II memorials. The photographs reveal an extended image-production industry that buttressed Soviet cultural memory and rooted it in the space of the USSR.

## MOUNTAINEERING AND THE SPATIAL CONQUEST

In the 1960s, new forms of individual and small-group travel came to coexist with the "patriotic tourism" described above. In particular, mountaineering and alpinism, whose early ideologists perished during the 1930s purges, experienced rebirth.[23] The image in figure 11.1 is a visual relic of one such mountaineering expedition. At first glance, it stands a world apart from the staged group tour photographs described in the preceding pages. But, while visually different, many of Elena's mountaineering images, too, worked toward assimilating geographically diverse locations into an overarching framework of spatial and ideological unity.

The expedition during which this photograph was taken had an explicit mission. The group led by Elena was to deliver a memorial stone slab to a site of an important World War II battle. Pausing on this photograph, Elena recollected:

**Figure 11.7.** Elena surveying the Caucasus landscape in Kizgych, the Arkhyz Gorge. Private collection, 1972, Moscow.

> [T]his was an interesting episode in my life. There [was] a battle in the Caucasus in 1942, and [ . . . ] I was invited to lead a mountaineering group whose mission was to deliver a memorial to this Cliff of Silence. The group even included one of the battle's participants, one journalist, myself as the leader, and a few assistants. The monument was a stone slab, a really heavy one, with text. We all took turns carrying it. . . . But we never managed to erect it in the end. There was another group that was supposed to meet us [with supplies] but they had an accident along the way and they never made it. So we had to just put it on the ground and leave it there.

The goal of Elena's expedition, in other words, was to physically mark a supposedly wild and pristine part of the Caucasus landscape, a site of long-standing "imperial, colonial, and later communist interventions,"[24] with a monumental reference to Soviet heroism during World War II. This effort to symbolically appropriate the space of nature and tie it into the Soviet ideological narrative is in line with other practices of Soviet mountaineering, such as the shaping of the topography of the Caucasus and Central Asia through the naming of conquered mountain peaks and passes in ideologically unambiguous terms (The Peak of Victory, the Lenin Peak, the Peak of Communism, and so on), and the practice of mounting the Soviet flag or other ideological markers on conquered heights. It is perhaps due to these rich possibilities of spatial and personal transformation that Soviet mountaineering enjoyed support and abundant resources for much of its development. Soviet mountaineering was construed in many ways as opposite to "bourgeois mountaineering" in the West: it was supposed to be available to the working masses, not just the privileged elites; it relied on group efforts, not the exploitation of local guides; and it was centered on collective cooperation and mutual support, and not individual achievement.[25]

Viewed in this context, Elena's photographs of the Cliff of Silence expedition embody the social and visual politics of spatial conquest and personal transformations through mountaineering. Like many travel photographs,

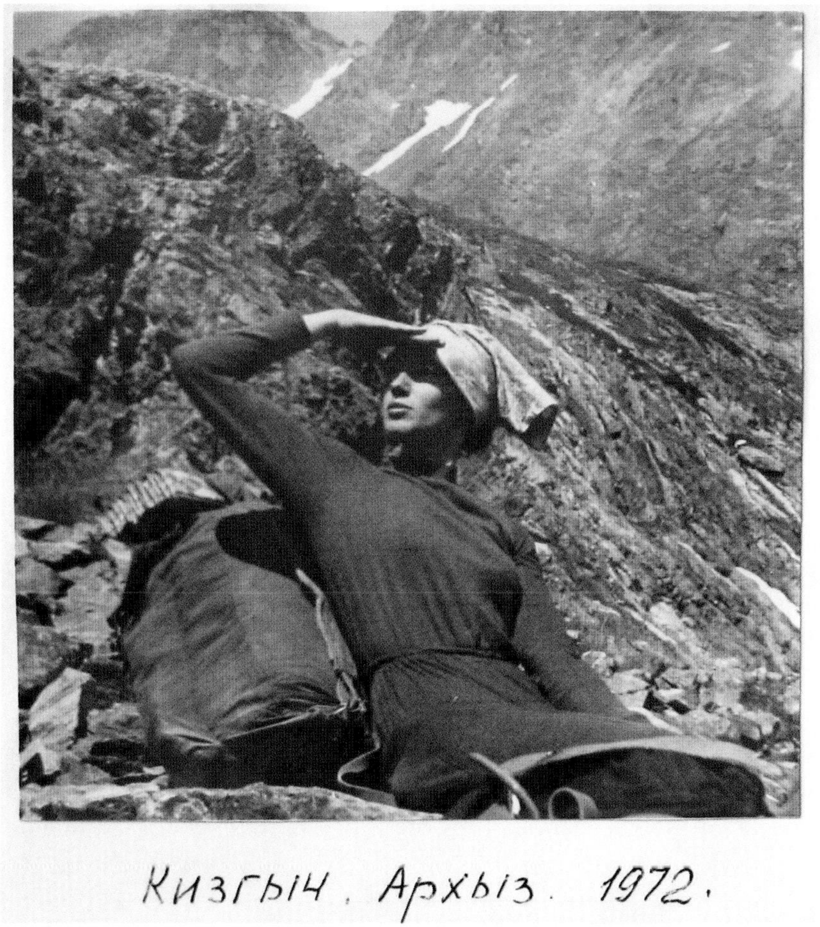


they are posed, but in this case they seek to pass as an action shot. Many are taken from a low angle so as to highlight the formidable task ahead and to include the outlines of mountain peaks behind the mountaineers. Group shots emphasize the collective aspect of the endeavor, featuring Elena, the group leader, animatedly discussing something while her companions look on. Others, like the one in figure 11.7, feature Elena alone. Perched on a rock, with the mountains in the background, Elena is looking into the distance, intently shielding her eyes from the sun in order to be able to see farther.

Like many Soviet citizens featured in newspapers photos of the 1930s, in this image, Elena is "preoccupied with looking far out of the frame," performing what Galina Orlova calls "the special labor of seeing, thus visualiz-

**Figure 11.8.** **World War II monument on the Cherkesskiy pass, Adygea, photographed in 2001. Private collection, St. Petersburg.**

ing the impossible"—a labor that was required from Soviet subjects who had to be able to see through their harsh everyday realities the contours of the fulfilled Soviet utopia.[26] But while the workers described by Orlova tend to look up, Elena, due to her position high in the mountains, can look all around and below her, deploying what Albert Boime described as the "magisterial gaze" of the American pioneers. In a recent study of Soviet visual rhetoric, Jan Plamper drew upon Boime's notion of magisterial gaze to describe the socialist realist paintings that routinely depicted Joseph Stalin looking over the vast landscapes of Soviet industry with the same effect, communicating mastery over large swaths of formerly untamed nature.[27] Plamper's study focused on Stalinist iconography and thus did not necessarily consider the possibility that the labor of deploying the "magisterial gaze" over the Soviet landscape and thus materializing utopia could be performed for the camera by rank-and-file Soviet citizens like Elena.

Unlike the group trip photographs, which have their subjects looking straight into the camera, confidently registering their presence at the site, Elena's photographs from the Caucasus depict people in the process of mastering a space not yet fully conquered, but well on its way to being so. Indeed, while the delivery of the World War II memorial had failed on that occasion, many similar undertakings succeeded, with the physical markers of their success remaining in the landscape as objects of photographic attention and already-accomplished signs of the territory's incorporation within the Soviet framework of reference.

A 2001 photograph in figure 11.8 offers a good example of this process, whereby "each encounter with and in the landscape is shaped by the cultural history of previous encounters, particularly those that get fed back into the visual culture of place."[28] The photograph depicts a makeshift memorial encountered in the Cherkesskiy pass by Mikhail, a sales manager from St. Petersburg, during his travels in Adygea, a small autonomous republic in the northwestern Caucasus. The memorial is one among many commemorative

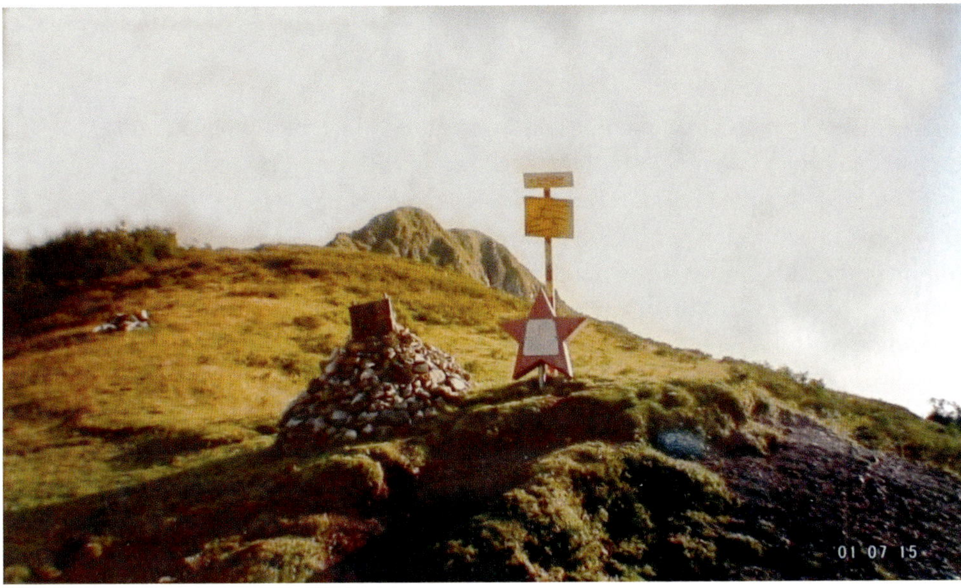


war sites in the mountains (likely delivered to this site by an expedition, like Elena's) where it marks, according to Mikhail, "*the site of battles in World War II.*" It is photographed as a central compositional element and an integral part of the landscape, which also unproblematically includes, in our interviewee's words, "*a beautiful Khuko lake . . . a sacred lake of the Adyghe people,*" where "*Putin has recently built himself a ski lift on an adjacent mountain, to downhill ski.*" This landscape is no longer viewed as contested (as in much of the nineteenth-century literature on the Caucasus), nor is it physically forbidding. It is presented as a picturesque place with a clearly marked ideological belonging. While it may be tempting to take Mikhail's attitude as natural, given the physical beauty of the place, it is important to remember that the Caucasus, and in particular the highlands, has long occupied a special place in the Russian imagination, having been cast as a place of violence, vengeance, and resistance to external rule.[29] In this context, the benign vision cast on the region by Mikhail's photograph comes across not so much as a display of a natural attitude but rather as a tenuous accomplishment, enabled by decades of cultural work that made this way of seeing possible, of which both mountaineering and travel photography are an integral part.

The impression of geographic variety conjured in a typical Soviet family album is not accidental. It reflects social practices of traveling and is produced both by the diversity of sights and landscapes (ranging from tropical gardens to snow-covered peaks) and by the inscriptions of location that, as a rule, caption group travel photographs, enabling the geographic identification of otherwise indistinguishably composed images. With foreign travel at best rare for a typical Soviet citizen, the official discourse compensated for it by presenting the Soviet Union as a self-sufficient "Sixth Part of the World."[30] The photographs, illustrating the variety of climates and landscapes readily available to a Soviet traveler, made this diversity and self-sufficiency immediately observable: one need not exit the Soviet realm to experience "our West" (i.e., the Baltics), "our tropics" (the Black Sea coast) and "our wilderness" (from the mountains of the Caucasus to Siberia and Lake Baikal). The visual uniformity of the images discussed above, therefore, was only one aspect of an overall visual strategy we may call "a managed diversity," in which stylistic uniformities went hand in hand with specific ways of framing differences so as to integrate them as parts of the overall whole.

While photographic production helped to homogenize and unite the space, it also reproduced and reinforced strong spatial hierarchies. Thus, in most of the family archives outside the capital, Moscow features prominently as a much-desired place to visit. In the context of the Cold War, the significance of Moscow in general, and of the Kremlin in particular, was officially framed in international, global ways, as the center of hopes for "all progressive humanity." All state-published albums representing the Soviet "unity in diversity" started with the images of Moscow, most often featuring the Kremlin as the starting point of the journey and as the symbolic center of the Soviet universe.[31] Resonating with this intensive cultural production, family albums linger on the visual evidence of family members' visits to Moscow. The most recurrent culmination and visual "proof" of the visit was a photograph by the Kremlin wall on the Red Square, which worked as a synecdoche for the center of the Soviet world.

Moscow remained a desired destination for many not only because of its ideological prominence but because it was better supplied, with higher living standards and more attractive career prospects. However, due to limitations imposed on permanent mobility—residence in Moscow was subject to rigid state-imposed quotas after the war, and few families ever left willingly—the capital was available to most visitors only as a short-term tourist destination. Those coming on individual or group tours to Moscow received a visual and narrative "package" of the capital's imperial and revolutionary past. Several preferred background sites for Red Square photographs shaped the visual vocabulary of the center. While today, most visitors choose as a photographic backdrop either the picturesque St. Basil's Cathedral or a glamorous boutique-filled GUM shopping center, Soviet-era group photographs construct the image of the city as the center of political power, and used the Kremlin wall, Lenin's Mausoleum, and the Museum of the Revolution as backdrops. Visits within the Kremlin were solely possible on guided tours, where tourists were escorted to the Palace of Soviets, the Tsar-Cannon, and the Tsar-Bell, and where they subsequently marveled at the Cathedral Square, the place of traditional pre-Petrine coronations, which remained a location of imperial might and spectacular power.

While many of the images preserved in family collections feature extended groups, recollections of visits to the Soviet capital refer primarily to individual or small-group experiences. However, it was not uncommon for entrepreneurial photographers working on the Red Square to single-handedly create transient communities of Soviet people by grouping chance visitors into large groups for mail-order group photographs, as in the photograph in figure 11.9, which unites visibly diverse visitors from multiple Soviet Republics in front of the Kremlin wall. In this way, the ideological work of producing the visions of cohesive Soviet communities fell on the photographer's shoulders, in this case fueled by utilitarian, as well as an ideological, logic.

Many of the recollections of trips to Moscow reference a combination of shopping agenda with visits to the ideological landmarks of the capital:

> We used to go to Moscow to look at the department stores, such as GUM, TsUM, it is only now that we have lots of different shopping malls, and earlier it was something! Just to go up and down on the escalator was a big thing. . . . When I was in Moscow we went to Lenin's Mausoleum, I took Olga [her daughter] there, it was interesting. [. . .] We got up at 6 a.m. to queue, there were lots of people there, millions every day, such a crowd, moving on and on. (F. 67 y.o., Vladimir)

For the older generation, descriptions of visits to Moscow often reference the intention to acquire consumer goods that were rare in their home towns. The travels were undertaken with the idea of not only expanding one's own wardrobe but also bringing supplies back to relatives, friends, acquain-

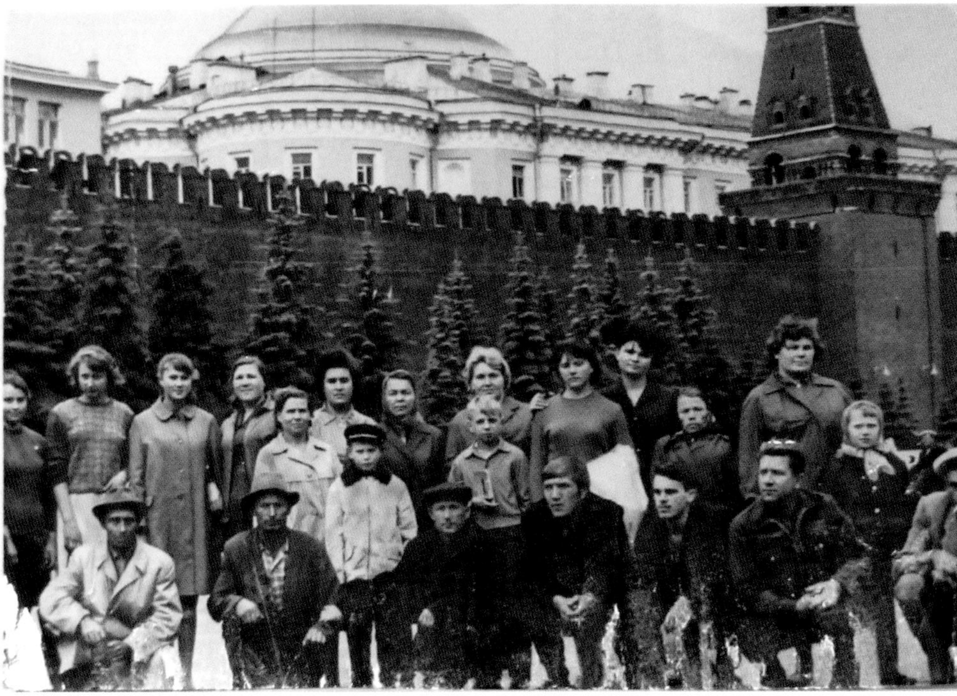

tances and at times even one's teachers. These accounts were also emotionally loaded, but usually not in a positive way.

> I remember how we traveled with my mother to Moscow to bring food, sausage, butter, fancy shoes for which we had to kill ourselves queuing. (F. 53 y.o., Samara)

> To buy a "Java" motorcycle we had to go to Moscow . . . get registered and go through several roll calls. In winter there were fewer buyers, but they were still available. [ . . . ] My brother went [to buy one] and then he almost rode into the Red Square [on the way back], he did not know Moscow well. (F. 53 y.o., Vladimir)

> We went to Moscow [in 1990] in the hope of buying something. [. . .] But then it turned out that we could not enter the shop. There was a security guard who allowed only those who had Moscow registration [propiska]. And when I, with my Rostov passport, was kicked out, I was sitting there [. . .] at "Belgrade" department store, and there were Moscovites coming out with boxes of shoes that I needed so much. [. . .] I

Figure 11.9. This group photo belongs to a retired technologist from St. Petersburg, but includes a host of other tourists visiting the Red Square on that day: "*The photographer asked, Who else wants to be in the photo?*" Private collection, 1970s, St. Petersburg.

was crying, cursing the country where I cannot even enter the store. . . . (F. 53 y.o., Rostov-on-Don)

Unlike the proper sightseeing activities, shopping adventures and disappointments rarely became a target of photographic attention.[32] By comparison, the visual record of post-Soviet visits to the capital documents an experience in which consumption and sightseeing are both pleasurable and intertwined. Thus, a 22-year old resident of Samara recalled:

> And this is our trip to Moscow [in 1996]. This was my first long trip to Moscow. We took metro, visited the zoo, went to the circus, to an amusement park—it had just opened back then and it was quite in vogue. We rode the rollercoasters, went to a park with fountains, [made our] first trip to McDonalds, it had also just opened, we had to go there and photograph this moment. Here is obviously Red Square, we also traveled by boat [on the Moscow River], and here's the GUM shopping arcade. (F. 22 y.o. Samara)

Along with Moscow, another type of location seems to be particularly ubiquitous in domestic photo collections. These are the photographs from the Black Sea coastal resorts that figured in practically every one of the two hundred plus family albums that we have had a chance to see in the course of this project, although in varying quantities. These photographs fell into several recognizable types: a group photograph in a sanatorium (composed similarly to other group travel photos), action shots outdoors,[33] and a distinctive genre of beach portraiture that could be labeled "knee-deep." In it, individuals often stand, solo or in a small group, at the very edge of the sea and face the camera frontally. While some of these photographs look like amateur snapshots, most were taken for a fee by a beach photographer, as evidenced

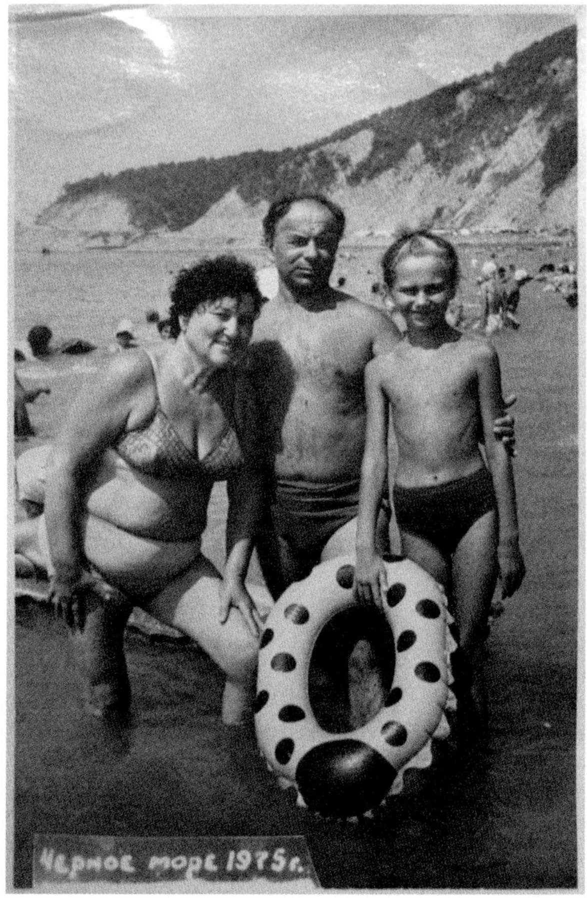


by the presence of color, occasional props ranging from a live monkey to a cardboard motorcycle, as well as date and location inscriptions. The point of these images was not to create a character study or a glamorous portrait (hence the frequent presence of other bathers in the background, often with their backs to the camera and unceremoniously cut in half), but rather to register one's presence in the visibly southern location, one that was highly sought after, for climatic reasons and as a status symbol.

Here, as with the group travel photographs, the important message appears to be the entitlement to one's physical presence at the site. The photographic reiterations of this entitlement repeatedly function as visual "proof" of one of the recurrent tropes of Soviet ideology, "Citizens of the USSR have a right to rest" (Grazhdane SSSR imeiut pravo na odykh) guaranteed in the Soviet constitution of 1936 and at times physically spelled out on the buildings

**Figure 11.10.** ***(opposite)*** **A family photograph from the Black Sea (specific location unknown). Private collection, 1975, Rostov-on-Don.**

**Figure 11.11.** ***(below)*** **A family photograph from Feodosia, Crimea. Private collection, early 1980s, Moscow.**

of the health resorts and sanatoriums in front of which the individuals pose. Photographs thus corroborated the newspaper accounts that contrasted, in the Cold War spirit, the "healing, life-giving" Soviet spaces with the "dysfunctional and neglected" spaces of the West.[34]

Indeed, evidence of one's entitlement to a share of Soviet welfare is not only visible in these images' composition but is also clearly perceived by their owners today. An elderly resident of St. Petersburg, for example, commented on a photograph of her aunt posing by the sea in the following terms:

> She, for example, worked at the Proletarii plant. She was a cleaning lady and was always sent to the Black Sea for free. . . . She had traveled to the Crimea, Simeiz, even though she was a manual worker, my auntie.

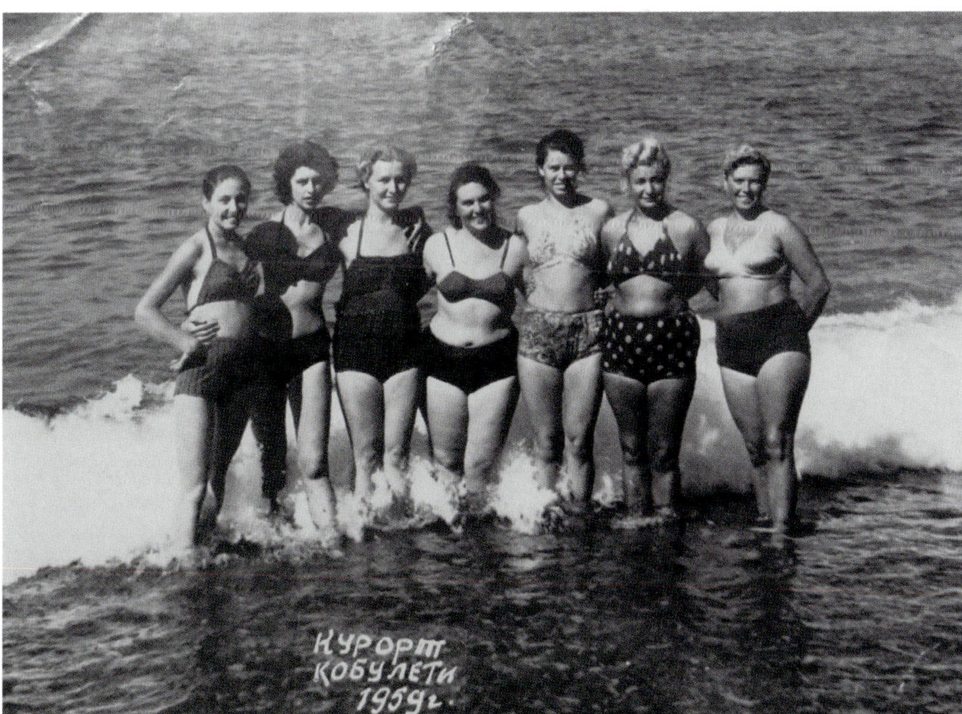

**Figure 11.12.** A group photograph from the Livadia sanatorium, with the words "Citizens of the USSR Have a Right to Rest" mounted on top of the main building. Prior to 1917, Livadia served as the Southern residence of the Romanovs and was thus a particularly potent symbol of the Soviet state's investment in the welfare of its citizens. Private collection, 1960, Moscow.

Later on, commenting on another image, she continued,

> And this is, as I told you, auntie Masha, who was a custodian, here she is somewhere . . . in Odessa and FOR FREE [with emphasis]. One should not say that under Stalin everyone lived badly. (F. 81 y.o., St. Petersburg)

While all sanatorium photographs lend themselves to a reading that emphasizes the availability and affordability of Soviet-era travel, the prized and sought-after location of the seaside resort made this point most dramatically because the photographs made there referred to a visibly different space of leisure and rest, one that was nonetheless accessible to a "simple manual worker," or at least this is what the photograph makes one believe.

## THE AFTERLIFE OF SOVIET TRAVEL PHOTOGRAPHY

What effects might Soviet-era travel imagery have on contemporary viewers of the family albums, who are often far removed in age and experience from the realities of the Cold War? The young viewers of the albums rarely questioned the terms on which subsidized travel was available to their parents and grandparents, not least because the photographs rarely made visible any downsides to the Soviet model of travel (such as difficulties of getting access to subsidized vouchers, limitations on seasonal travel, or the de facto inability to get travel vouchers for a whole family) as well as the material circum-

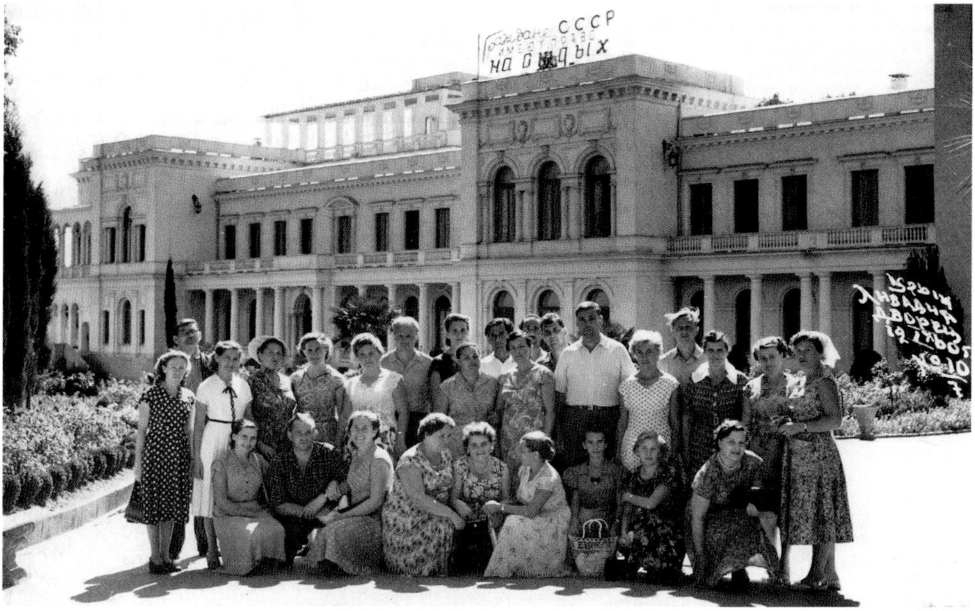

stances of travel that entailed, for example, sleeping in a shared room with four to eight randomly assigned roommates. The composite nature of the album itself—the logic of excess through the reproduction of visibly monotonous shots taken in ostensibly different but visually homogenized locations—further contributes to a sense of the fullness of experience that they now attribute to the Soviet era, which is retrospectively imagined as both utopian and unified. By contrast, it is travel through the formerly Soviet space today that is perceived both as disenchanted (especially in reference to the Baltic States, which are no longer the only destination where one could experience "Western" consumer goods and services) and riddled with logistical difficulties, inflated prices, a sense of betrayed entitlement and even danger.

Surprisingly, an idealized vision of Soviet-era travel is more characteristic for younger generations than for their parents and grandparents who interspersed their recollections with penetrating references to the everyday realities of Soviet travel. For example, a former trade-union official from Vladimir burst into laughter when coming across a photo of herself getting off the train from a trade-union sponsored trip with shopping bags in tow: "*Back then, we were buying, bringing everything from there* [the Baltics]. *And here we are loaded, she has a bag on her shoulder and a suitcase, I have these two bags. . . . Yes, we were buying boots there, and underwear, and even condensed milk and candies were brought from there, everything. . . .*" By contrast, her eighteen-year-old granddaughter had a far more sanitized vision of the same travel photographs, which she took to be the evidence of the state's overwhelming care for its working citizens, care which she found lacking today:

> In the twentieth century people were united. They were told about their history, special excursions were organized, and it is visible here that people of different generations—for example here they are older, at that moment already over thirty . . . But nevertheless, excursions were organized for them, they were edified and people were interested in what happened around them and were proud of the history of their country, because they visited these places, these excursions, and later they could talk about them to their children and grandchildren. [ . . . ] Now of course people also visit such places, but earlier it was done by the factory, organized by the state, and now if people travel they do it solely out of their own private enthusiasm.

But the power and appeal of Soviet-era travel photographs are perhaps most interesting not because they inspire longing for the welfare policies of late socialism, but because they simultaneously inform the taken-for-granted definitions of what constitutes the national territory today. Indeed, the nostalgia inspired by these images is poignant because they are perceived as referring to a space that was once readily accessible but is currently out of reach. Commenting on his mother's photographs taken in Kislovodsk, the balneological resort in the northern Caucasus, Alex, a sixteen-year-old student from Novocherkassk pointed with sadness: "*These pictures, they make it evident that a common person could travel anywhere, all over Russia. . . . Whereas now, one cannot go to so many places.*" Echoing this sentiment, an eighteen-year-old resident of St. Petersburg, Tamara, extended the imaginary reach even farther when, looking at a photograph of her grandmother taken in the 1980s in Georgia, she commented that "[grandma] *has traveled all over the place with her husband; they have been in Transcaucasia and they traveled all over Russia in general.*" In this casual remark, Tamara seamlessly connected the space of several independent states (Armenia, Azerbaijan, and Georgia) with Russia. The visual grammar of these images, similar as it is to the rest of their family travel photos, contributed to a subjective perception of the fully appropriated space and individual possibility to travel, and enabled these young Russians, for whom the depicted territories are already out of reach, to identify them as "their own."

"Travel by its very nature crosses boundaries," writes Anne Gorsuch in her overview of postwar Soviet tourism.[35] Yet Soviet tourists within the USSR traveled changing locations, but not crossing boundaries; they found recognizable Soviet spaces wherever they went. Family photos not only reflected the microtraces of homogenization of space through urban planning, design, and memorial politics but also contributed to that very same process in a visual idiom. From this vantage point, it is instructive to revisit Elena's stories about the childhood game of "exploring the territory" that we relayed earlier. The word Elena used when she spoke of these explorations is osvoenie, and, apart from exploration, it also connotes a sense of mastery, and a process of making a place one's own [svoi]. What the stories and the images explored here suggest is that, for a broad array of Soviet citizens, photographic practices were deeply implicated in the project of both shaping the cultural imagination connected to the various regions of the Soviet Union and making the far-flung areas of the USSR "their own." In this way, they gave a compelling visual form to the Cold War battle for hearts and minds in the realm of tourism and leisure, and extended this vision into the private living spaces where these images are kept and still revisited today. The comments that these photographs now evoke from many young Russians, like Tamara and Alex, suggest that in many ways the Soviet visual project succeeded. At a time when millions of Russian citizens embrace the Crimea as "always having been ours," the stakes in which these seemingly banal amateur snapshots are involved are anything but trivial.

### *Notes*

1 All names used in this chapter are pseudonyms. Unless otherwise noted, all translations are our own.

2 Gorsuch, *All This Is Your World*, 6.

3 Travel abroad was seen as a form of cultural diplomacy and could be undertaken only as part of an organized and state-approved group, led by a loyal and ideologically vigilant guide who was expected to report back on the tourists' behavior to the authorities upon return. Gorsuch offers a partial list of information one had to provide to apply for a group tour to Western Europe: one had to turn in stellar recommendations from Komsomol or the Party, as well as the workplace; one had to have an unblemished past and political connections; one had to have already traveled to Eastern Europe; in addition, one had to fill out a five-page form that included exhaustive questions about relatives, all former and current workplaces, any encounters with the Soviet legal system, family members living abroad, and family members who may have been interned or who were known to have lived in the occupied territories during World War II. Finally, one had to undergo a rigorous health examination. Usually, in the process of application, aspiring tour-

ists would be required to meet with ideological workers who tested them for their "political maturity," "so that we don't cover ourselves in shame over there," as one of our informants put it. As a result, only a tiny fraction of Soviet citizens ever crossed the borders of the USSR for vacations, and of those who did, most went to a socialist country in Eastern Europe. For a rich study of Soviet tourism practices, see Gorsuch, *All This Is Your World*; and Gorsuch, "Vystuplenie na mezhdunarodnoi stsene."

4 Koenker, "Whose Right to Rest?," 401, 402.

5 Koenker, "Whose Right to Rest?," 401.

6 Orlov and Popov, "'Skvoz' zheleznyi zanaves.'"

7 Sandomirskaia, "'Novaia zhizn' na marshe," 167.

8 Sandomirskaia, "'Novaia zhizn' na marshe," 166.

9 Reid, "'Our Kitchen Is Just as Good.'"

10 Verdery, *What Was Socialism, and What Comes Next?*, 4.

11 Urry, *The Tourist Gaze*.

12 Anne Gorsuch's *All This Is Your World* integrates published sources with oral history and archival documents to paint a comprehensive picture of the Soviet tourism industry without, however, concentrating specifically on the work of visual representation.

13 The larger project had two related foci. On one level, it explored what kinds of memories of the Soviet era were facilitated by viewing family photographs and, in particular, how these memories connected with the "big" frames through which historians understand the Soviet era, such as collectivization, industrialization, the Great Patriotic War, various political and social campaigns, and so on. On another level, it sought to understand how these narratives change as they are transferred from one generation to the next. Our fieldwork was supported by grants from the Wenner-Gren Foundation for Anthropological Research and a NCEEER Collaborative grant. We conversed with representatives of two, three, or four generations in fifty-four Russian families in five different regions of the country (Moscow, St. Petersburg, Rostov-on-Don, Novocherkassk, Vladimir, and Samara), asking each separately to comment on the photographs from their domestic archives and on the events that the photographs represented.

14 Althusser, "Ideology and the Ideological State Apparatuses," 162.

15 For canonical accounts of how this is accomplished by various photographic genres, see Tagg, *The Burden of Representation*; and Wexler, *Tender Violence*.

16 Billig, *Banal Nationalism*. See also J. E. Fox, "The Edges of the Nation."

17 Chistikov, "Razreshen vyezd"; Orlov, "Pervye shagi vyezdnogo turizma v SSSR (1955–1964)."

18 Gorsuch, *All This Is Your World*, 39.

19 These were Leningrad (now St. Petersburg), Odessa, Sebastopol, Volgograd (up

to 1961 called Stalingrad), Kyiv, the Brest Fortress, Moscow, Kerch, Novorossiisk, Minsk, Tula, Murmansk, and Smolensk.

20 Gorsuch, *All This Is Your World*, 34.

21 Brodsky, *Less Than One*, 11.

22 Gorsuch, *All This Is Your World*, 39.

23 Maurer, "Al'pinizm as Mass Sport and Elite Recreation," 142.

24 Grant, *The Captive and the Gift*, xv.

25 See Maurer, "Cold War, 'Thaw' and 'Everlasting Friendship.'"

26 Orlova, "'Karty dlia slepykh'" ["Maps for the Blind"], 76–77.

27 See Boime, *The Magisterial Gaze*, and the use of his analysis by Jan Plamper, *The Stalin Cult*.

28 Bednar, "Being Here, Looking There," 2.

29 On the place of the Caucasus in the Russian imagination and, in particular, on the cultural work done by the narratives of captivity in legitimizing the "gift of empire," see Grant, *The Captive and the Gift*.

30 Sarkisova, "Across One Sixth of the World."

31 *The Soviet Union: A Photo Album.*

32 We discuss one rare photograph depicting a tour group returning with consumer spoils from an organized visit later in the chapter (that particular trip, however, took travelers not to Moscow but to another privileged shopping destination, the Baltics).

33 These were a distinct minority. Most subsidized travel to resorts was done solo, since their purpose was to restore the worker to his or her health, rather than to provide them with family time. Hence, there was little opportunity to informally take each other's photographs at leisure. See Dianne Koenker's "A Right to Rest?" regarding the organization of Soviet travel.

34 Gorsuch, *All This Is Your World*, 41.

35 Gorsuch, *All This Is Your World*, 206.

12

GIL PASTERNAK & MARTA ZIĘTKIEWICZ

# Exhibiting Ethnic Minorities, Democratizing History

## COLD WAR LEGACIES AND THE JEWS IN POLAND'S VISIBLE SPHERE

The gradual decline of Soviet power in Poland during the late 1970s and most of the 1980s saw the installation of numerous public displays taking issue with historical memories that Soviet authorities had not previously tolerated.[1] The number of these displays increased and their subject matter radicalized, particularly during the mid-1980s, when Polish society was in the midst of a prodemocratic social revolution led by underground factions of the Solidarity trade union. With the policy of *glasnost* already implemented by the Communist Party of the Soviet Union, and with *perestroika* increasingly guiding

Poland's official state policies, Polish society slowly began adjusting to Western democratic values and a market economy.[2] Exhibitions concerning long-lasting societal divisions in Poland started to emerge. The most influential among them consisted of crowd-sourced family photographs and other photographic image-objects taken from domestic collections that explicitly overrode the Soviet Cold War position on identity politics, which had embraced peasants and workers as the exclusive face of the nation.[3] The growing proliferation of family photographs in Poland's visible sphere subsequently challenged the historiographical paradigms that mediated Soviet ideology and informed the production of Soviet historical narratives in Poland of the Cold War period.

The prodemocratic revolution of the late 1980s rendered the full range of dominant social formations in the country visible. Peasants and workers were now openly accompanied by Catholics and the intelligentsia, two social groups that had until then been largely tolerated by the state, at the same time as state leaders gravely restricted their freedom of speech and expression. Even in this prodemocratic atmosphere, however, ethnic minorities—whose belonging to the Polish nation and right to exist in Poland had been challenged by Soviet communism and the Polish state since the end of World War II—continued living in the country without drawing much attention. It took Poland nearly another decade to openly acknowledge the presence of these minorities in the country. Before the mid-1990s, ethnic minorities thus had no comprehensibly legitimized space in which to express their societal beliefs, to nurture their distinct cultural heritage, or to recall collective memories of their lived experience in recent history.

In the mid-1990s, members of the Jewish community in Poland readily adopted the innovative practice of organizing public displays of photographs as a productive means by which to open up such a space. Since the end of World War II and throughout the Cold War period, the generations of Jews who had survived the war and continued living in Poland under communist rule had been repressed by Soviet partisanship against ethnic minority groups. The political reality developing in Poland in the second half of the 1980s, therefore, gradually convinced this community that it was becoming safe for Jews to begin participating in Poland's social and cultural life again. The approval of the new, noncommunist government in September 1989 accelerated the process, and by the mid-1990s, Polish Jews largely endeavored to reclaim their cultural identity, to recall their collective memory as Jews, and to reinstate their place as equal citizens of the Polish nation and as committed members of Polish society.[4]

In this chapter we focus on the impact of Soviet Cold War visual principles and their legacies on the appearance of Jews in Poland's visible sphere in order to explore the significance of one of the most influential photographic initiatives organized by Poland's Jewish community. Taking the form of a crowdsourced public photography contest, this initiative was inaugurated in 1994 under the title *And I Still See Their Faces*. By 1996, the initiative culminated in an exhibition, a lavishly illustrated book publication, and the emergence of a collection of over seven thousand, mostly annotated, photographic records. Since then, the exhibition has traveled to more than ten cities in Poland and to more than thirty-five countries around the world. It has been on display at nearly sixty venues altogether, and its accompanying book publication has so far been reprinted in four editions.[5] Drawing on our archival research of the initiative's complete photographic collection and our study of the public debates that ensued in Poland when this initiative fully materialized, we show that the reintroduction of images of Jews into Poland's visible sphere helped Polish society shake off Soviet Cold War definitions of Polish cultural identity, which had continued to haunt Poland even when it was clear that the Soviet Union was no more.

While the photographs and the related information and interpretations that *And I Still See Their Faces* placed in the Polish public sphere openly contested the communist legacies of ethnic discrimination, we argue that the initiative achieved much more. In calling upon past and present Polish citizens from all walks of life to search for historical photographs of the Jews of Poland and to share their stories openly, *And I Still See Their Faces* established a prodemocratic space in which records of relational lived experience of the recent political history of the country could be deposited by Jewish and non-Jewish subjects alike. Individually, yet nevertheless together, these records unearthed the Polish people's socially and culturally diverse visual histories and historical memories that Soviet Cold War ideology compelled them to forget.

## REALITY CHECK

*And I Still See Their Faces* primarily featured snapshots and photo-portraits that were made privately within the territories of the Polish country throughout the first half of the twentieth century. A relatively large portion gave some visual expression to the experiences that Polish Jews encountered in

**Figure 12.1.** Chaja Tendler with friends in Kraków. Submitted by Henryk Kurek. Photographer unknown. Courtesy Shalom Foundation Archive, fs_1_0088_0056.

the country during World War II. Otherwise, however, the photographs emphasized their social conditions and the circle of life in the contexts of industrialization and urbanization, mostly concentrating on themes familiar from contemporaneous European domestic photographic collections: brides and grooms standing together for wedding-day photographs; adults taking pride in their children and grandchildren; young couples and groups of friends visiting the vast landscapes of the countryside, the beach, or the big city (figure 12.1); and individuals grouped together in front of their houses and alongside modern cars (figure 12.2). Photographs of shop owners, local artisans, and of scenes from the marketplace were also common, as were annotated class photographs presenting seemingly homogenous groups of pupils of mixed Jewish and non-Jewish origin who had studied side by side (figure 12.3).

Some photographs also provided insight into the more particular wartime experience of the Jews. Because the majority, however, focused on a select number of individuals and showed them in various private and public contexts, they mainly introduced impressions of the lived experience of Polish Jews as identical to that of any other Pole of the same period. Even when the subjects of the photographs were dressed in accordance with Jewish ultra-orthodox fashion, the activities they engaged in, alongside the material culture in which they appeared, portrayed them as fully engaged members of modernized Polish society. And if the sociocultural commonality of these photographs was not yet enough to demonstrate how integrated Polish Jews were within the broader fabric of Polish society, numerous portraits of Jewish men in military uniform could likewise be found among the photographs included in *And I Still See Their Faces* (figure 12.4).

While almost none of the photographs featured in the collection were originally intended for public display, the legacies of Soviet Cold War ideology and the gradual democratization of Poland in the later twentieth century rendered them into cultural products of sociopolitical significance for the

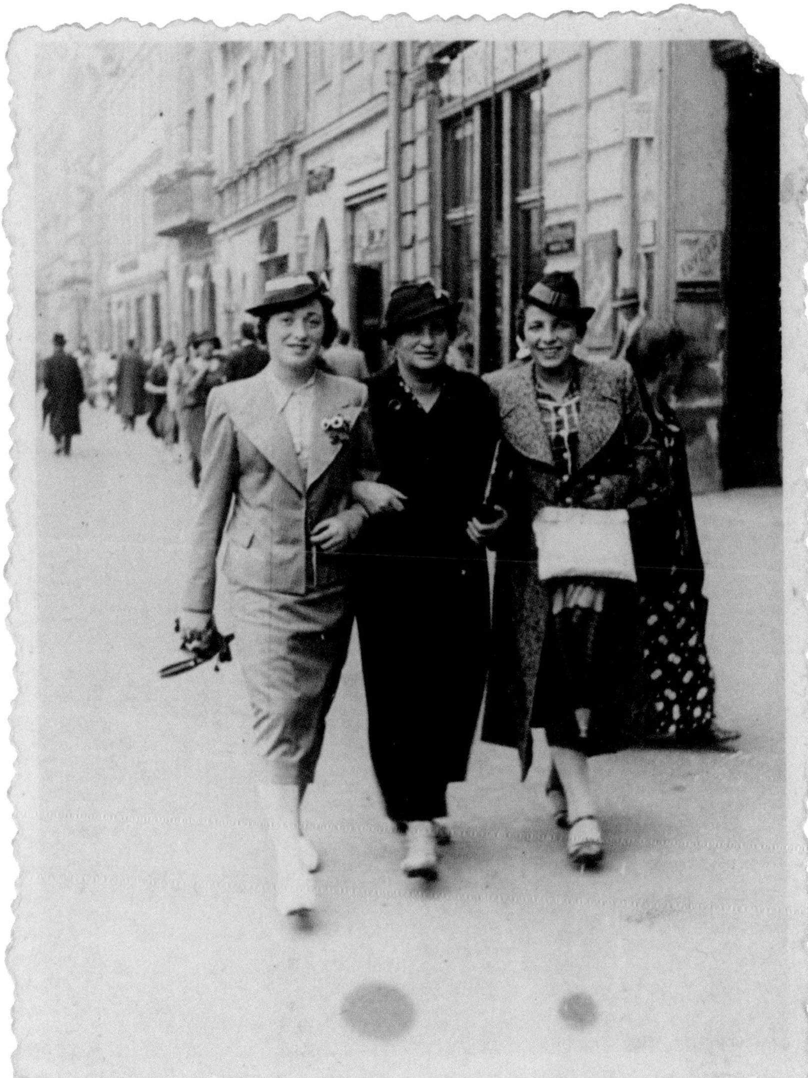

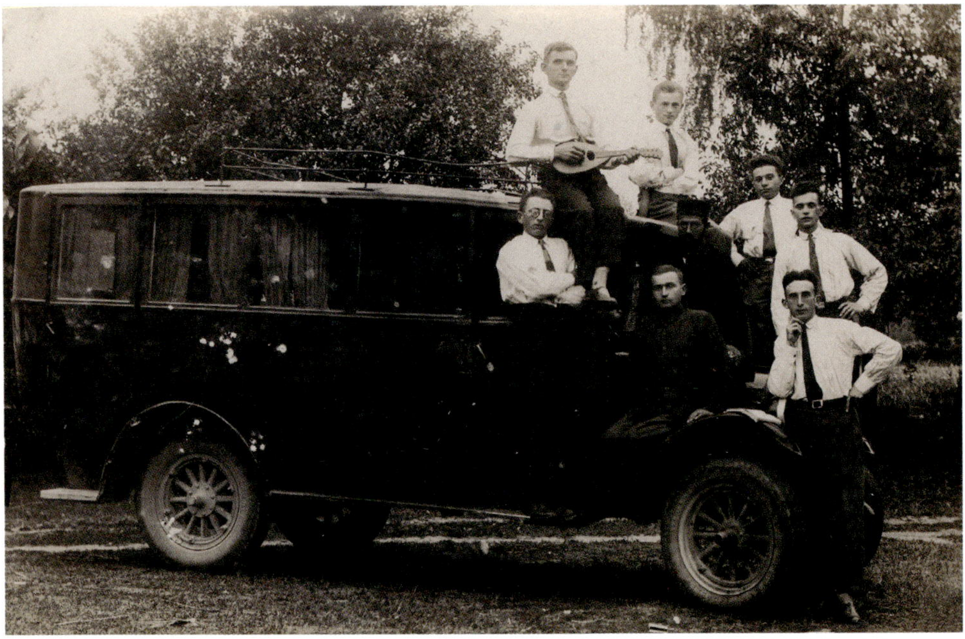

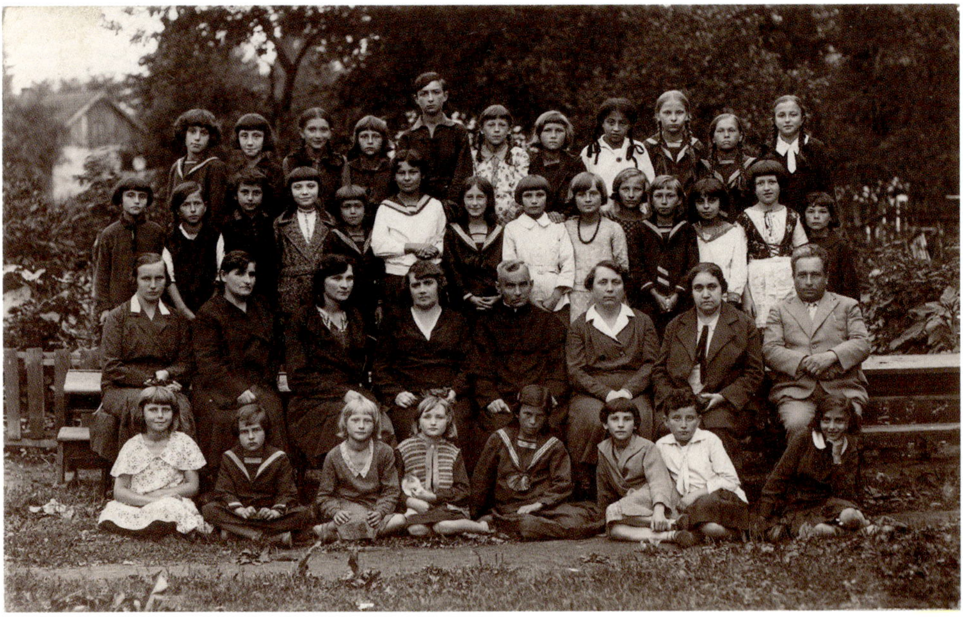

**Figure 12.2.** (*opposite, top*) Władysław Zaręba with fellows from a transportation company in Szczerców. Submitted by Ligia Kurasiewicz. Photographer unknown. Courtesy Shalom Foundation Archive, fs_1_0244_0001.

**Figure 12.3.** (*opposite, bottom*) A group of pupils from a primary school in Leżajski. Submitted by Maria Fijałkowska. Photographer unknown. Courtesy: Shalom Foundation Archive, fs_1_0139_0004.

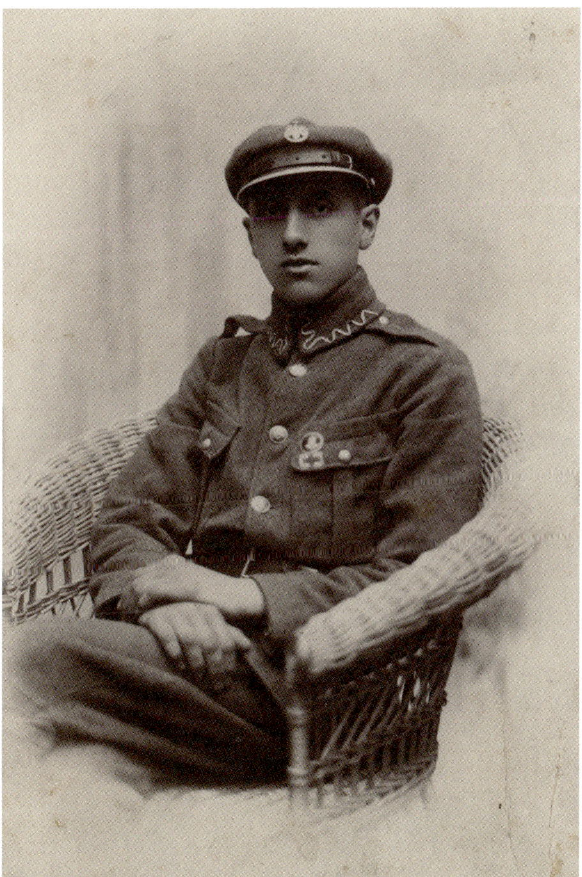

**Figure 12.4.** Benjamin Niedźwiedź, c. 1920. Photographer unknown. Courtesy Shalom Foundation Archive, fs_1_0094_0001.

whole Polish nation.[6] As Polish photographer and curator of the 1996 exhibition Tomasz Tomaszewski explained in an interview, the photographs were considered "extremely important because they remind us of a significant part of our culture."[7] Journalist Jerzy Sławomir Mac complemented Tomaszewski's words in his review of the exhibition, arguing, "These photographs . . . give testimony of the symbiotic relationship that once prevailed between these two peoples in Poland."[8]

The broader historical background that informed the initiative and framed it as antagonistic to the legacies of communist Cold War politics in fact takes us back to the final days of World War II, when Poland became a satellite state of the Soviet Union. As the German occupation of Poland ended in 1945, the newly formed Polish government was politically dominated by Soviet communism, rebuilding the Polish nation on the socialist principle of social equality.[9] In accordance with this political disposition, the government considered Poland as a country of one people. While ethnic minorities lived among the Poles, the state refused to acknowledge this sociocultural diversity so openly. In fact, to perpetuate the political ideology of one country for one people, the state insisted that, other than Poles, no other nationals lived in Poland. This, the government explained, was the consequence of Europe's postwar national partition.[10]

Although ethnic minorities are not by default members of another nation, their distinct cultural customs, social values, heritage, and appearance may mark them out as foreign to the majority population. To turn the ideological narrative of one country for one people into a coherent visible reality, the Polish state therefore called upon the country's ethnic minorities to assimilate into Polish society, dedicate themselves to contribute to its development, and abandon their histories and cultural heritage altogether. Individuals who refused to comply with Polish communism were pressured, through official expressions of anti-Semitic sentiments and state-organized anti-Jewish campaigns, to leave the country. Yet, although the state officially portrayed a different picture, some ethnic minorities chose to stay in Poland without fully assimilating, including numerous Polish Jews.[11]

To address the disruption to the consistent look of Poland's visible spheres constituted by the existence of Jewish and other ethnic groups in the country, the state repressed these communities throughout its communist phase. To this end, the state monitored their activities, limited the number of institutions and organizations that these groups were allowed to run for their own communities, and almost completely obliterated any spoken or written reference to their heritage, histories, and collective memories. The political regime's position with respect to Poland's ethnic minorities found official expression in the communist party's third plenary meeting of February 20, 1976, when party members affirmed that Poland had to become an ethnically homogenous state.[12] Subsequently, ethnic minorities were further deprived of political influence and visibility, which helped the Polish state cement the illusion of a socially unified and politically united Poland.

Yet, Poland of the 1970s was far from socially or politically cohesive. Edward Gierek, First Secretary of the Polish United Workers' Party between 1970 and 1980, intended to bridge social and political gaps in the country by attending to the diverse needs and aspirations of the Polish people, from peasants to workers and intellectuals. He increased wages and eased censorship as measures to unite the Polish people behind his leadership. To facilitate his sociopolitical ambitions, Gierek also purchased large amounts of Western technology with the intention of developing the country's economy. Three years after he took office, however, it was clear that his plan failed. Poland owed a significant foreign debt at the same time that an oil crisis and recession hit international trade. Attempting to overcome the financial challenge, in 1976 Gierek raised food prices by 60 percent and reorganized the distribution of wages. Strikes, protests, and demonstrations broke out across the country. Although it took Gierek's government exactly one day to revoke the price increases, food shortages followed as—in an attempt to repay foreign debt—the government decided to sell abroad almost any product and produce found in the country. Popular upheaval continued subsequently. Bringing together the radical intelligentsia, the Catholic societies, and the workers, this upheaval culminated in 1977 with the emergence of a fragile but nevertheless integrated political opposition to the Polish regime and its supporters, as well as to Soviet communism more broadly.[13]

To ensure calm and relative stability in the second half of the 1970s, the Polish regime concurrently employed two complementary strategies. First, it deployed workers nationwide to orchestrate rallies in support of the government and the rule of communism. By mobilizing them this way, the state could present news photographers with fabricated evidence of political solidarity with Gierek's leadership. The images they captured on film populated the pages of newspapers and were played on the nation's TV screens in homes.[14] The same images thereby framed the antigovernment demonstrations across the country as insignificant local activities carried out by an outnumbered group of individual agitators, unsupported by the masses, and condemned by the nation.[15] Second, the state simultaneously advocated tolerance of political and social diversity. As a consequence, the Polish people enjoyed the benefits of a relatively unrestricted freedom of speech and expression. Although the establishment of this condition did not signal the end of communist rule, it did mean that the Polish visual sphere could begin to reintroduce references to periods in the country's history that had preceded the creation of the communist Polish People's Republic. Local scholars and intellectuals were, by extension, able to unearth as well as develop a broader range of depictions concerning the diversity of Polish society and the history of the Polish nation. Already in 1977, for example, the Society of Lublin Enthusiasts (Towarzystwo Miłośników Lublina) organized an exhibition of photographs that renowned photographer Stefan Kiełsznia took in the city during the interwar period. Because Lublin was the home of many Polish Jews prior to the war, the exhibition and its accompanying catalog featured their images as well. As another example, in 1979, author and journalist Henryk W. Piekarniak published an album of photographs that well-established photographer Jerzy Benedykt Dorys took in Kazimierz, Kraków's Jewish quarter, between 1930 and 1931.[16]

Some restrictions persisted, however. As closer examination of these and similar projects reveals, their creators still had to provide a conservative context for the public presentation of photographs of Polish Jews. For this reason, the text in Kiełsznia's exhibition catalog, written by Henryk Gawarecki, and that of Dorys's photo album, written by Roman Kłosiewicz, focused on the photographs' artistic qualities and documentary properties alone.[17] The history and fate of the Jewish communities depicted in the photographs was not even mentioned. Moreover, whereas from the outset Kiełsznia's exhibition and its accompanying catalog were designed for the consumption of local audiences in Lublin—and subsequently constituted no threat to the Polish implementation of Soviet Cold War ideology—Piekarniak's publication had to comply with restrictions on the distribution of Dorys's work, which resulted in a print run of only 300 copies at a time when other photo albums in the country were only rarely printed in runs of less than 5,000 copies.

Indeed, despite the general openness of the state to issues concerning domestic affairs, Poland's ethnic minorities were not yet able to raise concerns about their own rights in Polish society or about their place in Polish history. Opening this discussion would have constituted a threat to Poland's perceived national homogeneity at a time when national pride was the sole sentiment that Polish society still shared. More importantly in the context of this study, legitimizing cultural diversity of this kind would also have slashed the government's ability to point the finger at ethnic minorities as the cause for at least some of the sociopolitical disturbances in the country. The Polish regimes of the post–World War II and Cold War periods widely employed this strategy whenever their leaders faced significant internal ideological confrontations, political instability, or economic challenges. And yet, Soviet communism is full of paradoxes and contradictions. At the same time that ethnic minorities did not officially exist in Poland, Jews were most often the state's main target of blame because of their relatively wide participation in Polish social and political life and because they were the largest ethnic group in the country for most of this period.[18]

## HISTORICAL REBIRTH

The organization of *And I Still See Their Faces* was made possible, then, largely due to the rapid proliferation of democratic tendencies within Polish society in the second half of the 1980s, as the Soviet grasp of Poland and the rest of the Eastern Bloc continued deteriorating to a point of no return.[19] Under such circumstances, the dominant factions of Polish society began to criticize Soviet politics regularly, and the various historical imaginaries that Soviet Cold War ideology nurtured gradually diminished. For members of the Jewish community who felt it was now safe enough to proclaim their ethnic origin in public, this period was marked by a yearning to salvage and preserve the history, heritage, and memory of the Eastern European Jewish world that had been annihilated during World War II.

One member of the Jewish community who shared this aspiration was Gołda Tencer, an actress and director of the Ester Rachel and Ida Kamińskie State Yiddish Theater. In 1987, she established the Shalom Foundation to facilitate this effort and, when a democratic political system officially replaced communism between 1989 and 1990, the Foundation became fully equipped to challenge head-on the ethnically insular, haunting legacies of Soviet Cold War ideology.

It was against this background that the seeds for *And I Still See Their Faces* were sowed on November 11, 1994, as the Foundation made a public appeal on the Polish public television channel TVP1, inviting viewers to send their photographs of Polish Jews to the Foundation's postal address. Between December 1994 and January 1995, the Foundation used the local and international print media to publicize the initiative, framing it as an invitation to partake in a public contest and offering awards as enticements for participants. The contest organizers were keen to receive photographs (and films) featuring

Jewish life in Poland before, during, and after World War II. Approximately a year after the public call for participation, the Foundation had more than seven thousand photographs.[20] Accompanied by explanatory letters, they arrived from Poland but also from countries such as Argentina, Brazil, Canada, Israel, Italy, the United States, and Venezuela (countries to which Jews had emigrated before, during, or after the war). Some of their senders were Jews, mostly the descendants and friends of the individuals shown in the pictures submitted, or descendants of those who took the photographs. Less expected, however, and significantly as we demonstrate below, was the large number of photographs submitted by non-Jewish Poles.

The resulting large-scale exhibition opened to the public at Zachęta—National Gallery of Art in Warsaw on April 18, 1996. Its accompanying catalog simultaneously began circulating in public, reaching the hands of journalists, scholars, art critics, and other intellectuals who took great interest in the initiative. Having analyzed the exhibition's and catalog's sociopolitical and sociocultural implications in written publications of their own, they amplified the information put together both by the Foundation and by its radical photographic initiative. Indeed, many of the photographs and letters that featured in the catalog and the exhibition triggered lively public discussions about Poland's multicultural past and social history, especially prior to World War II. These debates and the sociocultural histories the photographs and their accompanying interpretations brought to light suited the agenda of the Polish government that came to power with the collapse of the Soviet Union. Like other governments in formerly communist European countries, the new Polish regime sought to establish political relationships with democratic western European countries. If this government was to be successful, it had to undo Cold War regulations concerning ethnic minority rights and demonstrate the state's genuine adherence to international human rights laws more broadly. An obvious way to evidence such compliance was to allow the small percentage of minorities still left in Poland to exist in the open and enjoy the same speech and expression rights as other Polish citizens.[21]

One of the most significant achievements of *And I Still See Their Faces*, however, was the challenge it posed to the formal Soviet narration and commemoration of the Polish experience in World War II, which largely remained prevalent in the country even when Poland was consciously attempting to complete its transformation into a democratic state. US postwar and Cold War visualizations of World War II drew upon images related to the ghettoization, systematic starvation, and mass extermination of European Jews.

From the mid-1970s onward, images of this kind had become the most traditional of Western references to Nazi German atrocities and the war period. Between 1945 and 1989, however, the Polish state sanctioned an altogether different set of images to visualize the same war, in compliance with Soviet ideology. Tightly administering the country's discursive sphere, the Polish state ratified collective memorialization practices that focused on national wartime circumstances, on the one hand, and that glorified the redemptive character and healing power of Soviet communism, on the other. Artists, filmmakers, and photographers were compelled to promote this agenda, both through censorship and state initiatives.[22] Although initially some carefully curated visualizations of the wartime experience of Poland's ethnic minorities existed, over time the state consciously repressed references to Polish Jews, rendering Poland's national historiography on the Polish experience of World War II limited, if not parochial.

At first, when Poland was still adjusting to communist power between 1945 and 1949, the newly formed government regularly put images of the ruins of Warsaw on public display, with the intention of memorializing the barbaric German attempt to annihilate the Polish nation and its heritage.[23] Most noticeable and influential in this respect were photographs taken by Zofia Chomętowska. Working before the war for the Polish Ministry of Communication, in 1938 Chomętowska and photographer Tadeusz Przypkowski were tasked by the mayor of Warsaw to photograph some of the city's dominant streets, buildings, and monuments. The photographs were intended for inclusion in the exhibition *Warsaw Yesterday, Today, and Tomorrow* [*Warszawa wczoraj, dziś, jutro*], which celebrated the renewal of some parts of the city and foregrounded other cityscapes that had been marked for further development in the near future.[24] In 1945 the newly established Capital Rebuilding Bureau (Biuro Odbudowy Stolicy) commissioned Chomętowska to go back to the same locations, this time in order to photograph their wreckage from the very same point of view. Documenting the destruction of the city through these images, Chomętowska's photographs were featured in the photographic exhibition *Warsaw Accuses* [*Warszawa oskarża*], which was open to the public at the National Museum in Warsaw between May and June of the same year. Some of the images in this exhibition later became iconic when they were printed on Poland's postal stamps and on postcards, juxtaposed with the images that Chomętowska and Przypkowski took in Warsaw before the war (figure 12.5). Populating Poland's visible sphere with images of this kind assisted the Polish government in staging the war period as a battle between Germany and the Soviets, where the latter were framed as the protectors of

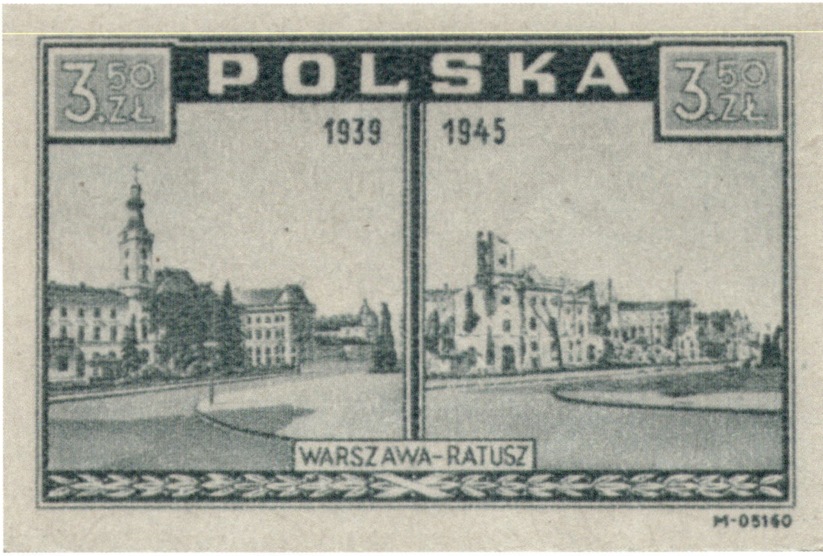


the Polish nation and its patrons. Images referencing the wartime experience of Polish Jews had little place in this environment, although occasionally they did appear, as long as they portrayed their subjects as nonreligious, assimilated Polish citizens—supporters of communist ideology.[25]

When the Polish communist regime consolidated its power in 1949, all forms of cultural production had to conform to a particular representational style. Known as Socialist Realism, it developed in the Soviet Union during the 1920s and since the early 1930s had become its only acceptable form of art. The style required artists of all media to use their work to render the values of communist ideology clear and accessible to the masses and to glorify the spirit and achievements of the communist party at the same time. Artists were practically expected to propagate idealized, yet realistic-looking depictions of communist leaders, significant social events, and scenes of everyday life, with the latter focusing on workers and peasants at work in particular.[26] The Soviet Union also imposed adherence to Socialist Realism as a formal policy across all the countries that fell under its political influence in the years that followed the end of World War II, including Bulgaria, Czechoslovakia, East Germany (GDR), Hungary, Romania, and Poland.[27] Subsequently, for several years after the 1949 consolidation of communist power in Poland, the imagery that populated the country's visible sphere glorified communist ideas, the communist party, and peasants and workers mainly by depicting the hard work the Polish people put into the rebuilding of Poland and its in-

**Figure 12.5.** ***Poland 1939, 1945—Warsaw, Town Hall*** **(Polska 1939, 1945—Warszawa-Ratusz). Stamp, rotogravure. Courtesy Post and Telecommunications Museum, Wrocław (Poland).**

frastructures. As demonstrated by *Peace Is Winning* (*Pokój zwycięża*), one of the most influential photography exhibitions of the time organized by the National Museum in Warsaw in 1949, photographs in the style of Socialist Realism focused on the postwar condition of life in the country and only vaguely pointed to Polish wartime experience.[28] The majority of these images promoted a sense of national unity and were intended to enhance the people's trust in the ability of the communist state to lead them toward a brighter future. Franciszek Myszkowski's photograph *The New Avenue Is Growing* (*Rośnie nowa arteria*) is but one telling example from the 1949 exhibition (figure 12.6). Newspapers and magazines also circulated photographs in this very style regularly and Polish citizens frequently encountered them in the country's art galleries too.

Socialist Realism dominated the Polish visible sphere (and that of the Soviet Union's other European satellite states) until the mid-1950s, when Stalin's death in 1953 led to changes in Soviet policies, including the end of totalitarian rule in the Eastern Bloc. As communist control over public life and individual forms of expression became significantly less repressive, Polish artists, filmmakers, photographers, and writers began to repopulate Poland's visible sphere with rich pieces on the Polish wartime experience.[29] Thanks to their work, Poland saw some descriptions and representations of Polish Jews. Due to a sudden deterioration of the relations between the Soviet Union and Israel in the mid-1960s, however, Soviet Cold War politics required the instigation of official anti-Jewish attitudes across the Eastern Bloc.[30]

Known in the history of Polish-Jewish relations as the period of "organized forgetting," the following two decades witnessed any obvious cultural and historical references to Polish Jews and their heritage in the country systematically repressed, most particularly, the memory of the Shoah.[31] The production of projects that imaged Polish Jews one way or another ceased, and

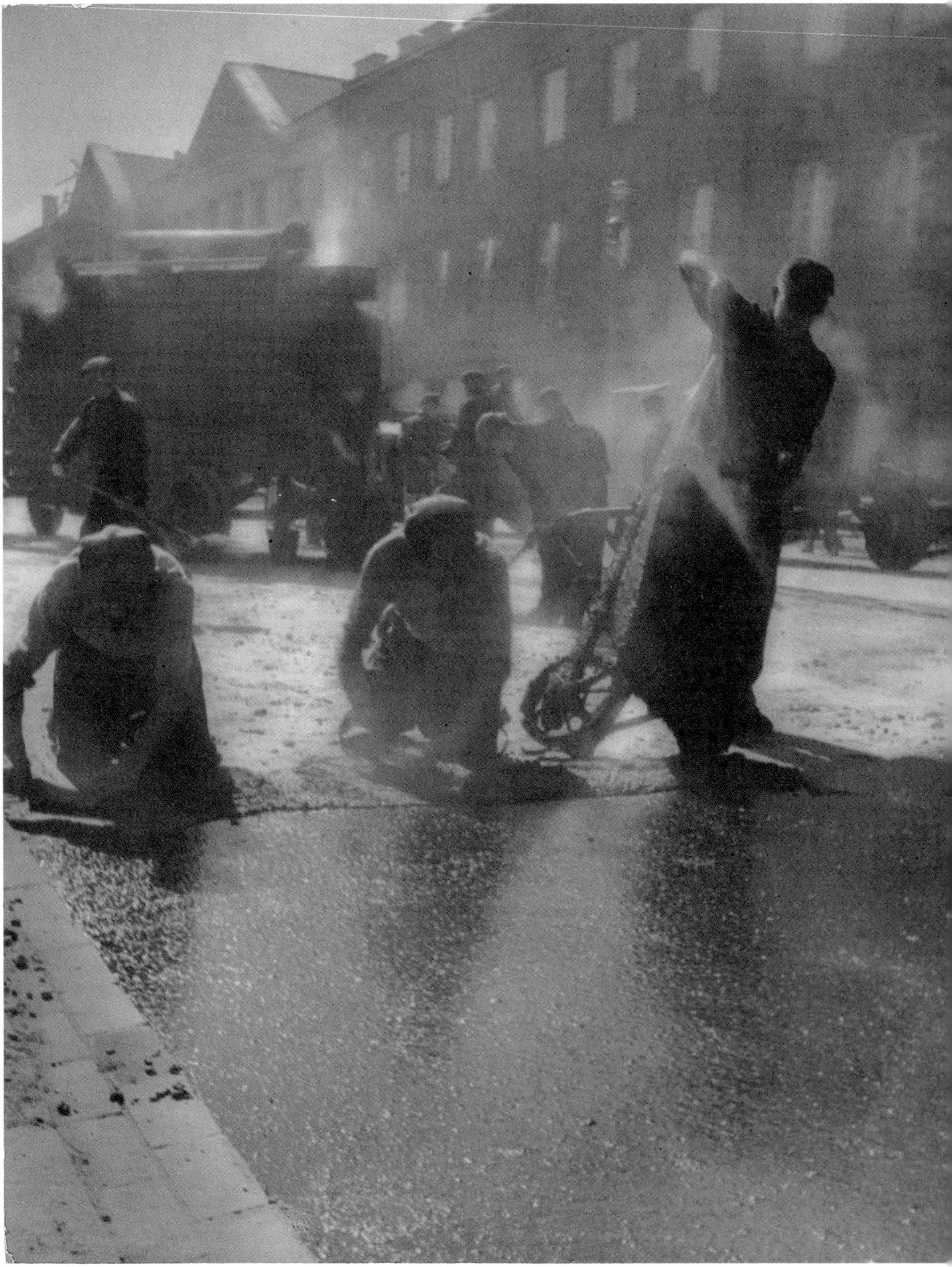

Figure 12.6. *The New Avenue Is Growing* [*Rośnie nowa arteria*], 1949. Photograph by Franciszek Myszkowski. 47.4 × 36.8 cm. Courtesy National Museum in Warsaw, di 83251/33 mnw.

those already completed were shelved. Shaping the collective memory and imagination of World War II for Polish citizens born after 1945, visualizations of the Polish wartime experience between the mid-1960s and the mid-1980s commemorated the nation's martyrdom and celebrated the victorious union of Polish soldiers, left-wing partisans, and the Red Army. To facilitate the absorption of this pseudo-historical imagery in the nation's mind, the Polish state turned to popular culture. TV series such as the comedy *Four Tankmen and a Dog* [*Czterej pancerni i pies*] and the action drama *More Than Life at Stake* [*Stawka większa niż życie*] won the people's hearts.[32] Communist Poland's approach toward the memorialization of World War II during that period also affected uses of photographs in the Polish education system. The country's standard secondary school history book of 1970, for example, featured a contemporaneous photograph of a generic view from Auschwitz. Showing a segment of the camp, empty and cleared of explicit traces of past atrocities (figure 12.7), it illustrated a text that introduced Nazi German death camps as places constructed by Germans to exterminate the Polish nation.[33] Furthermore, Poland's visualization of World War II from that period also largely determined the scope of photography exhibitions and publications, as can be seen in a number of issues of the prominent photographic journal *Fotografia* from 1974. On the occasion of the thirtieth anniversary of the 1944 Soviet break of the German front line, the journal dedicated a range of articles and images focusing on Soviet and Polish soldiers liberating Polish cities and posing at various locations in Berlin after the city's emancipation.[34]

The communist framing of the Polish wartime experience with this series of visual practices and restrictions meant that often the Shoah featured neither in formal narratives about Poland's history nor in configurations of the Polish sphere of collective memory.[35] Instead, victims of Nazi German camps were discussed within the context of Germany's cruelty toward the Polish nation. Ethnic minorities counted, but only in terms of the total number of vic-

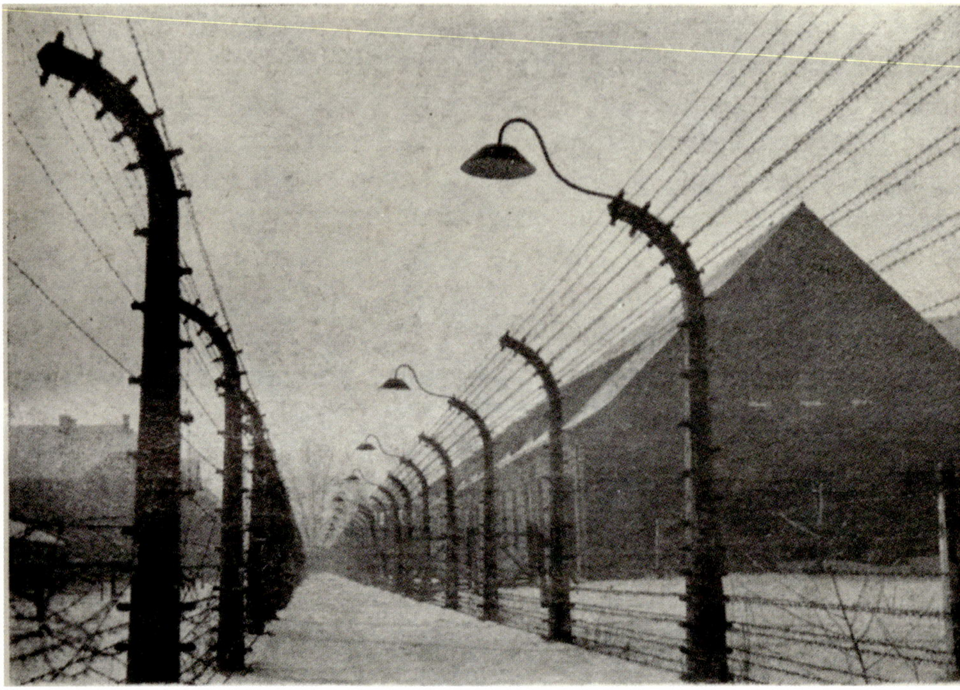

tims with Polish citizenship; there was mention neither of their ethnic identity nor of the fact that they were systematically imprisoned and exterminated precisely because of that identity. While in Jewish culture and historiography the memory of World War II has come predominantly to be associated with the experience of the Shoah, the systematic genocide of Polish Jewry had to a great extent been written out of Poland's national history during this period.[36]

Following the weakening of the Soviet Bloc in the mid-1980s, censorship in Poland became somewhat more relaxed and some more nuanced variations of the country's past gradually returned to the Polish visual sphere. In 1983, for instance, the musical *Fiddler on the Roof* premiered in Łódź; and a 1985 issue of *Fotografia* printed Stefan Kiełsznia's historical photographs of Polish Jewry in Lublin, as if to introduce them into the local canon of the history of photography. Yet, the state still insisted on maintaining the history of the Polish war experience free from references to the fate of Polish Jews. This was so much so the case that, when Claude Lanzmann's film *Shoah* was broadcasted on Polish television in 1986, many of the scenes were expurgated and used to exemplify Western attempts to frame the Poles as anti-Semites who were complicit in the German persecution of Jewish citizens.[37] Polish

Figure 12.7. *Obóz koncentracyjny w Oświęcimiu* [Concentration camp in Auschwitz]. Reproduced in Roman Wapiński, *Historia: od wybuchu II wojny światowej do roku 1964* [History: From the outbreak of World War II to 1964]. Warsaw: Państwowe Zakłady Wydawnictw Szkolnych, 1970, 49.

Jews had to wait patiently for the complete collapse of the communist regime to claim the right for their wartime experiences to be commemorated, for their dead to be remembered, and for their visual histories to flood and to be integrated into the Polish visual sphere.[38]

## LIBERATED NATIONAL HISTORY

In inviting prospective participants to publicly share their historical photographs of Polish Jews in public, the Shalom Foundation facilitated the gradual assimilation of the Shoah into Poland's national historiography and visual realm. One striking submission included Zahava Bromberg's recollections about the way in which she rescued some of her family photographs from destruction while her own life was at risk. The rescued photographs included one photographic portrait that she had of her mother (figure 12.8). As Bromberg put it in her letter, these photographs "are likely to be of importance because of the history of *their* survival."[39] Expanding on the history she referred to, Bromberg explained, "I myself carried [the photographs] through two selections by Dr. Mengele when I was in the Auschwitz concentration camp."[40] She later gave further details about these occurrences: "In one selection I kept the photographs in my mouth. During the second selection they were taped with a plaster to the bottom of my bare foot. Even today I cannot understand how I was able to do something so dangerous. Obviously, I could have been sentenced to death by what I did."[41]

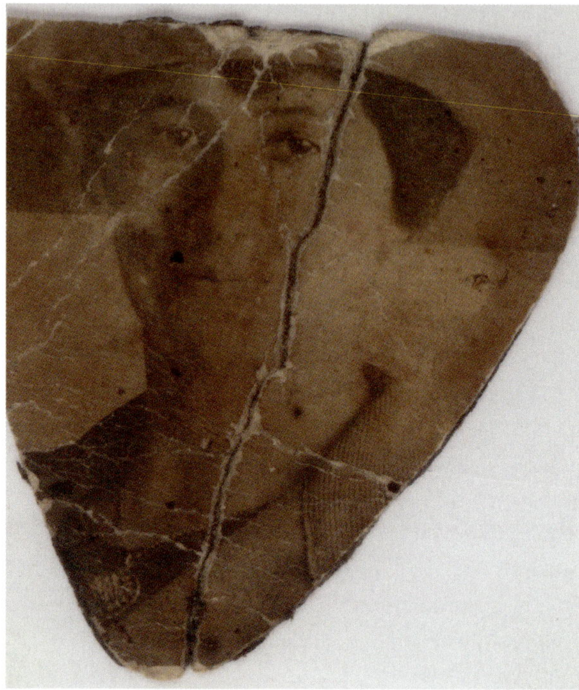

**Figure 12.8.** Debora Goldstein-Rosen. Submitted by Zahava Bromberg. Photographer unknown. Courtesy Shalom Foundation Archive, fs_1_0348_0009.

As Bromberg was willing to risk her life to protect these photographs, one can only assume she wished to safeguard what the images featured. And yet, as we indicated above, historians of Poland's communist period considered Auschwitz as a site at which Germans endeavored to eliminate the Polish nation, without revealing that most Polish citizens who lost their lives in this camp were of Jewish origin and that they were singled out for execution because they belonged to the "Jewish race." This strategy enabled the Polish communist regime to prioritize notions of Polish victimhood and sidestep the German elimination of Polish minority groups.[42] Submissions such as the one by Bromberg inserted into the Polish sociocultural domain narratives about the realities Polish Jews faced in Nazi German concentration, labor, and death camps, publicly elaborating on the Polish experience of World War II through the provision of information concerning the experience of *Jewish* Poles.

Other entries like Bromberg's further contributed to the accumulation of knowledge about the shared sufferings of Polish Jews and non-Jewish Polish citizens during the German occupation of Poland. Moreover, as journalist Anna Bikont argued in an article for the widely read Polish newspaper

*Gazeta Wyborcza*, narratives elicited through the participants' discussions of the photographs demonstrated the interconnected histories of Jewish and non-Jewish Poles, in particular their interrelated wartime experiences and memories.[43]

Illuminating in this regard were submissions sent by non-Jewish Polish citizens. While some non-Jewish Poles entered the contest with photographs related to relationships they or their families had with individual members of the Polish-Jewish community (which the Shoah brought to an untimely end), we find others to be of greater interest to this study. Depicting anonymous Jews, some of these had usually been found during the war, either by contest participants or by members of their families (who then incorporated them into their own photographic collections). Non-Jewish Poles had found these photographs in Jewish ghettos, shortly after their liquidations, and occasionally also in abandoned attics, perhaps the last hiding places of Jews who had hoped to escape their fate. Numerous submissions also explained that Polish citizens had collected the photographs Jews left at train stations before being deported to camps by the Germans, who most likely did not allow them to carry their luggage any further. Owing to the risk that being found with pictures of Jews entailed during the war, the photographs, some participants explained, were hidden at the time in various locations around their families' houses: beneath staircases, in sewage pipes, coal cellars, behind framed pictures, and under more ordinary photographs in albums. The photographs' arrival at the Foundation revealed that numerous non-Jewish Poles silently bore the memory of the Polish-Jewish community throughout the period of communist rule in Poland, if only because they understood that Poland's history would be incomplete without it.

Jan Kochański's submission is one telling example. Having entered the contest with a picture of two anonymous elderly Jews (figure 12.9), Kochański in his letter explained that he had worked at the Zawiercie steelwork factory throughout the German occupation of Poland.[44] Every so often the German army sent to the workers at the factory some clothes that used to belong to Jews; this clothing was intended to be used to wipe the machinery. Kochański found the photograph among the items of clothing that arrived at his workshop in one of these deliveries. By itself, the found photograph does not help retrieve any information about the subjects it depicts, nor does it offer any definitive knowledge about the individuals' eventual fate. Yet, Kochański's keeping the photograph, coupled with his decision to entrust it to the Foundation in association with a narrative about his own wartime experience, is meaningful for another reason: it shows that at least some Polish citizens saw in the

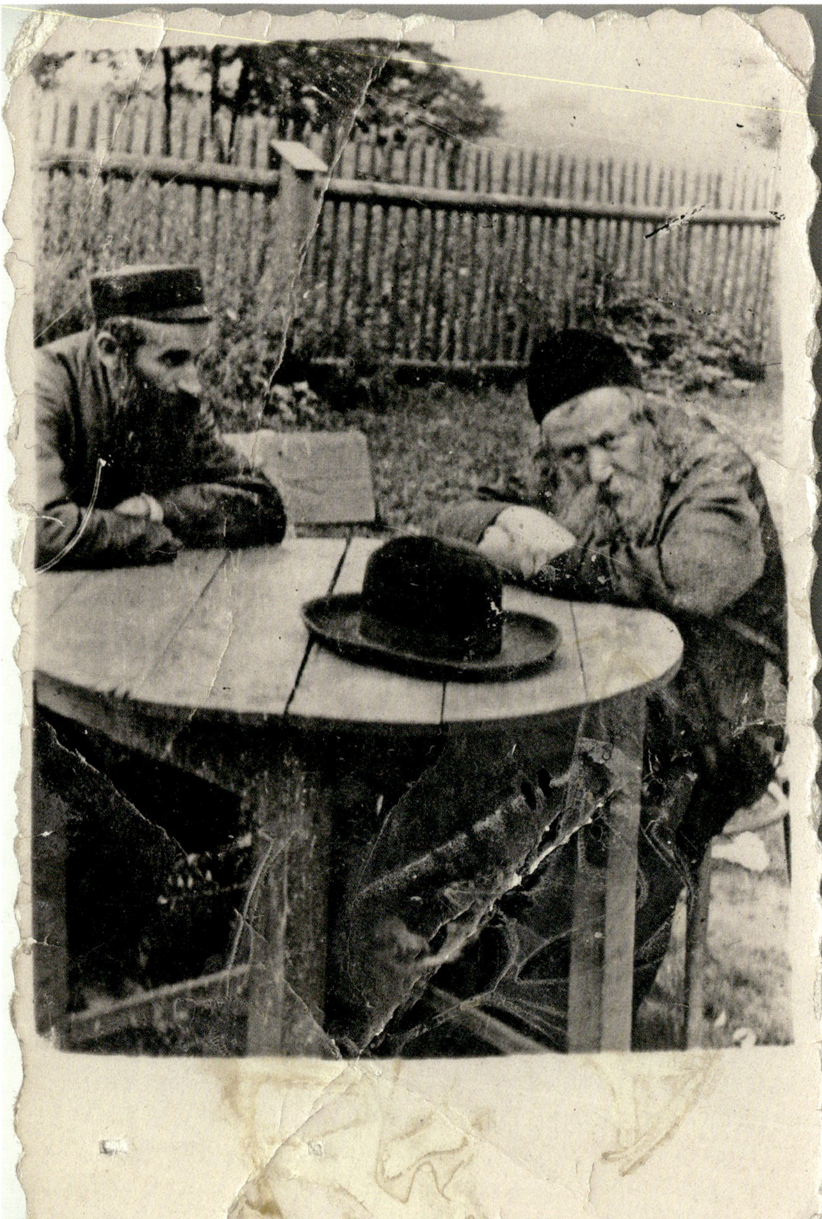

Figure 12.9. Subjects unknown. Submitted by Jan Kochański. Photographer unknown. Courtesy Shalom Foundation Archive, fs_1_0114_0001.

Foundation's initiative an opportunity to open up a discursive space capable of accommodating their own traumatic experiences of the war, which cannot be understood without the insertion of the Shoah into Poland's history. To be sure, referring to photographs submitted by Polish participants, journalist Joanna Dąbrowska, for example, clarified in her review of the exhibition: "The pictures tell a lot about those who saved the photographs. We therefore ought to remember that all these pictures are part of the history of Poland."[45] Communist Polish historiography could not afford to open up this space for these citizens, because their traumatic memories and, indeed, their photographs, were entwined with recollections of the Polish-Jewish community, its people, their way of life, and accounts of their suffering that consequently detracted from narratives about Polish martyrdom. In the context of the Foundation contest, however, such accounts could finally be heard and validated.

The desire to open up this discursive space also characterizes submissions made by Poles who witnessed the German mistreatment of Jews and photographed or obtained photographic records of some of these atrocities. Stanisław Leszczyński employed the two photographs that he included in his submission to provide testimony to what he saw in his hometown of Krosno. One photograph depicts four Jewish subjects in an urban environment, facing each other in pairs and pulling one another's beards (figure 12.10a). The other was taken from farther afield, revealing that these four subjects were part of a longer lineup of other Jewish individuals, also positioned in front of each other and engaged in the same degrading activity (figure 12.10b). Leszczyński noted that the individuals in the pictures were ordered to pull at each other's beards for the camera, clarifying that the photographs "were taken by some Kraut who gave them to a photographer to make prints and we made copies for ourselves on the sly."[46] It is unclear from the letter why Leszczyński asked for these copies in the first place. He had decided to send them to the Foundation, however, "as they evidence the martyrdom of Polish Jews."[47] Adhering to his perception of the photographs as credible testimo-

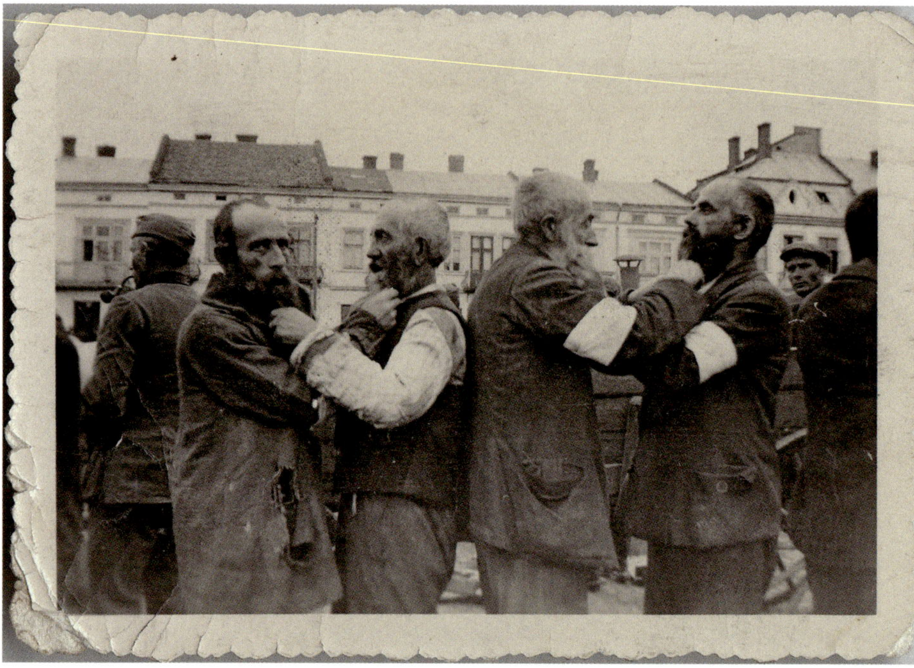

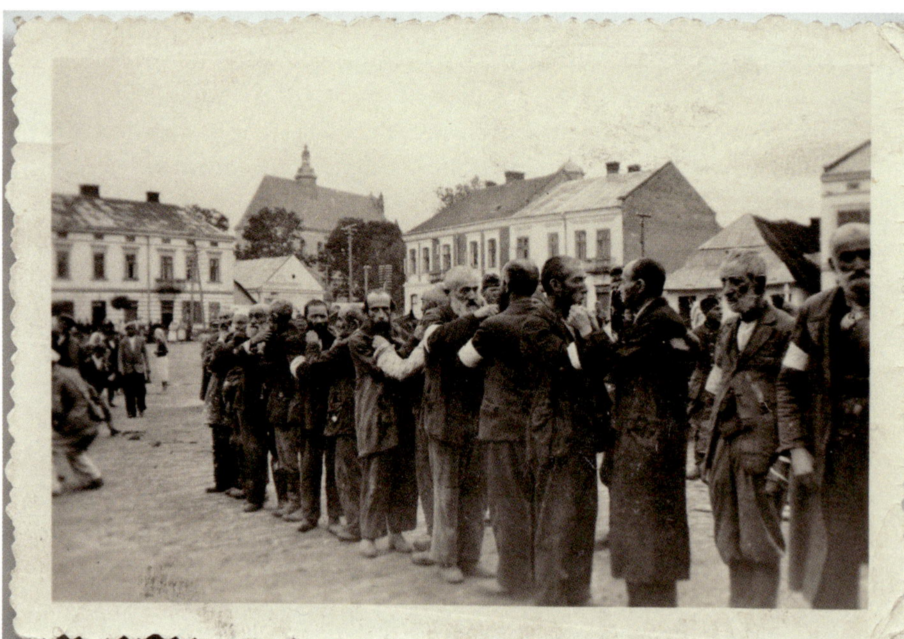

**Figure 12.10a.** ***(opposite, top)*** **Krosno upon the river Wisłok. Submitted by Stanisław Leszczyński. Photographer unknown. Courtesy Shalom Foundation Archive, fs_1_0273_0001.**

**Figure 12.10b.** ***(opposite, bottom)*** **Krosno upon the river Wisłok. Submitted by Stanisław Leszczyński. Photographer unknown. Courtesy Shalom Foundation Archive, fs_1_0273_0002.**

nies to Jewish suffering, throughout his letter Leszczyński uses the photographs as a point of departure for a broader narrative about the possible fate of those shown in the pictures. He notes, for example, that they had been made "on the marketplace in Krosno during the war, by the river Wisłok . . . where the Jews were first rounded up and later deported to the death camp in Bełżec . . . They were taken away through the city in open tracks, for the local people to see."[48] Positioning himself at the scene, however, Leszczyński also writes that, "I have eye-witnessed the deportations of the Jews from Krosno, often recognizing familiar faces. They were seen for the last time."[49] In doing so, Leszczyński frames the photographs as source-material capable of attesting to the atrocities carried out against Jews who lived in his town, as well as to his own wartime memories, which he could not have so easily shared in public before the democratization of Poland in 1989.

Marian Kosior entered the Foundation contest for the same reason. Showing a subject in traditional Jewish dress (figure 12.11), Kosior defined the visual element of her submission as an "original historical photograph from the early period of German occupation, around 1939 or 1940."[50] The photographed subject has his legs fully sunk in water, and he seems to be walking farther into the depths of the river. According to Kosior, the photograph "depicts the liquidation of the Jewish elite in Tarnobrzeg . . . [a process that] was carried out by driving them into the Vistula and shooting them therein."[51] The five rounded hats floating on the surface of the water in the image's foreground may indeed silently signify the execution of others who were sent into the river before this moment was captured on film. For Kosior this photograph is a credible portrayal of German brutality and indifferent attitude toward Jewish life, revealing how "the Gestapo and German soldiers entertained themselves in late 1939 and early 1940."[52]

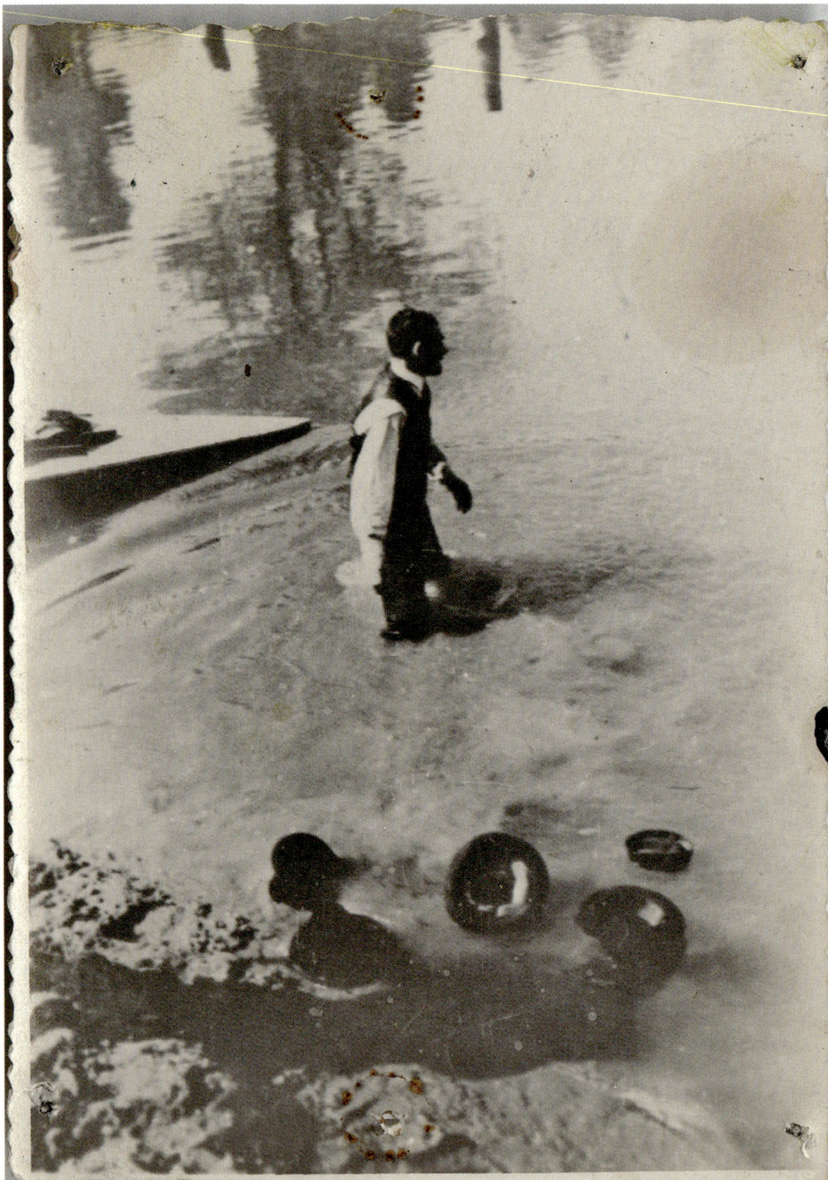

**Figure 12.11.** Tarnobrzeg, 1939 or 1940. Submitted by Marian Kosior. Photographer unknown. Courtesy Shalom Foundation Archive, fs_1_0246_0002.

## COLD WAR LEGACIES AND THE JEWS IN POLAND'S VISIBLE SPHERE

*And I Still See Their Faces* explicitly challenged Polish communist legacies of ethnic discrimination by increasing awareness of the rich history of Jews in the country, depicting them as integral inhabitants of Poland, members of Polish society, and equal contributors to the common cause of the Polish nation. As we have demonstrated, however, through the use of crowd-sourced historical photographs and the inclusive involvement of Jewish and non-Jewish, past and present Polish citizens, the initiative in fact achieved much more. The daring call for the creation of a Poland-based photographic collection about the history of Polish Jewry has given both Polish Jews and non-Jewish Poles the legitimacy to more openly recollect life in their country, before, during, and after World War II. As such, their contributions to the initiative—from the photographs they submitted to the recorded elicitations that accompanied their arrival at the Shalom Foundation—directly confronted some of the most restrictive communist rhetorical mechanisms that to this day still dominate Polish historical consciousness.

The modest desire of the Jewish community of Poland to record its history and rich heritage when the seeds of Polish democracy began to grow, normalized the appearance of Jews in Poland's visible sphere. The Shalom Foundation's employment of personal photographs and related recollections, however, also bridged the gap between personal life narratives and national, social, and cultural histories. As a whole, *And I Still See Their Faces* has therefore abolished, or at least significantly mitigated, the legacies of the artificial separation between lived experience, collective memory, and formal historiography that Polish communism had imposed on the country as a means to promote Soviet Cold War politics. The result of this process has reinscribed the lived experience of Polish Jews back into the country's history at the same time as it has exposed and documented chapters in the history of Polish society that had been suppressed by the communist Polish state.

At the beginning of the twenty-first century, these histories of Polish Jews and non-Jewish Poles live together and within each other, although admittedly still not altogether safely. *And I Still See Their Faces* indeed created a successful opportunity for Polish Jews to become active participants in Polish social and cultural life once again. That it facilitated the ability of Jews to reappear in Poland's visible sphere as historically legitimate citizens of the state is also true. Equally, however, the return of Polish Jews into this sphere has reawakened xenophobic and nationalist sentiments among some non-Jewish Polish citizens and politicians, which bring to mind the social and political tensions that characterized the relationship of these majority and minority groups prior to World War II and in the interwar period in particular.[53] Considered in the context of our discussion, this state of affairs stresses photography's concurrent potential to mitigate as well as to escalate sociopolitical anxieties in the country, highlighting the necessity of engaging Polish majority and minority groups alike in the search for agreeable stability arrangements.


### *Acknowledgment*

We would like to thank Gołda Tencer-Szurmiej and Ewa Paługa for granting us access to the Shalom Foundation photographic archive. All the photographs from *And I Still See Their Faces* printed in this chapter are taken from that archive and reproduced courtesy of Gołda Tencer-Szurmiej, General Director of the Shalom Foundation in Poland. We published another study about *And I Still See Their Faces* under the title "Beyond the Familial Impulse: Domestic Photography and Sociocultural History in Post-communist Poland, 1989–1996," in "Seeing Family," edited by Jennifer Orpana and Sarah Parsons, special issue, *Photography and Culture* 10, no. 2 (2017): 121–45. For a Polish translation of the article see, "Subwersywna moc prywatnych kolekcji fotografii. Żydzi w polskiej pamięci zbiorowej po upadku komunizmu," in *Konteksty: Antropologia Kultury-Etnografia-Sztuka* 71, no. 3 (2017): 212–24.


### *Notes*

1 One key example is the art exhibition *Poles' Self-Portrait* [*Polaków portret własny*], shown at the National Museum in Krakow in 1979–80.

2 Introduced by eighth General Secretary of the Communist Party of the Soviet

Union Mikhail Gorbachev, the policy of glasnost (openness) promoted transparent management of Soviet economy and politics and endorsed freedom of speech. Gorbachev believed that the implementation of this policy could engender a genuine discussion about the living conditions and needs of the people of the Soviet Bloc. Such a debate, he hoped, would pave the way toward an effective restructuring of the Soviet economic and political systems, a process that he named perestroika (restructuring) and whose prime intention was to revamp Soviet control over the Eastern Bloc.

3 The two most notable of these were initiated by academic and amateur photographer Aleksandra Garlicka, who installed them at Zachęta—National Gallery of Art in Warsaw. In 1985, she curated the exhibition *Photography of Polish Peasants* (Fotografia chłopów polskich), which she organized in collaboration with Maria Bijak. In 1989, she put on display the exhibition *Workers* (Robotnicy). For additional information about these and other exhibitions that Garlicka curated throughout the period of Poland's transition from dictatorial communism to democracy and free-market economy see, Pasternak and Ziętkiewicz, "Haunting Legacies."

4 In taking issue with the postwar and Cold War histories of Polish Jews, we certainly do not wish to suggest that Jewish and non-Jewish Poles lived together peacefully and harmoniously in the prewar era. We, equally, do not suggest that Polish Jews had not been subjected to socioeconomic discrimination or that they were not victims of private and organized, racist and nationalist, verbal and physical abuse, before, during, and after the war. The complex histories of Jewish lived experience in Poland throughout its history are well documented in scholarly literature. See, for example, Polonsky, *The Jews in Poland and Russia*; Gross, *Fear: Anti-Semitism in Poland after Auschwitz*; and Segel, *Stranger in Our Midst*. Our contribution intends to elaborate and offer nuances to such historical accounts rather than to challenge them in any way.

5 The exhibition was shown in venues such as Palacio de Canete (Madrid, 2012), London City Hall (London, 2008), Yeshiva University Museum (New York, 2007), Vystavochnyj centr Sankt-Peterburgskogo otdelenija Sojuza hudozhnikov Rossii (St. Petersburg, 2001), Memorial du Martyr Juif Inconnu (Paris, 1998), Yad Vashem (Jerusalem, 1998), The Simon Wiesenthal Center Museum of Tolerance (Los Angeles, 1997), and Towarzystwo Przyjaciół Sztuk Pięknych (Kraków, 1996).

6 On some of the public debates triggered by *And I Still See Their Faces*, see Mazur, *Historie fotografii polskiej 1839–2009*, 120–25; Hrynkiewicz, "I ciągle widzę ich twarze," 119–20; and Toeplitz, "Ciągle widzę ich twarze," 12–13.

7 Kuc, "Przez powiększenie," 12.

8 Mac, "Fotografie Żydów Polskich," 83.

9 Kemp-Welch, *Poland under Communism*; Micgiel, "'Bandits and Reactionaries.'"

10 Farmer, "National Minorities in Poland, 1919–1980," 51–55.

11 Łoziński, *Polityka państwa polskiego wobec mniejszości narodowych w latach 1989–1993*, 1–2.
12 Drozd, "Ukraińcy w Polsce w okresie przełomów politycznych 1944–1989," 237.
13 N. Davies, *God's Playground*, 2:469–72.
14 The most dominant examples emerged in June and July 1976 in connection with a state-orchestrated political campaign that was intended to tame workers' strikes in Ursus and Radom. The front page of the newspaper *Dziennik Bałtycki* of June 29, 1976, for example, featured a photograph of a mass demonstration in Gdańsk and Elbląg, showing protestors holding large banners with messages such as: "The programme of the party—the programme of the nation," "Comrade Gierek, we are with you," "Each Pole is responsible for the development of the country." The newspaper *Trybuna Robotnicza* of the same day, as another example, printed a similar photograph. Captured in Katowice it featured banner messages such as: "The Polish United Workers' Party—the nation's Party," "You can rely on us," and "We trust you." The front page of the newspaper *Słowo Ludu* of July 1, 1976, as a final example, printed a photograph of a pro-government rally from Radom, with banner messages such as "We are not all guilty but we are ashamed," and "We will do everything to regain your trust, comrade Gierek."
15 Mazur, *Propagandowy obraz świata*, 61–62.
16 Piekarniak, *Kazimierz nad Wisłą w 1931 roku*.
17 Henryk Gawarecki, [Untitled], in Gawarecki and Kiełsznia, *Dawny Lublin na fotografiach Stefana Kiełszni*, n.p.; Roman Kłosiewicz, [Untitled], in Piekarniak, *Kazimierz nad Wisłą w 1931 roku*, n.p.
18 Well-known examples include the crises of 1956, 1968, and the early 1980s. See Michlic, *Poland's Threatening Other*, 230–61.
19 N. Davies, *God's Playground*, 496–501.
20 "Ocalone fotografie," 7.
21 Fleming, "The New Minority Rights Regime in Poland," 534–35; Smooha, "Types of Democracy and Modes of Conflict Management in Ethnically Divided Societies," 428–29.
22 Haltof, *Polish Film and the Holocaust*, 2.
23 Szymanowicz, *Zaburzona epoka*, 77–82.
24 The exhibition was on public display at the National Museum in Warsaw between October 13, 1938, and April 30, 1939.
25 Haltof, *Polish Film and the Holocaust*, 6–7, 24–25, 78–89. Under these terms, mentions of Polish Jews entered into the Polish public environment in two main forms. One was through their depiction as members of left-wing resistance movements, most poignantly exemplified by Aleksander Ford's 1949 film, *The Border Street*. The other presented Polish Jews as individual war prisoners, detained in Nazi German concentration and death camps among a majority of non-Jewish Polish war prisoners. A telling example is Wanda Jakubowska's 1948 influential film, *The Last*

*Stage*, which also demonstrates the desire of the Polish communist government to describe Auschwitz-Birkenau (and similar Nazi German camps) as places designed for the extermination of the Poles alongside other nations that resisted Nazi Germany.

26 See also, C. V. James, *Soviet Socialist Realism*.

27 For more information about the absorption of Socialist Realism into Poland's visible sphere see Rottenberg, *Sztuka w Polsce 1945–2005*, 39.

28 Szymanowicz, *Zaburzona epoka*, 193–228.

29 Haltof, *Polish Film and the Holocaust*, 74–78. This was most visible in the work of an informal group of filmmakers known as the Polish Film School. Including such renowned film directors as Andrzej Wajda and Andrzej Munk, the group engaged more openly with questions concerning the characters of individuals within the Polish nation and the specific fate of Polish Jews in this respect. Wajda's 1961 film, *Samson*, and Munk's *Pasażerka* of 1963 are but two key examples.

30 Frankel, "The Soviet Regime and Anti-Zionism: An Analysis," 326–33.

31 Zaremba, "Zorganizowane zapomnienie o Holocauście w dekadzie Gierka."

32 Haltof, *Polish Film and the Holocaust*, 118.

33 Wapiński, *Historia*, 49–50.

34 See, for example, Latoś, "Żołnierze fotografowie," and Latoś, "Fotoreporterskie braterstwo broni."

35 Steinlauf, *Bondage to the Dead*, 63–74.

36 Cała, "Przekleństwo pamięci traumatycznej," 201–2; Steinlauf, *Bondage to the Dead*, 81–83.

37 Bikont, "A on krzyczał: 'Wszyscy jesteście kapo,'" 10.

38 While the communist administration of the Polish visual sphere certainly facilitated Poland's ideologically informed repression of the experience of the Shoah, it must be mentioned that other conditions in the country also did not help to incorporate it into Polish collective memory. By the time World War II ended, for instance, only a few Jews remained in Poland to recall their experiences. Those who survived the German persecution and systematic elimination of the Jews either chose to live the rest of their lives elsewhere or preferred to keep their memories to themselves rather than share and relive their traumatic recollections. Furthermore, Polish Jews who returned to Poland after the war often did not acknowledge their Jewish origin owing to waves of anti-Jewish violent acts that Poles carried out between 1944 and 1946, primarily as a consequence of their assumption that Jews were supporters of Soviet politics and those responsible for the establishment of the communist regime in postwar Poland. As Poland remained communist until 1989, many of its Jewish citizens opted to hide their Jewish background throughout this period. In fact, a large number of Polish Jews opted to carry on hiding their Jewish background even after the fall of the communist regime, and some prefer to withhold their Jewish identity to this very day.

39 Zahava Bromberg to Shalom Foundation, December 27, 1995, Shalom Foundation (Warsaw), And I Still See Their Faces Collection, FS_1_0348, our emphasis.

40 Bromberg to Shalom Foundation, December 27, 1995.

41 Bromberg to Shalom Foundation, December 27, 1995.

42 Steinlauf, *Bondage to the Dead*, 69.

43 Bikont, "Pamięć polska, pamięć żydowska," 10–12.

44 Jan Kochański to Shalom Foundation, December 3, 1994, Shalom Foundation (Warsaw), And I Still See Their Faces Collection, FS_1_114.

45 Dąbrowska, "Wystawa w warszawskiej 'Zachęcie': Pamięć," 2.

46 Stanisław Leszczyński to Shalom Foundation, February 15, 1995, Shalom Foundation (Warsaw), And I Still See Their Faces Collection, FS_1_0273. *Kraut* is a derogatory term for a German, most often used as a degrading reference to a German soldier in the historical contexts of World War I and World War II.

47 Leszczyński to Shalom Foundation, February 15, 1995.

48 Leszczyński to Shalom Foundation, February 15, 1995.

49 Leszczyński to Shalom Foundation, February 15, 1995.

50 Marian Kosior to Shalom Foundation, undated, Shalom Foundation (Warsaw), And I Still See Their Faces Collection, FS_1_0246.

51 Kosior to Shalom Foundation, undated.

52 Kosior to Shalom Foundation, undated.

53 See also Pasternak and Ziętkiewicz, "Making a Home in Poland."

# Bibliography


Abdulhadi, Faiha. *The Political Role of Palestinian Women in the 1930s*. Translated by Nitham Sais. Al-Bereh, West Bank: Palestinian Women's Research and Documentation Center, 2006.

Acharya, Amitay, and See Seng Tan, eds. *Bandung Revisited: The Legacy of the 1955 Asian-African Conference for International Order*. Singapore: National University of Singapore Press, 2008.

Adelman, Rebecca. *Beyond the Checkpoint: Visual Practices in America's Global War on Terror*. Amherst: University of Massachusetts Press, 2014.

Ageron, Charles-Robert. "Les états africains de la Communauté et la guerre d'Algérie (1958–1960)." In *L'Afrique noire française: L'heure des indépendances*, edited by Charles-Robert Ageron and Marc Michel, 230–53. Paris: CNRS Éditions, [1992] 2010.

Agnew, John. *Geopolitics: Re-visioning World Politics*. London: Routledge, 2003.

Ahmed, Sarah. *Queer Phenomenology: Orientations, Objects, Others*. Durham, NC: Duke University Press, 2006.

Akinsha, Konstantin, and Grigorii Kozlov, with Sylvia Hochfield. *Beautiful Loot: The Soviet Plunder of Europe's Art Treasures*. New York: Random House, 1995.

Alford, Kenneth D. *Allied Looting in World War II: Theft of Art, Manuscripts, Stamps and Jewelry in Europe*. Jefferson, NC: McFarland, 2011.

Alinder, Jasmine. *Moving Images: Photography and the Japanese American Incarceration*. Urbana: University of Illinois Press, 2011.

Althusser, Louis. "Ideology and the Ideological State Apparatuses." In *Lenin and Philosophy and Other Essays*. New York: Monthly Review Press, 1971.

Amad, Paula. "From God's-Eye to Camera-Eye: Aerial Photography's Post-Humanist and Neo-Humanist Visions of the World." *History of Photography* 36, no. 1 (2012): 66–86.

Anand, Mulk Raj. "Photography as an Art Form." *Marg* 14 (1960): 2–3.

Anderson, Carol. *Eyes Off the Prize: The United Nations and the African American Struggle for Human Rights, 1944–1955*. Cambridge: Cambridge University Press, 2003.

Anderson, Carol. "From Hope to Disillusion: African Americans, the United Nations, and the Struggle for Human Rights, 1944–1947." *Diplomatic History* 20, no. 4 (1996): 531–641.

Anderson, Carol. "The Histories of African Americans' Anticolonialism during the Cold War." In McMahon, *The Cold War in the Third World*, 178–91.

Anderson, Carol. "International Conscience, the Cold War, and Apartheid: The NAACP's Alliance with the Reverend Michael Scott for South West Africa's Liberation, 1946–51." *Journal of World History* 19, no. 3 (2008): 297–325.

Antonius, Soraya. "Fighting on Two Fronts: Conversations with Palestinian Women." *Journal of Palestine Studies* 8, no. 3 (1979): 26–45.

Antonov-Saratovskii, V. A. "Turizm, Partiia I Gosudarstvo." *Na Sushe i Na More* 16 (1930).

Archer, David, and Patrick Costello. *Literacy and Power: The Latin American Battleground*. London: Earthscan, 1990.

Armstrong, Elizabeth, and Vijay Prashad. "Solidarity: War Rites and Women's Rights." *CR: New Centennial Review* 5, no. 1 (2005): 213–53.

Ascencio, Daniel Flores, and Lucy R. Lippard. "Artists Call: For Solidarity and Culture." *Art and Artists* 14, no. 4 (1984): 1–4.

Ashford, Doug. "Aesthetic Insurgency: Artists Call against US Intervention in Central America (1982–1985)." In *System Error: War Is a Force That Gives Us Meaning*, by Lorenzo Fusi and Naeem Mohaiemen, 111–17. Milan: Silvana Editoriale, 2007.

Ashford, Doug, Wendy Ewald, Nina Felshin, and Patricia C. Phillips. "A Conversation on Social Collaboration." *Art Journal* 65, no. 2 (2006): 58–83.

Ashton, Dore. *New York School: A Cultural Reckoning*. New York: Penguin Books, 1979.

Assubuji, Rui, and Patricia Hayes. "The Political Sublime: Reading Kok Nam, Mozambican Photographer (1939–2012)." *Kronos* 39 (2013): 66–111.

Ault, Julie, ed. *Show and Tell: A Chronicle of Group Material*. London: Four Corners Books, 2010.

Azoulay, Ariella. *The Civil Contract of Photography*. London: Zone Books, 2008.

Azoulay, Ariella. *Civil Imagination: A Political Ontology of Photography*. London: Verso, 2015.

Azoulay, Ariella. "The Execution Portrait." In *Picturing Atrocity: Reading Photographs in Crisis*, edited by Geoffrey Batchen, Mick Gidley, Nancy K. Miller, and Jay Prosser, 249–60. London: Reaktion Books, 2012.

Azoulay, Ariella. "'The Family of Man': A Visual Universal Declaration of Universal Rights." In *The Human Snapshot*, edited by Thomas Keenan and Tirdad Zolghadar, 19–48. Berlin: Sternberg Press, 2013.

Azoulay, Ariella. "Palestine as Symptom, Palestine as Hope: Revising Human Rights Discourse." *Critical Inquiry* 40, no. 4 (2014): 332–64.

Azoulay, Ariella. *Potential History: Unlearning Imperialism*. London: Verso, 2019.

Azoulay, Ariella. "Revolutionary Moments and State Violence." In *New Media, Old Media: A History and Theory Reader*, by Wendy Chun, Anna Watkins Fisher, and Thomas Keenan, 2nd ed., 205–22. New York: Routledge, 2015.

Azoulay, Ariella. "Unlearning the Position of the Photographer as Expert." In *Susan Meiselas: Meditations*, by Susan Meiselas, 95–118. Bologna: Damiani, 2018.

Back, Jean, and Viktoria Schmidt-Linsenhoff, eds. *The Family of Man, 1955–2001: Humanism and Postmodernism; A Reappraisal of the Photo Exhibition by Edward Steichen*. Marburg, Germany: Jonas Verlag, 2004.

Ba Jin. *Random Thoughts*. Translated by Geremie Barmé. Hong Kong: Joint Publication Company, 1984.

Bajorek, Jennifer. "Decolonizing the Archive: The View from West Africa." *Aperture* 210 (Spring 2013): 66–69.

Bajorek, Jennifer. "Photography and National Memory: Senegal about 1960." *History of Photography* 34, no. 2 (2010): 160–71.

Baldwin, Kate A. *The Racial Imaginary of the Cold War Kitchen: From Sokol'niki Park to Chicago's South Side*. Lebanon, NH: University Press of New England, 2016.

Bard, Mitchell G. "U.S. Israel Strategic Cooperation: The 1968 Sale of Phantom Jets to Israel." *Jewish Virtual Library*. Accessed December 16, 2021. http://www.jewishvirtuallibrary.org/the-1968-sale-of-phantom-jets-to-israel.

Barnhisel, Greg. *Cold War Modernists: Art, Literature, and American Cultural Diplomacy, 1946–1959*. New York: Columbia University Press, 2015.

Barnouw, Dagmar. *1945: Views of War and Violence*. Bloomington: Indiana University Press, 1996.

Barros, César A. "Declassifying the Archive: The Bombardment of La Moneda Palace and the Political Economy of the Image." In *Technology, Literature, and Digital Culture in Latin America: Mediatized Sensibilities in a Globalized Era*, edited by Matthew Bush and Tania Gentic, 127–45. New York: Routledge, 2014.

Barthes, Roland. *Camera Lucida: Reflections on Photography*. Translated by Richard Howard. New York: Hill and Wang, 1981.

Barthes, Roland. "The Great Family of Man." In *Mythologies*, translated by Annette Lavers, 100–102. New York: Hill and Wang, [1957] 1972.

Barthes, Roland. *Mythologies*. London: Paladin, 1973.

Barthes, Roland. "The Third Meaning: Research Notes on Some Eisenstein Stills." In *Image, Music, Text*, translated by Stephen Heath, 52–68. New York: Hill and Wang, 1977.

Bass, Warren. *Support Any Friend: Kennedy's Middle East and the Making of the U.S.-Israel Alliance*. Oxford: Oxford University Press, 2003.

Bassnett, Sarah, Andrea Noble, and Thy Phu, eds. "Cold War Visual Alliances." Special issue, *Visual Studies* 30, no. 2 (2015).

Bassnett, Sarah, Andrea Noble, and Thy Phu. "Introduction: Cold War Visual Alliances." Special issue, *Visual Studies* 30, no. 2 (2015): 119–22.

Batchen, Geoffrey, ed. *Photography Degree Zero: Reflections on Roland Barthes's* Camera Lucida. Cambridge, MA: MIT Press, 2011.

*Battle Stations! Your Navy in Action: A Photographic Epic of the Naval Operations of World War II*. New York: Wm. H. Wise, 1946.

Bayart, Jean-François. *The State in Africa: The Politics of the Belly*. Translated by Mary Harper, Christopher Harrison, and Elizabeth Harrison. London: Polity, 2009.

Bednar, Robert. "Being Here, Looking There: Mediating Vistas in the National Parks of the Contemporary American West." In *Observation Points: The Visual Poetics of National Parks*, edited by Thomas Patin, 1–28. Minneapolis: University of Minnesota Press, 2012.

Behrooz, Maziar. "Iranian Revolution and the Legacy of the Guerrilla Movement." In Cronin, *Reformers and Revolutionaries in Modern Iran*, 189–203.

Beins, Agatha. "Radical Others: Women of Color and Revolutionary Feminism." *Feminist Studies* 41, no. 1 (2015): 150–83.

Benjamin, Walter. *The Origin of German Tragedy*. Translated by John Osborne. London: Verso, 1997.

Bergen-Cico, Dessa K. *War and Drugs: The Role of Military Conflict in the Development of Substance Abuse*. London: Routledge, 2011.

Berger, John. *Ways of Seeing*. London: BBC, 1972.

Berger, Martin A. *Seeing through Race: A Reinterpretation of Civil Rights Photography*. Berkeley: University of California Press, 2011.

Berlier, Monique. "*The Family of Man*: Readings of an Exhibition." In *Picturing the Past: Media, History, and Photograph*, 206–41. Urbana: University of Illinois Press, 1999.

Bikont, Anna. "A on krzyczał: 'Wszyscy jesteście kapo.'" *Gazeta Wyborcza*, October 4, 1997, 10.

Bikont, Anna. "Pamięć polska, pamięć żydowska." *Gazeta Wyborcza*, Magazyn, April 12, 1996, 10–12.

Bill, James A. *The Eagle and the Lion: The Tragedy of American-Iranian Relations*. New Haven, CT: Yale University Press, 1988.

Billig, Michael. *Banal Nationalism*. London: SAGE, 1995.

Bình, Nguyễn Thị. *Family, Friends, and Country*. Hanoi, Vietnam: Trí Thức, 2012.

Bin Xu. "Regretless Youth and Long Live Youth! Exhibits and Museums as Sites of Memory." Unpublished manuscript, 2019.

Blackburn, Robert M. *Mercenaries and Lyndon Johnson's "More Flags": The Hiring of Korea, Filipino, and Thai Soldiers in the Vietnam War*. Jefferson, NC: McFarland, 1994.

Blacker, O'Neill. "Cold War in the Countryside: Conflict in Guerrero, Mexico." *Americas* 66, no. 2 (2009): 181–210.

Boime, Albert. *The Magisterial Gaze: Manifest Destiny and American Landscape Painting c. 1820–1865*. Washington, DC: Smithsonian Institution Press, 1991.

Botting, Douglas. *Ruins of the Reich: Germany 1945–1949*. New York: Crown, 1985.

Bradley, Doug, and Craig Werner. *We Gotta Get Out of This Place: The Soundtrack of the Vietnam War*. Amherst: University of Massachusetts Press, 2015.

Brettin, Michael, and Peter Kroh. *Berlin 1945: World War II; Photos of the Aftermath*. New York: Berlinica, 2014.

Brodsky, Joseph. *Less Than One: Selected Essays*. New York: Farrar, Straus and Giroux, 1986.

Brothers, Caroline. *War and Photography: A Cultural History*. New York: Routledge, 1997.

Brown, Ryan Lenora. "A Native of Nowhere: The Life of South African Journalist Nat Nakasa, 1937–1965." *Kronos* 37, no. 1 (2011): 41–59.

Bruning, John R. *Bombs Away! The World War II Bombing Campaigns over Europe*. Minneapolis: Zenith Press, 2011.

Buckley, Liam. "Objects of Love and Decay: Colonial Photographs in a Postcolonial Archive." *Cultural Anthropology* 20, no. 2 (2008): 249–70.

Burant, Jim. "Using Photography to Assert Canadian Sovereignty in the Arctic: The A. P. Low Expedition of 1903–4 aboard the CGS *Neptune*." In *Imaging the Arctic*, edited by Jonathan C. H. King and Henrietta Lidchi, 77–87. Seattle: University of Washington Press, 1998.

Burgin, Victor, ed. *Thinking Photography*. London: Palgrave Macmillan, 1982.

Burma, Ian. *Year Zero: A History of 1945*. London: Penguin Press, 2013.

Byford-Jones, Wilfred. *Berlin Twilight*. New York: Hutchinson, 1947.

Cadava, Eduardo. *Theses on the Photography of History*. Princeton, NJ: Princeton University Press, 1997.

Cała, Alina. "Przekleństwo pamięci traumatycznej." In *Zagłada Żydów: Pamięć narodowa a pisanie historii w Polsce i we Francji*, edited by Barbara Engelking et al., 198–202. Lublin: Wydawnictwa Uniwersytetu Marii Skłodowskiej-Curie, 2006.

Callahan, William A. *Cultural Governance and Resistance in Pacific Asia*. New York: Routledge, 2006.

Campt, Tina. *Image Matters: Archive, Photography, and the African Diaspora in Europe*. Durham, NC: Duke University Press, 2012.

Campt, Tina. *Listening to Images*. Durham, NC: Duke University Press, 2017.

Caplan, Caren. *Aerial Aftermaths: Wartime from Above*. Durham, NC: Duke University Press, 2018.

Carreon, Michelle E., and Valentine M. Moghadam. "Resistance Is Fertile: Revising Maternalist Frames across Cases of Women's Mobilizations." *Women's Studies International Forum* 51 (2015): 19–30.

Chakrabarty, Dipesh. *Provincializing Europe: Postcolonial Thought and Historical Difference*. Princeton, NJ: Princeton University Press, 2000.

Chamberlin, Thomas. *The Global Offensive: The United States, the Palestine Liberation Organization, and the Making of the Post–Cold War Order*. Oxford: Oxford University Press, 2012.

Chatterjee, Partha. *The Politics of the Governed: Reflections on Popular Politics in Most of the World*. New York: Columbia University Press, 2006.

Chauvel, Patrick. *Ceux du Nord*. Paris: Aranesh, 2014.

Chen, Jian. *Mao's China and the Cold War*. Chapel Hill: University of North Carolina Press, 2001.

Chen, Tina Mai. "Dressing for the Party: Clothing, Citizenship, and Gender-Formation in Mao's China." *Fashion Theory* 5, no. 2 (2001): 143–71.

Chistokov, Aleksandr. "'Razreshen vyezd: Deiatel'nost' Komissii po vyezdam za granitsy v 1949–1962 gg." *Peterburgskii istoricheskii zhurnal* 4, no. 16 (2017): 100–119.

Chomsky, Noam. "State and Corp.: Noam Chomsky Interviewed by Uncredited Interviewer." ZNet Germany, May 18, 2005. https://chomsky.info/20050518/.

Chubin, Shahram. "Iran." In *The Cold War and the Middle East*, edited by Yezid Sayigh and Avi Shlaim, 216–49. Oxford: Oxford University Press, 1997.

Cockcroft, Eva. "Abstract Expressionism: Weapon of the Cold War." *Artforum* 12, no. 10 (1974): 39–41.

Coderre, Laurence. "The Curator, the Investor, and the Dupe: Consumer Desire and Chinese Cultural Revolution Memorabilia." *Journal of Material Culture* 21, no. 4 (2016), 429–47.

Cole, Ernest. *House of Bondage*. New York: Random House, 1967.

Cole, Ernest. Letter to the Editor. *New York Times*, December 12, 1967.

Cole, Ernest. "My Country, My Hell!" *Ebony*, February 1968, 68–73.

Coleman, Kevin. *A Camera in the Garden of Eden: The Self-Foraging of a Banana Republic*. Austin: University of Texas Press, 2016.

Conor, Gearty. *Can Human Rights Survive?* Cambridge: Cambridge University Press, 2006.

Coombes, Annie E. *History after Apartheid: Visual Culture and Public Memory in a Democratic South Africa*. Durham, NC: Duke University Press, 2003.

Cooper, Frederick. *Africa since 1940: The Past of the Present*. Cambridge: Cambridge University Press, 2002.

Cottam, Richard W. *Iran and the United States: A Cold War Case Study*. Pittsburgh: Pittsburgh University Press, 1988.

Coulthard, Glen Sean. *Red Skin, White Masks: Rejecting the Colonial Politics of Recognition*. Minneapolis: University of Minnesota Press, 2014.

Crimp, Douglas. "Appropriating Appropriation." In *Image Scavengers: Photography*, edited by Paula Marincola, 126–37. Philadelphia: Institute of Contemporary Art, University of Pennsylvania, 1982.

Cronin, Stephanie, ed. *Reformers and Revolutionaries in Modern Iran: New Perspectives on the Iranian Left*. London: Routledge Curzon, 2004.

Crowder, Michael, ed. *The Cambridge History of Africa*. Cambridge: Cambridge University Press, 1994.

Crowley, David, ed. *Style and Socialism: Modernity and Material Culture in Post-War Eastern Europe*. Oxford: Berg, 2000.

Cull, Nicholas J. *The Cold War and the United States Information Agency: American Propaganda and Public Diplomacy, 1945–1989*. New York: Cambridge University Press, 2008.

Cull, Nicholas J. "'The Man Who Invented the Truth': The Tenure of Edward R. Murrow as Director of the United States Information Agency during the Kennedy Years." *Cold War History* 4, no. 1 (2003): 23–48.

Cultural Correspondence. *We Will Not Be Disappeared! Directory of Arts Activism*. New York: Cultural Correspondence, in cooperation with Lake View Press, 1984.

Cumings, Bruce. *Parallax Visions: Making Sense of American–East Asian Relations at the End of the Century*. Durham, NC: Duke University Press, 2002.

Curley, John J. *A Conspiracy of Images: Andy Warhol, Gerhard Richter, and the Art of the Cold War*. New Haven, CT: Yale University Press, 2013.

Dąbrowska, Joanna. "Wystawa w warszawskiej 'Zachęcie': Pamięć." *Sycyna*, May 12, 1996, 2.

Dallas, Gregor. *1945: The War That Never Ended*. New Haven, CT: Yale University Press, 2005.

Darnton, Christopher. *Rivalry and Alliance Politics in Cold War Latin America*. Baltimore, MD: Johns Hopkins University Press, 2014.

David-Fox, Michael. "The Iron Curtain as Semipermeable Membrane: Origins and Demise of the Stalinist Superiority Complex." In *Cold War Crossings: International Travel and Exchange across the Soviet Bloc, 1940s–1960s*, edited by Patryk Babiracki, 14–39. College Station: Texas A&M University Press, 2014.

Davies, David J. "Old Zhiqing Photos: Nostalgia and the 'Spirit' of the Cultural Revolution." *China Review* 5, no. 2 (2005): 97–123.

Davies, Norman. *God's Playground: A History of Poland*, vol. 2. Oxford: Oxford University Press, 2005.

Deák, István. *Europe on Trial: The Story of Collaboration, Resistance, and Retribution during World War I*. Boulder, CO: Westview Press, 2015.

Deák, István, Jan T. Gross, and Tony Judt. *The Politics of Retribution in Europe*. Princeton, NJ: Princeton University Press, 2000.

De La Parra, Marco Antonio. "Fragments of a Self-Portrait," translated by Marcelo Montealegre. In *Chile from Within*, edited by Susan Meiselas, 13–15. New York: W. W. Norton, 1990.

Denton, Kirk. *Exhibiting the Past: Historical Memory and the Politics of Museums in Postsocialist China*. Honolulu: University of Hawai'i Press, 2014.

"Department of Justice File No. 2/1/2265," South Africa. Freedom of Information Programme Collection, South African History Archive, n.d.

Department of Northern Affairs and National Resources, Canada. *Visit of His Excellency the Rt. Hon. Vincent Massey, Governor-General, to the Canadian Arctic, March 20 to April 5, 1956*. Ottawa: Department of Northern Affairs and National Resources, 1956.

Desnoes, Edmundo. "The Death System." In *On Signs*, edited by Marshall Blonsky, 39–42. Baltimore, MD: Johns Hopkins University Press, 1985.

Diack, Heather. "Hand over Fist: A Chronicle of Cold War Photography." *Visual Studies* 30, no. 2 (2015): 182–94.

Dickerman, Leah. "Socialist Realism in the Shadow of Photography." *October* 93 (2000): 138–53.

Dikötter, Frank. *The Cultural Revolution: A People's History, 1962–1976*. London: Bloomsbury, 2016.

Dinges, John. "Chilling Accusation Is Coldly Contradicted by Facts." *Los Angeles Times*, September 3, 1981.

Dinges, John. "White Paper or Blank Paper: U.S. Report on Aid to El Salvador Guerrillas Falls Short." *Los Angeles Times*, March 17, 1981, C7.

Đoàn Công Tính. *Khoảnh khắc*: Ảnh phóng sự về chiến tranh Việt Nam. Hồ Chí Minh City, Vietnam: Nhà xuất bản Tổng hợp, n.d. [2004].

Doucette, Wilfred. "Cape Herschel: The Post Office That Never Was." *Postal History Society of Canada Journal* 46 (1986): 20–24.

Dower, John W. "The Bombed: Hiroshima and Nagasaki in Japanese Memory." In *Hiroshima in History and Memory*, by Michael J. Hogan, 116–42. Cambridge: Cambridge University Press, 1996.

Drozd, Roman. "Ukraińcy w Polsce w okresie przełomów politycznych 1944–1989." In *Mniejszości narodowe w Polsce: Państwo i społeczeństwo wobec mniejszości narodowych w okresach przełomów politycznych 1944–1989*, ed. Piotr Madajczyk. Warsaw: Instytut Studiów Politycznych Polskiej Akademii Nauk, 1998.

Dudziak, Mary L. *Cold War Civil Rights: Race and the Image of American Democracy*. Princeton, NJ: Princeton University Press, 2011.

Duganne, Erina. "*The Nicaragua Media Project* and the Limits of Postmodernism." *Art Bulletin* 100, no. 1 (March 2018): 146–68.

Duganne, Erina, and Abigail Satinsky, ed. *Art for the Future: Artists Call and Central American Solidarities*. Los Angeles: Inventory Press, 2022.

Dussault, René, and George Erasmus. "The High Arctic Relocation: A Report on the 1953–55 Relocation." In *Royal Commission on Aboriginal Peoples*. Toronto: Canadian Government Publishing, 1994.

Editorial Board. "Preface: About the Virtual Museum of the 'Cultural Revolution.'" *Virtual Museum of the "Cultural Revolution"/China News Digest* (Hua Xia Wen

Zhai), 1996–2000. Accessed December 20, 2021. http://www.cnd.org/CR/english/about.htm.

Edwards, Elizabeth. "Photography and the Material Performance of the Past." *History and Theory* 48, no. 4 (2009): 130–50.

Edwards, Elizabeth, and Janice Hart, eds. *Photographs Objects Histories: On the Materiality of Images*. London: Routledge, 2004.

Elder, Greg. "Faces of Defense Intelligence: John T. Hughes." US Defense Intelligence Agency, July 22, 2016. https://www.dia.mil/News-Features/Articles/Article-View/Article/853205/faces-of-defense-intelligence-john-t-hughes/.

Emering, Edward J. *Viet Cong: A Photographic Portrait*. Atglen, PA: Schiffler Military History, 1999.

Estrin, James. "Susan Meiselas: Breaching Boundaries in Photography." *New York Times*, July 3, 2018. https: //www.nytimes.com/2018/07/03/lens/susan-meiselas-mediations.html.

Falk, Andrew J. *Upstaging the Cold War: American Dissent and Cultural Diplomacy, 1940–1960*. Amherst: University of Massachusetts Press, 2011.

Fall, Bernard B., ed. *Ho Chi Minh on Revolution: Selected Writings, 1920–66*. London: Praeger, 1967.

Farmer, Kenneth C. "National Minorities in Poland, 1919–1980." In *Eastern European National Minorities, 1919–1980: A Handbook*, ed. Stephan M. Horak, 35–107. Littleton, CO: Libraries Unlimited, Inc. 1985.

Felski, Rita. "Suspicious Minds." *Poetics Today* 32, no. 2 (2011): 215–34.

Ferguson, Karen. *Top Down: The Ford Foundation, Black Power, and the Reinvention of Racial Liberalism*. Philadelphia: University of Pennsylvania Press, 2013.

Fleming, Michael. "The New Minority Rights Regime in Poland: The Experience of the German, Belarussian, and Jewish Minorities since 1989." *Nations and Nationalism* 8, no. 4 (2002): 531–48.

Foltz, William J. *From French West Africa to the Mali Federation*. New Haven, CT: Yale University Press, 1965.

Fosler-Lussier, Danielle. *Music in America's Cold War Diplomacy*. Oakland: University of California Press, 2015.

Foster, Hal, ed. *The Anti-Aesthetic: Essays on Postmodern Culture*. Seattle: Bay Press, 1983.

Foster, Hal. "Postmodernism: A Preface." In Foster, *The Anti-Aesthetic*, ix–xiv.

Fox, Claire F. *Making Art Panamerican: Cultural Policy and the Cold War*. Minneapolis: University of Minnesota Press, 2013.

Fox, Jon E. "The Edges of the Nation: A Research Agenda for Uncovering the Taken-for-granted Foundations of Everyday Nationhood." *Nations and Nationalism* 23, no. 1 (2017): 26–47.

Frankel, Jonathan. "The Soviet Regime and Anti-Zionism: An Analysis." In *Jewish Culture and Identity in the Soviet Union*, edited by Yaacov Ro'i and Avi Beker, 326–33. New York: New York University Press, 1991.

Fraser, Blair. "The Loneliest Job in the World." *Maclean's Magazine*, November 15, 1954.

Freudenheim, Susan. "Chilean Photos, Folk Art, Document Rage, Passion." *The* (San Diego) *Tribune*. September 11, 1989, C-1.

Gagnon, Melanie, and Iqaluit Elders. *Inuit Recollections on the Military Presence in Iqaluit*. Iqualit: Nunavut Arctic College, Language and Culture Program, 2002.

Galov, N. "American North in the U.S. Imperialists' Aggressive Plans." *The Current Digest of the Soviet Press* 4, no. 19 (1952): 14–26.

Gandhi, Evyn Lê Espiritu. Archipelago of Resettlement: Vietnamese Refugee Settlers and Decolonization across Guam and Israel-Palestine. Oakland: University of California Press, 2022.

Garb, Tamar. "Rethinking Sekula from the Global South: Humanist Photography Revisited." *Grey Room*, no. 55 (2014): 34–57.

Gawarecki, Henryk, and Stefan Kiełsznia, eds. *Dawny Lublin na fotografiach Stefana Kiełszni*. Lublin: Towarzystwo Miłośników Lublina, 1977.

Glendon, Mary Ann. *A World Made New: Eleanor Roosevelt and the Universal Declaration of Human Rights*. New York: Random House, 2002.

Goedde, Petra. *GIs and Germans: Culture, Gender, and Foreign Relations, 1945–1949*. New Haven, CT: Yale University Press, 2014.

Gorsuch, Anne E. *All This Is Your World: Soviet Tourism at Home and Abroad after Stalin*. Oxford: Oxford University Press, 2011.

Gorsuch, Anne E. "Vystuplenie na mezhdunarodnoi stsene: sovetskie turisty khruschevskoi epokhi na kapitalisticheskom Zapade." *Antropologicheskii Forum* 13 (2010): 359–88.

Grace, Claire. "Counter-Time: Group Material's Chronicle of US Intervention in Central and South America." *Afterall: Journal of Art, Context, and Enquiry* 26 (2011): 27–37.

Grandin, Greg. *Empire's Workshop: Latin America, the United States, and the Rise of the New Imperialism*. New York: Holt, 2010.

Grandin, Greg. *The Last Colonial Massacre: Latin America in the Cold War*. Chicago: University of Chicago Press, 2011.

Grandin, Greg. "Living in Revolutionary Time: Coming to Terms with the Violence of Latin America's Long Cold War." In *A Century of Revolution: Insurgent and Counterinsurgent Violence During Latin America's Long Cold War*, edited by Greg Grandin and Gilbert M. Joseph, 1–42. Durham, NC: Duke University Press, 2010.

Grant, Bruce. *The Captive and the Gift*. Ithaca, NY: Cornell University Press, 2009.

Gittings, John. "Excess and Enthusiasm." In *Picturing Power in the People's Republic of China: Posters of the Cultural Revolution*, edited by Harriet Evans and Stephanie Donald, 27–46. Lanham, MD: Rowman and Littlefield, 1999.

Gresh, Alain. "Reflections on the Meaning of Palestine." *Institute for Palestine Studies* 41, no. 1 (December 2011): 67–81.

Gross, Jan Tomasz. *Fear: Anti-Semitism in Poland after Auschwitz*. Princeton, NJ: Princeton University Press, 2006.

Grygier, Pat Sandiford. *Long Way from Home: The Tuberculosis Epidemic among the Inuit*. Montreal: McGill-Queens University Press, 1997.

Guilbaut, Serge. *How New York Stole the Idea of Modern Art: Abstract Expressionism, Freedom and the Cold War*. Chicago: University of Chicago Press, 1983.

Gunter, Michael M. "Self-Determination or Territorial Integrity: The United Nations in Confusion." *World Affairs* (1979): 203–16.

Gupta, Atreyee. "Belatedness and Simultaneity: A Short History of Photography from India." In *Postdate: Photography and Inherited History in India*, by Jodi Throckmorton, Atreyee Gupta, Latika Gupta, Susan Krane, and Rags Media Collective, 24–35. Oakland: University of California Press, 2015.

Hagopian, Patrick. "Vietnam War Photography as a Locus of Memory." In *Locating Memory: Photographic Acts*, edited by Annette Kuhn and Kirsten Emiko, 201–22. New York: Berghahn Books, 2006.

Hallin, Daniel C. *The Uncensored War: The Media and Vietnam*. New York: Oxford University Press, 1986.

Haltof, Marek. *Polish Film and the Holocaust: Politics and Memory*. New York: Berghahn, 2012.

Hamilton, Carolyn, Verne Harris, Michèle Pickover, Graeme Reid, Razia Saleh, and Jane Taylor, eds. *Refiguring the Archive*. Dordrecht: Kluwer Academic Publishers, 2002.

Hamilton, Kevin, and Ned O'Gorman. *Lookout America! The Secret Hollywood Studio at the Heart of the Cold War*. Hanover, NH: Dartmouth College Press, 2018.

Hammond, William M. *Reporting Vietnam: Media and Military at War*. Lawrence: University Press of Kansas, 1998.

Haraway, Donna. *Simians, Cyborgs, and Women: The Reinvention of Nature*. New York: Routledge, 1991.

Hardesty, Von. *Camera Aloft: Edward Steichen in the Great War*. Cambridge: Cambridge University Press, 2016.

Hassner, Rune. "Ernest Cole: Photojournalist." Interview by Hans Beukes, Göteborg, Sweden, August 1993.

Hatzky, Christine, and Jessica Stites Mor. "Latin American Transnational Solidarities: Contexts and Critical Research Paradigms." *Journal of Iberian and Latin American Research* 20, no. 2 (2014): 127–40.

Heather, David. *Vietnam Posters: The David Heather Collection*. Munich: Prestel, 2009.

Heatwole, Joanna, and Mariola Mourelo. "Extending the Frame: An Interview with Susan Meiselas." *Afterimage* 33, no. 5 (2006). http://www.americansuburbx.com/2010/03/interview-extending-frame-interview.html.

Hevia, James L. "The Photography Complex." In *Photographies East*, edited by Rosalind Morris, 79–119. Durham, NC: Duke University Press, 2009.

Hien, Nina Mai. "Reanimating Vietnam: Icons, Photography and Image Making in Ho Chi Minh City." PhD diss., Cornell University, 2007.

Hirsch, Marianne, ed. *The Familial Gaze*. Hanover, NH: Dartmouth College Press, 1999.

Hirsch, Marianne. *Family Frames: Photography, Narrative and Postmemory*. Cambridge MA: Harvard University Press, 1997.

Hirsch, Marianne. "Nazi Photographs in Post-Holocaust Art: Gender as an Idiom of Memorialization." In *Phototextualities: Intersections of Photography and Narrative*, by Alex Hughes and Andrea Noble, 19–40. Albuquerque: University of New Mexico Press, 2003.

"Hispanic Art from Outrage." *Upfront*, no. 5 (February 1983): 3–6.

Ho, Denise Y. *Curating Revolution: Politics on Display in Mao's China*. Cambridge: Cambridge University Press, 2018.

Holt, Maria. *Women and Conflict in the Middle East: Palestinian Refugees and the Response to Violence*. New York: I. B. Tauris, 2014.

Honig, Emily. "Maoist Mappings of Gender: Reassessing the Red Guards." In *Chinese Femininities, Chinese Masculinities: A Reader*, edited by Susan Brownell and Jeffrey N. Wasserstrom. Berkeley: University of California Press, 2002.

Howe, Russell Warren. "African Atlantic Chess." *New Republic*, March 6, 1976, 12–14.

Hrynkiewicz, Wojtek. "I ciągle widzę ich twarze." *Przegląd Polityczny* 31, [undated; 1996], 119–20.

Hu Angang, *Mao and the Cultural Revolution: Mao's Motivation and Strategy*, Vol. 1. Honolulu: Silk Road Press, 2017.

Hung, Chang-tai *Mao's New World: Political Culture in the Early People's Republic*. Ithaca, NY: Cornell University Press, 2011.

Hurm, Gerd, Anke Reitz, and Shamoon Zamir, eds. *The Family of Man Revisited: Photography in a Global Age*. London: I. B. Tauris in association with Centre National de l'Audiovisuel (CNA), Luxembourg, 2018.

Huyssen, Andreas. *Present Pasts: Urban Palimpsests and the Politics of Memory*. Palo Alto, CA: Stanford University Press, 2003.

Iber, Patrick. *Neither Peace nor Freedom: The Cultural Cold War in Latin America*. Cambridge, MA: Harvard University Press, 2015.

Irving, Sarah. *Leila Khaled: Icon of Palestinian Liberation*. London: Pluto Press, 2012.

Isoart, Paul. "Le Conseil Exécutif de La Communauté." In *L'Afrique noire française : L'heure des indépendances*, edited by Charles-Robert Ageron and Marc Michel, 237–67. Paris: CNRS Éditions, 2010.

Isoart, Paul. "Rapport général." In *L'Afrique noire française : L'heure des indépendances*, edited by Charles-Robert Ageron, and Marc Michel, 221–35. Paris: CNRS Éditions, 2010.

Iyad, Abu. *My Home, My Land*. New York: Times Books, 1981.

Jackson, Robert H. *Quasi-States: Sovereignty, International Relations and the Third World*. Cambridge: Cambridge University Press, 1993.

James, Caradog Vaughan. *Soviet Socialist Realism: Origins and Theory*. London: Palgrave Macmillan, 1973.

James, Sarah E. *Common Ground: German Photographic Culture across the Iron Curtain*. New Haven, CT: Yale University Press, 2013.

Jammal, Laila. *Contributions by Palestinian Women to the National Struggle for Liberation*. Washington, DC: Middle East Public Relations, 1985.

Jay, Martin. *Downcast Eyes: The Denigration of Vision in Twentieth-Century French Thought*. Berkeley: University of California Press, 1993.

Johnson, Ian. "At China's Museum, History Toes Party Line." *New York Times*, April 3, 2011.

Joseph, Gilbert M. "Latin America's Long Cold War: A Century of Revolutionary Process and U.S. Power." In *A Century of Revolution: Insurgent and Counterinsurgent Violence during Latin America's Long Cold War*, edited by Greg Grandin and Gilbert M. Joseph, 397–414. Durham, NC: Duke University Press, 2010.

Joseph, Gilbert M., and Daniela Spenser, eds. *In from the Cold: Latin America's New Encounter with the Cold War*. Durham, NC: Duke University Press, 2008.

Judt, Tony. *Post War: A History of Europe since 1945*. London: Penguin Press, 2005.

Kaiser, Robert G. "White Paper on El Salvador Is Faulty." *Washington Post*, June 9, 1981.

Kaplan, Caren. *Aerial Aftermaths: Wartime from Above*. Durham, NC: Duke University Press, 2018.

Katsakioris, Constantin. "The Soviet-South Encounter: Tensions in the Friendship with Afro-Asian Partners, 1945–1965." In *Cold War Crossings: International Travel and Exchange across the Soviet Bloc, 1940s–1960s*, edited by Patryk Babiracki, 134–65. College Station: Texas A&M University Press, 2014.

Kauffmann, Stanley. "Hue and Cry." *New Republic*, October 28, 1967.

Kawar, Amal. *Daughters of Palestine: Leading Women of the Palestinian National Movement*. Albany: State University of New York Press, 1996.

Kazi, Hamida. "Palestinian Women and the National Liberation Movement: A Social Perspective." In *Women in the Middle East*, edited by Khamsin, 26–39. London: Zed Books, 1987.

Keddie, Nikki R., and Mark Gasiorowski, eds. *Neither East nor West: Iran, the Soviet Union, and the United States*. New Haven, CT: Yale University Press, 1990.

Keller, Candace. "Visual Griots: Social, Political and Cultural Histories in Mali through the Photographer's Lens." PhD diss., Indiana University, 2008.

Kemp-Welch, Anthony. *Poland under Communism: A Cold War History*. Cambridge: Cambridge University Press, 2008.

Kennedy, Liam. *Afterimages: Photography and U.S. Foreign Policy*. Chicago: University of Chicago Press, 2016.

Kennedy, Liam, and Caitlin Patrick, eds. *The Violence of the Image: Photography and International Conflict*. London: I. B. Tauris, 2014.

Khaled, Leila. *My People Shall Live: The Autobiography of a Revolutionary*, edited by George Hajjar. London: Hodder and Stoughton, 1973.

Khalidi, Rashid. "The United States and Palestine." *Cairo Review of Global Affairs*, April 2015.

Kim, Jodi. *Ends of Empire: Asian American Critique and the Cold War*. Minneapolis: University of Minnesota Press, 2010.

King, David. *The Commissar Vanishes: The Falsification of Photographs and Art in Stalin's Russia*. New York: Metropolitan Books, 1997.

Kirking, Clayton C., and Edward J. Sullivan. *Latin American Still Life: Reflections of Time and Place*. New York: Katonah Museum of Art, 1999.

Klinghoffer, Judith A. *Vietnam, Jews and the Middle East: Unintended Consequences*. New York: St. Martin's Press, 1999.

Knape, Gunilla, ed. *Ernest Cole: Photographer*. Göteborg: Hasselblad Foundation; Göttingen: Steidl, 2010.

Knott, Marie Luise, ed. *Hannah Arendt/Gershom Scholem: Der Briefwechsel*. Berlin: Jüdischer Verlag, 2010.

Kodat, Catherine Gunther. *Don't Act, Just Dance: The Metapolitics of Cold War Culture*. New Brunswick, NJ: Rutgers University Press, 2015.

Koenker, Diane P. "Whose Right to Rest? Contesting the Family Vacation in the Postwar Soviet Union." *Comparative Studies in Society and History* 51, no. 2 (2009): 401–25.

Kriebel, Sabine. "Photomontage in the Year 1932: John Heartfield and the National Socialists." *Oxford Art Journal* 31, no. 1 (2008): 92–127.

Kuc, Monika. "Przez powiększenie: Fotografia Żydów polskich w Zachęcie." *Gazeta Wyborcza*. Co jest Grane, April 19, 1996, 12.

Kuehn, Karl Gernot. *Caught: The Art of Photography in the German Democratic Republic*. Berkeley: University of California Press, 1997.

Kunkel, Sönke. *Empire of Pictures: Global Media and the 1960s Remaking of American Foreign Policy*. Oxford: Berghahn, 2016.

Kunuk, Zacharius. *Exile* (MPEG video). Igoolik: Isuma Productions, 2009. http://www.isuma.tv/isuma-productions/exile-0.

Kuttab, Eileen S. "Palestinian Women in the Intifada: Fighting on Two Fronts." *Arab Studies Quarterly* 15, no. 2 (1993): 69–85.

Kwinty, Jonathan. "Tarnished Report? Apparent Errors Cloud U.S. White Paper on Reds in El Salvador." *Wall Street Journal*, June 8, 1981, 33.

Kwon, Heonik. *The Other Cold War*. New York: Columbia University Press, 2010.

Lackenbauer, P. Whitney, ed. *Human Flagpoles or Humanitarian Action: Discerning Government Motives Behind the Inuit Relocations to the High Arctic, 1953–1960*. Cal-gary: Documents on Canadian Arctic Sovereignty and Security n. 16, 2020. https://pubs.aina.ucalgary.ca//dcass/85283.pdf.

Langford, Martha. "Richard Harrington's Guide: Universality and Locality in a Canadian Photographic Document." In *Photography, History, Difference*, edited by Tanya Sheehan, 33–56. Hanover, NH: Dartmouth College Press, 2015.

Langford, Martha. *Suspended Conversations: The Afterlife of Memory in Photographic Albums*. Montreal: McGill-Queen's University Press, 2001.

Langford, Martha, and John Langford. *A Cold War Tourist and His Camera*. Montreal: McGill-Queen's University Press, 2011.

Lary, May. *Recasting America: Culture and Politics in the Age of Cold War*. Chicago: University of Chicago Press, 1989.

Laszczuk, Katarzyna. "The Visual Politics of Success and Solidarity: A Case Study of Chris Niedenthal's Photography from the People's Republic of Poland 1978–1982." MA thesis, Ryerson University, 2015.

Latoś, Henryk. "Fotoreporterskie braterstwo broni." *Fotografia* 11 (1974): 328–30.

Latoś, Henryk. "Żołnierze fotografowie." *Fotografia* 10 (1974): 310–12.

Lawson, Thomas. "Group Material, Timeline, P.S. 1." *Artforum* 22, no. 9 (1984): 83.

Lee, Christopher J., ed. *Making a World after Empire: The Bandung Moment and Its Political Afterlives*. Athens: Ohio University Press, 2010.

Lee, Jung Joon. "No End to the Image War: Photography and the Contentious Memories of the Korean War." *Journal of Korean Studies* 18, no. 2 (2013): 337–70.

Lenin, Vladimir Ilyich. "The Right of Nations to Self-Determination," 1914. Marxists.org. https://www.marxists.org/archive/lenin/works/1914/self-det/ch01.htm.

LeoGrande, William M. *Our Own Backyard: The United States in Central America, 1977–1992*. Chapel Hill: University of North Carolina Press, 1998.

Leshkowich, Ann Marie. "The Ao Dai Goes Global. How International Influences and Female Entrepreneurs Have Shaped Vietnam's 'National Costume.'" In *Re-Orienting Fashion: The Globalization of Asian Dress*, edited by Sandra Niessen, Ann Marie Leshkowich, and Carla Jones, 79–115. Oxford: Berg, 2003.

Leshkowich, Ann Marie. "Wandering Ghosts of Late Socialism: Conflict, Metaphor, and Memory in a Southern Vietnamese Marketplace." *Journal of Asian Studies* 67, no. 1 (2008): 5–41.

Lewinsky, Jorge. *The Camera at War: War Photography from 1848 to the Present Day*. London: W. and J. MacKay, 1978.

Li, Jie. "Virtual Museums of Forbidden Memories: Hu Jie's Documentary Films on the Cultural Revolution." *Public Culture* 21, no. 3 (2009): 539–49.

Lieu, Nhi T. "Remembering 'The Nation' through Pageantry: Femininity and the Politics of Vietnamese Womanhood in the 'Hoa Hau Ao Dai Contest.'" *Frontiers* 21, nos. 1–2 (2000): 127–51.

Lindgren, David T. *Trust but Verify: Imagery Analysis in the Cold War*. Annapolis, MD: Naval Institute Press, 2000.

Lindo-Fuentes, Héctor, Erik Chang, and Rafael A. Lara-Martínez. *Remembering a Massacre in El Salvador: The Insurrection of 1932, Roque Dalton, and the Politics of Historical Memory*. Albuquerque: University of New Mexico Press, 2007.

Linebauch, Peter. *The Magna Carta Manifesto: Liberties and Commons for All*. Oakland: University of California Press, 2009.

Linfield, Susie. *The Cruel Radiance: Photography and Political Violence*. Chicago: University of Chicago Press, 2010.

Linker, Kate. "Forum." *Artforum* 22, no. 5 (1984): 70.

Lippard, Lucy. "Artists Call against U.S. Intervention in Central America." *Village Voice*, January 24, 1984.

Lippard, Lucy. *Get the Message: A Decade of Art for Social Change*. New York: E. P. Dutton, 1984.

Lippard, Lucy. "Hotter Than July." *Village Voice*, August 9, 1983.

Lippard, Lucy. "Revolting Issues." *Village Voice*, July 27, 1982, 75.

Lippard, Lucy. "Too Political? Forget It." In *Art Matters: How the Culture Wars Changed America*, edited by Brian Wallis, Marianne Weems, and Philip Yenawine, 38–61. New York: New York University Press, 1999.

Lochner, Robert. Interview with Robert Lochner, n.d. Accessed December 20, 2021. http://www2. gwu.edu/~nsarchiv/coldwar/interviews/episode-4/lochner2.html.

Long, Tania. "Governor-General Starting Tuesday on First Trip of a Viceroy to Region." *New York Times*, March 18, 1956, 17.

Łoziński, Sławomir. *Polityka państwa polskiego wobec mniejszości narodowych w latach 1989–1993: Raport nr 55 Biura Studiów i Ekspertyz Kancelarii Sejmu*. Warsaw: Kancelaria Sejmu, 1994.

Lubben, Kristen. *Susan Meiselas: In History*. New York: International Center of Photography; Göttingen: Steidl, 2008.

Mac, Jerzy Sławomir. "Fotografie żydów polskich: Twarze nieobecnych." *Wprost*, April 21, 1996, 83.

Macaya, Ángeles Donoso. "Arte, Documento y Fotografía: Prolegómenos Para Una Reformulación Del Campo Fotográfico En Chile (1977–1998)." *Aisthesis* 52, no. 2 (2012): 407–24.

Macaya, Ángeles Donoso. *The Insubordination of Photography: Documentary Practices under Chile's Dictatorship*. Gainesville: University Press of Florida, 2020.

Macaya, Ángeles Donoso. "A Little History of Photographic Displacements: From Chile from Within (1990) to Chile Desde Adentro (2015)." In *Photography and Its Publics*, edited by Melissa Miles and Edward Welsh, 127–46. London: Bloomsbury Press, 2019.

MacLear, Kyo. *Beclouded Visions: Hiroshima-Nagasaki and the Art of Witness*. Albany: State University of New York Press, 1998.

Magana, Mariano Castro. *Gods, Spirits and Legends: 20th-Century Art from El Salvador*. New York: Museo del Barrio, 1998.
Mai Nam. *Một Thời Hào Hùng*. Ha Noi, Vietnam: Nhà xuất bản Thanh niên, n.d.
Maldonado-Torres, Nelson. "Thinking through the Decolonial Turn: Post-continental Interventions in Theory, Philosophy, and Critique—An Introduction." *Transmodernity* (Fall 2011): 1–15.
Man, Simeon. *Soldiering through Empire: Race and the Making of the Decolonizing Pacific*. Oakland: University of California Press, 2018.
Mao Zhedong. "Jieshao yige hezuoshe" [Introducing a cooperative]. *Hongqi* [Red flag] 1, no. 1 (1958): 3–4.
Marcus, Alan R. *Relocating Eden: The Image and Politics of Inuit Exile in the Canadian Arctic*. Hanover, NH: Dartmouth College Press, 1995.
Masco, Joseph. *The Theater of Operations: National Security Affect from the Cold War to the War on Terror*. Durham, NC: Duke University Press, 2014.
Maslow, Jonathon Evan, and Ana Arana. "Operation El Salvador." *Columbia Journalism Review* 20, no. 1 (1981): 55.
Maslowski, Peter. *Armed with Cameras: The American Military Photographers of World War II*. New York: Free Press, 1993.
Mathur, Saloni. "Charles and Ray Eames in India." *Art Journal* 70, no. 1 (2011): 40.
Maurer, Eva. "Al'pinizm as Mass Sport and Elite Recreation: Soviet Mountaineering Camps under Stalin." In *Turizm: The Russian and East European Tourist under Capitalism and Socialism*, edited by Anne E. Gorsuch and Diane P. Koenker, 141–62. Ithaca, NY: Cornell University Press, 2006.
Maurer, Eva. "Cold War, 'Thaw' and 'Everlasting Friendship': Soviet Mountaineers and Mount Everest, 1953–1960." *International Journal of the History of Sport* 26, no. 4 (2009): 484–500.
May, Elaine Tyler. *Homeward Bound: American Families in the Cold War Era*. New York: Basic Books, 1988.
Mazower, Mark. *No Enchanted Palace: The End of Empire and the Ideological Origins of the United Nations*. Princeton, NJ: Princeton University Press, 2013.
Mazur, Adam. *Historie fotografii polskiej 1839–2009*. Kraków: Fundacja Sztuk Wizualnych, 2009.
Mazur, Mariusz. *Propagandowy obraz świata: Polityczne kampanie prasowe w PRL 1956–1980; Model analityczno-koncepcyjny*. Warsaw: Trio, 2003.
Mbembe, Achille. *On the Postcolony*. Berkeley: University of California Press, 2001.
Mbembe, Achille. "The Power of the Archive and Its Limits." In *Refiguring the Archive*, edited by Carolyn Hamilton, Verne Harris, Michèle Pickover, Graeme Reid, Razia Saleh, and Jane Taylor, 19–26. Dordrecht: Kluwer Academic Publishers, 2002.
McClennen, Sophie, and Alexandra Schultheis Moore, eds. *The Routledge Companion to Literature and Human Rights*. New York: Routledge, 2016.

McGehee, Ralph. "The CIA and the White Paper on El Salvador." *The Nation*, April 11, 1981.

McGrath, Melanie. *The Long Exile: A Tale of Inuit Betrayal and Survival in the High Arctic*. New York: Alfred Knopf, 2007.

McKay, Vernon. "South African Propaganda: Methods and Media." *Africa Report* 11, no. 2 (1966): 42.

McMahon, Robert J., ed. *The Cold War in the Third World*. New York: Oxford University Press, 2013.

McPherson, Alan. "The Paradox of Latin American Cold War Studies." In *Beyond the Eagle's Shadow: New Histories of Latin America's Cold War*, edited by Virginia Garrard-Burnett, 307–19. Albuquerque: University of New Mexico Press, 2013.

Meiselas, Susan, ed. *Chile from Within: 1973–1988* [ebook]. New York: MAPP, 2013.

Meiselas, Susan. "Exchanges between Susan and Chilean Photographers: Alejandro, Alvaro, Claudio, Héctor, Helen, Marcelo, Óscar, and Paz." In Meiselas, *Chile from Within, 1973–1988* [ebook].

Meiselas, Susan. "Hoja de Contacto: Alejandro Hoppe, Summer 1990." In Meiselas, *Chile from Within, 1973–1988* [ebook].

Meiselas, Susan. *Meiselas: On the Frontline*. Edited by Mark Holborn. New York: Aperture, 2017.

Meiselas, Susan. "Photography, Expanded: Conversation with Christ Boot." *Aperture Magazine*, no. 214 (Spring 2014). https://aperture.org/blog/photography-expanded-conversation-chris-boot/.

Meisner, Maurice J. *Mao's China and After: A History of the People's Republic*, 3rd ed. New York: Free Press, 1999.

Meyer, Lysle E. "The American Image of South Africa in Historical Perspective." *Social Studies* 67, no. 1 (1976): 19–26.

Micgiel, John. "'Bandits and Reactionaries': The Suppression of the Opposition in Poland, 1944–1946." In *The Establishment of Communist Regimes in Eastern Europe, 1944–1949*, edited by Norman Naimark and Leonid Gibianskii, 93–110. Boulder, CO: Westview Press, 1997.

Michlic, Joanna B. *Poland's Threatening Other: The Image of the Jew from 1880 to the Present*. Lincoln: University of Nebraska Press, 2006.

Mignolo, Walter D. *The Darker Side of Western Modernity: Global Futures, Decolonial Options*. Durham, NC: Duke University Press, 2011.

Mignolo, Walter D. "Delinking: The Rhetoric of Modernity, the Logic of Coloniality, and the Grammar of De-Coloniality." *Cultural Studies* 21, nos. 2–3 (2007): 449–514.

Mignolo, Walter D., and Catherine E. Walsh. *On Decoloniality: Concepts, Analytics, Practices*. Durham, NC: Duke University Press, 2018.

Ministère des Affaires Ètrangères. "Télégrammes nos. 1035–1040, du 12 décembre 1966, de M. Vyau de Lagarde, Ambassadeur de France à Dakar, à M. Couve de Murville."

In *Documents diplomatiques français: 1966; Tome II (1 Juin–31 Décembre)*. Brussels: PIE Peter Lang, 2006.

Mirzoeff, Nicholas. *How to See the World*. New York: Basic Books, 2016.

Mirzoeff, Nicholas. *An Introduction to Visual Culture*. London: Routledge, 1999.

Mirzoeff, Nicholas. *The Right to Look: A Counterhistory of Visuality*. Durham, NC: Duke University Press, 2011.

Mitchell, W. J. T. *Seeing through Race*. Cambridge, MA: Harvard University Press, 2012.

Mitter, Rana. "China and the Cold War." In *The Oxford Handbook of the Cold War*, edited by Petra Goedde and Richard H. Immerman, 124–40. Oxford: Oxford University Press, 2013.

Moeller, Robert G. "War Stories: The Search for a Usable Past in the Federal Republic of Germany." *American Historical Review* 101, no. 4 (1996): 1008–48.

Moghissi, Haideh. "Troubled Relationships: Women, Nationalism, and the Left Movement in Iran." In Cronin, *Reformers and Revolutionaries in Modern Iran*, 209–22.

Mor, Jessica Stites, ed. *Human Rights and Transnational Solidarity in Cold War Latin America*. Madison: University of Wisconsin Press, 2013.

Morton, Christopher, and Darren Newbury, eds. *The African Photographic Archive: Research and Curatorial Strategies*. London: Bloomsbury, 2015.

Mosley, Leonard O. *Report from Germany*. London: Victor Gollancz, 1945.

Moyn, Samuel. *The Last Utopia: Human Rights in History*. Cambridge, MA: Belknap Press, 2012.

Nail, Thomas. *The Figure of the Migrant*. Stanford, CA: Stanford University Press, 2015.

Nash, Mark. *Red Africa: Affective Communities and the Cold War*. London: Black Dog Publishing, 2016.

Newbury, Darren. *Defiant Images: Photography and Apartheid South Africa*. Pretoria: University of South Africa Press, 2009.

Newbury, Darren. "Ernest Cole and the South African Security Police." *History of Photography* 35, no. 1 (2011): 76–79.

Nguyễn Thị Định. *No Other Road to Take: Memoir of Mrs. Nguyễn Thị Định*. Ithaca, NY: Southeast Asia Program Publications, 1976.

Nimis, Érika. *Photographes de l'Afrique de l'Ouest: L'expérience yoruba*. Paris: Karthala, 2005.

Noble, Andrea. "Introduction: Visual Culture and Violence in Contemporary Mexico." *Journal of Latin American Cultural Studies* 24, no. 4 (2015): 417–33.

Noble, Andrea. "Recognizing Historical Injustice through Photography: Mexico 1968." *Theory, Culture, and Society* 27, nos. 7–8 (2010): 184–213.

Noble, Andrea. "Travelling Theories of Family Photography and the Material Culture of Human Rights in Latin America." *Journal of Romance Studies* 8 (2009): 43–59.

Noble, Andrea. "Visual Culture and Latin American Studies." *New Centennial Review* 4 (2004): 219–38.

Noer, Thomas. *Cold War and Black Liberation: The United States and White Rule in Africa, 1948–1968*. Columbia: University of Missouri Press, 1985.

Nora, Pierre. "Between Memory and History: 'Les Lieux de Mémoire.'" *Representations* 27 (1989): 7–24.

Nora, Pierre, ed. *Realms of Memory: Rethinking the French Past*. Vol. 1, *Conflicts and Divisions*. New York: Columbia University Press, 1996.

Nordbruch, Claus. *Bleeding Germany Dry: The Aftermath of World War II from the German Perspective*. Pretoria: Contact Publishers, 2012.

North Atlantic Treaty Organization. "The Atlantic Charter." NATO/OTAN, August 14, 1941. http://www.nato.int/cps/en/natolive/official_texts_16912.htm.

Nudelman, Franny. "Against Photography: Susan Sontag's Vietnam." *Photography and Culture* 7, no. 1 (2014): 7–20.

Oberdorfer, Don. "Salvador Is 'the Place to Draw the Line' on Communism." *Washington Post*, February 20, 1981.

O'Brian, John, ed. *Camera Atomica*. London: Black Dog Publishing; Toronto: Art Gallery of Toronto, 2015.

"Ocalone fotografie." *Gazeta Stołeczna*, April 14, 1996, 7.

O'Donnell, Joe. *Japan 1945: A U.S. Marine's Photographs from Ground Zero*. Nashville, TN: Vanderbilt University Press, 2005.

Ogbar, Jeffrey. *Black Power: Radical Politics and African American Identity*. Baltimore, MD: Johns Hopkins University Press, 2004.

Olick, Di Jeffrey K. *In the House of the Hangman: The Agonies of German Defeat, 1943–1949*. Chicago: University of Chicago Press, 2005.

Olin, Margaret. "Touching Photographs: Roland Barthes's 'Mistaken' Identification." *Representations* 80, no. 1 (2002): 99–118.

Onishi, Yuichiro. *Transpacific Antiracism: Afro-Asian Solidarity in 20th-Century Black America, Japan, and Okinawa*. New York: NYU Press, 2014.

Orlov, Igor'. "Pervye shagi vyezdnogo turizma v SSSR (1955–1964)." *Servis plus* 4 (2013): 67–79.

Orlov, Igor', and Aleksei Popov. "Skvoz' 'zheleznyi zanaves.'" *Russo turisto: Sovetskii vyezdnoi turizm, 1955–1991*. Moscow: Vysshaia shkola ekonomiki, 2016.

Orlova, Galina. "'Karty dlia slepykh': Politika i politizatsia zreniia v Stalinskuiu epokhu" ["Maps for the Blind": The Politics and Politicization of Vision in the Stalin Era]. In *Vizualnaia antropologiia: Rezhimy vidimosti pri sotsializme* [*Visual Anthropology: Regimes of Visuality under Socialism*], edited by Elena Iarskaia-Smirnova and Pavel Romanov, 57–104. Moscow: TsSPiGI, 2009.

Organization of Iranian People's Fedaii Guerrillas (OIPFG). "Zan-e Baluch [Baluch Women]." Pamphlet, Women's Committee of Supporters of the OIPFG in Sistan-Baluchestan, 1985.

Ortega, Luisa Maria Dietrich. "Looking Beyond Violent Militarized Masculinities." *International Feminist Journal of Politics* 14, no. 4 (2012): 489–507.

Ó Tuathail, Gearóid. *Critical Geopolitics. The Politics of Writing Global Space*. Minneapolis: University of Minnesota Press, 1996.

Owens, Craig. "The Discourse of Others: Feminists and Postmodernism." In Foster, *The Anti-Aesthetic*, 57–82.

Page, Timothy, and Horst Faas. *Requiem: By the Photographers Who Died in Vietnam and Indochina*. New York: Random House, 1997.

Page, Timothy, and Douglas Niven. *Another Vietnam: Pictures of the War from the Other Side*. New York: National Geographic Society, 2002.

Panzer, Mary. "Introduction." In *Things as They Are: Photojournalism in Context since 1955*, 9–33. New York: Aperture, 2005.

Parker, Jason C. *Hearts, Minds, Voices: U.S. Cold War Public Diplomacy and the Formation of the Third World*. New York: Oxford University Press, 2016.

Parker, John, and Richard Rathbone. *African History: A Very Short Introduction*. Oxford: Oxford University Press, 2007.

Parliament of Canada. *Debates of the House of Commons*. 22nd Parliament, 1st Session, December 8, 1954. Ottawa: Queen's Printer, 1954.

Parr, Martin, and Gerry Badger, eds. *The Photobook: A History*. Vol. 2. London: Phaidon, 2006.

Pasternak, Gil, ed. "Photography in Transitioning European Communist and Post-Communist Histories." Special issue, *Photography and Culture* 12, no. 2 (2019).

Pasternak, Gil, and Marta Ziętkiewicz. "Haunting Legacies: Family and Archival Photographs in Aleksandra Garlicka's Taxonomy of Polish Society (1985–95)." Special issue, *Photography and Culture* 12, no. 2 (2019), 171–201.

Pasternak, Gil, and Marta Ziętkiewicz. "Making a Home in Poland: Photographic Education and Practices in the *Landkentnish* Movement." *IMAGES: A Journal of Jewish Art and Visual Culture* 12, no. 1 (2019): 151–79.

Payne, Carol. *The Official Picture: The National Film Board of Canada's Still Photography Division and the Image of Canada, 1941–1971*. Montreal: McGill-Queen's University Press, 2013.

Paz, Octavio. *The Labyrinth of Solitude and Other Writings*. New York: Grove Press, [1972] 1986.

Peace, Roger. *A Call to Conscience: The Anti-Contra War Campaign*. Amherst: University of Massachusetts Press, 2012.

Pensado, Jaime M. *Rebel Mexico: Student Unrest and Authoritarian Political Culture during the Long Sixties*. Palo Alto, CA: Stanford University Press, 2013.

Perla, Héctor, Jr. "Heirs of Sandino: The Nicaraguan Revolution and the U.S.-Nicaragua Solidarity Movement." *Latin American Perspectives* 36, no. 6 (2009): 80–100.

Perla, Héctor, Jr. "'Media Framing and Opposition to the Use of Force in U.S. Foreign Policy' in 'Revolutionary Deterrence: The Sandinista Response to Reagan's Coercive Policy Against Nicaragua.'" PhD diss., University of California, 2005.

Perla, Héctor, Jr. "Si Nicaragua Vencío, El Salvador Vencerá: Central American Agency in the Creation of the U.S.-Central American Peace and Solidarity Movement." *Latin American Research Review* 43, no. 2 (2008): 136–58.

Perla, Héctor, Jr., and Susan Bibler Coutin. "Legacies and Origins of the 1980s US–Central American Sanctuary Movement." *Refuge: Canada's Periodical on Refugees* 26, no. 1 (2009): 7–19.

Peterson, Bhekizizwe. "The Archives and the Political Imaginary." In *Refiguring the Archive*, by Carolyn Hamilton, Verne Harris, Michèle Pickover, Graeme Reid, Razia Saleh, and Jane Taylor, 29–35. Dordrecht: Kluwer Academic Publishers, 2002.

Phu, Thy. "Vietnamese Photography and the Look of Revolution." In *Photography and the Optical Unconscious*, edited by Shawn Michelle Smith and Sharon Sliwinski, 286–320. Durham, NC: Duke University Press, 2017.

Phu, Thy. *Warring Visions: Photography and Vietnam*. Durham, NC: Duke University Press, 2022.

Piekarniak, Henryk W., ed. *Kazimierz nad Wisłą w 1931 roku*. Warsaw: Pracownie Sztuk Plastycznych, 1979.

Piškur, Bojana. "Solidarity in Arts and Culture: Some Cases from the Non-Aligned Movement." *L'internationale*, 2016. http://www.internationaleonline.org/research/alter_institutionality/78_solidarity_in_arts_and_culture_some_cases_from_the_non_aligned_movement.

Plamper, Jan. *The Stalin Cult: A Study in the Alchemy of Power*. New Haven, CT: Yale University Press, 2012.

Pluhařová, Eva. "A National Discovery and Loss of a Landscape: Photographic Images of the Curonian Spit." Unpublished manuscript, n.d.

Poelchau, Warner. *White Paper Whitewash: Interviews with Philip Agee on the CIA and El Salvador*. New York: Deep Cover Books, 1981.

Polonsky, Antony. *The Jews in Poland and Russia: A Short History*. Oxford: Littman Library of Jewish Civilization, 2013.

Quijano, Aníbal, "Colonialidad y modernidad-racionalidad." In *Los conquistados: 1492 y la poblacicin indigena de America*, edited by Heraclio Bonilla, 437–47. Bogota: Tercer Mundo/FLACSO, 1992,

Rabe, Stephen G. *The Killing Zone: The United States Wages Cold War in Latin America*. New York: Oxford University Press, 2012.

Rabine, Leslie W. "Photography, Poetry, and the Dressed Bodies of Léopold Sédar Senghor." In *African Dress: Fashion, Agency, Performance*, edited by Karen Tranberg Hansen and D. Soyini Madison, 171–85. London: Bloomsbury Academic, 2013.

Raymont, Peter, dir. *The Magic in the Sky*. Investigative Productions and the National Film Board of Canada, in collaboration with the Inuit Tapirisat of Canada. Toronto: White Pine Pictures, 1981.

Reich, Morris. *Race and Photography: Racial Photography as Scientific Evidence*. Chicago: University of Chicago Press, 2016.

Reid, Susan E. "'Our Kitchen Is Just as Good': Soviet Responses to the American Kitchen." In *Cold War Kitchen: Americanization, Technology, and European Users*, edited by Ruth Oldenziel and Karin Zachmann, 83–112. Cambridge, MA: MIT Press, 2009.

Reid, Susan E. "(Socialist) Realism Unbound: The Effects of International Encounters on Soviet Art Practice and Discourse in the Khrushchev Thaw." In *Socialist Realisms: Soviet Painting 1920–1970*, edited by Matthew Bown and Matteo Lafranconi, 261–76. Milan: Skira, 2012.

Reinhardt, Michael, Holly Edwards, and Erina Duganne, eds. *Beautiful Suffering: Photography and the Traffic in Pain.* Chicago: University of Chicago Press, 2007.

"Resolution on Certain Questions in the History of Our Party since the Founding of the People's Republic of China, Passed by the Sixth Plenum of the Eleventh CCP Central Committee." *Beijing Review*, no. 27 (1981): 10–39.

Revolutionary Organization of the Tudeh Party of Iran (ROTPI). "Zan Dar Vietnam [Women in Vietnam]." Pamphlet, 1967.

Richard, Nelly. *Margins and Institutions: Art in Chile Since 1973*. Melbourne: Art and Text 21 (Special Issue), 1986.

Richard, Nelly. *Utopías: Revisar el pasado, criticar el presente, imaginar el futuro*. Santiago: Cuarto Propio, 2004.

Ricoeur, Paul. *Freud and Philosophy: An Essay on Interpretation*. New Haven, CT: Yale University Press, 1970.

Robertson, Struan. "Ernest Cole in the House of Bondage." Unpublished manuscript, n.d.

Rodogno, Davide, and Thomas David. "All the World Loves a Picture: The World Health Organization's Visual Politics, 1948–1973." In *Humanitarian Photography: A History*, edited by Heide Fehrenbach and Davide Rodogno, 223–48. Cambridge: Cambridge University Press, 2015.

Rollins, Tim. "Particles, 1980–83." *Real Life*, no. 11/12 (Winter 1983): 8.

Romano, Renee. "No Diplomatic Immunity: African Diplomats, the State Department, and Civil Rights, 1961–1964." *Journal of American History* 87, no. 2 (2000): 546–79.

Rose, Gillian. *Doing Family Photography: The Domestic, the Public, and the Politics of Sentiment*. London: Routledge, 2010.

Rosenheim, Jeff. *Photography and the American Civil War*. New Haven, CT: Yale University Press, 2013.

Rosler, Martha. *3 Works*. Halifax: Press of the Nova Scotia College of Art and Design, 1981.

Rottenberg, Anda. *Sztuka w Polsce 1945–2005*. Warsaw: Stentor, 2005.

Saar, John. "Of Bullets and Ballots: Portrait of El Salvador." *People*, March 15, 1982.

Sabbagh, Suha, ed. *Palestinian Women of Gaza and the West Bank*. Bloomington: Indiana University Press, 1998.

Said, Edward. *The Question of Palestine*. New York: Times Books, 1979.

Salaff, Janet, and Judith Merkle. "Women in Revolution: The Lessons of the Soviet Union and China." *Berkeley Journal of Sociology* 15 (1970): 166–91.

Sandeen, Eric J. *Picturing an Exhibition: The Family of Man and 1950s America*. Albuquerque: University of New Mexico Press, 1995.

Sanders, James, and Matthew Campbell. "Ernest Cole's Photographs Reveal America's Apartheid." *Sunday Times* (UK), October 22, 2017.

Sandomirskaia, Irina. "Novaia zhizn' na marshe: Stalinskii turizm kak 'praktika puti.'" *Obshchestvennye Nauki i Sovremennost'* 4 (1996): 163–72.

Sarkisova, Oksana, "Across One Sixth of the World: Dziga Vertov, Travel Cinema, and Soviet Patriotism." *October* 121 (2007): 19–40.

Sarkisova, Oksana, and Olga Shevchenko. "Soviet Past in Domestic Photography: Events, Evidence, Erasure." In *Double Exposure: Memory and Photography*. New York: Routledge, 2017.

Saunders, Frances Stonor. *The Cultural Cold War: The CIA and the World of Arts and Letters*. New York: The New Press, 2013.

Sayigh, Rosemary. "Encounters with Palestinian Women under Occupation." *Journal of Palestine Studies* 40, no. 4 (1981): 3–26.

Sayigh, Rosemary, and Julie Peteet. "Between Two Fires: Palestinian Women in Lebanon." In *Caught Up in Conflict: Women's Responses to Political Strife*, edited by Rosemary Ridd and Helen Callaway, 106–37. London: Macmillan Education, 1986.

Sayigh, Yezid. *Armed Struggle and the Search for State: The Palestinian National Movement 1949–1993*. Oxford: Oxford University Press, 1997.

Schumann, Frank, and Peter Kroh. *Berlin nach dem Krieg: Unbekannte Bilddokumente*. Berlin: Das Neue Berlin, 2010.

Schwenkel, Christina. "Exhibiting War, Reconciling Pasts: Photographic Representation and Transnational Commemoration in Contemporary Vietnam." *Journal of Vietnamese Studies* 3, no. 1 (2008): 36–77.

Scott, David. *Omens of Adversity: Tragedy, Time, Memory, Justice*. Durham, NC: Duke University Press, 2014.

Scott, Peter Dale. *American War Machine: Deep Politics, the CIA Drug Connection, and the Road to Afghanistan*. Lanham, MD: Rowman and Littlefield, 2010.

Segel, Harold B., ed. *Stranger in Our Midst: Images of the Jew in Polish Literature*. Ithaca, NY: Cornell University Press, 1996.

Sekula, Allan. "The Body and the Archive." *October* 39 (1986): 3–64.

Sekula, Allan. "The Instrumental Image: Steichen at War." *Artforum* 14, no. 4 (1975): 26–35.

Sekula, Allan. *Photography against the Grain: Essays and Photographic Works 1973–1983*. Halifax: Press of the Nova Scotia College of Art and Design, 1984.

Sekula, Allan. "The Traffic in Photographs." *Art Journal* 41, no. 1 (1981): 15–25.

Selejan, Ileana. "Postmodern Warfare in Images: The Aesthetics of War Photography in the Late 1970s and 1980s." PhD diss., Institute of Fine Arts, New York University, 2014.

Sembène, Ousmane. *Camp de Thiaroye*. New York: New Yorker Video, 1988.

Sembène, Ousmane. *Les bouts de bois de dieu* [*God's Bits of Wood*]. Paris: Pocket Presses, 1960.

Shahidian, Hammed. *Women in Iran: Emerging Voices in the Women's Movement*. Westport, CT: Greenwood Press, 2002.

Sharoni, Simona. "Palestinian Women's Resistance." In *Gender and the Israeli-Palestinian Conflict: The Politics of Women's Resistance*, 56–68. Syracuse, NY: Syracuse University Press, 1995.

Shaw, Tony. *Hollywood's Cold War*. Amherst: University of Massachusetts Press, 2007.

Shevchenko, Olga. *Crisis and the Everyday in Postsocialist Moscow*. Bloomington: Indiana University Press, 2009.

Shevchenko, Olga, ed. *Double Exposure: Memory and Photography*. New York: Routledge, 2017.

Shevchenko, Olga, and Oksana Sarkisova. "Remembering Life in the Soviet Union, One Family Photo at a Time." *New York Times*, December 27, 2017.

Shipway, Martin. *Decolonization and Its Impact: A Comparative Approach to the End of the Colonial Empires*. Malden, MA: Blackwell, 2008.

Shi Zhe. "With Mao and Stalin: Liu Shaoqi in Moscow." *Chinese Historians* 6 (Spring 1993): 67–90.

Simpson, Audra. *Mohawk Interruptus: Political Life across the Borders of Settler States*. Durham, NC: Duke University Press, 2014.

Sliwinski, Sharon. *Human Rights in Camera*. Chicago: University of Chicago Press, 2011.

Smith, Gary, ed. *Benjamin: Philosophy, Aesthetics, History*. Translated by Leigh Hafrey and Richard Sieburth. Chicago: University of Chicago Press, 1989.

Smith, M. L. R., and Sophie Rogers. "War in Gray: Exploring the Concept of Dirty War." *Studies in Conflict and Terrorism* 31 (2008): 377–98.

Smith, Shawn Michelle. *At the Edge of Sight: Photography and the Unseen*. Durham, NC: Duke University Press, 2013.

Smith, Terence. "Enemy in Vietnam Opens Wide Drive, Ending Long Lull." *New York Times*, April 2, 1970.

Smooha, Sammy. "Types of Democracy and Modes of Conflict Management in Ethnically Divided Societies." *Nations and Nationalism* 8, no. 4 (2002): 423–31.

Solomon-Godeau, Abigail. "'The Family of Man': Refurbishing Humanism for a Postmodern Age." In *In the Family of Man, 1955–2001: Humanism and Postmodernism: A Reappraisal of the Photo Exhibition by Edward Steichen*, edited by Jean Back and Viktoria Schmidt-Linsenhoff, 28–55. Marburg, Germany: Jonas, 2004.

Solomon-Godeau, Abigail. "Living with Contradictions: Critical Practices in the Age of Supply-Side Aesthetics." *Screen* 28, no. 3 (1987): 2–23.

Solomon-Godeau, Abigail. *Photography at the Dock: Essays on Photographic History, Institutions, and Practices*. Minneapolis: University of Minnesota Press, 1991.

Sontag, Susan. *On Photography*. New York: Farrar, Straus and Giroux, 1977.

Sontag, Susan. *Regarding the Pain of Others*. New York: Farrar, Straus and Giroux, 2003.

*The Soviet Union: A Photo Album*. Moscow: Planeta, 1973.

Sparke, Matthew. "Graphing the Geo in Geo-Political: Critical Geopolitics and the Re-Visioning of Responsibility." *Political Geography* 19 (2000): 373–80.

Stafford, David. *Endgame, 1945: The Missing Final Chapter of World War II*. New York: Back Bay Books, 2007.

Steinlauf, Michael C. *Bondage to the Dead: Poland and the Memory of the Holocaust*. Syracuse, NY: Syracuse University Press, 1997.

"Story of Newsmen's Slaying Is Reconstructed in Salvador." *New York Times*, March 22, 1982, 22.

Stuelke, Patricia. "The Reparative Politics of Central American Solidarity Movement Culture." *American Quarterly* 66, no. 3 (2014): 767–90.

Swedenburg, Ted. *Memories of Revolt: The 1936–1939 Rebellion and the Palestinian National Past*. Minneapolis: University of Minnesota Press, 1995.

Swedenburg, Ted. "Seeing Double: Palestinian/American Histories of the Kufiya." *Michigan Quarterly Review* 31, no. 4 (1992): 557–77.

Szymanowicz, Maciej. *Zaburzona epoka: Polska fotografia artystyczna w latach 1945–1955*. Poznań: Wydawnictwo Naukowe Uniwersytetu im. Adama Mickiewicza, 2016.

Taffet, Jeffrey. *Foreign Aid as Foreign Policy: The Alliance for Progress in Latin America*. London: Routledge, 2007.

Tagg, John. *The Burden of Representation: Essays on Photographies and Histories*. Minneapolis: University of Minnesota Press, 1988.

"Taking Aim at Nicaragua." *Newsweek*, March 22, 1982.

Tang, Xiaobing. *Visual Culture in Contemporary China: Paradigms and Shifts*. Cambridge: Cambridge University Press, 2014.

Taubman, Philip. "U.S. Offers Photos of Bases to Prove Nicaragua Threat." *New York Times*, March 10, 1982.

Taylor, Diana. *Disappearing Acts: Spectacles of Gender and Nationalism in Argentina's "Dirty War."* Durham, NC: Duke University Press, 1997.

Taylor, Sandra C. *Vietnamese Women at War: Fighting for Ho Chi Minh and the Revolution*. Lawrence: University of Kansas Press, 1999.

Taylor, Sandra C. *Vietnamese Women, Vietnam Studies*. Hanoi: Xunhasaba, 1966.

Tester, Frank J., and Peter Kulchyski. *Tammarniit (Mistakes): Inuit Relocation in the Eastern Arctic, 1939–63*. Vancouver: University of British Columbia Press, 1994.

Tétreault, Mary Ann, ed. *Women and Revolution in Africa, Asia, and the New World*. Columbia: University of South Carolina Press, 1994.

Thompson, Drew. "AIM, FOCUS, SHOOT: Photographic Narratives of War, Independence, and Imagination in Mozambique, 1953–1993." PhD diss., University of Minnesota, 2013.

Toeplitz, Krzysztof T. "Ciągle widzę ich twarze." *Wiadomości Kulturalne*, May 5, 1996, 12–13.

Trần Lệ Xuân. "In the Face of Hate." *Vietnam Archives*, March 21, 1963.

Tucker, Anne Wilkes. *War/Photography: Images of Armed Conflict and Its Aftermath*. New Haven, CT: Yale University Press, 2012.

Tudjaat. "Kajusita/My Ship Comes In." Lyrics by Madeleine Allakariallak, Jon Park-Wheeler, and Randall Prescott. Compact Disk CK80226. New York: Columbia Records, 1995.

Turner, Fred. "*The Family of Man* and the Politics of Attention in Cold War America." *Public Culture* 24, no. 1 (2012): 55–84.

Turner-Gottschang, Karen, and Phan Thanh Ho. *Even the Women Must Fight: Memories of War from North Vietnam*. New York: Wiley, 1998.

*Two Visions of El Salvador: Modern Art and Folk Art*. Washington, DC: Inter-American Development Bank, Cultural Center, 2000.

United Nations. "Charter of the United Nations, June 26, 1945." Avalon Project, Yale Law School. https://avalon.law.yale.edu/20th_century/unchart.asp#art27.

Urry, John. *The Tourist Gaze: Leisure and Travel in Contemporary Societies*. London: SAGE Publications, 1990.

"U.S. Accepts the Account by Salvador on 4 Newsmen." *New York Times*, March 20, 1982, 6.

U.S. Department of State. *Communist Interference in El Salvador: Documents Demonstrating Communist Support of the Salvadoran Insurgency*. Washington, DC: U.S. Department of State, 1981.

"The U.S. Gets Tougher." *Newsweek*, March 9, 1981.

Vahabzadeh, Peyman. *A Guerrilla Odyssey: Modernization, Secularism, Democracy, and the Fadai Period of National Liberation in Iran, 1971–1979*. Syracuse, NY: Syracuse University Press, 2010.

Van Gosse. *Where the Boys Are: Cuba, Cold War America and the Making of a New Left*. London: Verso, 1993.

Verdery, Katherine. *What Was Socialism, and What Comes Next*? Princeton, NJ: Princeton University Press, 1996.

Viner, Katharine. "I Made the Ring from a Bullet and the Pin of a Hand Grenade." *Guardian*, January 25, 2001. https://www.theguardian.com/world/2001/jan/26/israel.

Virgilli, Fabrice. *Shorn Women: Gender and Punishment in Liberation France*. Oxford: Berg, 2008.

Virilio, Paul. *War and Cinema: The Logistics of Perception*. Translated by Patrick Camiller. London: Verso, 1989.

Vokes, Richard, and Darren Newbury. "Photography and African Futures." *Visual Studies* 33, no. 1 (2018): 1–10. https://doi.org/10.1080/1472586X.2018.1424988.
Volo, Lorraine Bayard de. "A Revolution in the Binary? Gender and the Oxymoron of Revolutionary War in Cuba and Nicaragua." *Signs* 37, no. 2 (2012): 413–39.
Von Eschen, Penny. *Satchmo Blows Up the World: Jazz Ambassadors Play the Cold War.* Cambridge, MA: Harvard University Press, 2006.
Vucetic, Radina, and Paul Betts. *Tito in Africa: Picturing Solidarity.* Belgrade: Museum of Yugoslavia, 2017.
Wagnleitner, Reinhold. *Coca-Colonization and the Cold War: The Cultural Mission of the United States in Austria after the Second World War.* Chapel Hill: University of North Carolina Press, 1994.
Wakeham, Pauline. "At the Intersection of Apology and Sovereignty: The Arctic Exile Monument Project." *Cultural Critique* 87 (2014): 84–183.
Wang, Jian. "Telling the American Story to the World: The Purpose of US Public Diplomacy in Historical Perspective." *Public Relations Review* 33, no. 1 (2007): 21–30.
Wang, Youqin. "Introduction to the Online Memorial for Victims of the Cultural Revolution" [Wangshang wengge shounan zhe jinian yuan qianyan]. Chinese Holocaust Memorial. 2001. http://chinese-memorial.org.
Wapiński, Roman. *Historia: Od wybuchu II wojny światowej do roku 1964.* Warsaw: Państwowe Zakłady Wydawnictw Szkolnych, 1970.
Ward-Lowery, Mary. "The Search for Photos of China's Past." BBC News, July 11, 2012. https://www.bbc.com/news/magazine-18784990.
Westad, Odd Arne. *The Global Cold War: Third World Interventions and the Making of Our Times.* Cambridge: Cambridge University Press, 2007.
Wexler, Laura. "The Purloined Image." In *Photography and the Optical Unconscious*, edited by Shawn Michelle Smith and Sharon Sliwinski, 264–79. Durham, NC: Duke University Press, 2017.
Wexler, Laura. *Tender Violence: Domestic Visions in an Age of U.S. Imperialism.* Chapel Hill: University of North Carolina Press, 2000.
Whalen, Catherine. "Interpreting Vernacular Photography: Finding 'Me'—a Case Study." In *Using Visual Evidence*, edited by Richard Howells and Robert W. Matson. New York: McGraw Hill, 2009.
Whitfield, Stephen. *The Culture of the Cold War.* Baltimore, MD: Johns Hopkins University Press, 1991.
Whitman, Alden. "A South African Talks about U.S." *New York Times*, December 11, 1967.
Whitman, Daniel. *Outsmarting Apartheid: An Oral History of South Africa's Cultural and Educational Exchange with the United States, 1960–1999.* Albany: State University of New York Press, 2015.
Wilder, Gary. *Freedom Time: Negritude, Decolonization, and the Future of the World.* Durham, NC: Duke University Press, 2015.

Wilkinson, Douglas. *Land of the Long Day*. Toronto: Clark Irwin, 1955.

Williams, Raymond. "Structures of Feelings." In *Marxism and Literature*, 128–35. Oxford: Oxford University Press, 1977.

"Woman-as-Revolutionary." *Journal of Palestine Studies* 4, no. 1 (1974).

*A Woman in Berlin: Eight Weeks in the Conquered City; A Diary*. New York: Picador, 2006.

Wright, Richard. *The Color Curtain: A Report on the Bandung Conference*. New York: World Publishing, 1956.

Wu, Judy Tzu-Chun. *Radicals on the Road*. Ithaca, NY: Cornell University Press, 2013.

Wulf, Andrew James. *U.S. International Exhibitions during the Cold War: Winning Hearts and Minds through Cultural Diplomacy*. Lanham, MD: Rowman and Littlefield, 2015.

Yale, Richard. *Cultural Exchange and the Cold War: Raising the Iron Curtain*. University Park: Pennsylvania State University Press, 2004.

Yu, Fu, and Gao Chu. "Photographic Manipulation in China: A Conversation between Fu Yu and Gao Chu." *Trans Asia Photography Review* 6, no. 1 (2015). http://hdl.handle.net/2027/spo.7977573.0006.104.

Zamir, Shamoon. "Structures of Rhyme, Forms of Participation." In *The Family of Man Revisited: Photography in a Global Age*, edited by Gerd Hurm. London: I. B. Tauris, 2018.

Zaremba, Marek. "Zorganizowane zapomnienie o Holocauście w dekadzie Gierka: Trwanie i zmiana." *Kwartalnik Historii Żydów Polskich* 2 (2004): 216–24.

Zelizer, Barbie. *About to Die: How New Images Move the Public*. New York: Oxford University Press, 2010.

Zelizer, Barbie. *Remembering to Forget: Holocaust Memory through the Camera's Eye*. Chicago: University of Chicago Press, 1998.

Zertal, Idith. *Israel's Holocaust and the Politics of Nationhood*. Cambridge: Cambridge University Press, 2010.

Zolov, Eric. "Introduction: Latin America in the Global Sixties." *Americas* 70, no. 3 (2014). 349–62.

Zuromskis, Catherine. *Snapshot Photography: The Lives of Images*. Cambridge, MA: MIT Press, 2013.

# Contributors

## Ariella Aïsha Azoulay

is Professor of Modern Culture and Media and the Department of Comparative Literature, Brown University. She is also an independent curator whose research focuses on the potential history of key political concepts such as archive, sovereignty, art, and human rights. She is author, coauthor, and coeditor of books on photography, including *The Resolution of the Suspect* (with photographer Miki Kratsman); *Aïm Deüelle Lüski and Horizontal Photography*; *From Palestine to Israel: A Photographic Record of Destruction and State Formation, 1947–1950*; *Civil Imagination: The Political Ontology of Photography*; *The Civil Contract of Photography*; *The One State Condition: Occupation and Democracy between the Sea and the River*; and, most recently, *Potential History: Unlearning Imperialism*.

## Jennifer Bajorek

is Associate Professor of Comparative Literature and Visual Studies at Hampshire College and Research Associate in the VIAD Research Centre at the University of Johannesburg. Her research on photography in Africa includes over fifteen years of collaborative research and practical projects with artists, curators, and museum and heritage professionals in the region. Her latest book is *Unfixed: Photography and Decolonial Imagination in West Africa* (Duke University Press). Her latest curatorial project, *Look and*

*Feel*, integrated an exhibition of graffiti works by Mow 504 (Mouhamadou Moustapha Souaré) with commissions, a residency, and new curriculum at Hampshire and the Five Colleges, in September–October 2021.

## Erina Duganne

is Professor of Art History at Texas State University. She is a coauthor of *Global Photography: A Critical History*; the author of *The Self in Black and White: Race and Subjectivity in Postwar American Photography*; and a coeditor of *Beautiful Suffering: Photography and the Traffic in Pain*. Her recent exhibition project *Art for the Future: Artists Call and Central American Solidarities* opened in 2022 at the Tufts University Art Galleries.

## Evyn Lê Espiritu Gandhi

is Assistant Professor of Asian American Studies at the University of California, Los Angeles. She is the author of *Archipelago of Resettlement: Vietnamese Refugee Settlers and Decolonization across Guam and Israel-Palestine*.

## Eric Gottesman

is a visual artist; a mentor in the Arab Documentary Photography Program; and a cofounder of For Freedoms, where he is the artistic and education director. He has been the recipient of awards for his photographic work from the John Simon Guggenheim Foundation, International Center of Photography, Creative Capital, the Aaron Siskind Foundation, and Artadia.

## Tong Lam

is Associate Professor of History at the University of Toronto and a visual art practitioner. His lens-based work engages the issues of the Cold War, ruins, infrastructure, media technology, and contemporary China. His current visual project focuses especially on the materiality of Cold War mobilizations globally and their environmental and social consequences. He has exhibited his research-based photographic and video works internationally.

## Karintha Lowe

is a doctoral candidate in the American Studies program at Harvard University. A Mellon Predoctoral Fellow in Women's History at the New-York Historical Society, she specializes in Asian American visual culture and multiethnic literatures.

## Andrea Noble

was a Latin Americanist based at Durham University. Her research in visual culture studies, particularly in film and photography, and Mexican cultural history left an indelible and influential mark in these interdisciplinary fields. She authored three books: *Photography and Memory in Mexico: Icons of Revolution*; *Mexican National Cinema*; and *Tina Modotti: Image, Texture, Photography*. In addition to this volume, she coedited two books: *Photography: Theoretical Snapshots* and *Phototextualities: Intersections of Photography and Narrative.*

## Ángeles Donoso Macaya

is Professor of Latin American Literature and Visual Culture at The Graduate Center/CUNY and at The Borough of Manhattan Community College/CUNY. She is Faculty Lead of Archives in Common: Migrant Practices/Knowledges/Memory, part of the Mellon Seminar on Public Engagement and Collaborative Research at The Center for the Humanities at The Graduate Center/CUNY and a 2021–2022 Mellon/ACLS Community College Faculty Fellow. Her research centers on the theory and history of Latin American photography, counter-archival production, human rights activism, documentary film, and transfeminisms, with a focus on the Southern Cone. She is the author of *The Insubordination of Photography: Documentary Practices under Chile's Dictatorship* and coeditor of *Latina/os of the East Coast: A Critical Reader*.

## Darren Newbury

is Professor of Photographic History at the University of Brighton. He is the author of *Defiant Images: Photography and Apartheid South Africa* and *People Apart: 1950s Cape Town Revisited*, with photographs by Bryan Heseltine. And he is coeditor, with Christopher Morton, of *The African Photographic Archive: Research and Curatorial Strategies*; coeditor, with Richard Vokes, of "Photography and African Futures," a special issue of *Visual Studies*; and coeditor, with Lorena Rizzo and Kylie Thomas, of *Women and Pho-*

*tography in Africa: Creative Practices and Feminist Challenges*. He was the editor of the international journal *Visual Studies* from 2003 to 2015, and has curated exhibitions at the Pitt Rivers Museum, University of Oxford, and the District Six Museum, Cape Town. In 2020 he received the Royal Anthropological Institute Photography Committee Award for his distinguished contribution to the study of photography. His current research is concerned with the role of photography in US public diplomacy in Africa during the Cold War and decolonization.

## Sarah Parsons

is Associate Professor of art history and visual culture at York University, Toronto. She is the author of *William Notman: Life and Work*, editor of *Photography after Photography: Gender, Genre, and History*, and coeditor of the journal *Photography and Culture*.

## Gil Pasternak

is Professor of Photographic Cultures and Heritage at De Montfort University (UK). His recent publications include *The Handbook of Photography Studies*; *Visioning Israel-Palestine: Encounters at the Cultural Boundaries of Conflict*; and two special issues of the journal *Photography and Culture* titled "Photography in Transitioning European Communist and Post-Communist Histories" and "Photographic Digital Heritage in Cultural Conflicts."

## Thy Phu

is Distinguished Professor of Race, Diaspora and Visual Justice at the University of Toronto. She is the author of *Picturing Model Citizens: Civility in Asian American Visual Culture*; coeditor of *Feeling Photography*; co-founder of the research collective, Critical Refugee and Migration Studies Network of Canada; and Principal Investigator of the Family Camera Network, a project that collects and preserves family photographs and their stories. Her most recent books are *Warring Visions: Photography and Vietnam* (Duke University Press) and *Refugee States: Critical Refugee Studies in Canada*.

## Oksana Sarkisova

is Research Fellow at Vera and Donald Blinken OSA (Open Society Archives) and Head of the Visual Studies Platform at Central European University. She is the author of *Screening Soviet Nationalities: Kulturfilms from the Far North to Central Asia* and coeditor of *Past for the Eyes: East European Representations of Communism in Cinema and Museums after 1989*. She teaches courses on visual theory, memory politics, cinema and human rights, and on the construction of historical narratives in documentary cinema; she also directs the Verzio International Human Rights Documentary Film Festival in Budapest. Sarkisova and Shevchenko's manuscript on Soviet family photography and generational memories of socialism in Russia is currently being prepared for publication.

## Olga Shevchenko

is Professor of Sociology in the Department of Anthropology and Sociology at Williams College. She is the author of *Crisis and the Everyday in Postsocialist Moscow* and editor of *Double Exposure: Memory and Photography*. Shevchenko teaches courses on social theory, visual culture, ethnographic methods, and socialism and post-socialism; she writes on post-Soviet political culture, consumption, memory, and photography. Sarkisova and Shevchenko's manuscript on Soviet family photography and generational memories of socialism in Russia is currently being prepared for publication.

## Laura Wexler

is Charles H. Farnam Professor of Women's, Gender, and Sexuality Studies, and American Studies; and Acting Co-chair of the Public Humanities Program at Yale University. Wexler's book *Tender Violence: Domestic Visions in an Age of U.S. Imperialism* was a recipient of the American Historical Association's Joan Kelley Memorial Prize. She is the original Principal Investigator of the Photogrammar Project and an author, along with Ariella Azoulay, Wendy Ewald, Susan Meiselas, and Leigh Raiford of *Collaboration: A Potential History of Photography*.

## Guigui Yao

is Professor at the School of Foreign Languages and Director at the Center for American Culture at Jianghan University in Wuhan, China. Recently, she held the position of Associate Research Scholar at Yale University. Her publications include contributions to the *Routledge Handbook of Religion and Ecology*; *Going Soft? The US and China Go Global*, edited by Priscilla Roberts; and *Collection of Women's Studies*.

## Donya Ziaee

is a former doctoral candidate in Gender, Feminist and Women's Studies at York University in Toronto. She has worked as a radio journalist at the Canadian Broadcasting Corporation (CBC) and is currently a researcher for the Council of Canadians, a grassroots political organization fighting against corporate power.

## Marta Ziętkiewicz

has been awarded her doctorate in Art History from the Institute of Fine Art at the Polish Academy of Sciences. In 2017 she copublished the edited volume *Discovering "Peripheries": Photographic Histories in Central and Eastern Europe*. Her research has also appeared in journals such as *Photography and Culture*, *Konteksty*, and IMAGES: *A Journal of Jewish Art and Visual Culture*.

# Index

Page numbers followed by *f* indicate figures.